LIVING LANGUAGE®

GETTING AHEAD IN THE U.S.

Written by
Barbara Raifsnider

Edited by
Christopher A. Warnasch
Shaina Malkin

ACKNOWLEDGMENTS

I would like to thank Caroline Devereaux, Dr. J. Ronald Meyers, Dr. Richard J. Ewing, Margaret McWhorter, John H. Raifsnider I, and Jan Forstrom.

Thanks to the Living Language® staff: Tom Russell, Nicole Benhabib, Christopher Warnasch, Zviezdana Verzich, Suzanna McQuade, Shaina Malkin, Elham Shabahat, Sophie Chin, Denise De Gennaro, Linda Schmidt, Alison Skrabek, Lisbeth Dyer, and Tom Marshall.

Editors: Christopher A. Warnasch and Shaina Malkin
Production Editor: Lisbeth Dyer
Production Manager: Thomas Marshall
Interior Design: Sophie Ye Chin

First Edition

ISBN: 978-1-4000-2369-1

Library of Congress Cataloging-in-Publication Data available upon request.

This book is available at special discounts for bulk purchases for sales promotions or premiums. Special editions, including personalized covers, excerpts of existing books, and corporate imprints, can be created in large quantities for special needs. For more information, write to Special Markets/Premium Sales, 1745 Broadway, MD 6–2, New York, New York 10019 or e-mail specialmarkets@randomhouse.com.

PRINTED IN THE UNITED STATES OF AMERICA

10 9 8 7 6 5 4 3 2 1

CONTENTS

Introduction

Living Language® Getting Ahead in the U.S. is a complete program designed to help newcomers to the U.S. with much more than language. If you think about it, there are really three major barriers that people who move to new countries have to face. The one that most often comes to mind is the language barrier. Unless a person's new home and native country share a language, mastering a new language is just about always difficult. Even if you've studied English and have achieved a certain degree of comfort with it, being immersed in an English-language environment is challenging. And "fine-tuning" a language to sound more natural and become more confident expressing yourself and understanding others is not an easy thing.

The second major barrier is the cultural barrier. This is often even more frustrating than the language barrier, because the differences between cultures can sometimes be very subtle, and they affect people in much deeper ways. After all, it's much easier to learn how to *speak* like other people than it is to understand how they *think*! As a newcomer to the United States, you've probably quickly realized that people in other cultures often think very differently about such basic issues as time, personal space, communication, food, friendship, and much, much more. They also have different expectations. This can make even the simplest interaction with others challenging, embarrassing, bewildering, or just plain exhausting.

The third major barrier we can call the "how-to" barrier. People in different countries and cultures go about the business of their daily lives in different ways, so if you're an immigrant, you may find yourself constantly asking how to do this or how to do that. This often involves little things—getting something repaired, registering a child for school, or having television, telephone, or internet service hooked up. But it can also involve more important (or expensive) issues—finding a new home, communicating with a doctor, finding a good deal on a new car, or figuring out how to pay for college tuition. For a person who doesn't know how to go about doing these things, they can be very intimidating, especially if there's no one to turn to and ask for advice.

That's where *Getting Ahead in the U.S.* comes in. This program has been designed specifically with you in mind in order to address all three barriers that you're facing at once. It's really a three-in-one program:

- First, it's a high intermediate to advanced level ESL program meant to expand your vocabulary, help you master more challenging grammatical constructions, build your confidence in both speaking and understanding, and fine-tune your pronunciation. All of this English language content is based on practical, everyday issues that you face in your life, so while you're addressing the language barrier, the content is designed to help you overcome the other two barriers as well, the cultural barrier and the "how-to" barrier.

- Second, it's a cultural training program that gives you practical advice on American cultural expectations so you'll understand important issues related to time and punctuality, professional and personal etiquette, making friends and communicating with people, table manners, and much more. The program isn't designed to change your culture, but rather to help you understand American culture, and most importantly, to inform you about the cultural expectations people in your new home will have about you and others.

- Finally, it's a practical survival guide to life in the U.S. Each chapter in the program covers an everyday issue, such as cars, schools, doctors, dentists, shopping, taxes, jobs, government, and so on. You'll learn essential information about things that might be confusing to you because they're done differently in the U.S. than in your country.

Getting Ahead in the U.S. is divided into eight topical sections: *At Work, In the Car, Making Friends, School, Health and Emergencies, Everyday Life, Finding a Home,* and *Government and Immigration.* Each section includes between three and six chapters that focus on important aspects of the topic of the section. For example, in the section *Finding a Home,* there are the chapters *Looking for a Home, Renting an Apartment, Buying a House,* and *Utilities and Other Household Essentials.* There are a total of 35 such chapters, each of which gives you essential cultural and practical information on a particular aspect of one of the major topics covered in the program, as well as related vocabulary, grammar, pronunciation, and other important English language skills.

It's not entirely necessary to go through the chapters in sequential order; if there is a particular topic that you have questions about, simply look it up in the table of contents and go to the relevant chapter. But if you'd like a comprehensive course in ESL that is also designed to answer your questions about life in the U.S., it's a good idea to move through the program sequentially. Each of the 35 chapters follows an identical format to make the program as easy as possible to use:

A. English Close-Up: First, you'll see a piece of "real life" English—a memo, an ad, a form, a report, an official document, or anything you'd be likely to encounter when dealing with the topic of the chapter. It's a way to move into the chapter and show you examples of the types of vocabulary and other information relevant to the topic, and also a way to help take some of the mystery out of documents or forms you might need to deal with.

B. Vocabulary Essentials: Next comes a list of related vocabulary items. Naturally, it's impossible to list every single vocabulary item you may encounter in any given situation, but each chapter includes about 25 of the essentials. You'll find examples of jargon, official terms, phrasal verbs, and important idioms. Each item is defined clearly and simply, and an example of usage is given as well.

C. Grammar Essentials: Next is a grammar point that you're likely to encounter in the context of the topic of the chapter. The grammar points are generally at the intermediate or advanced level, with a clear and concise explanation followed by plenty of examples. They're designed for nonnative English speakers who have some background in the language, so they're an ideal way to review and practice with structures that still pose problems.

D. How-To: The How-To section is the focal point of each chapter. It features the vocabulary and structures covered in the chapter, and it provides important practical and cultural information about the topic of the chapter. The How-To section is never meant to be completely exhaustive; entire books have been written about many of the topics covered in this program. It is also not intended to provide legal, medical, accounting, or any other kind of professional advice. For that, you must go to a professional! The How-To section is instead an overview of a topic, with practical advice and general information on issues or situations that immigrants to this country find confusing or intimidating. With the general overview provided in the How-To section, you'll be better equipped to deal with the topic at hand.

E. English in Action: The English in Action section takes the form of a dialogue or other piece of authentic English related to the topic of the chapter. More key information is provided in this section, and the important vocabulary is used in a realistic context.

F. Practice: There are two types of practices, one for the vocabulary and one for the grammar covered in the chapter. The practice exercises will give you a chance to test how well you've learned the material.

G. Task: The task is a real-life exercise or "discovery" activity designed to put you in a situation where you'll have to use the material presented in the chapter. Often the tasks contain several different suggested steps that you could take to practice what you've learned in a real-world context, but they may also involve one particular activity with a fixed answer, such as visiting a related website and finding a particular piece of information. All of the tasks are designed to put you out in the world, where you can see the practical applications of what the chapter covers.

H. Real Life: The Real Life section can take a few different forms—a piece of advice, an article, a letter, or perhaps a personal message. It's meant to give you more advice and information on the topic of the chapter from the perspective of people who know because they work or have experience in the field, or perhaps because they've gone through exactly what you're going through.

I. Resources: Finally, each chapter includes a list of important resources that you should know about. They may be phone numbers, websites, books, or any other resource that will come in handy.

Answer Key: The answer key contains the answers to the two practice exercises for each chapter.

Pronunciation: Each chapter also includes a pronunciation exercise that does not appear in the book, but that you'll find on the recordings.

Recordings: The complete program includes six hours of recordings, featuring Vocabulary Essentials, English in Action, and Pronunciation.

How to Use *Getting Ahead in the U.S.*

1. English Close-Up: Begin each chapter by reading the English Close-Up for a warm-up to the topic. Some chapters include forms or other official documents, ads, and so on, so take the opportunity to look over a piece of written English that you're likely to encounter in the real world.

2. Vocabulary Essentials: Next, read the Vocabulary Essentials to familiarize yourself with the important vocabulary you'll find in the chapter. Read each entry, definition, and example, and focus on the ones that are new or unfamiliar to you. After you've read the section once or twice, you can listen to it on the recordings for further practice. It's always a good idea to use a notebook along with any language program so that you have a place to record new or unfamiliar words and expressions along with a few examples of their use.

3. Grammar Essentials: Next, read over the Grammar Essentials, taking as much time as you need to understand the information and become comfortable with the examples. Many of the grammar notes may be familiar to you, but a little review is always a good thing! If the note is new or especially confusing, be sure to read it over a few times until you've

mastered it. This is also a good section to take notes on. Write down summaries of the grammar points in your notebook, along with any new examples that you can think of.

4. How-To: This is the centerpiece of each chapter, and this is where you'll find most of the cultural and practical information related to the topic of the chapter. As you read over the section, keep in mind that details may vary from place to place, but the information in this section should serve as a good general summary of the topic. Although the course is designed so that much of the relevant vocabulary is covered in the Vocabulary Essentials section, it is possible that some words or expressions may be new or unfamiliar to you. If so, look them up and write them down in your notebook, along with any examples that you can think of. If the topic of the How-To section is of particular interest to you, you might also consider writing down a few of the major points in your notebook so that you can apply them to your own life.

5. English in Action: First, read over the section once or twice in the book to familiarize yourself with it. Then, listen to your recordings while you read along in your book one more time. The section is recorded twice, once at normal conversation speed without pauses, and a second time with pauses so that you can repeat. The repetition is a chance for you to practice pronunciation and natural conversational intonation. Of course, it will also give you a chance to practice the vocabulary and grammar presented in the chapter, as well.

6. Practice: Next, do the printed practice exercises. These are also good things to write down in your notebook, because writing will help you process and master the information much better than simply reading the exercises and answering them "in your head."

7. Task: The task is a great chance to challenge yourself by putting everything you've learned to practical use in a real-life situation. The more tasks you can do, the better. Some will be more interesting (and useful) to you, so it's natural to focus more on those than others, but make an effort to do as many of them as you can.

8. Real Life: Treat the Real Life section just like the English in Action section. Read it over once or twice, because it's a great way to expand your vocabulary, practice comprehension, and get some important advice related to the topic of the chapter.

9. Pronunciation: Finally, listen to the Pronunciation section on the recordings. Note that this section does not appear in print anywhere in the book for a reason; it's designed as a listening/speaking exercise. Listen to the explanation of the pronunciation or intonation point and repeat the examples, carefully imitating the pronunciation or intonation of the native speakers. If you need to listen a few times to get all of the examples, that's exactly what you should do. Use the repetition and careful listening as a chance to build your aural comprehension skills.

After you've completed a chapter, you can do one of three things. If you're not totally comfortable with the material, don't be afraid to go over the chapter again. The great thing about this program is that you can do it all on your own, so you can move at exactly the pace that you're comfortable with. So, go over sections or chapters as many times as you'd like. A second option is to listen to the audio for the chapter on its own, without the help of the book. This is a great opportunity to review the most important contents of each chapter, and it's also a great way to build your listening comprehension and speaking proficiency. Since you don't need the book for the audio review, you can do this anywhere—on the train, in the car, while you do the dishes, at the gym, or anywhere else you can listen to the audio. Of course, your final option is to move on to the next chapter if you're comfortable and ready to get ahead!

Good luck, and enjoy the program!

CHAPTER 1

At Work: Losing Your Job

NOTICE OF TERMINATION OF FULL TIME EMPLOYMENT

January 7, 2008

To: J. Arnold   Title: Bus Driver
From: Joe Tomlinson, supervisor

Subject: Discharge from Full Time Employment

This is notice that you will be discharged from your full time employment with the WDC Bus Line effective January 21, 2008.

This discharge is based on the following reason(s): 1) Failure to show up on time on more than four occasions. 2) Failure to ask supervisor's permission before leaving work early. 3) Failure to follow supervisor's orders. WDC provided counseling for these concerns on February 8, 2006, November 9, 2006, and August 14, 2007. A Standard Form 50, Notification of Personnel Action, effecting your discharge will be forwarded to you when available.

B. **VOCABULARY ESSENTIALS**

Absenteeism—Being absent from work for a long period of time, or repeated absences. *Bill's absenteeism is a big problem. He misses more days than he works.*

Accrued vacation time—Unused vacation time that continues to grow year after year. This can often be taken as cash at retirement or job termination. *Tara has close to two months of accrued vacation.*

To be down—To feel temporarily depressed. *Rama's really been down ever since he lost his job. I hope he finds a new job soon.*

To be out of a job—To be temporarily unemployed. *Lannie, I just heard you were out of a job. Would you like to help me out at the office until something more suitable comes along?*

Between jobs—In a period of unemployment. *Since Marco's between jobs, he's taking some classes to update his skills.*

COBRA—Consolidated Omnibus Budget Reconciliation Act. A law that allows most workers who were covered by a company's health insurance during employment to continue to purchase that insurance for 18 months or longer after leaving the job. Usually companies with more than 20 employees must offer COBRA coverage. *When I retired, I decided to opt for COBRA coverage in order to have some sort of health insurance until I qualified for Medicare.*

To downsize—To reduce personnel, to cut jobs. *To be downsized* means to lose one's job because of downsizing. *Many internet-based companies had to downsize during the dot-com crisis of the early 2000s.*

Eligible—Qualified, as for a job. *Human resources removed the resumes of those who were not eligible for the position due to lack of experience.*

Entitled—Able to claim the right to something, eligible. *As an employee of this company, you are entitled to outplacement assistance, which will help you find another job before this one ends.*

To feel blue—To be depressed. *It's so easy to feel blue when you don't have a job; the important thing is to stay active and get your resume to as many employers as possible.*

Freelance, to freelance—Work done, or to do work, independently of a company or agent. *Many journalists prefer freelancing so they can sell their work to whomever they want.*

To get the boot, to get booted out—To lose a job, or, more generally, to lose any kind of relationship or affiliation. *If you don't meet the company's sales quota within your first or second year, you're likely to get the boot.*

To get/be fired—To lose your job because of poor performance, misconduct, etc. *Did you hear that Todd got fired for altering his time card?*

Hardship—A difficulty, a trying situation. *My wife's pregnancy is turning out to be a real hardship for us; we'll be losing her income until a few months after the baby is born.*

Human resources—Department dedicated to serving the needs of employees and prospective employees. *Stan checked with human resources to see what kinds of employee benefits the company offered.*

Job referrals—Job prospects or potential employment opportunities, often found through contacts within the company offering employment. *Emil got his job by checking into job referrals at the unemployment agency.*

Job seeker—Anyone looking for a job. *When unemployment rises, many job seekers will be out looking for a job.*

To lay off, to be laid off—To remove from a job or to lose a job that an employer has eliminated, usually because of a company's poor economic performance. *Merle was only one of many laid off during the last economic downturn, but when things got better she got her old job back.*

Networking, to network—Making connections or to make connections through friends, coworkers, etc. *Fortunately, Selma began networking as soon as she discovered she was being laid off; she quickly found a good job through a former coworker.*

Outplacement resources—Employment services, such as job referral, job training, resume preparation, and so on, that a company provides to terminated employees in order to help them find a new job. *We encourage you to take advantage of the generous outplacement resources that our company provides to those whose jobs are being terminated.*

To outsource—To turn to a source that is outside of the company, or even the country, for a service, often in order to save money. *A lot of Americans have lost their jobs since Agra athletic shoes outsourced their factories to China.*

Overqualified—Having too much education, training, and/or experience for a job. *You know, Mr. Biddle, I'd love to hire you, but you're overqualified for this position. I'd be afraid you'd leave your job as soon as you found something more suitable to your skills.*

Overspecialized—Having overly specific skills and training. *I'm sorry, Mr. Uyar. We need someone with a wider range of skills. You're just too overspecialized for our company.*

Pink slip—Written notification of termination from a job. *Edgar, Raf, and Jin were among the people who got pink slips today. I wonder if anyone else will be losing a job in this company before too long.*

To pound/hit the pavement—To go out looking for support, financial assistance, or a job, often actually going door-to-door looking for work. *Tanya discovered that modeling is a lot harder than she had thought. Her agent told her to get a good portfolio and pound the pavement to get her face known.*

Severance pay—Money that some companies provide when an employee is terminated. *Mac didn't qualify for severance pay when he lost his job because he hadn't been with the company long enough.*

Termination—Job loss caused by a layoff, firing, or the conclusion of temporary employment. *At least 50 employees are facing termination due to the company's need to downsize.*

Unemployment insurance, to be on unemployment—Financial assistance paid to eligible, unemployed workers through a state-controlled insurance fund, or to receive such assistance. *I'd rather be working than living off my* unemployment checks. Who can survive on $400 a week with a spouse and two kids to support?

Unskilled labor—Work that does not require any special skills, education, or training. *In this day and age, it's difficult for many unskilled laborers to find work that pays enough for them to live on.*

Willful misconduct—Behavior that violates rules or laws, either intentional or without concern for the consequences. *Jack was fired for willful misconduct after he didn't show up for work two days in a row and never bothered to call in.*

C.   GRAMMAR ESSENTIALS: *USED TO*

To talk about a repeated action in the past, use the expression *used to* + verb.
> *Nobody used to work as hard as I did.*

The expression *used to* + verb indicates a past habitual action that does not occur in the present, for example, *I used to work in a bank. Used to* implies that you no longer do something that you once did. If you say *I used to get paid every Friday,* the implication is that you do not get paid on Fridays anymore.

The negative and question forms are the same as the simple past tense of the verb *use:*
> *He didn't use to work so hard.*
> *Did you use to repair computers?*

Don't confuse these expressions with *be* + *used to* + noun/*-ing* verb. This indicates something that you are accustomed to.
> *Tran is used to working long hours because he's been doing it for years.*
> *Tran is used to long workdays.*

In the negative and question forms of this type of expression, the word *used* does not change because it isn't a verb but an adjective.
> *I'm not used to going on job interviews.*
> *Is anyone used to this unseasonably warm weather?*

If you want to describe the act or process of becoming accustomed to something, use the expression *get used to* + noun/*-ing* verb. In this case, *get* can be in any tense.
> *Sheila has gotten used to being unemployed.*
> *Frank finally got used to the idea of losing his job.*
> *I will never get used to networking all the time!*

In the question and negative forms, that's:
> *Raul hasn't gotten used to working for himself.*
> *Did you eventually get used to freelancing?*

If you want to describe something that's difficult to become accustomed to, use the expression *can't get used to* + noun/*-ing* verb.

I can't get used to sitting around all day doing nothing but watching TV.

If it's something you'd like to continue, use *can get used to.*

I can get used to working fewer hours.

If there's something that you would really like to have as a part of your life, use *could* instead of *can:*

I could (really) get used to making more money!

Finally, there's the related expression *get used to it!* This is a kind of command or warning that means that because something is inevitable, there is no choice but to accept it.

I'm out of work, so we won't have enough money to go to the movies for a while. You'd better just get used to it!

D. HOW-TO

If you should ever lose your job, it may feel like the end of the world, but there are several options available to help you get through the crisis. The first thing to look into is unemployment insurance. Even if you get fired, unless it's for willful misconduct, you will probably still qualify for unemployment insurance. Checks are usually issued weekly, and in order to keep those checks coming in, you will probably have to document your current job searches to prove that you are seeking gainful employment. Just keep in mind that unemployment insurance usually doesn't kick in until one week after you have applied for it, so you should apply on the first business day after you lose your job. That way, the gap between your last paycheck and your first unemployment check will be minimal. However, unemployment insurance usually only lasts for 18 months, and unemployment checks are often too small to do anything but pay the basic bills, so you will want to get another job as soon as possible.

Unemployment insurance is controlled by each state, so qualifications and compensation amounts may vary depending on where you live. You can find out about your state's program by checking with your local unemployment office. To find the nearest unemployment office, you can either check your phone book under "state offices" or go to an internet search engine and type in your state's name and the words "unemployment office." The U.S. Department of Labor also has a website that will help lead you to your state's unemployment office. Type in the following: workforcesecurity.doleta.gov/map.asp. Then click on the name of your state. You may be able to apply for unemployment insurance online. If not, you might have to go directly to your local branch of the unemployment office.

You may also have accrued sick leave or vacation time during your months or years with your company. This accrued time can sometimes be taken as a lump sum of cash when employment ends. Because this all depends on the company that you worked for, you should ask your human resources department for details.

Although not all companies provide severance pay, this is another possible source of income to help tide you over until you find another job. The amount provided to you is usually based on your length of employment with the company. Some companies also offer outplacement resources to help you find another job as soon as possible. The services available to you might include career assessment, career counseling, help with updating your resume, contact information for employment agencies and companies with job openings, training for job interviews, and so on. Of course, you may not be lucky enough to have these services provided to you by your former company, but you can still find them in other places. Look under "employment services" in the yellow pages, or do an internet search for such topics as "resume services" or "career counseling." You'll also find some useful resources listed at the end of this lesson. As you can see, there's no need to feel down about losing your job. There are a lot of resources available to help you transition through this difficult time.

E. ENGLISH IN ACTION

Now listen as Lorena learns that Jorge has just lost his job.

Lorena: Aren't you supposed to be at work, Jorge? Jorge? Did you hear me? Jorge, what's going on? You look really down.

Jorge: Yeah, I am. I got a pink slip yesterday. I'm going to be out of a job in two weeks.

Lorena: Jorge, you must be joking.

Jorge: Nope. I got fired.

Lorena: Why? What happened? Did they tell you why?

Jorge: Yep.

Lorena: Are they downsizing?

Jorge: No. And I don't want to talk about it.

Lorena: Look, Jorge, I promise I won't nag you, but with the kids in college, and the mortgage . . . We can't pay for those things without your paycheck. This is going to be a real hardship for us. You've got to get another job.

Jorge: I know, I know, but I'm just feeling too blue to do anything about it right now. I've got some sick leave and vacation time accrued. That'll give us a little more time. I figure I've got at least a month or more to find a job.

Lorena: Well, you can't just sit here. You've got to start thinking like a

job seeker. Let's check the internet, and we can start
networking right away. Maybe somebody will know where you
could get another job.

Jorge: Okay. But don't tell anybody I got fired! I'm not used to people
feeling sorry for me.

F. PRACTICE

Fill in the blanks with the correct form of one of the following expressions:
*to feel blue, to be out of a job, freelancing, to pound the pavement, to get
fired, hardship, to be laid off, downsized, between jobs, to network, human
resources*

1. Not having a job is a real _____ for Teka, especially since his wife's been
   sick.

2. It's not unusual _____ when you aren't working, because work keeps
   your mind off of other problems.

3. Many workers lost their jobs when the company _____. There just wasn't
   enough money to pay everyone's salary anymore.

4. I'm not too worried about _____. I have a lot of skills, so I know I'll get
   another one very soon.

5. Celia is _____ right now, but she's out _____ every day because she
   knows there's a good job waiting for her out there.

6. It's important to follow the company rules so that you'll never _____.

7. Did you hear that Tony _____? The company he worked for must really be
   in trouble.

8. If you take the time _____, you might find someone who knows someone
   who'd like to hire you.

9. You should really check with your _____ department to see what kind of
   severance pay, if any, your company offers, just in case anything happens.

10. Instead of trying to look for a new job at an agency, I was thinking of
    _____ so that I could work for myself and do translation jobs for a variety
    of companies.

Now fill in the blanks with the correct expression with *use to*.

1. You look awfully familiar. Didn't you _____ work at the airport?

2. Maria is _____ taking the bus to work every day.

3. I didn't _____ have to work so hard!

4. Is there anyone who is _____ working the graveyard shift?

5. We are _____ sleeping in on Saturday mornings.
6. We _____ go bowling after work every Thursday.
7. I just can't _____ the idea of not having a job!
8. Jack _____ waking up very late when he was between jobs.
9. We just _____ the fact that we all lost our jobs!
10. I _____ traveling all over the world for my job like John does. That would be great.

G. TASK

If you are currently employed, check with your human resources department to see if they offer severance pay. You might also want to check to see if they offer outplacement services and, if so, what is included in those services. If you are not currently employed, you can check on these same benefits with the human resources departments of companies where you would like to work. Check with your state unemployment office to see what qualifications are necessary for receiving unemployment insurance. These are all valuable things to know should you ever lose your job.

H. REAL LIFE

Now, let's turn to "Ask Sammy," where people share their real-life questions and get practical advice.

Dear Sammy,

I was recently given notice at work. I was told that I lost my job because I hadn't been finishing my work on time, but I know that others didn't get their work done on time, yet I was the only one that was let go. The others are still working there, and one of them even got a promotion. I think I lost my job because I'm a lot older than the others. How can I find out whether my termination was legal, and, if not, how can I get help getting my job back?

Sincerely,
Feeling Blue

Dear Blue,

Employment termination due to age discrimination would be considered wrongful termination. It may be difficult to prove, though not impossible. What you need to do is discuss your case with a lawyer. It is possible that all you would need to do is have your lawyer send a letter to your employer stating how the company has violated federal discrimination laws. Your company may not want to get tangled up with court cases, and you could even get your job back.

Good luck,
Sammy

I. RESOURCES

U.S. Department of Labor
www.dol.gov
www.workforcesecurity.doleta.gov/unemploy (for information on unemployment)
www.dol.gov/esa/contacts/state_of.htm or
workforcesecurity.doleta.gov/map.asp to find your state's department of labor.

Check your local One-Stop Career Center, established by federal law. To find one near you, go to www.servicelocator.org or call 1-877-US-2JOBS for direct assistance.

For information on employees' rights and how to deal with problems at work, visit www.workplacefairness.org.

And don't forget to check the resources available to you through your former employer and the local library.

ANSWER KEY
Practice 1: 1. hardship; 2. to feel blue; 3. downsized; 4. being out of a job; 5. between jobs, pounding the pavement; 6. get fired; 7. was laid off; 8. to network; 9. human resources; 10. freelancing

Practice 2: 1. use to; 2. used to; 3. use to; 4. used to; 5. used to; 6. used to; 7. get used to; 8. got used to; 9. can't get used to; 10. could get used to

CHAPTER 2

At Work: Looking for a Job

A. ENGLISH CLOSE-UP

A job fair is an excellent opportunity for job seekers to meet potential employers. Companies seeking employees set up booths where they show job seekers what their companies offer in the way of salaries, benefits, stable career tracks, and more. Job seekers can show potential employers what they have to offer by networking with people from companies with openings appropriate to their skills and experience. Often, other job search services are offered as well, such as assistance with resumes or even career guidance.

Job Fair
Open to the public!

April 6–8
10 a.m.–4:30 p.m.
At the Civic Center,
Broadway Ave.

Over 100 companies will be in attendance!
Check our website to see the full listing, updated every day.

1 p.m. – discussion panel of employers from finance,
advertising, the arts, education, and more

3:30 p.m. – workshop conducted by the city's
premier career consultant

Bring your resume!!

For more information: www.findyourjob.com
Sponsored by the Employment Council and Local Bank

B. VOCABULARY ESSENTIALS

Applicant—A person who applies for something, such as a job. *Applicants must fill out the employment application forms and leave a copy of their resume with human resources.*

Candidate—A person who is being considered for something, such as a job. *Out of the fifty applicants, there are three pretty good candidates.*

Career field—Area of specialization or career path. *Check with your career center for help finding the best career field for you before you start your job search.*

Entrepreneur—A person who takes the risk of starting a business. *Ben Cohen and Jerry Greenfield of Ben & Jerry's Ice Cream are two world-famous entrepreneurs.*

Follow-up interview—A second interview, usually offered only to strong candidates. *We'll schedule follow-up interviews with the five strongest candidates next week.*

To follow up on something—To inquire, by phone, e-mail, or letter, about the status of something, such as an application. *Hello. This is Brad Simms. I just wanted to follow up on my interview last week to see if any decisions have been made.*

To get a handle on—To gain control of (something), to understand (something). *It takes time and patience to get a handle on a new job.*

Headhunter—An independent recruiter of candidates for high-level positions, especially for corporations. *Damian believed he was capable of getting a position with more responsibility and more money, so he contacted a headhunter.*

To jump-start—To set (something) in motion, to reinvigorate (something). *Trey and Mario had to do something to jump-start their business or else they would have been forced to shut down operations.*

To land a job—To get a job, particularly one you really want. *After calling repeatedly over several months, Anton finally landed a job at the film company.*

Marketable—Capable of being sold, having enough appeal to sell well. *Greg lost his job, but he doesn't have to worry. With his experience, background, and education, he's very marketable.*

Mentor—A teacher, someone more knowledgeable and experienced who can serve as a guide. *Kenji was Harris's mentor in the company. He taught Harris how to act in meetings, how to pitch ideas, and how to get to know the important people.*

Resume—A written summary of your education, training, and experience given to a prospective employer when applying for a job. *Tara went to Acumen Resume Service because she needed a resume that would make her stand out as the best candidate for the job.*

Self-marketing skills—Knowing how to sell or market yourself, as in your abilities, experience, etc., to others, such as potential employers. *You'll need to have strong self-marketing skills to get a job in today's competitive market.*

Self-starter—Someone with initiative, who doesn't need to be told what to do. A person who can begin a project without extensive direction and prompting. *Buzz has turned out to be a real self-starter. He always has good ideas for how to accomplish the company's goals.*

Strategy—A plan of action. *Without a good strategy it is impossible to be successful.*

Teamwork, a team player—Cooperating on a team, or someone demonstrating the ability to work well with others. *It takes teamwork for a company to run smoothly and successfully, so we expect every one of you to be a strong team player.*

Temp agency—An employment agency specializing in temporary employment. *Chas decided he would work for a temp agency to help pay the bills while waiting for a permanent job.*

To think outside the box—To think creatively, to come up with an idea that has never been tried before. *The director at the ad agency was always complaining that her employees didn't think outside the box. All of their ideas were unoriginal.*

Want ad—An advertisement for a job that needs to be filled. *Harold found a want ad for the perfect job in the Sunday Daily News.*

 ## C. GRAMMAR ESSENTIALS: *GET*

While *be* is the verb that is used the most in English, the verb *get* is probably the most versatile verb, especially in North American English. Here are some common meanings of the verb *get:*
> To obtain or acquire. *I'm getting a new job.*
> To receive. *I just got some good news.*
> To earn. *We don't get enough money for this job!*
> To bring, to obtain for someone. *Could you get me a cup of coffee, please?*
> To grow to feel or experience. *She gets bored with office work.*
> To become. *It's getting darker, so we should head back.*
> To contract (as an illness). *I get a cold every winter.*
> To understand or hear. *I didn't get your last name. Could you repeat it?*
> To comprehend. *No matter how hard I try, I don't get geometry!*

Get can also be used along with other words, such as prepositions or adverbs, to form many different phrasal verbs with idiomatic meanings. Here are the most common:
> Get along—To manage, to make do. *Billy's thirteen years old, so I think he can get along without a babysitter now!*

Get along with—To enjoy a positive relationship with. *Mark really gets along well with his new colleagues, so he's happy with his job.*

Get around—To be socially active, to be involved with many people. *Bill seems to have talked to everyone at the party tonight! He sure gets around!*

Get around to—To come to a project, to find time to work on something. *I'll start working on the new file as soon as I have the time to get around to it.*

Get away—To escape. *The prisoners broke out of the jail and got away.*

Get away with—To avoid punishment. *No matter what Dan does, he somehow manages to get away with it!*

Get back—To return, to come back. *I got back from the movies at 10:30.*

Get back at—To take revenge. *Bob wants to get back at his brother for playing such a nasty trick.*

Get by—To manage, to succeed. *Rina told Carlos everything he needed to know to get by in business.*

Get down—To seek cover or protection. *A tornado is coming! Get down!*

Get even—To exact revenge. *Bob wants to get even with his brother.*

Get in—To arrive home. *What time did you finally get in last night?*

Get into (1)—To become involved in a hobby or interest. *When she was in college, Rachel really got into Tai Chi.*

Get into (2)—To become involved in trouble or mischief. *The kids are always getting into something!*

Get off (1)—To stop working for the day. *What time do you get off?*

Get off (2)—To leave (a bus, train, or plane). *The passengers are just getting off now.*

Get on—To board (a bus, train, or plane). *We got on the bus at 86th Street.*

Get out—To go out, to leave one's home for social engagements. *I'm so busy these days; I really don't get out much anymore.*

Get out (of)—To leave. *If you don't like what I say, then you can just get out of my home!*

Get over—To move beyond (a difficult situation). *Jacinta was very sad after she and Rob broke up, but she's finally begun to get over him.*

Get through (to)—To communicate effectively (with). *Jolene's parents tried to convince her to stay in college, but they couldn't get through to her.*

Get to—To arrive at. *We didn't get to the hotel until 11:30 at night.*

Get up—To wake up. *What time do you get up in the morning?*

Get is also used in many important grammatical constructions. Perhaps the most common one is *have got to*, which means "must."

I've got to get to work early tomorrow or I'll be in trouble with my boss!
Mary's got to find a job quickly, because she's running out of money.

Get can be used in place of *be* in passive constructions. Note that this is more informal and is used mostly in conversational English:

Bob got laid off last week, but he's going to job fairs looking for work.
Oh! My shirt got torn somehow!

Get is also used in causative constructions with infinitives, meaning "to convince" or "to coerce."
Jill somehow managed to get her boss to give her a raise.
Nadine's kids always get her to do what they want her to do!

Get can be used with past participles as well, in passive causative constructions:
I have to get my brakes fixed before I drive anywhere.
Valerie is getting her hair done.

D. HOW-TO

Finding a career that suits you is not an easy task. Many people fall into jobs and may end up getting stuck in careers that they don't really enjoy. It is not uncommon for people in the U.S. to change jobs often, possibly because they don't know what they really want to do and don't know how to go about finding out. Because we spend so much of our lives working, it's important to find work that we really enjoy. After all, work has the capacity to bring us a great sense of fulfillment, not just help us pay the bills!

One way to find a job you'll enjoy is to consult a career counselor. A career counselor can help you find jobs that match your personality and skills, polish your resume and interviewing skills, teach you about networking, and provide other kinds of employment aid. A career counselor may have you take a personality test like the Myers-Briggs or an aptitude test that will then help match you with a career. Although career counseling is not always free, there are plenty of free career services available to you if you do enough research. Just start looking online and in the newspaper, and you'll see both job listings and career counseling services. In fact, many career tests are now available online. In addition, many universities offer career counseling services and post job listings for their students and alumni. Another great resource for both career advice and job opportunities is a job fair. You'll see these advertised locally, and it's a great idea to start attending them if you can, because you can begin to network that way, get a sense of what's out there, attend free career workshops, and meet people who can help you find a job.

Once you find a career or specific job that interests you, you'll want to see if there are any particular requirements or skills and experience levels necessary for that job and industry. If your job requires retraining or a college degree that you don't have, start looking around for the best and preferably the least expensive training you'll need. Most states offer either free or low-cost vocational training schools, so you do not need to make a huge financial investment. If you need a college degree, be sure the career choice you've made is really the right one for you, because this could mean a considerable investment of time and money. There are low-cost loans and grants available to you to help cover the costs of education, but you need to do some more homework. Your local library is one of the best places to look, but a career counselor will have the relevant material at his or her fingertips as well. You can also see Chapter 16 of this book for more information.

Once you've discovered what you want to do, and you've taken the necessary steps to prepare yourself for your new career field, you need to seek out employers that offer the kinds of jobs you're interested in. Check with employers' human resources departments for job openings. You can usually find openings online, at company websites, or even by telephone if the company has a job line. You might also want to think about setting up a few informational interviews. An informational interview entails meeting with someone that you have contacted in the industry or even the specific company you are interested in to discuss the industry and the company, what that person's duties are in the company, and what he or she looks for in potential job applicants. Informational interviews are a great way to learn more about a potential career before you start, discover what employers are looking for in that field, and sharpen your interviewing skills. Plus, there's no pressure to sell yourself, and you come away from the meeting with a new contact. You can find potential contacts for these interviews through networking (friends, family, teachers, etc.), career services centers, or online research.

E. ENGLISH IN ACTION

Now listen in as two old friends talk about their career paths.

Raf: Eric?

Eric: Raf? Is that you? I didn't recognize you under all those sideburns.

Raf: Yeah. It's me. What's the matter? Don't you like sideburns?

Eric: That's not it. I just remember you as the short-hair type. Hey, what have you been up to?

Raf: Oh, me? I've been working at a health food store. You know, stocking shelves, running the cash register, and just being surrounded with food. What about you?

Eric: Well, I finally got my BA. And I just landed a job at a movie studio.

Raf: Yeah? What do you do there? How'd you get that job?

Eric: I'm doing film editing. You know, I actually found out about the job on Craig's List and then just kept calling the studio. I even went down there and delivered my resume to the guy personally.

Raf: Wow! How'd you ever get the nerve?

Eric: Yeah, it was hard. I am kind of shy, I know, but I just knew I really wanted this job, so I decided to talk to a career counselor about it. He said the only way to get it was to go after it. He suggested I should keep calling until they gave me an interview. I knew I had to jump-start my career somehow, so I tried it. The guy just kept putting me off, saying call back in a week, a few weeks, or a month. It just took forever. I never thought I'd get a handle on it, but it finally happened. And here I am. I just love my job. It really makes it all seem worth the effort, and I'm so glad I went in to see the career counselor. He really helped me. So, what about you? Do you have any other plans, Raf?

Raf: Well, I'm kind of a self-starter. I may just get my own health food store some day.

Eric: Really? That's great! If you need any help, that career counselor I told you about could probably give you some good ideas about starting your own business. And, you know? I can see you doing that. I always thought you were kind of an entrepreneur.

Raf: Yeah. That's me. The entrepreneur. Hey, good seeing you. I've got to go. Good luck!

Eric: Thanks. You too. See you around.

F.   PRACTICE

Fill in the blanks with the correct form of one of the following expressions: *to think outside the box, team player, to land a job, self-starter, to follow up on, to jump-start, headhunter, to get a handle on, mentor, self-marketing skills*

1. Rao's business is really struggling. If he doesn't _____ it pretty soon, it's probably going to fail.

2. Every new job applicant needs to learn _____ quickly in order to compete for good jobs.

3. If you don't start _____, your career as an ad writer will go nowhere.

4. Charles was excited because he _____ as a film editor. He's wanted to do film editing for several years.

5. If you want to move up the corporate ladder, you need to be a _____. Otherwise you'll be stuck in a low-level position your entire career.

6. Tina was having a hard time with the Mitchell account, but it looks like she finally _____ it.

7. Jim, can you _____ the Big Benny account? We need to find out what's taking so long.

8. If you're a professional, you might want to consider talking to a _____ about getting a better-paying job.

9. You have to be a _____ in this company. Nobody works alone.

10. Heather, this is Marie. She'll be your _____ while you learn how to do your job.

Fill in the blanks with an expression using *get*. In some cases, there is more than one correct answer.

1. The Willits-Busby project _____ be finished by Friday or we'll lose the account.

2. The plane _____ around 9:00 last night.

3. Jan has finally _____ cleaning the attic after putting it off for months.

4. Reina _____ her boyfriend to buy her a diamond ring.

5. It's taken me weeks to _____ this flu; it really lasted a long time!

6. How do you _____ your brothers and sisters?

7. My friends _____ me to go to a career counselor to find out what I'm good at.

8. I have a problem now, and I really don't know how I'm going to _____ it.

9. Do you think that you can _____ on that salary? It seems low.

10. We _____ the subway at Union Square, and then _____ at Columbus Circle.

G. TASK

Even if you're not looking for a new job at the moment, you might want to try some of the following options. It's always good to be prepared just in case you have to change careers or decide that you want to follow a new career path. Write down your strengths, skills, interests, and values. Ask friends and family about any career advice they might have for you. Take a personality test. Speak to a career counselor, or take a career test online. Imagine what type of education or training you might want or need if you chose to or had to change careers, and look into local colleges or vocational schools to see what's offered. You can check out the resources at the end of this chapter to get a sense of where to find things. It never hurts to find out more about the job market and yourself!

H. REAL LIFE

John Raifsnider, former owner of *Acumen* resume and career counseling service in San Diego, had this to say about the job search:

"A resume should be a 'sales document,' which 'sells' an employer on granting you an interview because of who you are and your proven abilities and achievements in your chosen field. Applying for job openings advertised on the internet or in newspapers can be very time consuming, frustrating, and unproductive, because doing so puts you in competition with perhaps hundreds of other applicants, many of whom are bound to have more education and experience than you do. The odds are overwhelmingly against you for getting a response.

The answer to this problem is as follows:

1. Get on the internet and identify companies that are leaders in your career field.

2. Get the names and addresses of contacts within the company, through friends and family, former coworkers, career services, online research, even the company's human resources department, and so on.

3. Research each company to find out more information about its products, history, finances, etc.

4. Send a letter, certified mail, addressed to each of your contacts. You should include your resume and ask to meet with him or her over lunch to talk about that person's position, company, and industry, as well as to discuss any advice that person has as to how best to go about finding a position in that field. Many contacts will probably be flattered and grant you an interview, probably in their office and not at lunch. However, take them to lunch if you have to. It would be well worth the investment if you can afford it. If your finances are tight, leave that option out of your letter.

If you follow this advice, you're sure to get results."

I. RESOURCES

Job postings and/or career resources:
www.hotjobs.com
www.monster.com
www.careerbuilder.com
www.truecareers.com
www.craigslist.com.
www.careerplanner.com
www.employmentguide.com
www.aftercollege.com

As noted in Chapter 1, check your local One-Stop Career Center, established by federal law. To find one near you, go to www.servicelocator.org or call 1-877-US-2JOBS for direct assistance.

Other resources:
www.princetonreview.com
www.jobsearch.about.com
www.online.onetcenter.org
www.projectcareer.com

Career counselors, information and listings:
www.ncda.org (National Career Development Association)
Myers-Briggs test www.myersbriggs.org

Books:
What Color Is Your Parachute? by Richard Nelson Bolles
Guide to Your Career by The Princeton Review

ANSWER KEY
Practice 1: 1. jump-start; 2. self-marketing skills; 3. thinking outside the box; 4. landed a job; 5. self-starter; 6. got a handle on; 7. follow up on; 8. headhunter; 9. team player; 10. mentor

Practice 2: 1. has got to; 2. got in; 3. gotten around to; 4. got; 5. get over; 6. get along with; 7. got; 8. get out of; 9. get along/get by; 10. got on/get on, got off/get off

CHAPTER 3

At Work: Your Resume

Eric Anton

11223 Camarino St., #210 • North Hollywood, CA 91602 • (818) 555-4704
eric@ericanton.com • www.ericanton.com

CAREER OBJECTIVE
To experience and record life through photography and other visual media.

PROFESSIONAL PROFILE
- Dedicated photographer, filmmaker, and photojournalist.
- Confident artist with proven ability to effectively capture emotion.
- Cum Laude graduate of Cooks Institute of Photography.
- Computer-proficient worker with expertise in Adobe Photoshop, Final Cut Pro, HTML, Macromedia Flash, and Macromedia Director.

EDUCATION

2001–2004	Bachelor's of Arts in Visual Journalism, Cum Laude, Cooks Institute of Photography
1997–2001	High School Diploma, La Jolla High School

EMPLOYMENT

2006–Present	Digital Postproduction Technician – Edwards.com Since January of 2006, have performed high-end digital retouching and various post production photography for eventual web use on Edwards.com, a leading industry website.
2005–2006	Self-Employed – San Diego and Los Angeles, California Took on various projects in the visual art field, such as websites, digital retouching, and photography.
2004–2005	Digital Retoucher – Ibis Photo Lab – Los Angeles, California Performed digital retouching and setup of images, as well as digital printing on a Fuji Frontier printer.
2003–2004	Teacher's Assistant – Cooks Institute of Photography Assisted in Non-HTML Web Design class, dealing with Macromedia Flash towards the production of a fully professional website for each student completing the course.
2003–2004	Teacher's Assistant – Cooks Institute of Photography From September, 2003, until June, 2004, assisted in the instruction of a multimedia class. Each student finished the class with a fully functional, interactive CD-ROM.
2003	AV Show Committee Chair – Cooks Institute of Photography Managed the production of 15-minute audio-visual show using images taken on group trip overseas. Hired a musician, programmed and directed the show behind the scenes.

B. VOCABULARY ESSENTIALS

Chronological resume—Standard resume that has data in a chronological order beginning with most recent (see above). *Al needs a chronological resume for jobs in his field.*

Circular file—Idiom that essentially means the "trash can." *Most resumes get put in the circular file and never lead to interviews.*

To climb the ladder—To get steady promotions along the corporate chain of command. To gain power within a company. *Nada's promotion shows that she is climbing the ladder fast.*

Combination resume—A resume that is a combination of both a functional and a chronological resume. Usually contains a description of skills plus an employment history. *A combination resume could be good for new graduates, steady workers, and older workers.*

Cover letter—A letter of introduction that provides additional information not in the resume. *Career guidance counselors recommend that you send a cover letter along with your resume. Furthermore, many companies now require one.*

Electronic resume—A resume formatted specifically for e-mail and internet posting. *These days it seems everybody needs an electronic resume as well as a paper resume.*

Fast-paced environment—An energetic work environment where many projects are going on at once and where many people interact. *Jillian enjoys the challenge of a fast-paced environment.*

Functional resume—A resume used for career changes or for those wanting to get back into the workforce. It lists work history with no dates and emphasizes skills. *Maria Luisa chose a functional resume because she had not worked since her children were born.*

To get a foot in the door—To make a first step toward achieving some goal, to begin something, usually at the bottom. To act in a way that allows entry into a company, especially by taking a low-level position or by establishing personal contacts. *If you want to work for that company, you should accept a low-level position as a way to get your foot in the door.*

Go-getter—Someone who is hardworking and outgoing. *Ray is such a go-getter; he landed a big account within his first few months on the job.*

Job quest—Job hunting, the process of looking for a job. *Before you begin your job quest, be sure your resume is updated.*

To name-drop—To mention the name of a well-known person that you happen to know in order to impress people. *Terrence always tries to impress people by name-dropping, but everyone sees right through it.*

On-the-job training—Training or skills obtained while working. *Tina's on-the-job training helped her to know exactly what she needed to do if any problems came up at work.*

Outgoing—Extroverted, expressive, and sociable. *Leila has such an outgoing personality that she's sure to find a good job anywhere.*

To pad a resume—To make a resume look more impressive by embellishing or exaggerating. *Many people try to pad their resumes by exaggerating involvement in community activities or charity work.*

Potential—A quality that makes someone or something capable of growth in a certain area. *Marlon showed potential, but no one imagined he'd be a millionaire this young.*

To revamp—To revise, to update. *Revamp your resume, and then begin your job quest.*

Scannable resume—A type of resume similar to the electronic resume, designed to be easy to scan. *You need both paper and scannable resumes.*

Skills—Abilities obtained through experience or training. *List all your pertinent job skills on your resume.*

Template—A model or format of a document used repeatedly. *You can find many resume templates on the internet if you know where to look.*

Well-versed—Very knowledgeable about a subject. *Are you well-versed in any computer programs, or is your knowledge of them only passable?*

C. GRAMMAR ESSENTIALS: MODALS IN THE PAST AND PRESENT

Modals can be a bit confusing, because there are subtle differences in meaning among them, and there may also be slight differences in meaning or structure in the past or in negation. Let's look at each modal separately.

1. Can (can't/cannot; could)

Can expresses ability. It can be replaced with *able to* when meaning ability. *How many words a minute can you type (are you able to type)?* It can also express possibility, especially as *could*. *I could still get a call for an interview, but it's not very likely.* The past of *can* is *could*, or *was/were able to*.

Dawn could work (was able to work) well with all of the clients, so it was hard to see her leave the company. To express possibility in the past, *could have* is used. *They could have made a decision by now, but you should call them to find out.* The negative form of *can* is *cannot* or *can't. I can't find that report and I really need it.* The negative form of *could* is *could not* or *couldn't. I couldn't find that report I was looking for and now I have to start all over again.*

2. Have/has to (don't/doesn't have to; had to)

 Have to expresses an obligation, but it can also be used to express a very strong desire. *My boss needs this report by tomorrow, so I have to finish it.* Or: *Marsha really hates her job, so she has to find a new one!* The past of *have to* is *had to. Bill had to get to his interview early so that he could fill out some forms.* In the negative, *don't have to* expresses that something isn't an obligation or necessity, that there is a choice. *You don't have to send a thank-you letter after an interview, but it is a good idea.*

3. Must (must not; had to)

 Must expresses a strong obligation. *You must submit your application by the deadline—no exceptions!* In the past tense, *had to* is used to express this concept. *I had to get to work on time today, or I would have been in trouble.* In the negative, *must not* expresses a strong prohibition, that it's necessary <u>not</u> to do something. *You must not be late to this meeting! Must* can also be used to express a very strong likelihood, or near certainty. *Look at that stack of resumes! There must be hundreds of applicants!* With this meaning, there is also a past form: *must have. It's been four weeks since your interview, so they must have made a decision by now.*

4. Need to (don't/doesn't need to; needed to)

 Need to expresses necessity. *You need to get a better job, because you need to make more money.* The past and negative forms are regular. *Rachel needed to do some volunteer work to get some variety on her resume.* And: *You don't need to pad your resume—just be truthful and to the point.* The forms *needn't* and *need not* also exist, but they aren't very common in North American English.

5. Should (shouldn't; should have)

 Should expresses advice or a suggestion. *You seem so unhappy at work; you really should get another job!* In the negative, *shouldn't* expresses advice against doing something, or a warning. *You shouldn't cancel your appointment with human resources; it will look really bad.* The past tense form of *should* is *should have. I should have updated my resume earlier!*

6. Ought to (ought not; ought to have)

 Ought to is similar to *should;* it expresses advice. *You ought to get a better paying job.* The negative of *ought to* is *ought not. You ought not pad your resume too much, because it can land you in trouble.* However, *ought* is not very commonly used by all speakers in the negative, so it's often replaced by *shouldn't*. The past tense form of *ought to* is *ought to have. I ought to have left much earlier, because I'll never make it to my interview on time.* Again, some speakers prefer to use *should have* instead.

7. Want to (don't/doesn't want to; wanted to)

Want to expresses desire. *Sarah wants to go to the job fair this weekend.* Its negative and past tense forms are regular. *Jacob doesn't want to take any career guidance tests.* And: *Gail wanted to ask for a raise, but she chickened out.*

D. HOW-TO

Some career counselors say that few people ever get an interview based on a resume. In fact, most resumes end up in the circular file rather than on the desk of whoever is in charge of hiring. According to statistics, about one interview is granted for every fifty to one hundred resumes received. Nevertheless, resumes are still very important. Virtually every job that you will ever apply for will ask for one, so unless you want your application tossed for being incomplete, you simply need a resume. And you need to make sure that your resume is as appealing as possible. After all, you want it to be the one in fifty or a hundred that actually catches someone's eye and lands an interview!

A good resume will showcase your skills, highlight your potential, and say something unique about who you are and what you offer. There are a few basic rules you should stick to when building your resume so that it presents you as favorably as possible. First of all, you don't have to go out and purchase paper in an attractive color. Just stick to basic white or off-white, but pay the extra money to purchase high quality paper and print it up using the best copy quality possible. When you print your resume, use a font and font size that will be easy to read. You don't need to get fancy or outlandish with text effects; sometimes your "creativity" can even land you in the garbage can. You just want your resume to be legible. But even more important than the quality of the paper and print is something more basic; your grammar and spelling must be perfect. Typos will demonstrate the opposite of what you are trying to project. You want to look efficient and detail oriented, not sloppy or lazy. If you know anyone who has good grammar and spelling, have him or her check your resume carefully for errors. Don't just rely on your computer's spell check, because if your spelling mistake nevertheless produces a real word, your error won't be corrected. You want your resume to demonstrate that you are a competent communicator and writer, so if you need to, don't be afraid to brush up on your writing skills before starting on your resume.

Speaking of writing, there are some key points to keep in mind when you write your resume. Above all, be clear and concise. Choose action verbs.

Avoid passive constructions most of the time. Leave out unnecessary details and go right for the point. Whatever you do, don't pad your resume. You could get caught in an exaggeration—or worse yet, a lie—that could end your career if anyone ever found out. Be honest. Never say you are proficient or experienced at something when you are really not that well-versed. If you're qualified or capable rather than proficient, say so. Focus on what you have to offer, but don't embellish anything. A very important point to keep in mind is that while you're only writing one or even a couple of resumes, your audience has read hundreds, maybe thousands. Any trick you can come up with to make yourself appear to be more than what you are will probably be very, very obvious!

Another thing to think about when writing your resume is whether you want to use a chronological resume, a functional resume, or a combination of both. If you're choosing a job in your current field of experience or education, you will most likely want to use a chronological resume, which lists your experience and history chronologically, beginning with the most recent. Otherwise, you may want to consider a functional resume, which lists work history without giving dates and focuses on skills. If you're just out of college and have little or no experience, or if you've been out of the job market for a long time, a functional resume might suit your needs better. A combination resume, which includes employment history and a skills section, might also be a good idea for certain job applicants, including those listed above. A list of qualifications can be a helpful addition to your employment history, because it allows you to point out and emphasize to employers both the skills and the experience you have that make you perfect for the job. In this age of technology, you should consider making an electronic or scannable resume as well as a paper resume. Several resources for resume templates and guidelines are listed in the Resources section of this lesson, so you can find plenty of examples of the types of resumes mentioned above. It's probably best to look carefully at current examples of resumes on the internet, rather than selecting samples from old resume books. Styles and wording change over time, like everything else, and you don't want to look outdated. Look at resumes that are similar to what you need, and find samples written for people your age and with similar amounts of experience.

Another very good piece of advice is to try to put yourself in the place of your prospective employer. What would he or she want in a job candidate, and how would he or she want to read about it? Try to select words that describe you in a way that will appeal to your audience and get your point across. It's not a good idea to brag; being positive, confident, and modest in describing yourself and your qualifications will win employers over faster than bragging. And don't think that longer is better! If you have so much experience that you could easily fill five pages, that's great, but don't do it! Edit yourself down so that you keep the best, strongest pieces of information—and don't fill more than one or two pages at the very most.

In the end, your resume should be neat, clean, attractive, and compelling. You are selling your most important commodity, yourself. Once your resume is finished, write a cover letter that mentions some specific contribution you can make to the organization. Even though your cover letter may not be carefully read or even read at all, you should not send out a generic form letter. The cover letter is a good opportunity for you to customize your presentation for different prospective employers, hitting on points that will resonate with certain individuals, companies, business cultures, and so on. Once you've finalized your cover letter and resume, check to make sure you've gotten the employer's name and title right, and then, if sending by mail, send your resume and cover letter to your prospective employer in a large envelope so that they remain crisp and clean. After sending off your resume, be optimistic, but don't sit back and wait for a phone call. This is where many new job applicants get discouraged and fail to follow through due to lack of confidence. It's likely that you won't get a call. Even after sending out hundreds of resumes, you still may not get any calls. You need to remind employers that you are there, so you need to make follow-up calls asking about the status of your resume and reemphasizing your interest in the position. Also, make sure to keep a record of it all—date resume sent, note on follow-up, interviews scheduled, etc. Your job quest is one of the most important experiences in your life. Just like anything else that's important, you have to work hard to make it successful.

E.   ENGLISH IN ACTION

Listen as Gloria and Jon from human resources look at resumes that have been sent in for a position that just opened up in their company.

Jon: Hey! Look at this one. It looks like someone used it for a coaster or something. It's got coffee rings all over it! And look at this one! Script font on canary yellow paper? No way, Picasso.

Gloria: Here's a guy that must have padded his resume. How can you be 21 years old and have worked as a vice president?

Jon: Well, maybe his dad owned the company.

Gloria: Yeah, right. Why's he applying here if he had such a good job? Oh, man. This other resume has the worst spelling. It says "fast paced envirment" and "climb the latter." Jeez! These are all going in the circular file. Ugh! And this one stinks like cigarette smoke!

Jon: These would all be more useful if we made paper airplanes out of them. Doesn't anybody know how to write a resume anymore?

Gloria: Well, isn't that part of the problem? Nobody knows how to write. How are we ever going to fill a position that demands good writing and organizational skills when no one seems to have them, at least judging by their resumes?

Jon: Hey, what's this? Look, this guy took the trouble to put his resume in a large envelope so he didn't have to fold it. Wow, this actually looks good. It's clean. It's legible. He's young, but he seems to have some good work experience. And at least he knows how to present himself on paper. Let's put it in the to-call pile.

Gloria: Good. At least we've got one to show for all the time it's taken to go through these. Here are a few more. Let's see if there are at least one or two more good ones.

Jon: Here's one that's passable. A little long, but still under two pages . . .

F. PRACTICE

Fill in the following sentences with these expressions: *get a foot in the door, go-getter, follow up, cover letter, pad, climb the ladder, on-the-job, circular file, name-drop, job quest, revamp*

1. You might want to take a low-level position. Then you'll at least _____.

2. Be honest. Don't _____ your resume.

3. It's a good idea to _____ on your job interview with a phone call.

4. Many people get _____ training rather than going to school to learn a skill.

5. Joe's a real _____. I bet he'll _____ to become vice president in a couple of years.

6. Take a look at your old resume. It's probably time to totally _____ it and bring it up to date.

7. It probably doesn't do any good to _____ when you go on a job interview, because some interviewers might not appreciate hearing rivals' names.

8. The _____ begins with a good resume.

9. If you don't turn in all the forms and a proper resume, your application will go into the _____.

10. The company I'm applying to requires a(n) _____ with every job application, so I'm trying to come up with a few short paragraphs that will help me stand out.

Use the negative form of the following modals: *have to, must, should, need to, want to, can.* In a few cases, there may be more than one correct answer.

1. Why _____ you take the bus to work yesterday? It runs right by your house.

2. It's forbidden to show that file to anyone. You _____ leave it lying around.

3. Don't worry. You _____ work weekends. You can enjoy those days off.

4. Our deadline has been extended, so we _____ finish the project as soon as we thought we did.

5. Robert _____ go to the office party, because he knows Lucy will be there.

6. You know, you really _____ go home early without first clearing it with your boss. You could get in trouble.

7. Why _____ you use your teacher for a reference? I'm sure she'd do it.

8. In my opinion, Bill _____ accept that job if it doesn't pay enough.

9. He absolutely _____ accept less than minimum wage.

10. You _____ to take a job with great benefits just because you'd have to work weekends?

G. TASK

Now that you've learned about resumes and cover letters, write out some practice ones. Go online to one or a couple of the websites mentioned in Resources and look at samples. Think about which resume style best fits your needs. You might want to write both a paper resume and an electronic one.

H. REAL LIFE

Hi there! My name is Sandra, and I work in the human resources department of a medium-sized company, so I see a lot of resumes and cover letters. I'm in a pretty good position to give you some advice on cover letters because—believe me—I read a lot of them. Well, to be honest, I don't really *read* many of them, because I normally turn right to the resume. If I don't like the resume, I don't bother with the cover letter. But every once in a while, when I come across an interesting resume, I like to turn back to the cover letter to see what else the candidate has to say. So, the (sad) truth about cover letters is that they're not always read, and when they are read, it may not be in the order you'd expect. Surprising, maybe, but true. Despite all of this, you should still put effort into your cover letter! Let me tell you what works for me . . .

First of all, don't write anything too long or fancy. I don't want to read a novel, and I'm not interested in your creative writing skills. Just give me what I need to know. I like to see a nice, standard business letter, and please, make sure you get my name and title right! If I see my name instead of "Dear Madam or Sir" or "To Whom It May Concern," it catches my eye and lets me know that you've done a little homework instead of sending out mass form letters. Better yet, show me that you know something about my company and that you have a specific idea of what you—you, as an individual—have to offer us. Don't give me your work history again; I can read that in the resume. Just let me know that you've given some thought to the question I'm asking myself: Why should I want to meet this person? Because you have something that my company needs and you'd be a good fit with the organization. So tell me that. Make me see the connection between your resume and my company. If your resume is strong, I'll be impressed. And if your cover letter shows me that you understand exactly how your strengths are a good match for my company, well, you'll probably be getting a phone call from me. Now, let me get back to all these resumes. Good luck!

I. RESOURCES

Resume Templates and Resume Resources
resume.monster.com
www.careerjournal.com/jobhunting/resumes
www.collegegrad.com/resumes/quickstart.shtml
www.jobweb.com/Resumes_Interviews/default.htm
www.quintcareers.com/scannable_resumes.html
www.rileyguide.com/letters.html

ANSWER KEY
Practice 1: 1. get a foot in the door; 2. pad; 3. follow up; 4. on-the-job; 5. go-getter, climb the ladder; 6. revamp; 7. name-drop; 8. job quest; 9. circular file; 10. cover letter

Practice 2: 1. couldn't; 2. must not; 3. don't need to/don't have to; 4. don't have to/don't need to; 5. doesn't want to; 6. shouldn't; 7. can't/couldn't; 8. shouldn't; 9. must not; 10. don't want to

CHAPTER 4

At Work: The Interview

A. ENGLISH CLOSE-UP

> Bill Bailey and Associates
> 2903 10th Avenue
> Seattle, Washington
>
> Mr. Ralph Sager,
> This letter is to confirm that you have an interview with Bill Bailey and Associates, scheduled on Thursday, November 19th, at 10:00 a.m. Please check in with the Human Resources Office on the 7th floor when you arrive, and bring a list of references with you. We look forward to seeing you.
>
> Sincerely,
>
> *Mary E. De Lanou*
>
> Mary E. De Lanou
> Recruiting Director

B. VOCABULARY ESSENTIALS

Asset—Something or someone useful. A quality an employee or prospective employee has that would benefit a company. *Making people feel comfortable is a real asset for any insurance salesperson.*

Collaborative effort—A joint effort, something that is accomplished cooperatively. *The Mills project was a collaborative effort by Nguyen, Haynes, and Bogg.*

Conflict mediation—A type of conflict resolution involving communication through a mediator or neutral third party. *Because the union and the managers could not agree, they turned to conflict mediation to resolve the disputed contracts.*

Conflict resolution—Processes designed to resolve conflicts, avoiding confrontation or violence. *Effective conflict resolution saves time and money for all parties.*

Entry-level position—A low-level job in a company, often taken by a recent graduate or by someone looking to work his or her way up in the company. *It's only an entry-level position, but there are opportunities for growth.*

In the bag—Certain, bound to occur. *I just had such a great interview that I really think this job is in the bag.*

Jargon—Specialized language, language related to a specific field or industry. *Reading a contract can be challenging because there's so much legal jargon to work through.*

On your toes—Alert, careful. *The director said that we should all be on our toes this week because we're being evaluated.*

Opportunities for advancement—Chances to grow or be promoted within a company. *Even though you're overqualified, there are so many opportunities for advancement that I'd encourage you to take this position.*

Productivity—Effectiveness at producing, showing a good rate of production relative to time and money spent. *Our department's productivity has gone way down since we lost some of our senior managers.*

To relocate—To move to a new state or city, usually because of work. *I know your family is happy here, but are you willing to relocate?*

Room for growth—Potential to improve. *Bill decided to take our job offer because he sees that there's a lot of room for growth with us.*

Salary range—Range of pay available for a particular job, usually depending on experience, education, etc. *The salary range for the position is $55k to $65k. Your final salary will be based on your years of experience in the field.*

To set the pace—To lead the way, to set an example that competitors follow. *Ablex is the top producer in its field; it sets the pace for all its competition.*

To shadow—To closely follow someone through a routine in order to learn from him or her. *During her first week on the job, Sarah shadowed one of her coworkers so she could learn everything she'd need to do.*

Short list—A list of candidates that has been narrowed down from a longer list, such as the list of candidates being seriously considered after first interviews. *Phoung was excited that she'd made the short list and that they'd asked her back for a second interview.*

Transferable job skills—Job skills acquired through one job that can be used in an entirely new position. *It's always a good idea to highlight any transferable job skills you might have on your resume or during an interview.*

Up to speed—Informed and aware, up to date. Equipped with what is needed for a particular position or project. *Jill says she's going to take some computer classes so that she'll be up to speed for her new job.*

Well-rounded—Balanced in character, having cultivated different qualities in a fairly equal way. *Companies look for well-rounded candidates, so don't just focus on economics. Take a few literature classes, too!*

C.   GRAMMAR ESSENTIALS: DIFFERENT MEANINGS OF *EVEN*

There are a few English words that you may notice are used over and over, and with many different meanings. The word *even* is one of those words. *Even* can be used as an adjective, with related but slightly different meanings:

1. Smooth and uniform, as a surface. *My desktop is an even surface.*
2. With equal parts or portions. *There's an even division of work in our department.*
3. Straight and level. *Use a ruler so that your lines are even.*
4. On the same level, aligned. *The couch is even with the windowsill.*
5. Equal, tied. *The game was exciting because the score was even right up through the last quarter.*
6. Numbers that are not odd. *All even numbers can be divided by two.*
7. Describing an exact amount. *The total is an even $10.00.*
8. Remaining the same. *Jack has an even temperament; he never gets too angry or too happy.*
9. Taking revenge. *I'll get even with you for what you did; you'll see.*
10. Not in debt or obligation. *Here's the $20.00 I owe you. That should make us even.*

Even can be used as a verb, as well:

1. To make things level or uniform. *We need to call a carpenter to even out those bookshelves.*
2. To make equal or tied. *That last goal evened the scores.*

Even is often used to emphasize or focus attention on certain parts of a sentence, usually suggesting that something is additional or unexpected:

1. Used with *when, while,* and similar connective words, it suggests that something is unexpected or remarkable. *You look beautiful even when you're angry.*
2. Used with *if,* it means "although" or "despite the fact that." *Even if we can't go*

tomorrow, we can still go on Friday. Even if I win the lottery, I'll stay at my job.

3. It can be used to focus attention on or emphasize a particular word or phrase. *The interview went so well that they even offered him the job right away. I knew it would be hard to finish this project, but it was even harder than I expected!*

4. The phrase *even so* adds to an argument or discussion. *Yes, but even so, I think you still have to consider that . . .*

5. Used with *not*, it emphasizes that something is contrary to fact. *That's not even his real name. That's not even the point!*

D. HOW-TO

You've proven to an employer that you're a good enough candidate for a job to the extent that you have an appointment for an interview. What's next? Do you sit back and relax because you feel certain you'll get the job? Do you do nothing because you think that there's nothing else to be done before the interview? No! Chances are, five, ten, or even more people may be interviewing for the same position you are, and there are things that you can do to set yourself apart from them before your interview. Basically, you need to beat the odds and be the one selected for the job or at least get your name on the short list so that you're called back for another chance to shine. That means that you need to prepare for your interview. There are a few key steps that you can follow to be as prepared as possible.

The first step is to make sure you know the company you're applying to. If you haven't already researched their products or philosophy, now is the time to do so. The greater your knowledge about the company you hope to join, the better your chances are of responding well to the interview questions. Your interviewers may ask you specific questions about their products, and they'll be looking for people with intelligent and well-thought-out opinions. And even if they don't ask you such questions, they'll most likely give you the chance to ask your own questions. If you use that as an opportunity to show that you've educated yourself about the company, you will appear more thoughtful and more interested in the position.

While research on the company will help you ask and answer certain questions, you need to practice answering multiple types of questions before the interview. There are two basic categories of interview questions—the traditional and the behavioral. You will probably be asked some traditional questions, such as: *What are your strengths and weaknesses? What motivates you? How do you handle stress?* Think about these questions and have some good answers ready. You will also be asked behavioral questions that gauge how you may react to situations, such as: *Can you tell me about a time you had to make a split-second decision? What risky decisions have you had to make, and how did you come to your decisions? Tell me about a disappointment you faced at work and what you learned from it.* Again, imagine several of these kinds of questions, and have your answers ready. Any other questions your interviewers ask will probably be related to the company or the position, and if you've done your research on the company, you'll be prepared for them, as well.

After you have prepared your answers to the interviewer's questions, you need to think about preparing your own questions. Although there may not be time to ask any questions at all, there are many interviewers who will make sure there is time, and some may even dedicate most of the interview to your questions. Therefore, you need to be prepared. As noted before, you can prepare thoughtful questions about the company and industry that emphasize your interest in it. You can also ask about what your career path might be if you are hired, the position's day-to-day duties, your interviewer's history at the company, and so on. Write down all the questions you can think of so you can easily refer to them and so that you won't forget what you wanted to ask.

The next step is to plan your route and make sure you have what you need. Before your interview, be sure you understand how to get there, and above all, how long it will take you. Always arrive a few minutes early for an interview, never late. If you're late for an interview, it's often impossible to undo the damaging message you've sent, which is, "I don't care enough about your time to take a few simple steps to get here early." Also, plan to bring along additional materials, such as copies of resumes, business cards, lists of references, copies of letters of recommendation, and anything else you think might be relevant. Carry them in a briefcase or a folder. It's also a good idea to bring a notepad and take notes. Taking notes can show that you are interested in and care about what the interviewer has to say.

In addition, you should pay attention to your appearance. Get a haircut or have your hair trimmed and styled so that it looks fresh and natural. Select your clothing carefully and appropriately, always choosing something on the conservative side. For more traditional work environments, it's best to select a two-piece suit in dark colors. On the other hand, if your prospective company is less conservative, you may appear stuffy if you show up in a suit. If you've visited the company before the day of your interview, you'll have a good idea of how people dress, and you should adapt to their style, perhaps taking it one step toward the more conservative just to be safe. Whatever you wear, be sure that your clothes fit and that they are clean and nicely pressed. If you don't have anything to wear and can't afford to buy anything, there are organizations available to help you out, as shown in the Resources section. The truth is that clothing makes an impression, and first impressions are indeed important. Look neat, clean, and put together.

If you've taken care of all of these steps in advance of your interview, then you're ready to focus on the next step, which is simply to get there on time and perform well! Once you've arrived for your interview, be friendly to everyone, smile, and be relaxed. You may be nervous, but this isn't the time to smoke or chew gum . . . and definitely make sure to turn off your cell phone. When you're in the interview itself, keep in mind that the interviewers have seen your resume. They know that you are qualified. What they are looking for in an interview is to see who you are. Will you fit in with the company? Will you be pleasant or difficult to work with? Will you be efficient or lazy? They are looking at you, the person behind the experience listed on your resume. So smile and look everyone in the eyes. Sit up straight, but don't be too rigid. Your arms should be relaxed and not crossed in front of you. Be warm, friendly, and communicative throughout the interview, but keep your responses to a reasonable length. Don't drone on and bore anyone with excess information. Allow your wonderful, warm personality to come out. Show that you can handle the stress of an interview with ease, because this means you will probably handle problems on the job even better.

Once the interview has come to an end, you may even already have some idea as to whether you are being seriously considered. Thank your interviewers for their time and consideration, and say that you look forward to hearing from them. When you get home, write a letter thanking them for the interview and expressing your interest in the job. Mail it the next day, so that it arrives within a few days to a week of your interview. Then . . . wait to hear. You may get good news and be offered a new job. Of course, you may also learn that someone else was chosen over you. If that's the case, show that you are gracious by writing another letter thanking them for the opportunity to interview for the position and letting them know that you would be interested should anything else come up. This just might get your foot in the door next time.

E. ENGLISH IN ACTION

Let's listen as Ralph Sager arrives at the human resources department of Bill Bailey and Associates for his interview.

Ralph:	Hello. I'm Ralph Sager. I have a 10:00 a.m. appointment for an interview.
Mary:	Oh, hello, Mr. Sager. I'm Mary De Lanou.
Ralph:	Nice to meet you, Ms. De Lanou.
Mary:	Thank you. Nice meeting you, too. Well, you're a few minutes early. The last appointment hasn't quite finished up yet. Have a seat. Would you like some coffee, tea, water?
Ralph:	Oh, thank you. Water's fine.
Mary:	Here you are. Oh, it looks like they're ready for you already. Come this way.
Ralph:	Okay.

Mary: Mr. Sager, this is our Director of Human Resources, Brenda
          Martin.

Ralph: Very happy to meet you, Ms. Martin.

Brenda: It's Brenda, please. It's good to meet you, too. May I call you
          Ralph? Come with me and we'll get started.

Ralph: Of course . . . Please call me Ralph. Everyone seems very
          accommodating here!

Brenda: Yes, we have a great bunch of people. I guarantee you'd enjoy
          working here. I just have a few questions for you, and I'm sure
          you have questions for me as well.

Ralph: Yes, definitely.

Brenda: Okay, I've seen your resume. You've got a lot of transferable
          skills, so I know you're certainly qualified for this position, but
          I'd like to explore whether this job and this company would be
          a good fit. So let's start with a nice general question. How
          would you describe yourself?

Ralph: Well, I'm pretty easygoing. I don't let too much bother me, but
          I'm also a hard worker. I think I'm pretty well-rounded and
          even-tempered. I tend to do a lot of research before I begin a
          project to see what's already been done. I really like working
          with people. I like being involved in a collaborative effort. I
          think two or three people working together are smarter than
          one person working alone. I prefer a relaxed environment, like
          what you seem to have here.

Brenda: What about conflict? Have you had much conflict at work?
          And how do you deal with on-the-job conflict?

Ralph: Unfortunately, when you're with a lot of other people, conflict
          is bound to come up, so, yeah, I've seen some on-the-job
          conflict. If it involves me, I try to immediately go to the other
          person and see if we can resolve the issue. So far that's always
          worked, but if it didn't, I'd suggest we go through conflict
          mediation.

Brenda: Um-hum. So, what made you want to work here?

Ralph: Your company is one of the best names in the business. Of
          course, I want to work for the best. I like your products, too.
          And I see lots of room for growth.

Brenda: I can't disagree with you there! I'd love to hear some of your
          specific ideas on that, but first, tell me more about you as a
          person. What do you like to do in your spare time?

Ralph: Well, you may think I'm square, but I love to go bowling. In fact,
          I heard that you had a good office bowling team, and I would
          love to join it.

Brenda: Oh, boy. There's someone in Accounts Receivable who would
          be thrilled to hear that! I think he seriously wants us to

consider bowling scores as one of our hiring criteria! Seriously, though, what do you think of "the other guys"?

Ralph: Oh, you mean your competitors? As bowlers or as ...? [laughter] Okay, seriously, Craft and Company's pretty good. In fact, I used to work for them until I got a better offer at Bentson. But honestly, I don't think Bentson is doing their best, so it's you and Craft and Company. You two are the best. In fact, Craft has even offered me a position, but I'd really rather work here. I like a company that sets the pace.

Brenda: Would you be willing to travel? Relocate?

Ralph: Absolutely. I've already done both for the other companies I've worked for.

Brenda: Okay, well, it all sounds good. And it looks like our time's up. We'll be making a decision about our short list and will get back to you. We'll be discussing salary range, what's negotiable, etc., at the final interviews. Thanks so much, Ralph, for meeting with me.

Ralph: Thanks. I hope to see you again very soon.

F. PRACTICE

Fill in the space with the following vocabulary expressions: *on your toes, up to speed, short list, entry-level position, jargon, in the bag, to shadow, room for growth, to set the pace, well-rounded*

1. Juan is going _____ his uncle in the newspaper office tomorrow because he thinks he might want to go into journalism.

2. In order to apply for this job, your typing speed needs to be at least 50 WPM. You'd better get your typing _____ if you want the job.

3. Although I did well in my interview, the job isn't exactly _____; there were a lot of other people interviewing for the same position.

4. We can't allow other companies _____ for us, or we'll always be trying to catch up.

5. We think there's _____ in this area of the business. If not, we wouldn't be investing so much in it.

6. You really have to be _____ during an interview because you never know what they'll ask you.

7. I hope I can get on the _____. If I can get a second interview, I know I can get that job.

8. This applicant looks very _____. He's got a degree, he's had a lot of work experience, he's volunteered, and he's traveled around quite a bit.

9. Most people start out working in a(n) _____. Very few people start their career at the top.

10. You may want to do some research on any _____ used in the industry you're applying to work in. You don't want to get to an interview and not understand some of the words they're using.

Now choose from the following list to explain the meaning of *even* in each sentence: *a. emphasis; b. without debt or obligation; c. equal; d. at the same level; e. although; f. also; g. add to an argument; h. emphasizing that it's contrary to fact; i. an exact amount; j. revenge*

1. _____ He tries really hard. He keeps at it even when he knows he's been beat.

2. _____ Look! Those clouds are just about even with the hills.

3. _____ Do you think if there's enough time we could even go to Disney World?

4. _____ Thanks for mowing my lawn. How about I make dinner for you and we'll call it even?

5. _____ Why are you asking her to the holiday ball? She doesn't even like you!

6. _____ There are ten cookies left, so let's divide them into even portions.

7. _____ Yes, I did eat the last piece of cake. Even so, you didn't have to drink all of my cola.

8. _____ Ralph was determined to get even with Frank for getting the one job he had really wanted.

9. _____ That makes an even eight people we've invited to interview for this position.

10. _____ That employment history isn't even accurate!

G. TASK

Research some companies you would like to work for. (Check Resources below for help.) Then think about some typical interview questions and practice answering them. You could write out the answers or even practice while sitting in front of a mirror. If you do that, watch your body language and facial expressions. You can also consider recording your answers so you can hear how you sound. If you'd like to do role-play practice, ask a friend to play the part of the interviewer.

H. REAL LIFE

You've interviewed for a few jobs you really wanted, but you didn't get any of them. What do you do now? I know because this has happened to me a lot. I've learned that one very important thing to remember is that you should not allow yourself to get discouraged. Interviewers seem to pick up on this. You have to try to maintain a positive attitude about your future, never give up, and keep sending out resumes, making phone calls, and talking to people. If you put out enough of the right kind of energy, you're sure to start drawing some of that energy back to you in the form of interviews, callbacks, and eventually job offers. That's the way it happened for me. In fact, after sending out lots of resumes, I finally started getting lots of calls . . . all at the same time.

I. RESOURCES

Here are some websites you might want to check out to see job interview samples and other related information:
www.dressforsuccess.org
interview.monster.com
hotjobs.yahoo.com/interview
www.job-interview.net/sample/Demosamp.htm
www.quintcareers.com/researching_companies.html
www.quintcareers.com/job_interview_preparation.html

ANSWER KEY
Practice 1: 1. to shadow; 2. up to speed; 3. in the bag; 4. to set the pace; 5. room for growth; 6. on your toes; 7. short list; 8. well-rounded; 9. entry-level position; 10. jargon

Practice 2: 1. e; 2. d; 3. f; 4. b; 5. a or h; 6. c; 7. g; 8. j; 9. i; 10. h or a

CHAPTER 5

At Work: Workplace Etiquette

A. ENGLISH CLOSE-UP

AMERICAN CO., INC.
Company Policy
Employee Rules and Guidelines

We are an equal opportunity employer. It is our policy to recruit, hire, and promote employees on the basis of qualifications, without regard to age, sex, race, skin color, religion, disability, sexual orientation, or any other characteristic protected by state and federal law.

B. VOCABULARY ESSENTIALS

Big guns—Important people, those with power (informal). *We have to be on our toes today; the big guns are on their way down from the corporate office.*

Boundaries—Borders, limits, barriers. *It's important to keep boundaries between yourself and your coworkers. It's not appropriate to discuss everything!*

Colleague—Coworker, someone you work with. *I have a good relationship with my colleagues; we all respect one another.*

Consideration—Kind and thoughtful treatment. *A company always runs more smoothly when employees show consideration for one another.*

Discrimination—Treating people unfairly because of race, religion, gender, sexual orientation, etc. *Bertha felt that she was passed over for a promotion because she was a woman, so she filed a discrimination lawsuit.*

Diversity—The existence of many different forms or types, such as many different religions or races. *The United States is a nation with increasing cultural and racial diversity.*

To document—To record as evidence. *In cases of discrimination, you should try to document instances of its occurrence as much as possible.*

Equal Opportunity—Without discrimination based on race, skin color, gender, sexual orientation, disability, age, etc. *Any organization that receives government funds must provide equal opportunity.*

Inappropriate—Not proper, not acceptable. *Please, no rude or inappropriate comments!*

Interpersonal dynamics—How people behave around each other. *The fantastic interpersonal dynamics at Sundra Energy make for a very successful organization.*

Loser—Someone who fails at everything he or she tries (informal). *I feel like a real loser; I can't get a job doing anything.*

To make waves—To cause problems, to stir things up. *Be careful what you say; you don't want to make waves.*

To ream someone out—To verbally punish, to point out mistakes harshly. *Wow! I think Joaquin is in big trouble. I just heard the boss ream him out.*

To screw up—To make a mess of something, to fail. *Nate couldn't seem to do anything right. He kept screwing up every account he worked on.*

Sexual harassment—Unwanted or coercive sexual advances or language. *Glenda felt that the crude sexual jokes made by one of her coworkers were a form of sexual harassment.*

Subordinate—Someone of an inferior rank. *The director assigned the project's most tedious work to his subordinates.*

Work ethic—A diligent and hard-working attitude. *Many Americans have a strong work ethic.*

Workplace—Area designated for work, such as an office, factory, and so on. *Keep your socializing to a minimum in the workplace.*

To zip it—To be quiet, to stop talking. *I don't want anyone else to know that I'm leaving the company, so zip it!*

C. GRAMMAR ESSENTIALS: *JUST, SO,* AND *STILL*

In a way similar to the word *even*, the words *just, so,* and *still* have a variety of uses with nuanced differences in meaning. Let's begin with the word *just*. As an adjective, *just* is related to the word *justice*, so it means "fair":
> *Working to free wrongly imprisoned inmates is a just cause.*
> *Everyone thought that prison was a just punishment for the crime.*

Just can also be used to focus attention on verbs, adjectives, prepositions, and so on, and it usually means something similar to "only":
> *Don't worry. He just broke a cup, not your fine china.*
> *The office isn't far at all. It's just around the corner.*

Just can also be used with verbs to mean "recently":
> *Greg just got his new job, so he'd better not goof off!*
> *I just got in five minutes ago, so I need to relax for a moment.*

Just also has a sense meaning "exactly" or "precisely":

> *The music is at just the right level—don't turn it up.*
> *We made it to the airport just in time!*

There are a few common fixed expressions with *just*:

> Just about—Almost. *It's just about 10:00 a.m.*
> Just now—A short time ago. *He just now walked through the door.*
> Just the same—Even so, despite that, all the same. *I know it's raining, but I'd like to go on a picnic just the same.*
> Just so—Exactly in that manner. *Hold that position just so. Don't move!*

Now let's look at the word *so. So* is commonly used in place of "very":

> *It's so hot today! Let's go swimming.*

So can also be used to mean "to such an extent," in which case it's usually used with a *that* clause:

> *I was so tired last night that I fell asleep on the couch.*
> *The book was so boring (that) I stopped reading after three pages.*

So can also mean "in a certain way" or "in that way":

> *The director likes the report to be prepared just so.*
> *To recharge the battery, attach the cord so, and then plug it in.*

So can signal the consequence or outcome of an action:

> *Ken made a racist comment at work, so he was fired.*

It can also be used to mean "in order to":

> *I bring my own lunch to work so I can save money.*

So can be used with a form of *be, do,* or an auxiliary, along with a verb, adjective, or other predicate, to mean "the same thing":

> *Kara works in human resources, and so does Jane.*
> *I attended the workplace etiquette seminar last week, and so did Paul and Jill.*
> *We were concerned about the news, and so was everyone else.*
> *Tim has worked here for six years, and so has Georgette.*

There are also a few idiomatic uses of *so:*

> So as to—In order to. *We left 30 minutes early so as to prevent any problems.*
> So what!—I don't care! It's not important! *They haven't called you yet? So what! It's only been two days!*

After *be* or an auxiliary, to show emphatic disagreement:

> —*"You're not telling the truth!"*—*"I am so!"*
> —*"Bill won't make it here on time."*—*"He will so!"*

Finally let's look at *still*. As an adjective, *still* means "quiet" or "motionless":

> *The desert night is so still. I can't hear anything.*
> *Without any wind, the lake was completely still.*

When it's used with a verb, *still* has a sense of "more" or "continuing up to the present time":

> *I still have time before I have to get back to the office, so let's go for a walk.*
> *Bill and Gary got into a big fight last week and they still aren't talking.*

Still can also be used with a verb to mean "despite the fact that" or "even though":

> *Frank hardly makes any money, but he still buys his friends dinner when they go out!*
> *You cough, you can't climb a staircase, you know the risks, but you still smoke!*

A *still* can also mean a nonmoving picture, and a *still life* is a painting of nonmoving objects:

> *Magazines use lots of stills to fill their pages.*
> *The most typical objects depicted in still life paintings are pieces of fruit in a bowl.*

D. HOW-TO

The diversity of the American workplace reflects the multiethnic, multicultural nature of U.S. society as a whole. Unfortunately, differences between people too often create tension, both in society at large and on the job. To ensure a productive and safe workplace, there are federal, state, and local employment opportunity laws in place to prohibit discrimination and guarantee equal rights and fair treatment for all employees and potential employees. These laws prohibit discrimination in hiring, firing, promotion, and other job-related actions and behavior based upon such legally protected characteristics as age, race, color, religion, gender, physical ability, and so on. Some characteristics, such as sexual orientation, are not federally protected, but may be protected by state or local laws. There are also laws concerning working hours and salaries, and others protecting against sexual harassment.

As an employee, it is always a good idea to be familiar with the equal employment opportunity laws that apply where you work. Should you face what you believe is unfair or illegal treatment on the job, and if other attempted remedies fail, you may require the protection of these laws. To find out how to file a claim, check out the U.S. Equal Employment Opportunity Commission's (EEOC) website listed in the Resources section of this chapter.

But because your city or state may provide for additional protection, you should also familiarize yourself with your local or state agency.

It's also important to keep in mind that companies may have their own guidelines. They must naturally comply with federal, state, and local law, but they may also have policies related to acceptable and unacceptable workplace behavior. For example, your company may have rules regarding romantic relationships between coworkers, personal phone calls and e-mail, use of company equipment, personal workspace, and so on. To find out what these rules are, you should check your employee handbook or talk to your human resources department.

Much of what is covered by federal, state, and local laws, as well as by company guidelines or regulations, comes down to simple common courtesy and decency. In other words, responsible behavior often guarantees that no law or policy will be broken. But codes of behavior are often culturally determined, so here are a few very general points that outline expectations in the American workplace:

- Respect physical workspace. Whether a colleague works in an office, a cubicle, or even simply at a desk, treat that space as his or her own. Knock or ask permission before you move into someone's space, do not stand in front of someone's desk or door carrying on a conversation with a third party, and don't leave your belongings in someone else's space unless they offer or you speak with them about it first.

- Respect physical comfort zones. In addition to a physical workspace, Americans feel comfortable maintaining a "buffer zone" (or "personal space") around their bodies. That means that you should not stand too close to or lean too close over a colleague while talking. Notice that Americans tend to stand at least about three feet, or an arm's length, apart from one another. Respect that distance or you'll make people feel uncomfortable, or just plain annoyed.

- Be on time. Americans are generally time-sensitive, and if you're late for work or for an appointment, many Americans take that to mean that you're irresponsible or do not care about the value of others' time. Keep your schedule, get to meetings on time, and if you have to be late, make sure there's a very good reason. If you can, try to notify the people you're meeting with in advance if you know you'll be running late.

- Don't create noise pollution. That means, do not talk too loudly, and certainly do not play music so that others can hear it. If you have to carry on a conversation, close your door so others can work in peace. If you prefer to listen to music while you work, put on headphones.

- Dress professionally. Some companies have dress codes, and some environments are more or less casual than others, but in general, dress in a way that shows your colleagues that you respect yourself, them, and the workplace you share. No ripped jeans, dingy T-shirts, miniskirts, or tight, low-cut blouses!

- Be friendly, but professional. In general, American coworkers are on very friendly, seemingly casual terms with one another. They usually call one another by first names, they make small talk and tend to have a general sense of one another's lives outside of the office, and they may even socialize together outside of work. But that doesn't mean that there are no professional boundaries. Work comes first, and if there's a job to do, people turn off the small talk and get to work.

- Be appropriate. Despite this seemingly relaxed and even talkative atmosphere, there are definitely conversational boundaries that must be respected. Do not discuss "taboo" topics, including sex, religion, and politics. Sex is considered a private matter, of course, and for many people, religion and politics are just about as private.

- Mind your business. Don't gossip about coworkers or be overly concerned with their affairs. Gossip hurts people very much, but having the reputation of being a gossip hurts even more. That label will stay with you for a long time, and people will consider you untrustworthy, unprofessional, and petty.

Awareness of the cultural and professional expectations of the American workplace, along with some simple common sense and courtesy, will contribute to a warm, inviting atmosphere, allowing you and your coworkers to be creative, productive, and satisfied.

E. ENGLISH IN ACTION

Now let's listen in on a more serious situation, one that goes beyond the rules of courtesy. Molly Eakins is meeting with her EEO counselor to file a complaint against her employer.

Dean: Hello, Ms. Eakins? I'm Dean Caldwell. How can I help you?

Molly: Uh, yeah. Um . . . Well, I need to file a complaint against my boss, I think.

Dean: Okay, well, the first step is to see if we can resolve the problem without your having to file a complaint. If that doesn't work, then you can go ahead and file. Now, has it been 45 days or less since the discriminatory act occurred?

Molly: Oh, yes. It's only been maybe three or four weeks, I think.

Dean: Okay, then we can go ahead and proceed. Can you . . .

Molly: Um, wait . . . Before we begin, uh, what if I lose my job over this? I can't afford to do that. And my boss probably wouldn't give me a letter of recommendation or anything.

Dean: Ms. Eakins, you have nothing to worry about, believe me. If it's true that the law has been broken, your boss is the one who should be nervous right now, not you. You are protected by law from any form of retaliation. Your boss could even be responsible for compensatory damages and any back pay owed you, among other things.

Molly: So I would be able to keep my job?

Dean: That's right. So you can relax now. Okay, let's get back to how this process works. Now that you've begun the counseling process, you have 30 days to finish it. Once the counseling has ended, if the problem hasn't been resolved, you can then file your claim. Then we'll begin an investigation. Then, after that's finished, you can request a hearing. The administrative judge must issue a decision within 180 days. Oh, just so you know, you'll be getting all of this in writing before you leave today.

Molly: How will I know what happened?

Dean: Oh, the judge is required to send the decision to both parties. Your boss might just appeal, and he has 40 days to do so, but if he doesn't, then the judge's decision will be final.

Molly: Wow, the whole process takes a long time.

Dean: That's right. But that's the way we ensure that everything has been done carefully and within the law. Do you have any more questions?

Molly: No, I think that's about it. You've really made me feel better about this.

Dean: Well, that's what we're here for—to keep people from getting hurt. There are just a few more little details. You can also . . .

F. PRACTICE

Fill in the sentences with the correct form of one of the following vocabulary items: *big guns, loser, consideration, subordinate, to zip it, boundaries, to screw up, to ream someone out, inappropriately, to document, to make waves*

1. I really _____! I forgot to get one signature on this form, and it almost blew the deal.

2. Could you show a little _____ and close your door while you're speaking so loud?

3. If you think there's a problem, you should _____ everything so there's a record.

4. Maggie told Frank to change clothes because he was dressed _____.

5. I feel like such a(n) _____! It seems like every presentation I give falls apart!

6. You shouldn't discuss your sex life in the office! Respect people's _____!

7. All of the employees in the office are on their best behavior because the _____ are all here.

8. If it's only a minor concern I wouldn't _____ by telling the boss. It's not worth it, so I recommend you just _____.

9. Harry's upset because the boss just _____ over his low monthly sales.

10. You should not treat your _____ poorly just because you have a higher-level position than they do.

Fill in the blanks of the following sentences with *just, so,* or *still.*

1. Minnie _____ arrived. Now we can get started.

2. Your desk is _____ small! It's amazing that you get any work done!

3. Why is that phone _____ ringing? Where's the receptionist?

4. It looks like there are _____ a few presentations left before lunch.

5. No one had any questions, _____ the speaker _____ walked off the stage.

6. Could you _____ lower your voice a bit _____ the rest of us can work?

7. We can _____ make it if we hurry!

8. I hate the muffins they serve in the cafeteria and _____ does Nate.

9. I'm _____ about finished, so I'll be ready to go soon.

10. It's gotten very _____ in here all of a sudden. Where did everyone go?

G. TASK

Go to the EEOC website to review the laws against discrimination and sexual harassment in the workplace. Then check out your state or city equivalent and see if there are other local anti-discrimination laws. Finally, if you work for a company that has an employee guide, see what rules and regulations your company has. Is there a lot of overlap, or are there major differences at the different levels?

H. REAL LIFE

Dear Sammy,

I'm one of four temporary employees. I really like the job and the people I work with, but there's one temporary employee that gossips all the time. (Let's call her Betty.) Betty's always talking loudly to me about our colleagues' personal lives and their behavior in the office. And that's not all. She misunderstands my sense of humor. The other day I made an innocent joke, and she accused me of being a racist! At least now she doesn't share gossip with me, but I don't want her gossiping to other people about what a racist I am, either. I know this is a temporary job, but I'd like to enjoy being there while I can, and I don't want to make any waves. So how can I handle this situation?

Thanks,
Worried

Dear Worried,

Yes, there's usually at least one Betty in every company. Because it is a temporary job, I agree that you shouldn't do anything to make waves with your superiors right now. Wait to see if they keep you on. There are a few things you can do in the meantime, though. If Betty gossips, you can always say, "Excuse me, but I really don't have time to chat right now. I have a tight deadline." You could also be honest and say, "Betty, I really try to make it my policy not to talk about the people I work with. I really like getting along with everyone and I don't want to jeopardize that by talking about them."

Now, about the joke, it's true that people can misinterpret innocent comments, but I think you should ask yourself if your joke (that must involve some kind of racial angle) is really appropriate to be telling at work, or maybe even at all. Some people are overly sensitive, sure, but at the same time, other people say things that are hurtful and insensitive without understanding that what they're saying can be hurtful and insensitive. So the best policy is simply to avoid making any jokes that could offend other people. It will make things more pleasant for you and people around you, and it could even make you a better person by training you to become more sensitive. That way, everyone wins.

Sincerely, and Good luck,
Sammy

I. RESOURCES

Here are some links and other resources related to the topic of this lesson:
The U.S. Equal Employment Opportunity Commission:
www.eeoc.gov or 1-800-669-4000

A U.S. government site for businesses, including information on Equal Employment:
www.business.gov/topics/employees/equal_employment_opportunity

A site that gives advice on workplace etiquette:
www.askcarmencourtesy.com

As mentioned in Lesson 1: www.workplacefairness.org

ANSWER KEY
Practice 1: 1. screwed up; 2. consideration; 3. document; 4. inappropriately; 5. loser; 6. boundaries; 7. big guns; 8. make waves, zip it; 9. reamed him out; 10. subordinates

Practice 2: 1. just; 2. so; 3. still; 4. still; 5. so, just; 6. just, so; 7. still; 8. so; 9. just; 10. still

CHAPTER 6

At Work: Asking for a Raise

A. ENGLISH CLOSE-UP

Some organizations, particularly schools, government agencies, and many unions, have predetermined salary "schedules," meaning that raises are based on years of experience, possibly education or training, and time with the company. A salary schedule might look like the one below:

SALARY SCHEDULE FOR MEDINA ADULT SCHOOL

Full Time Contract Salary Schedule

Step	Less than Masters	BA + MA	45 units after BA + MA	60 units after BA + MA	75 units after BA + MA	90 units after BA + MA	Ph.D., Ed.D., or 105 units after BA + MA
A	30,300	32,120	34,200	36,410	38,790	41,320	43,169
B	31,190	33,150	35,250	37,200	39,860	42,290	44,159
C	32,300	34,230	36,300	38,540	40,920	43,410	45,229
D	33,420	35,350	37,850	39,700	42,030	44,569	46,391
E	34,620	36,580	38,640	40,880	43,270	45,731	47,542
F	35,880	37,850	39,880	42,090	44,520	46,991	48,801
G	37,144	39,100	41,190	43,360	45,690	48,279	50,105
H	38,533	40,048	42,540	44,730	47,100	49,611	51,449
I	39,890	41,859	43,880	46,160	48,540	51,021	52,851
J	41,340	43,290	45,370	47,560	49,990	52,489	54,289
K	42,850	44,820	46,870	49,050	51,460	53,989	55,801
L	44,440	46,360	48,410	50,640	53,040	55,521	57,362
M	45,677	47,629	49,749	52,039	54,500	57,049	58,949

B. VOCABULARY ESSENTIALS

Accomplishments—Achievements, experience, gained expertise in an area. *Max's many accomplishments earned him the recognition of his boss and a raise.*

Base salary—The beginning or lowest salary possible for any given position. *The base salary is 55k per year, but yours will be commensurate with your experience and expertise.*

To bide your time—To wait for something, especially strategically. *If you just bide your time, an opportunity for advancement will become available eventually.*

Cocky—Too sure of yourself, overly self-confident. *When you talk to your boss about a raise, don't act too cocky. Try to be a little modest.*

COLA—Cost of living adjustment or allowance, a small raise of a few percentage points to cover increased cost of living. *Well, at least I'll get a raise due to COLA this year. That should help a little.*

Compensation—Something given as payment for a service rendered or as a means of paying for an injury or loss. *My company offered me stock options along with a 3% raise as compensation for the hard work I put into the new account.*

Evaluation, performance review—An observation and record of performance. *Cummings, you'll receive your evaluation on the 29th, and any increase you may receive will be based on it.*

Going rate—The average, expected cost or price of something, including salaries. *What's the going rate for someone in your position?*

Grand, k—Ways of saying $1,000.00. For example, 3k equals $3,000.00. *I think I'm worth at least 63k, a grand more than I'm making now.*

To have the goods—To have the money, skills, or experience needed for something. *Make sure you have the goods before you go in and ask for a raise.*

To march in—To enter a place with great confidence and determination. *I had been thinking about asking for a raise for so long, but on Thursday I finally marched right into my boss's office and asked.*

Maxed out—Having used up all of your energy or resources. *I've given 150% on this and it's still not finished. I'm all maxed out. I just can't do it any more.*

Merit-based pay raises—Raises given based on performance rather than hours spent on the job. *Merit-based pay raises are great if you have a boss that recognizes your value.*

Negotiable—Unfixed, changeable, as price or salary. *The salary is negotiable, depending on how much experience an applicant has in this field.*

Paper-pusher—A low-level employee, especially administrative, who does a lot of paperwork. A similar idiom is a pencil-pusher. *If I end up being a paper-pusher, I'll lose all my creativity. No thanks!*

Perk—An extra benefit, either monetary or otherwise. Short for perquisite. *Travel agents don't get paid very well, but they enjoy lots of perks in the form of deep discounts on hotels, airlines, and tour packages.*

Promotion—Elevation to a higher-level position. *I've been working very hard and I think I deserve a promotion.*

Red-hot—Full of excitement, enthusiasm, energy, creativity, or interest. Also, very recent. *I've got to get to my desk to write. I'm on fire; I'm red-hot with ideas.*

To take the bull by the horns—To take firm and decisive control of a difficult situation. *If you think you deserve a raise, you can't be shy about it. You have to take the bull by the horns and explain why you deserve more money.*

Wake-up call—A warning that changes your perception or life dramatically. *Losing my job was a real wake-up call. Now I know I've got to go into business for myself.*

 C. GRAMMAR ESSENTIALS: PARTICIPIAL ADJECTIVES

You know that from the verb *to interest* you can form two different types of adjectives, based on the past and present participial forms:

> *I am interested in this movie.*
> *This movie is interesting to me.*

The following are some verbs that are descriptive of emotions. They can all be used as participial adjectives with the addition of -*ed* or -*ing*:

amuse	irritate	comfort	fascinate
puzzle	satisfy	annoy	bewilder
bother	interest	captivate	intrigue
depress	frustrate	tire	aggravate
shock	exhaust	surprise	excite
bore	amaze	confuse	disappoint

The key to using participial adjectives is simple. Use the -*ed* form to describe yourself if something has caused you to feel the emotion in question. Use the -*ing* form to describe the person or thing that is causing the emotion. So you might want to say *I'm interested in this book* (the book interests me), or *I'm bored with this class* (the class bores me), or *I'm feeling frustrated* (something is frustrating me). On the other hand, you might want to say that *the teacher is boring*, or *my neighbor is annoying*, or *my job is frustrating* (because they are the sources of these emotions). Let's look at some examples with the verb form as well as both participial adjective forms:

> *This case interests us.*
> *This case is interesting.*
> *We are interested in this case.*

> *Dinner satisfied me.*
> *Dinner was satisfying.*
> *I was satisfied by dinner.*

Joe's job exhausts him.
Joe's job is exhausting.
Joe is exhausted by his job.

Your smile captivates me.
Your smile is captivating.
I am captivated by your smile.

Your behavior shocks people.
Your behavior is shocking.
People are shocked by your behavior.

Notice that you can sometimes tell the forms apart by trying to use *by* or *to*. If you can say *by* someone or something, you should use *-ed*.

He's bewildered <u>by</u> her actions. She felt depressed <u>by</u> the movie. Tom was intrigued <u>by</u> the new woman in his office.

If you can say *to* someone you should use the *-ing* form.

Jan's religion is comforting <u>to</u> her. This book is intriguing <u>to</u> me. Raul is exciting <u>to</u> most of the women he knows.

D. HOW-TO

If you feel you deserve a higher salary, but you're afraid to ask for a raise, then try these suggestions. You may find that it's easier than you thought. The first step is to learn your company's policy on giving raises. Do they give merit raises, or only COLA? Do they have a fixed schedule of raises given according to the number of hours or years with the company? Is there a salary schedule? Once you've answered these questions and it looks as though a raise could be possible, it's time to . . . do a little more research! You need to find out what other companies are paying someone in your position. (It's probably not a good idea to compare salaries with your coworkers, though!) You can find out about the going rate for your position or the type of work you do by checking the salary websites listed in the Resources section of this lesson. Notice what people in your position in other cities are making, but pay special attention to how much they are making in your city and comparable cities. If your salary is just about the same, you may need to cut back on your expectations, but if you are underpaid you have an important bit of information to aid in your negotiation process.

Next, take a look at your company. Is your company doing well? Are there opportunities for growth? You need to be relatively certain that it's a good time to ask for a raise before you attempt it. If it looks like the company is experiencing a downturn, you will probably want to wait for a more auspicious time.

After you've established that the timing is right, you need to look at what you have to offer. Have you done anything to help improve the company's profitability? Has what you've done been obvious to others? Outside of COLA, and depending on the type of company, pay raises are generally merit-based. So a good beginning would be for you to sit down and make a list of your contributions to the company. Have you been asked to do additional tasks beyond what is expected of someone in your job? That might mean you deserve a promotion, and a promotion usually means a higher salary. You might think you are an amazing employee, but facts speak with more force than opinions do, so document your successes and contributions to the company. If possible, collect letters and emails showing that you are appreciated by clients or supervisors for jobs you have been involved in. Remember, asking for a raise is like applying for a job, so put together a "works in progress" resume listing details of recent accomplishments, especially the ones you've had with your current employer. If you don't have much to show, then you might need to think about trying to do more. Try taking classes to upgrade your skills, and take on assignments that will help demonstrate what you are capable of.

The best time for you to ask for a raise is when you are red-hot. You've just successfully closed an important deal, brought in additional clients, streamlined some workflow issue, or otherwise improved your company's profitability in some way. It's amazing how well it works to strike while the iron's hot. Don't wait too long, because your boss may forget how well you've done on this job when he or she turns attention to the next big project.

Once you've made an appointment to meet with your boss, be sure to think about your appearance. Your appearance is just as important when asking for a raise as it is when you interview for a job. Dress well and get a haircut or trim. Be polite, not pushy or cocky, and whatever you do, don't threaten to quit if you don't get what you want. You might just be taken up on that. Present your argument for more money by documenting your successes, and be sure you ask for what you truly deserve. If your boss agrees that you're a valuable employee but says no to a raise, try negotiating for other perks. You might be just as satisfied with paid vacation time, paid training or education, childcare, or even a more flexible work schedule. Also, don't allow your disappointment to show if your request for a raise is rejected. Any sign of disappointment on your part could make your boss feel uncomfortable around you.

Finally, don't forget to write a thank-you to your boss for listening and considering your suggestions. And be sure to include a list of your recent accomplishments to help him or her remember what you are worth.

E. ENGLISH IN ACTION

Let's listen in as Carl asks Mr. Peterson for a raise.

Mr. Peterson: Hello, Carl. How are you?
           Carl: I'm doing well, Mr. Peterson. How's your wife?

Mr. Peterson:	Oh, she's doing great. She just got back from Cincinnati . . . visiting her mother, you know.
Carl:	Oh, right. I hear it's really snowing there right now.
Mr. Peterson:	Yes, that's right. It's pretty cold.
Carl:	Um hum.
Mr. Peterson:	So, what did you want to talk to me about?
Carl:	Well, I've been thinking, Mr. Peterson. I've been with the company for several years now. And I've helped land several accounts, such as, you know, the Binbro and Maestro account, the Tellwin account, and I pretty much brought in the last big account, the Baldwin account, with very little help. And here, this is a letter from Jack Baldwin thanking me for the time and effort I put into it.
Mr. Peterson:	Hmm, yes, that was quite an accomplishment and yes, this is a great letter. Why don't you give me a copy so I can put it in your file, okay?
Carl:	Sure.
Mr. Peterson:	So, Carl, are you looking for some sort of compensation?
Carl:	Well . . . yes. I am. And, as a matter of fact, I've been doing some checking, and it looks like I'm a little underpaid. Look, see, here are the comps and here's what I'm making. You can see that I should be making several thousand more than what I'm making right now.
Mr. Peterson:	Hmmm. Yes, I see your point. You certainly have the goods, but I don't know if we can bring you up quite that much. I think you deserve a raise. I've noticed you've put in a lot of hours; you definitely have not just been a paper-pusher. And the Baldwin account is considerable, but it'll be a while before we start making anything off of it. What if we raise your salary by one thousand this year and another thousand next year? Hmm? How does that sound?
Carl:	Hmm. Well, maybe you could give me, say, an extra week of vacation this year and another two weeks next year.
Mr. Peterson:	Well, I think we could give you the extra week. I'm not sure yet about two additional weeks next year. What if we paid for some courses you need to pick up? If you took those classes that would make it easier for me to argue to corporate that you deserve a better salary.
Carl:	That sounds good. That would help a lot. I've been wanting to take some classes to get up to speed. Oh, um, do you think you could put this in writing?
Mr. Peterson:	Absolutely.
Carl:	Thanks a lot, Mr. Peterson. I really appreciate your time, and I'm really happy to be part of the team.

Mr. Peterson: Well, we certainly appreciate you, Carl. I'm glad we could work something out.

F. PRACTICE

Fill in the blanks with the following expressions: *going rate, paper-pusher, bide your time, red-hot, negotiable, maxed out, take the bull by the horns, perks, march into, has the goods*

1. Becca's really _____ right now. I can't get her to stop working long enough to even have a cup of coffee with me.
2. I don't think Ross is up to this job. I just don't think he _____, so I'd prefer to find someone else for the project.
3. If you want to spend your whole life being a(n) _____, take a desk job. Otherwise, take a risk on something more fun.
4. I've had it! I'm _____. I can't finish the job. I'm just too tired.
5. Just _____. You'll work your way into a better position, you'll see.
6. Before you ask for a raise, you'd better find out the _____ for the work you do!
7. My salary may not be the highest, but there really are great _____ that come with this job.
8. Honey, if you want to get a raise, you're just going to have to ask. Just _____ and tell your boss you're worth more than she's paying you.
9. You're right! I should just _____ her office and tell her that I deserve a raise!
10. All entry-level salaries here are non-_____, so if you accept this position, you have to accept this salary as well.

Fill in the blank with the correct participial form of the verb in parentheses.

1. I'm _____ (surprise) at your ability to get all this work done on time.
2. The flies in this office are _____ (annoy), don't you think?
3. We're all _____ (amuse) by his great sense of humor.
4. Ralph is _____ (fascinate) by the success of his boss.
5. I find my colleague's conversation in the next cubicle very _____ (distract).
6. I'm _____ (interest) in seeing this movie; aren't you?
7. Joan has been feeling a bit _____ (depress) since her raise request was rejected.
8. Yolanda found her evaluation very _____ (encourage).

9. It's _____ (comfort) to know that you have a job even in this slow job market.

10. Are you _____ (satisfy) by your work or would you prefer to be doing something else?

 G. TASK

Imagine that you want to ask for a raise. Follow the guidelines given in the How-To section of this lesson, and use the resources listed below in the Resources section to prepare a salary comparison chart for your occupation. Then make a list of the recent things you have done to benefit the company, and finally, practice asking for a raise with a friend or partner.

H. REAL LIFE

Once again, let's see what people want to "Ask Sammy" about their real-life questions and concerns.

Dear Sammy,

When I was offered my current job, my boss told me I would be getting a raise in six months. Well, six months have come and gone and I still haven't seen a raise. I really feel like I deserve it, too, because I've really been maxing out on this job. Would it be acceptable for me to ask my boss about the promised raise?

Sincerely,
Feeling Burned

Dear Burned,

Unfortunately, this sort of thing does happen. But most likely, your boss is just busy and hasn't noticed how long it has been since you started your job. A gentle nudge would be acceptable, but if you work for a union, a school, or the government, first check with human resources to see if there is a salary schedule. It may already be in writing, in which case, you should simply mention it to the human resources director and he or she should take it from there. If there is no schedule of raises, it would be a good idea to bring it up with your boss. Arm yourself with a list of your successes since joining the company. On the off chance that he or she has selective memory and does not remember telling you that you'd be getting a raise, let this be a wake-up call. And for the future, always ask your boss to put any monetary promises in writing when they are offered.

Good luck,
Sammy

I. RESOURCES

Here are a few important resources you may find helpful if you want to ask for a raise.
www.soyouwanna.com/site/syws/raise/raise.html

Salary information:
www.acinet.org/acinet/occ_rep.asp
http://salaryexpert.com
www.vault.com/companies/salary-survey.jsp

A sample salary increase memo:
www.quintcareers.com/salary_raise_letter.html

ANSWER KEY
Practice 1: 1. red-hot; 2. has the goods; 3. paper-pusher; 4. maxed out; 5. bide your time; 6. going rate; 7. perks; 8. take the bull by the horns; 9. march into; 10. negotiable

Practice 2: 1. surprised; 2. annoying; 3. amused; 4. fascinated; 5. distracting; 6. interested; 7. depressed; 8. encouraging; 9. comforting; 10. satisfied

CHAPTER 7

In the Car: Buying a Car

A. **ENGLISH CLOSE-UP**

Rob Riker's Cars
Special Event Sale!

Up to $4,300 off MSRP on select models!
No money down, 2% APR for 12 months!

For a limited time only!!
*Excludes taxes, title, and license

B. **VOCABULARY ESSENTIALS**

APR (Annual percentage rate)—Percentage of interest times 12 months. *It's a 60-month loan with an APR of 1.5% and no money down.*

Big-ticket item—A very expensive purchase, like a car or a boat. *I don't see where he gets the money to buy so many big-ticket items.*

Blue Book (Kelley Blue Book®)—A standard reference used to determine the value of a car based on year, make, model, condition, etc. *I have an old hatchback from 1990 that's still driveable, but the Blue Book® value is only a few hundred dollars!*

Clunker—An old car that has a lot of dents, scrapes, and broken parts. *Isn't it time you traded in that old clunker for a newer model?*

Dealer invoice price (factory invoice price)—The amount that dealers are charged by auto manufacturers for their cars. *The MSRP is usually much higher than the dealer invoice price, which is what dealers had to pay for the cars on their lot.*

To drive away, to drive off—To leave a place by driving. *You can drive away in a beautiful new car for only a $5,000 down payment.*

Driver's license—An official document, usually a small card, permitting a person to drive a vehicle. Often referred to just by "license." *My driver's license expires pretty soon. I know I should go get it renewed, but I just hate waiting in line at the DMV.*

Extended warranty—A guarantee purchased to cover time beyond an original warranty given by the manufacturer for a product. *You can also purchase a seven-year extended warranty to cover parts that fail after the manufacturer's warranty expires.*

FICO®—Fair Isaac Credit Organization, a credit score based on an applicant's credit history, used to verify credit worthiness. *Let us take a look at your FICO® score to see what kind of a rate we can give you on this car.*

Fuel-efficient—Able to operate on very little fuel. *Small cars are usually more fuel-efficient than large ones.*

To haggle—To bargain for something. *If you want a car at a good price, be prepared to haggle.*

Hybrid—A type of car that uses two different types of power, such as gas and electricity, to allow the car to use energy more efficiently. *More and more people are buying hybrids for their fuel efficiency.*

Incentive—A reward, often monetary, given to encourage someone to do something. *You can get either $1,000 or a 0% loan as an incentive to buy this car.*

Lemon—A car, often used, that is found to be in very poor condition. "Lemon laws" exist to protect people from cars that are in dangerously poor condition. *I thought I was getting a great deal on this used convertible, but all I got was a lemon!*

License plate—A vehicle registration plate, often metal, that is attached to the back and often the front of the car and is used to officially identify and document the car. The plate has a list of numbers and/or letters unique to that car. *I decided to pay for a personalized license plate so I could choose the letters and numbers on it.*

MSRP—Manufacturer's suggested retail price. *The MSRP on that model is $18,000.00, but that doesn't include any add-ons, taxes, or license fees.*

Odometer—An instrument on the dashboard of a vehicle that counts total distance a car has driven in miles or kilometers. *When the odometer hits 15,000 miles, you'll need to have the car serviced.*

Payoff, to pay off—An amount of money needed to settle a debt, the action of settling a debt. To make all payments or pay the full amount of a purchase. *Give us the payoff for your car, and we'll take care of it for you and put you in a brand new car.*

Rebate—A portion of money returned to the buyer after a purchase is made, usually sent by mail, but possibly paid out at the point of purchase. *There's a $1,500 point-of-purchase rebate on that model if you buy it this week.*

To renege—To fail to meet a commitment, for example, to back out of a contract. *The guy who was going to buy my car reneged on the deal. Now I have to find another buyer.*

Scam, to scam—An illegal means of tricking someone into buying or paying for something. To trick someone into buying or paying for something. *Some car dealers will scam you if they can, so try to go to a reputable car dealership if possible.*

Trade-in value—The price a dealer should be willing to pay for a used car. *Check out the trade-in value before you go to the dealer so you can better negotiate your price.*

VIN number—Vehicle identification number, unique to each car, giving information such as country of origin, date manufactured, etc. You can usually find the VIN number of your car on the driver's side dashboard, motor, and frame of your car, as well as in the car title. *There are several places you can go on the web to search your car's history using the VIN number.*

Warranty—A guarantee for a certain period of time that a product will be repaired or replaced if necessary. For cars, any warranty, whether a factory/manufacturer's basic warranty, a corrosion warranty, or some other kind of warranty, will usually cover up to a certain amount of time and/or miles, for example, a 4-year/50,000-mile warranty. *You shouldn't have to pay to make those repairs. The car is still under warranty.*

C. GRAMMAR ESSENTIALS: FILLER PHRASES

Just as in any language, spoken English contains a lot of filler words and other expressions that speakers use to stall for time while they think or to give listeners clues about what they're saying. These words and phrases will make your English sound more natural, and they'll make communication easier for both you and your listener. Let's focus on a few of them:

The conjunction *and* is used to add a thought to a previously spoken thought.

It can signal that the speaker isn't quite through making a point:
> *And when I went to the dealer to buy a car, she asked me if I wanted to sell my old one.*

It can also be a means of returning the conversation to an earlier topic, especially with the addition of *as I was saying*:
> *And as I was saying, I think you should check out the new hybrids.*

By itself, the expression *as I was saying* (*before*) is another filler used to continue or return to an earlier topic:
> *As I was saying, it's usually cheaper to drive a stick than an automatic.*

The expressions *but anyway* and *but as I was saying* can also be used at the beginning of a sentence to steer the conversation back to an original point:
> *But anyway, as I was saying, this car drives very well and it gets pretty good gas mileage.*

But can also be used on its own at the beginning of a sentence to interject an opinion or to give a contrary opinion:
> —*"This year's models look great!"*
> —*"But I think they don't look as good as last year's do."*

The word *so* can be used at the beginning of a sentence to signal a new topic or a break from the logical flow of conversation after a pause:
> *So anyway, I really need to get a new car, and I was looking online the other day . . .*

So can also be used to signal a logical consequence or deduction:
> —*"My car died, and I'm getting my tax return in a few weeks, but right now I'm broke . . ."*
> —*"So you want me to lend you some money?"*

So is also used as a request for the listener's response or to make an invitation:
> *So, what do you think of my new car?*
> *So, would you like to go for a drive in my new car?*

The word *or* is often used at the beginning of a sentence as a corrector. It's sometimes followed by *rather*:
> *It never rains in Southern California. Or, rather, I should say it almost never rains.*

It can also introduce a different possibility or choice:
> *Or, if you don't want to buy a new car, you could consider leasing one.*

On top of these "filler phrase" uses of conjunctions, English has lots of phrases that are used by a speaker to stall, giving the speaker time to think. Typical examples include: *well, you see, that is, I mean, you know, like*.
> *Well . . . you know . . . that is . . . I have some bad news about your car. You see, there was an accident, and . . .*

D. HOW-TO

So you want to buy a car! You should know, buying a car can be a tedious and emotional process. And it takes a lot of time from start to finish. In fact, some experts say you need at least six months to buy the best car for you at the lowest possible price. However, there are some steps you can take to ensure that the purchase goes as smoothly as possible.

First, think about what you're looking for in a car—what, exactly, you need the car to have. Will you need to transport a lot of people or equipment in the car? If so, you might need a car with a lot of space. Do you have a long commute or otherwise spend a lot of time driving? If you do, you might want to consider looking into cars that have good gas mileage so that you won't have to spend as much money on gas. You could also think about safety features, design, and so on. In addition, you'll want to think about what you can afford. Decide what your price range is and what monthly payments you can afford to make.

Once you've figured out what you need and what you can afford, do a lot of research. Visit Kelley Blue Book® at kbb.com, cars.com, edmunds.com, or consumerguide.com. You can also purchase a Consumer Reports New Car Buying Guide or go to their website at consumerreports.org for information. At these sites, you can find the MSRP and dealer invoice price as well as what people in your area are actually paying for the car. You'll also find car-buying tips, customer reviews, and additional information on the car's reliability, gas mileage, safety features, and so on.

While doing your research, you might also want to visit various dealerships, which are the companies that buy and sell cars. You are allowed to take a test-drive, or briefly drive the car around. This is a good way to get a sense of the car—how well it works and whether you feel comfortable in it. Make sure to take advantage of a test-drive and test out many of the car's features, such as its mirrors, locking system, etc. You should also test out parking, driving in congested areas, driving over bumpy or narrow streets, and other questions of how the car will perform on a day-to-day basis. Sometimes the car salesperson will come along with you on the test-drive, but not always. However, you should have your driver's license with you, as the salesperson will ask to make a photocopy of it before allowing you to take a test-drive.

Once you know what car you want, go into a dealership and start negotiating. The main rule here is never to accept the first price a dealer offers you. Unless the car is in very high demand, most people do not pay the listed retail price, or MSRP. If you've done your research, you know what the dealer invoice price is, or how much the dealer paid the car manufacturer for the car, so you can use that in your negotiations. You should also know from your research what most people in your area paid for the car, which will give you a good sense of how much you should be able to negotiate. You want to make the dealer think you can just walk away if you don't like the price. In addition, don't negotiate with just one dealer. Speak with several dealers. It's also a good idea to get quotes online through many of the sites mentioned here. In other words, get as many different offers as possible so you can negotiate better and get the best possible price.

You should also be aware of options, or add-ons, when negotiating and looking for a car. The dealer will hand you a list of available options for the car, such as leather seats, a sunroof, an enhanced stereo system, heated seats, and so on. The model you test-drove and are interested in will usually have many of the standard options already in it, such as a CD player and automatic windows, and the price quoted to you for that model will have those options included in it. However, you can customize the car by, for example, adding a CD changer or choosing a different car color, and these extras will cost you. Furthermore, keep in mind that you can always negotiate regarding options, so additional options might end up being included in the deal depending on how you negotiate. However, if you do get a deal on options, or any other sort of special deal, get it in writing to ensure that you will still get the deal when it comes time to sign for the car.

Throughout this whole process, you'll want to be thinking about and planning how you're going to pay for the car. You have several options. You can just pay for the car in cash (which means you don't use any financing) or get a car loan from the dealer or a bank. On many of the sites mentioned here, there are loan calculators that will tell you what your monthly payment will most likely be for a specific car. You'll also want to check out what your FICO credit score is, which you can do online at annualcreditreport.com. The better your credit score, the lower your loan payment will be. Next, you'll want to compare various financing options. Talk to your bank about the car loans it offers and talk to various dealers about their financing options and any special financing plans that might be available at that time. You can usually find special financing offers, such as a low APR or low monthly payments, advertised in newspapers, on television, on the radio, or online.

If you don't want to actually buy the car, you can always lease it. You might not want the financial commitment of owning a car. You also might not think a car is a good investment. In fact, it is often said that cars drop 20% in value the moment you drive them off the lot. If you lease a car, you are essentially renting a new car for a certain period of time for monthly payments. The monthly payments are often lower than they would be with a car loan. When the lease is up, usually after a few years, you usually have the option of leasing the same car again or leasing a new car if you want to. If you plan to keep the car for more than five years, leasing is probably not a good option. One thing to keep in mind is that if you lease a car, the number of miles you can drive that car is restricted. If you go over that number, you will most likely have to pay a penalty.

Of course, another option is to buy a used car instead of buying or leasing a new one. Buying a used car will usually save you a lot of money, but you still need to put the same amount of effort into buying a used car as you would into buying a new one. Again, be sure to do your research. Most of the sites mentioned will provide a good amount of information on used cars as well as new ones. They'll tell you what the retail price is for many used cars, the trade-in value, the mileage, the equipment installed in the car, and so on. They will also tell you if the used car is a certified pre-owned car (CPO), which means you get a lot of the benefits of a new car, such as warranties and a thorough inspection, for less than the price of a new car. However, CPOs are still used cars, so you still want to find out as much as possible about their condition. Once you've chosen the type of car you want to buy, you have two options. You can buy it commercially or through a private individual. Although buying it through a private party will often be cheaper than buying it through a dealer, there are not as many guarantees. If you feel it is necessary, you can take the car to a mechanic to get it checked out. If you decide to buy commercially, it is probably best to choose a large used car dealership with a good reputation, as there are many unscrupulous used car dealers out there who will sell you a lemon. Many reputable new car dealers also have used car lots, so you can always choose that option.

In addition to buying a used car, you can also sell your own used car to offset some of the cost of buying a different car. You can either sell your car on your own or trade in your used car for a new one. If you trade in the car, there are several things to keep in mind. First, check the standard trade-in value for your car on one of the car websites discussed here so you can make sure you get a good price for your old car from the dealer. Also, if you still owe money on your old car, you'll want to make sure you are aware of what the loan payments will be, because, in that case, you will be borrowing money for your new car as well as for the payoff on your old car. It's also important to be sure that your dealer pays off your old car immediately. Sometimes they tell you they'll pay it off, but a few months later you receive a notice saying your payment is overdue. Why? Because paying off your car is not the dealer's first priority. Even if you have signed the title, or the form that certifies ownership of the car, over to the dealer, the old car loan is still your legal responsibility.

Once you've finalized the car, price, payment, options, trade-in, and any other factors, and you're confident in your choice, you're ready to sign the papers. At this time, be sure to sign all the documents at the dealership, read everything you're signing, and get your own copies of every signed document. Note that car dealers will almost never make any changes to their standard contract forms. It's not a good idea to leave the dealership before all the paperwork is finalized. If you leave anything blank on the forms, you never know what financial surprises might be added on after you thought the deal was sealed. However, don't let all of this frighten you too much. It is certainly possible to get a good deal on a car, and it can be a reasonably enjoyable experience. You just need to keep a cool head and be sure to do all of your homework.

E. ENGLISH IN ACTION

Ms. Jurgens and her son Pete are at the car dealership looking at the new Bluebirds. Listen in as Jim, the car salesman, tries to sell them a car.

Pete:	Wow, Mom. Look at that Bluebird. She's a beauty!
Ms. Jurgens:	Yes. It really is a beautiful car.
Jim:	Would you like to take her for a spin?
Ms. Jurgens:	Oh, I don't know. I'm really just kind of looking right now.
Jim:	What's the harm? She really handles the road well.
Pete:	Couldn't we just try it?
Ms. Jurgens:	Well . . .
Jim:	My name's Jim, by the way. And you are?
Ms. Jurgens:	Melanie Jurgens, and this is my son Pete.
Pete:	Hi.
Jim:	Hi, Pete. I'll bet you'd like to try it out.
Pete:	Yeah.
Jim:	Well, how about it, Mom?
Ms. Jurgens:	Okay, I guess I do want to see what it's like. But I'm not buying anything, at least not today.
Jim:	Okay, I'll go get the keys. Can I have your license? I need to make a copy of it . . . Insurance, you know.
Ms. Jurgens:	Okay, here it is.
Pete:	Cool.
Ms. Jurgens:	Cool is right. But Pete, we don't want him to know we really want to buy one of these. So we need to act cool. Relax! You're giving away too much. No drooling, okay?
Pete:	Okay.
Jim:	Here are the keys. Have a seat, Mom.
Ms. Jurgens:	Thank you.
Jim:	Did you notice the dash? It's all lit up like a computer screen. How about that?
Ms. Jurgens:	Hmm. Yes. How much is this car, exactly?
Jim:	Well, this car has pin striping and chrome wheels.
Ms. Jurgens:	But I don't want those.
Jim:	Oh . . . well, we'll take those off, no problem. Lucky for you, it has an alarm system, though.
Ms. Jurgens:	What do I need that for? Nobody ever pays any attention to the alarm anyway.
Jim:	Well, it is a deterrent.
Ms. Jurgens:	I don't think I need it.

Jim: Okay, well, we can take that off, too. I guess the stripped down model would cost you about $26,000.

Ms. Jurgens: $26,000? Why do you charge so much? The true market value is at least $2,500 less than that.

Jim: Well, but our price includes the delivery fee, and a few other things. Look, I'll make you a deal. I'll give it to you for twenty-four five. And I'll throw in a bottle of car wax as well.

Pete: So that's a thousand dollar bottle of car wax?

Ms. Jurgens: Exactly!

Jim: Look, no car wax, okay. But I can't drop the price below twenty-three seventy-five.

Ms. Jurgens: I'll think about it.

Jim: For you, I'll take twenty-three five, but not a penny less.

Ms. Jurgens: Okay. It's a deal.

Pete: Yippee! We're getting a new Bluebird!

F. PRACTICE

Fill in the blanks with the following words: *big-ticket items, scams, rebates, renege, hybrid, haggle, trade-in value, pay off, clunker, lemon*

1. Car dealers may offer _____ to car buyers when they need to use incentives to get people to buy a car from them.

2. Some unscrupulous car dealers have a number of _____ they use to get more money from a buyer.

3. If you don't do any research on your used car, you may get less than the _____ for it.

4. It's embarrassing to be seen in this _____. I'd really like a new one.

5. If you don't like to _____, then you might want to buy your car through a car search service.

6. You can be better off financially if you _____ your old car yourself than if you allow the dealer to do it.

7. Cars are really _____. I mean, where can you get a decent new car for less than $10,000?

8. Nowadays, many people are considering buying a(n) _____ because gas is just getting so expensive.

9. Sometimes you can return your new car within three days of purchasing it. However, once you've signed a contract and driven your car off the lot, it's very, very difficult to _____ on the deal.

10. Most states have _____ laws that are there to protect the consumer against cars that are just no good.

Fill in the blanks in the following sentences with the best possible filler phrase: a. and; b. or, rather c. but as I was saying before; d. that is; e. well; f. so; g. as I was saying; h. or; i. but anyway; j. but

1. _____ we were interrupted, I think we need to look at hybrids as a real possibility.

2. It's a beautiful car, isn't it. _____ it can go from 0 to 60 MPH in 10 seconds flat.

3. —"I just don't think I really need them." —"_____, what you're saying then is that you aren't interested in heated seats?"

4. This car comes in five colors. _____, I should say, at least four; two of them are different shades of silver.

5. —"Blue is a much better color than red." —"_____ I think a red car looks sportier than blue!"

6. _____, I don't know . . . I think I need more time to think it over.

7. Yes, it is beautiful weather outside. But, _____, I can't wait to pick up my new car next week.

8. You could get an SUV. _____ you could get a more fuel efficient car.

9. _____, could we return to what I was talking about before?

10. You'll like the car. I'm almost positive you'll like the car . . . _____ . . . I hope you like the car.

G. TASK

Imagine that you want to buy a new car, and you'd like sell your current car to offset some of the costs. First, use one of the resources listed in this chapter to find out how much money you could get for your current car. Also check to see how much you might be able to get if you sell the car on your own. Then use one of the consumer guides to see how much the new car you're interested in will most likely cost. With the amount you'll get from your old car, can you afford a new one?

H. REAL LIFE

If you weren't already familiar with the term "lemon," you learned it in the vocabulary section of this chapter. A lemon is a car that has serious defects that cause it to break down and need constant repairs. Without naming names, you've probably heard of car models that the manufacturers were forced to recall after it became clear that there were serious safety problems with the car. Maybe even people died as a result. To protect the public from dangerously defective cars, there are laws called "lemon laws" on the books in each state. You can find out how your state defines a lemon, and what you can do if you have one, by checking out www.carlemon.com. If you think you have a lemon and are entitled to a legal remedy, make sure you document all repairs. In fact, because you usually don't realize that you have a lemon until after your warranty has expired, it's a good idea to begin documenting all repairs and problems with every single car you own. In the end, it's the best protection.

I. RESOURCES

For tips on buying new and used cars, check out:
www.carbuyingtips.com/buyingnewcar.htm
www.ftc.gov/bcp/conline/pubs/autos/usedcar.htm

For car comparison guides, pricing, and to determine the value of your car:
www.kbb.com
www.cars.com
www.edmunds.com
www.carbuyingtips.com
www.carclicks.com
www.consumerguide.com

To find out about your state's Lemon Law:
www.carlemon.com

ANSWER KEY
Practice 1: 1. rebates; 2. scams; 3. trade-in value; 4. clunker; 5. haggle; 6. pay off; 7. big-ticket items; 8. hybrid; 9. renege; 10. lemon

Practice 2: 1. c; 2. a; 3. f; 4. b; 5. j; 6. e; 7. g; 8. h; 9. i; 10. d

CHAPTER 8

In the Car: Rules of the Road

A. **ENGLISH CLOSE-UP**

KINGS CANYON PARK
VISITORS *DOs* & *DON'Ts*

- don't feed the bears
- use only dead & down wood for campfires
- no holding campsites

Have a safe vacation!

B. **VOCABULARY ESSENTIALS**

To back up—To drive a car backwards. *Jan backed up and pulled out of the driveway.*

To buckle up—To use seat belts. *All along the freeway there are signs that remind passengers to buckle up for safety.*

To cut off—To make a sharp and sudden turn in front of another driver. *Many accidents are caused by one driver cutting another off.*

Designated driver—The person chosen not to drink in order to drive a group of friends who will have been drinking. *Paul offered to be the designated driver because he had a big test the next day and didn't want to drink anyway.*

DMV (or MVD)—Department of Motor Vehicles/Motor Vehicles Department. *Go to your local DMV to take your driver's license exam and road test.*

To drive around—To change direction momentarily in order to avoid an obstacle. *A big rock had fallen into the road, so I had to drive around it.* Or, to drive aimlessly or without progress toward a specific destination. *You know, we've been driving around for an hour and we still haven't found the Children's Museum.*

Driver's Ed—Driver's education course that teaches car safety, car maintenance, driving technique, traffic law, and so on. It must be taken in many states in order to receive a learner's permit and eventually a driver's license. *Although David thought Driver's Ed was kind of boring, he knew that he was learning a lot about driving.*

DUI/DWI—A citation for Driving Under the Influence of alcohol, or for Driving While Intoxicated. *Every state in the union has stiff penalties for DUI/DWI.*

Emissions test—A test to check for and limit the amount of carbon dioxide and other pollutants a car emits. *Certain states have to require vehicle emissions tests because their air does not meet federal clean air standards.*

The finger—The middle finger pointed at someone with the two surrounding fingers bent. This is an obscene gesture meant to offend. *Hackett was so angry when he got cut off that he pulled up beside the other driver and gave him the finger.*

Flow of traffic—The movement of cars through a specific area. *The construction stretched for miles and really disrupted the flow of traffic, causing massive delays.*

To hitchhike—To solicit rides for free from other drivers, typically by holding out a thumb pointed upwards. (This is illegal in many states and cities.) *Tad and Mike hitchhiked all the way from Los Angeles to Seattle.*

Ignition—The slot for the key that starts the car's engine. *I can't get my key out of the ignition; it's stuck!*

Learner's permit—A document that allows you to drive a car before obtaining your license, usually in order to learn how to drive. Driving is usually only allowed when accompanied by a licensed driver who is over 21 years old. The minimum age to obtain a permit, often around 15 or older, varies by state. *I can't wait to turn 15 so I can get my learner's permit and start learning how to drive!*

NHTSA—The National Highway Traffic Safety Administration is the federal agency that administers traffic safety. *To find out what the national traffic safety standards are, check the NHTSA website.*

Off-roading, off-road driving—Driving a vehicle where there are no paved roads. *If you're going to go off-roading in the desert or mountains, check the rules for the state you are in.*

To pass—To overtake a car by switching lanes and accelerating. *You can only* pass another car if you switch into the left lane. *Passing is not permitted in the right lane.*

Pedestrian—A person traveling on foot. *Pedestrians often have the right of way.*

Radar—A method using high frequency radio waves for determining the speed and location of an object. *Cops often check speed by aiming radar guns at passing cars.*

Right of way—The right of a person or driver to move before another person or driver. *If you arrive at a stop sign before another driver, you have the right of way.*

Road rage—Explosive anger of one driver provoked by another driver. *Road rage erupted between two drivers when one accused the other of cutting him off.*

Rolling stop—Gradually applying the brakes to bring the car to a near, but not complete, stop. *Step on the brakes completely so you don't make a rolling stop.*

Rubbernecking—Slowing down (while driving) to look at an accident on the freeway. *The reason traffic gets so bad when there's been an accident is usually because so many drivers are rubbernecking.*

Rush hour—The hours just before and just after work when there is a great amount of traffic. *Let's wait until after rush hour to leave so we're not caught in traffic.*

To swerve—To make a sudden move to the side, usually in order to avoid hitting something. *A deer ran out onto the highway and I had to swerve to miss it.*

Tailgating—Driving dangerously close to the car in front of you. *If you tailgate and the driver ahead of you stops suddenly, you could rear-end him.*

To take off—To leave. *Do you want to take off?*

Ticket (traffic citation)—In the context of vehicles, a legal summons to appear in court or to pay a fine, written by a traffic officer for a traffic violation. *It's not only safer, but also cheaper to follow the traffic laws, because tickets can be expensive.*

Toll roads—Roads that charge a small fee to pass onto them. The fee is used to pay for maintaining the road. *It's much faster to take the toll road to Long Beach than the regular freeway.*

Wreck—A car accident. *There was a huge wreck on the highway during rush hour.*

C. GRAMMAR ESSENTIALS: CONFUSING VERBS

There are a few English verb pairs that confuse some non-native speakers, usually because the same distinction isn't made in their native languages or because of idiomatic usage. The most common examples are: *come* and *go*, *bring* and *take*, *make* and *do*, *take* and *have*, and *borrow* and *lend*. The three verbs *see*, *look*, and *watch* are also often misused, as are *listen* and *hear*.

Go—Expresses motion away from the speaker, or motion between two points away from the speaker:

> *Let's go to the movies this weekend.*
> *They went from door to door collecting signatures on their petition.*

Come—Expresses motion toward the speaker. It can also be used to express motion toward the listener:

> *If you come to visit me, take the back roads; it's more scenic.*
> *Bill is coming here by car.*
> *When are the kids coming to see you in Chicago?*

Take—Expresses the action of carrying something away from the speaker, or carrying something between two points away from the speaker:

> *What are you taking with you on your trip?*
> *Jerry took all of his DVDs with him when he went to college.*

Bring—Expresses the action of carrying something toward the speaker. It can also be used to express motion toward the listener:

> *Could you bring me a cup of coffee?*
> *What did your students bring you on your first day of school?*

Note that both *come* and *bring*, which usually imply motion toward the speaker or listener, can also refer to a location away from both speaker and listener, oriented toward a third party. This is often the case in narration, when a story is told from the perspective of a third party:

> *Three strangers came to Mark's door in the middle of the night.*
> *Sue brought all of her books with her when she moved into her own apartment.*

Make—To create or construct something, usually with a physical result:

> —*"What are you making?"*—*"A new spice rack for my mother."*
> *The fifth graders made models of the solar system for their science projects.*

Do—To perform an action, not necessarily with a physical result:

> —*"What are you doing?"*—*"I'm watching TV."*
> *The fifth graders are always doing something interesting in art class.*

There are a lot of idiomatic uses of both of these verbs, only some of which follow the general definitions given above:

Make a cake, make dinner, make money, make the bed, make a frown, make a deal, make fun of, make sure, make up, make believe, etc.
Do exercises, do homework, do dishes, do housework, do laundry, do over, do the math, do away with, do in, etc.

Have—Apart from its literal meaning, there are many idiomatic and fixed expressions that use *have*. One of its most confusing uses is in the context of eating or drinking, when it means to partake (in food and drink):
Do you want to have another drink?
For appetizers, I'll have the spring rolls, and for the main course I'll have red curry.

Take—In English, *take* is used when speaking of consuming medicine:
You should take aspirin if you have a headache.
Take some cough medicine if you are coughing.

Take can be used when speaking of accepting food or drink, not consuming it:
I'll take a cup of tea, thank you.
I'll take a cookie, but I'll eat it later on my break.

Borrow—To accept something from someone for temporary use.
Could I borrow $20 from you until I get paid?
Jules borrowed a book from me and I don't think he ever gave it back!

Lend/Loan—To offer something to someone for temporary use. Usually, but not always, *loan* is used with money:
Henry loaned me $20 until I get paid.
I lent Jules a book, and he never gave it back to me.

See, look, watch—All three of these verbs involve the sense of sight but suggest different levels of involvement.
See is the most general; it can refer to an involuntary action, as when something moves into your field of vision:
While we were driving along the coast we saw whales in the bay.
I saw something really interesting on the highway today.

Look implies intentional vision, but perhaps not very focused or for a very long time. It is always used with the preposition *at*:
Look at those whales out there in the bay!
I can't look at the map right now; I'm driving.

Watch implies a prolonged focus on something—a person, an object, an event, or a performance. It also implies careful study or attention:
We pulled over and watched the whales until they swam out of sight.
I'm watching television right now, so I can't talk.

Perhaps oddly, you *see a movie*, even though this is obviously a prolonged event. You can also *see a person* if you're romantically involved, which is most likely also a prolonged event.

Listen, hear—Both of these verbs refer to the act of sensing sound. *Listen* is always paired with *to* in English, and it refers to a more deliberate act of perceiving sound. You can *hear* something unintentionally, but you make a decision to focus on something and *listen to* it:

I can hear the sounds of the highway even when I'm this far away from it.
I love to listen to the radio when I drive.

You normally *listen to* music, a radio, a CD, a digital music player, etc., but you *hear* a specific song.

D. HOW-TO

Traffic laws vary from state to state in the USA. Each state's Department of Motor Vehicles (DMV) publishes a driver's manual that contains all the relevant laws so you can familiarize yourself with the laws you're subject to in your state. However, this section will cover some of the most common and important traffic laws to help guide you through the experience of driving in the U.S. Nevertheless, this is only a general overview and it is not meant to replace an official legal handbook.

Let's start with things that you should have with you when you drive. To drive legally, you must be at least 16 years old in most states, and you must have a valid driver's license, or in certain cases a learner's permit if an adult driver is with you. If you are only coming for a visit, you can use your driver's license from your own country for at least 90 days. If you plan to live in the U.S. for a while, you need to get a valid driver's license from the state in which you reside within 30 days of your arrival. Apart from your driver's license, you must always carry both proof of insurance and vehicle registration with you while you drive.

In addition, you should always have your seat belt on. Although this law varies from state to state, it's always better to be safe than sorry. If you're driving a motorcycle, you should wear a helmet. This is the law in many states, but it is a good idea everywhere. And speaking of safety, if you're driving with young children, you should put them in some form of child safety seats. Check on your DMV website for what to use, and be sure to follow product safety instructions very carefully.

Now let's look at some things you should *not* have with you when you drive. The most important thing not to have is alcohol in your system. Drunk driving is illegal everywhere in the U.S., and this law is seriously enforced. The exact legal definition of Driving While Intoxicated (DWI) or Driving Under the Influence (DUI) varies from state to state, but in general, if you have been drinking, take a cab, call a friend, or rely on a designated driver. Most states have open container laws as well, meaning that it is illegal even to have an open bottle of alcohol in the car with you. If you have to transport open containers of alcohol, put them in the trunk. Finally, it's illegal in many places to talk on your cell phone while you drive. Depending on where you are, you can get a fine for doing this.

Now let's look at driving in the town or city. The posted speed limit is the legal limit for the area. In residential and downtown areas it may be 25 or 35 miles per hour (MPH), but watch for the signs because the speed limit can change quickly. In general, slow down to 25 MPH or less (in some states it's 15 MPH) when passing a school while children are present. If you need to make a turn, always use your signal. In some states, you can make a right turn on a red light, but this varies from place to place. Speaking of traffic lights, you may observe that many Americans go on green, stop on red, and speed up on yellow, but of course a yellow light means that you should slow down. A U-turn is usually acceptable if not otherwise posted. Make a full stop at stop signs, because you can be ticketed for a rolling stop. If you want to make a left turn at a stop sign and reach a two-way stop at the same time as another driver, yield the right of way to the driver going straight. When arriving at a four-way stop, the first driver to stop is the first driver to continue driving. Drivers arriving at the same time must yield the right of way to the driver on the right. Stop when a stopped school bus has its red lights flashing, and always yield to emergency vehicles and funeral processions, which always have the right of way. When police vehicles, ambulances, or fire engines have their sirens on, pull over to the side of the road to allow them to pass. Funeral processions are permitted to stay together, and they will often have a police escort to ensure this. While going through a traffic signal, if any car in a funeral procession has not passed before the signal changes to red, you must wait for the entire procession to pass before you can move. All cars in a funeral procession should have their lights on and will sometimes have an orange sticker that says "funeral" to help identify them.

When driving on the freeway, as it's called in the western United States, or highway, as it's called in the eastern United States, go with the flow of traffic; driving much more quickly or slowly than other cars is dangerous. In most states, the speed limit on the freeway is 65 MPH, but watch for the signs, because the speed limit can vary even within the same state, usually dropping down in heavily populated areas. The far left lane is for passing, and the far right lane is for slower traffic or cars getting ready to exit on the right. Some areas now have carpool lanes, which are special lanes for cars that have more than one person. These lanes may also be open to hybrid cars with no passengers, meant as an incentive for people to buy hybrids. You may be able to pay for a special permit to ride in these lanes as a solo driver as well. Don't drive in these lanes illegally; you could get a very expensive ticket. Some highways are toll roads, which are sometimes called "turnpikes" or "parkways." You need to pay to drive on them, either by picking up a ticket when you enter and paying a particular price when you exit, or by slowing down and passing through tollbooths at fixed intervals.

Besides traffic laws, there are driving rules of etiquette as well. It's a good idea to follow these rules too, because although you won't get a ticket if you violate them, you can certainly make other drivers angry. Or worse, you could provoke "road rage." While most American drivers are polite and courteous, some drivers can get very aggressive and angry behind the wheel. Road rage might manifest itself as yelling obscenities or making rude gestures. In more severe cases it might result in highly aggressive driving, physical confrontations, or worse.

Here are some helpful suggestions for behind-the-wheel courtesy. First of all, be aware of all the cars around you at all times, and be very careful not to cut anyone off. Leave enough space between your car and other cars, use your signals when changing lanes or turning, and do not tailgate. If you see a driver trying to change lanes or merge onto the freeway, slow down or speed up to allow him or her to enter. Use your horn very carefully. Tap your horn as a polite signal, and only honk it loudly if there's danger. Use your high beams only when there's no one in front of you. You can also flash your lights at other drivers to warm them to slow down, for example, because of an animal in the road or an accident. Some drivers even use this method to warn other drivers that a police officer is lying in wait for speeders, so if you're driving over the limit and someone flashes you, you'd better slow down. A driver might also flash his or her high beams to remind you to turn yours off. If you come to a red light, be sure that you're not blocking the intersection. If there's traffic, stay out of the intersection until you're sure that there's enough time and room for you to get all the way through. And don't limit your courtesy to driving. If you're parking, make sure you only take up the space of one car. Don't pull into a space at such an angle that you take up two spaces. If you parallel park, leave enough space for the car in front or in back of you to get out. If you should happen to scrape someone's bumper when the other driver is not around, leave a note on the windshield with your name, phone number, and insurance information. All of these suggestions may seem like common sense to a courteous and responsible driver, but you'd be surprised at how often people disregard them and opt for rude driving behavior.

E.   ENGLISH IN ACTION

Let's listen as Hector receives a call on his cell phone while he's driving home during rush hour.

Hector: Hello?
Marla: Hi, Hector. It's me, Marla.
Hector: Uh, hi, Marla. What's up?
Marla: Oh, I just called 'cause I wanted to say . . .
Hector: Oh, man! Jeez!
Marla: What? What is it?
Hector: Oh, this guy's tailgating me.

Marla: Well, slow down. Maybe he'll pass you.
Hector: Why should I slow down? It's his problem.
Marla: Well, change lanes or something.
Hector: Yeah, yeah. What an idiot.
Marla: Hector, I called you because . . .
Hector: Jeez, look at that, would you?
Marla: What now?
Hector: Oh, it's raining and this car just swerved right in front of me.
Marla: Hector. I called to say . . .
Hector: Yeah, I know Marla. I'm coming right home. By the way, I went to a Chinese restaurant for takeout, and I'm bringing home your favorite.
Marla: Oh, wow! Thanks! But that's . . .
Hector: Oh my God!
Marla: Hector, you're scaring me.
Hector: There's a huge accident on the freeway. Man, you should see the mangled metal!
Marla: Hector, I know. It's raining and I just called to tell you to be careful.
Hector: Uhh . . . huh? What did you say? Why did you call me, again?
Marla: To tell you to be careful. I saw that there was a big accident on the freeway and that it was raining. I just wanted you to watch where you were going.

F.   PRACTICE

Complete the following sentences with the correct form of the following words: *tailgate, pedestrian, rush hour, swerve, road rage, buckle up, cut off, right of way, took off, wreck*

1. It's snowing, so everyone should _____ just to be safe.

2. You'll be caught in _____ if you go out on the freeway at 4:30.

3. There's a big _____ that's blocking traffic on I-95 for several miles.

4. _____ is dangerous, because if the driver ahead of you has to stop, you'll rear-end him.

5. Some idiot changed lanes right in front of me and _____ me _____!

6. Honking, cutting people off, and tailgating can all escalate into cases of _____.

7. Slow down and let all those _____ cross the street at the crosswalk.

8. There was a huge boulder in the road, and I had to _____ to miss it!

9. Pull over and give emergency vehicles the _____.

10. That jerk hit my car and then _____ before even giving me his insurance information!

Now choose the appropriate verb to complete the following sentences. In a few cases, there is more than one correct answer.

1. Can you please _____ (come/go) over there if you want to smoke?
2. I'll _____ (make/do) breakfast if you _____ (make/do) the dishes afterward.
3. When you _____ (come/go) over here, _____ (take/bring) me your new CD.
4. You can _____ (take/bring) my car to the movies tonight.
5. Could I _____ (loan/borrow) a few dollars from you?
6. The kids are _____ (looking at/watching) their favorite cartoon.
7. —"What are you _____ (doing/making)?"—"A sandcastle."
8. Could you please _____ (go/come) over to your grandmother's and _____ (take/bring) her this soup?
9. It's never a good idea to _____ (borrow/lend) someone your car.
10. We _____ (saw/watched) a safety video in Driver's Ed today.

G. TASK

Find your state's Department of Motor Vehicles website by typing the name of your state and "DMV" into a search engine. Find out what the procedure is in your state for renewing your license. Do you need to do in it person, or can you do it online or by mail? Do you need to take any kind of test, including a vision test? What sorts of forms are needed? What restrictions are there?

H. REAL LIFE

Did you know that drunk driving, speeding, and *distractions* are among the most common causes of car accidents? Believe it or not, the number one accident-causing distraction is not talking on a cell phone; it's rubbernecking. For example, while passing an accident, everybody wants to see what has happened, so people crane their necks around to see if anybody got hurt, how mangled the cars are, or what kind of cars were involved. This is simply a recipe for another accident! And there are other major accident-causing distractions, too. Driver fatigue, taking in roadside sights, passenger or child distractions, adjusting the radio, tape, or CD player, and eating all make the nation's highways unnecessarily risky. And while it's still a big problem, talking on a cell phone is actually toward the bottom of the list of accident-causing distractions.

With so many potential distractions out there, drivers have to practice "defensive driving." There are a few simple techniques in defensive driving. Drive slowly and carefully, keep a safety buffer zone around your car at all times, check your mirrors frequently, be aware of other drivers, never drive when you're tired or impaired, and assume that other drivers can and will make mistakes. All of these techniques can help prevent accidents. Along with defensive driving, remember that wearing a seat belt can save your life. In nearly half of all traffic fatalities, the deceased was not wearing a seat belt at the time of the accident. So do the right thing; drive defensively, buckle up, and keep the roads safe for yourself and other drivers!

I. RESOURCES

To find the official Department of Motor Vehicles for your state, type the name of your state and the initials "DMV" into a search engine.
You could also start from www.dmv.org (not an official government site). For information on traffic safety, visit the National Highway Traffic Safety Administration at www.nhtsa.dot.gov or call 1-888-327-4236.
For driving tips in the USA, try www.usatourist.com/english/tips/driving.html.
For information for drivers from outside the U.S., go to www.firstgov.gov/Topics/Foreign_Visitors_Driving.shtml and americadrives.com.

ANSWER KEY
Practice 1: 1. buckle up; 2. rush hour; 3. wreck; 4. Tailgating; 5. cut . . . off; 6. road rage; 7. pedestrians; 8. swerve; 9. right of way; 10. took off

Practice 2: 1. go; 2. make, do; 3. come, bring; 4. take; 5. borrow; 6. watching; 7. making; 8. go, take/bring; 9. lend; 10. saw/watched

CHAPTER 9

In the Car: Getting Pulled Over

A. **ENGLISH CLOSE-UP**

MUNICIPAL TRAFFIC SUMMONS & COMPLAINT

First name	Middle	Last name	DOB	Age

YOU ARE HEREBY DIRECTED TO APPEAR AS INDICATED

circle one

Municipal Court (333-5999) _____day of_____ 200__ at   8:30 AM   1:30 PM
Failure to pay fine or appear in court will result in a bench warrant for
your arrest and an outstanding warrant will result in your driver's license
being revoked.

SEE BACK FOR INSTRUCTIONS
If this date falls on a weekend or holiday you are to appear the
next business day.

B. **VOCABULARY ESSENTIALS**

Arrest warrant—An order calling for someone's arrest and detention. *The police issued an arrest warrant for our neighbor, but we're not sure of the charges.*

Bad apple—A person who doesn't obey rules. *There is an old expression: one bad apple spoils the bunch.*

To be arraigned—To be called to court to respond to legal charges. *Beth was arraigned on drunk driving charges.*

To bribe—To offer something valuable, especially money, to gain favor or influence. Accepting a bribe is considered an unethical, and often illegal, act. *Never try to bribe an officer to get out of a ticket.*

To clock (at)—To determine and record someone's speed. *The state trooper clocked me going 60 MPH in a 45 MPH zone.*

To contest—To dispute something legally. *With the help of an attorney, I contested my traffic ticket and won.*

Cruiser—A police car, a patrol car. *Wow! Look at all the cruisers. There must have been an accident or something.*

Fine—A penalty to be paid for a crime that has been proven or that has not been contested. *Most fines for moving violations are expensive.*

Firearm—Any type of gun. *It's illegal to carry an unregistered firearm.*

Incriminating—Suggestive of criminal activity. *Telling the police officer who has pulled you over that you had too much to drink is an incriminating statement.*

Miranda Rights—Before questioning a suspect who they have arrested, police must read the suspect these rights, which protect the individual's right to not self-incriminate, as detailed in the Fifth Amendment. The reading of these rights guarantees that the suspect is aware of his or her rights. *The basic rights detailed in the Miranda Rights are the right to remain silent and the right to an attorney.*

Moral turpitude—A criminal act that violates what is considered acceptable and decent behavior by the standards of a society. *Depending on the state and the situation, drunk driving is sometimes considered an issue of moral turpitude and immigrants can be deported for it.*

Moving violation—Violation of a traffic law involving a moving vehicle. *An illegal U-turn is a moving violation.*

Plainclothes officer—A police officer not wearing a uniform and driving an unmarked car. *There are sometimes plainclothes officers on public transportation, dressed as commuters to blend in.*

Probable cause—A sound legal reason to arrest someone or search someone or something, believing a crime has been committed. *The smell of marijuana in the car gave the officer probable cause for searching the car and arresting the offender.*

To pull away—To leave from a parked position. *The police car pulled away just after I did.*

To pull in—To turn a car into a driveway or entryway. *I waited until it was safe and then pulled into the nearest entryway.*

To pull over—To bring a car to a stop alongside the road. *Once Sarah heard the siren she decided she'd better pull over.*

To pull up—To move one's car alongside another, or to move the car forward. *Hey, there's Don. Pull up next to him. I want to talk to him.*

Quota—A fixed goal that must be met. *Do traffic officers really give a lot of tickets at the end of the month because they have a quota to meet?*

Registration—A document that certifies that a car has been registered with the DMV. *Be sure to carry your auto registration in your car at all times.*

To ride someone's tail—To drive very close behind another car. *I haven't done anything wrong but that police car is riding my tail.*

To run over—To hit something on the road and go over it with a car. *Be careful! You almost ran over a squirrel.*

To slow down—To reduce speed. *Is that a police car behind us? I'd better slow down.*

Tags—Registration stickers that you must place on your license plate each year. *Don't forget to pay for your auto registration so you can put your tags on your license plate next month.*

Traffic school—A school that some traffic violators are obligated to attend after breaking the law. *If you go to traffic school, you can keep your present insurance rates, but you still have to pay for the ticket.*

Trooper—A state police officer. *You can address a state officer by calling him or her "officer" or "trooper."*

U-turn—A 180-degree turn. *If there are no signs that say "no U-turns," then it's usually legal to make a U-turn.*

To weave—To drive erratically, changing back and forth between lanes. *The police officer pulled Drew over for weaving, which is often a sign of drunk driving.*

C. GRAMMAR ESSENTIALS: PREPOSITIONS OF MOTION AND DIRECTION

Prepositions can be difficult to master, because a lot of the time their meanings and usage do not "translate" directly from one language into another. Throughout this course we'll focus on different types of prepositions and cover the basics of how they're used in English, with explanations of meaning and examples. Prepositions can be divided into a few different categories: prepositions of time, prepositions of location, prepositions of motion or direction, and so on. We'll start with prepositions that describe motion or direction. Just keep in mind that the same prepositions don't always fit neatly into just one category. For example, *in* can describe motion (*he went in the house*), location (*he is in the house*), time (*he'll be there in five minutes*), etc. In this section, we'll only focus on motion and direction, and we'll come back to the other uses later.

Along—Beside the length of. *Highway 101 runs along the Pacific from southern California through Oregon.*

Around (1)—Following the outer edge of something. *You can get across the park by walking around the lake.*

Around (2)—Tracing a path over a large part of something. *We drove around the parking lot before we found a space.*

Below—Passing to the underside of something, and sometimes contained in it. *The alligator sank below the surface of the water.*

Beneath—Passing to the underside of something, and sometimes contained in it. *The dog ran beneath the table.*

Down (to)—From a higher to a lower point. *Janie and Bill liked walking down to the pier in the early morning.*

From—Out of a specific place or location. *Teka came here all the way from Ethiopia.*

In(to)—Entering a place, usually an enclosed place. *Isn't that Jim I see walking into the bank over there?*

On(to)—Toward the top or upper surface of something. *When Louis turned onto Mercer Way he knew he was lost.*

Out of—Toward the exterior of a place. *It was 9:30 before Jack got out of the car.*

Over (1)—Moving on or above the surface of something to the other side. *Drive over the bridge and then turn right.*

Over (2)—Inverted, from right-side up to upside down. *A car turned over on the freeway.*

Over (3)—Covering a distance. *Let's walk over to my car and talk.*

Through—Passing inside something and exiting out the other side. *Why not try taking the Eurostar through the Chunnel to London?*

To—In the direction of something. *We're going to the store.*

Toward—In the (general) direction of something. *We're driving toward the west, because we can see the sun setting over the Pacific.*

Under—Moving below something. *Turn left on Baker Street and go under the freeway until Frazee Road.*

Up (to)—Movement from a lower to a higher point. *Turn up Hillside Avenue and then drive up to the top of the road.*

D. HOW-TO

Most of us get a sinking feeling when we see a police car in the rearview mirror. We panic and assume we've done something wrong. We slow down or change lanes. Sometimes just seeing that police car causes us to make driving mistakes. So it's good to know how to avoid attracting the attention of the police in the first place. The most obvious step to take is simply to know the law and to follow it. Don't speed, don't run any red lights or ignore any stop signs, don't weave, and don't forget to use your turn signals. Always carry your driver's license, registration, and proof of insurance. Put your tags on your license plate, and make sure your headlights, taillights, and signals all work. And don't forget to buckle up, either! It's the law in many states. Also, eliminate the things that may distract you from noticing a stop sign or a red light. Don't talk on the cell phone, don't try to eat, drink coffee, or otherwise "multitask" while you're driving. It's all just common sense—pay attention, follow the law, and you won't get pulled over. Right?

Mostly. Although police officers might not agree, there are certain types of cars that seem to sometimes get pulled over more than others. Brightly colored sports cars—especially red ones—seem to cry out "speed!" and police officers may be more likely to pay careful attention to these cars. Also, banged up cars might attract more attention than clean, freshly painted cars with few or no dents. Maybe the subconscious message is, "sloppy car, sloppy driver." Other "law enforcement attention grabbers" could include big trucks with big wheels, low-riding cars, and cars with noisy mufflers or engines. Maybe the best way to avoid attention is simply to try not to attract it.

Above all, don't attract attention by being a drunk driver. Police officers can always spot a driver who's impaired by alcohol, and if you're lucky enough not to hurt yourself or anyone else, you're sure to get a very big fine and wind up in very serious legal trouble. If you're an immigrant, you have even more reason to be careful about drinking and driving. Your arraignment for DUI/DWI can sometimes be a deportation hearing, because the government can consider drunk driving an issue of moral turpitude, with this classification usually depending on state law. So if you want to drink, don't drive, or ask a friend to be the designated driver.

But if you haven't managed to avoid attention, it's important to know what to do if a police officer wants you to pull over. You'll know that this is the case because he or she will be right behind you, lights flashing. You might even hear sirens or a booming voice on a bullhorn telling you to pull over. Move over to the right hand lane, and pull to the side of the road as soon as it's safe. Do not get out of your car. The officer could interpret that as a threat. And do not start moving around in your seat. You may just be looking for that registration card that fell out of the glove compartment, but to the officer, it might look like you're trying to conceal drugs or alcohol, or even reaching for a weapon. Just stay put, wait for the officer to come to the side of your car, and roll down your window.

The first thing that the police officer will probably say will be to request to see your driver's license, registration, and proof of insurance. If your registration is in your glove compartment, tell the officer you need to open it. Don't make any sudden moves, or behave in a way that the officer could interpret as potentially dangerous to his or her safety. It's a good idea to keep your hands in plain sight. Remember that being a police officer is a very difficult job, and police officers have to deal with frustrated, angry, aggressive, and even dangerous people all day. So it helps to be polite, apologetic, and respectful. The officer will tell you why he or she pulled you over, and if you disagree, that's your right, but the time to show your disagreement is in court, not on the side of the road. And definitely don't try to bribe the officer, either! That will just get you into more trouble.

In the U.S., if you're pulled over, you have certain rights that you should know about. For example, if an officer asks if he or she can search your car, it is your right to say no. If there is probable cause—beer cans on the floor, the smell of an illegal substance, etc.—then the officer does have the right to perform a search. Just keep in mind that your behavior can be probable cause, which is all the more reason to behave calmly and respectfully. If you are arrested during a traffic stop, you have the right to remain silent and you have the right to see an attorney. The officer will read you these rights (the Miranda Rights) and ask if you understand them.

If you think you were cited for a moving violation in error, don't argue about it with the police officer. Instead, you can plead "not guilty" and go to court to prove your innocence. The officer will be at your hearing as well, and he or she will most likely be prepared with notes and other evidence supporting your citation. If the judge agrees with you, your case will be dismissed and you won't have to pay the fine. Or, if it's your first offense, the judge may even throw it out, with the same result. Even if you do not want to contest your ticket, there are some circumstances in which you might still have to appear in court. Some states require you to go to court if you are caught going a certain amount over the speed limit. In addition, speeding through certain locations, driving with a suspended license, committing a moving violation as a minor, and other circumstances may require a court appearance. If you are driving any significant distance away from home and are caught committing a violation, keep in mind that if you are ordered to appear in court, then you (or your attorney) may have to appear in the court of the location in which you committed the violation. In other words, if you live in New York City, but commit the moving violation while driving in Las Vegas, then you or your attorney may have to appear in the Las Vegas court. The moving violation could also have an impact on your driving record in your home state, because most states relay information on violations by nonresidents to their home state. So it pays to be extra careful if you're driving any significant distance from home.

If you don't have to or want to appear in court and you opt to pay the fine, you might want to go to traffic school to have the ticket taken off your record, so your insurance rates don't go up. It's also possible to be ordered to go to traffic school by a court. Whatever you decide to do about your ticket, be sure you resolve it one way or another. If you ignore the problem and do nothing, you could be arrested. Getting a traffic ticket can be a very expensive and time-consuming experience, and it can possibly turn into something much more complicated than a simple fine. So, as usual, prevention is the best medicine. Know the law, follow it, and drive carefully!

 ## E. ENGLISH IN ACTION

Let's listen in as Miriam and Hannah notice a patrol car behind them.

Miriam: Why's that police car following us?

Hannah: I don't know, did you do something wrong?

Miriam: Not that I know of. Oops! There goes his siren. I'd better pull over.

Hannah: Oh, Miriam, I'm so sorry. Well, it's the end of the month. He probably just needs to fill his quota.

Miriam: Yeah, I know. Do you think I should get out of the car?

Hannah: No way! Don't do anything the officer doesn't tell you to do.

Miriam: Yeah, you're right.

Hannah: Oh, here he is. Better roll down your window.

Miriam: Okay.

Trooper: Hello, ma'am. Could I see your license, registration, and proof of insurance, please?

Miriam: Oh, sure, officer. I . . . Just a minute, I have to get my registration out of my glove compartment, and my license and proof of insurance are in my wallet inside my purse.

Trooper: Sure, no problem.

Miriam: Okay, here they are. Officer, I don't know what I did wrong. I wasn't speeding, was I?

Trooper: Nope. You were driving just fine. I just noticed that your tags have expired and I need to check that out.

Miriam: You're kidding. I just put my new tags on last month.

Trooper: That might be. I need to make sure you're the owner, that's all. I'll be right back.

Hannah: Well, at least you're not gonna get a ticket . . . that is, unless you stole this car.

Miriam: Very funny. I know I put them on. I don't understand what happened.

Hannah: Maybe you just thought you'd put them on.

Miriam: No, I know I . . .

Trooper: Okay, ma'am, here're your license, registration, and proof of insurance. It looks like you are the registered owner, but you'll need to get those tags on.

Miriam: Officer, I'm sure I put them on.

Trooper: Yeah, it looks like you did, because I can still see a piece of them on there, but if you don't stick them on well, they can get stolen. It's a real common thing. Sometimes guys who steal

cars also steal tags because not having any tags on their
stolen car's license plate would get them pulled over pretty
quickly.

Miriam: So you think someone stole them?

Trooper: Looks like it. Don't worry though. They aren't expensive to
replace. Just take your registration into your nearest DMV.

Miriam: Oh, okay. Thanks a lot.

Trooper: No problem.

Hannah: Whew! Glad that's over!

Miriam: Yeah, I know. My heart's still pounding.

F. PRACTICE

Fill in each sentence with the correct form of one of the following words:
*bribe, ride someone's tail, arraign, pull over, fine, quota, probable cause, contest,
Miranda Rights, arrest warrant*

1. If you get stopped by a police officer, and your breath smells like alcohol, your
   car may be searched because of _____.

2. The police issued a(n) _____ for Tim because he failed to appear in court.

3. A month after being arrested, Greg was _____ on multiple charges,
   including reckless endangerment and operating a vehicle without a license.

4. If you don't agree with the charges, _____ them in court.

5. If you are arrested, the police officer will read you your _____ so that you
   know what your rights are in this situation.

6. Are you crazy? Don't try to _____ an officer!

7. If you get a traffic ticket you usually have to pay a(n) _____.

8. Tell Bill he doesn't need any more tickets. He's already filled his _____.

9. That car behind us is way too close. I don't feel comfortable having someone
   _____.

10. As soon as the police car turned its sirens on right behind her, Lisa _____
    to the side of the road and stopped the car.

Fill in each sentence with one of the following prepositions: *along, over to,
below, out of, over, through, down to, around, onto, toward*

1. Sir, open your door slowly and step _____ the car with your hands up.

2. I don't like driving _____ tunnels. They're so narrow and claustrophobic.

3. The car spun out of control and rolled _____ the median, stopping right
   in the middle of it.

4. The only way to get to the concession stand is if you go _____ the lake.

5. Druann likes to walk _____ the seawall early in the morning.

6. Could you take this book _____ that desk over there?

7. You park _____ the mall. There's a very large parking structure under there.

8. I think I see a yellow car coming _____ us. That must be the Williams' car.

9. Let's take the elevator _____ the bottom floor. They keep the rare books there.

10. Just go _____ the bridge, and on the other side, turn right. It'll be on your left.

G. TASK

Would you like to see how traffic court really works? All court cases, unless specifically noted by the judge, are open to the public, so you can most likely sit in and watch how things work. Contact your local courthouse to find out the details, such as when the cases are held, and, of course, whether there are any restrictions regarding who can attend and observe. Court is a real learning experience, and good citizens should be familiar with the legal process. Plus, it's far more pleasant if you're not the one on trial!

H. REAL LIFE

Hi, I'm Officer Smith. I'm here to offer you some tips about getting pulled over, and how to comply with a police officer while still protecting your safety. Suppose you're driving alone at night in an isolated area, and you see a red light flashing in your rearview mirror. Do you pull over right away? No, don't pull over immediately, but instead slow down and turn on your hazard lights, so that the officer knows you are planning to comply. If you have a cell phone, it's a good idea to call 911 and tell the dispatcher that you want to make sure you're being followed by a police officer, and that you will pull over as soon as it's safe. The dispatcher will verify whether an officer is tailing you. Continue driving until you reach a place like a gas station or coffee shop where there are other people around, and pull over there. When the officer gets out of his or her car and comes to greet you, keep your window rolled up until the officer properly identifies him or herself. Check out the officer's uniform, too. It's unlikely that a plainclothes officer in an unmarked car will pull anyone over for a traffic violation, so if he or she is not wearing a uniform, be very careful. If he or she is wearing a uniform, but it seems mismatched, or if items are missing or don't seem standard, be suspicious. If you're in a well-lit public place, you're most likely going to be fine, and a legitimate police officer will understand why you were careful.

I. RESOURCES

To find out about driving laws for specific states:
www.statedrivinglaw.com
www.mit.edu/~jfc/laws.html
Or visit your state's DMV website (as described in Lesson 7).

To read about your Miranda Rights:
www.usconstitution.net/miranda.html

DWI/DUI state laws:
www.iihs.org/laws/state_laws/dui.html

ANSWER KEY
Practice 1: 1. probable cause; 2. arrest warrant; 3. arraigned; 4. contest; 5. Miranda Rights; 6. bribe; 7. fine; 8. quota; 9. ride my tail; 10. pulled over

Practice 2: 1. out of; 2. through; 3. onto; 4. around; 5. along; 6. over to; 7. below; 8. toward; 9. down to; 10. over

CHAPTER 10

Making Friends: Friendly Appointments

A. ENGLISH CLOSE-UP

From: **Jay Hyde**
Sent: **August 14**
To: **Bill Angeleri**
Subject: **Visit**

Bill,
Julie and I are organizing an outing to John's new place on Thursday. We're going to take a picnic lunch, go hiking and just hang out by the lake. Would you like to come? If so, we'll pick you up around 9:00 a.m. If that's not a good time, you could try and meet up with us later in the day. Send me back an email to let me know.
Jay

B. VOCABULARY ESSENTIALS

To chat—To have friendly small talk, also used for talking online. *Jane and Sue like to get together every week to chat about all the things happening in their lives.*

To come together—Often used to mean that plans are in progress, becoming final, or working out well. *It looks like the party's coming together nicely. Let's call Sam and Debbie to see if they can come.*

Don't hold your breath—Don't expect something to happen soon. *If you expect Bill to ask you out, don't hold your breath. He's got a girlfriend already.*

To get together, a get-together—To spend time together, often used to talk about some future unplanned event. A gathering of people in an informal and social setting. *Let's get together sometime soon, maybe for coffee or something.*

To go dutch—An expression meaning that everyone pays for his or her share of a bill. *If we go out to eat, let's go dutch, because I don't have much cash.*

To be going out—To date, to spend time socializing outside the home. *I'd love to stay in and watch a DVD with you, but I'm going out with some friends.*

Gossip—Conversations or rumors, usually about people's personal lives. *Have you heard the latest gossip? Tamara left Tom for Bill.*

To hang out with—To spend time with someone doing nothing in particular, just enjoying one another's company. *Bill, Maria, and Tam really like to hang out with each other. I often see them at the coffee shop laughing and having a good time.*

Hot-button issues—Controversial and divisive topics that most people have strong opinions about. *Whatever you do, don't bring up the election in front of Ralph and Sandy. It's a real hot-button issue for them.*

Join the club—An (often sarcastic) expression used to mean that you share someone's unpleasant experience. *You're upset that you weren't invited to the party? Well join the club—I wasn't either!*

To make friends—To become friends with others. *It isn't always easy to make friends in a new country.*

To make good on—To follow through, to do what you promised. *Gerry always offers to pay for dinner the next time, but he never makes good on it.*

To make your blood boil—To make you very angry. *That Cheryl is so rude; she just makes my blood boil.*

To meet up with—To plan to join friends somewhere, such as in a restaurant or a theater. *We're going to meet up with Mona after the movie.*

To mingle—To join together with different people at a social gathering, making small talk, socializing, or talking briefly. *Well, if you want to meet people, you've got to get out there and mingle at the party tonight.*

Outing—A trip with one or more people that frequently involves being outside, such as traveling to a park to have a picnic, going boating, etc. *We're having a family outing at the beach this weekend. Want to join us?*

To pay your way—To pay for your share of something. *I don't need you to buy me dinner. I can pay my way.*

To pick up the tab—To pay the bill. *I went out to dinner with Ron, and he insisted on picking up the tab.*

The scene—Sometimes refers to the social culture, including popular trends, places to go, etc., of a particular group or in a field of interest. *I feel like doing something fun. Let's go check out the club scene in this city.*

To split the bill—To divide a bill evenly among a group. *It's too complicated to figure out who ate what, so let's just split the bill.*

To treat, a treat—To pay for someone else's dinner, movie ticket, etc., as a gift. The act of treating someone. *Let's go out to dinner tonight, my treat.*

To turn down—To refuse an invitation or an offering of any kind. *Thanks for the invitation to the dinner party, but I have to turn you down. I have plans.*

White lie—A very small lie told in order to not hurt anyone's feelings, often used when needing to give an excuse. *I really didn't feel comfortable going to Marla's party because I didn't know anyone. I had to tell a little white lie so I wouldn't have to go.*

C. GRAMMAR ESSENTIALS: PREPOSITIONS OF TIME

The last lesson focused on prepositions of motion and direction. Now let's look at prepositions used with time expressions:

About, around—Almost or near a certain time. *It's about 9:30. It's around 9:30. It's about time for another haircut.*

After—Following, happening subsequently. *We're all going out for drinks after the meeting.*

At—On a given point in time, usually used with a specific time. *The store will open at 11:00 a.m. today. We'll read a fairy tale today at story time.*

Before—Prior to a certain time. *Where did you go before the party?*

Between—After a certain time and before another. *Where were you between one and one thirty? The package should arrive sometime between Monday and Wednesday.*

By—No later than a certain time. *Jim said he'd be here by 5:00. We'll be out of here by the weekend.*

During—Within the time when something happens. *Jack stood in the corner with a glass of wine during the whole party.*

For (1)—Happening during a specific length of time. *Rita said she'd stop by for a few minutes. We stayed for two hours.*

For (2)—Not happening until a specific time. Used with verbs in the negative. *They won't be landing for a few more hours, so let's get something to eat.*

From—Indicating the starting time of something, used with *to* to indicate the end. *The movie runs from 7:10 to 9:40. The class is from Monday to Wednesday, from 9:00 to 12:00 noon.*

In (1)—Indicating the amount of time between the present and some other event. *The movie starts in fifteen minutes. We have to be there in two hours.*

In (2)—Indicating duration or length of time. *Greg got his Ph.D. in only three years. Rachel learned to speak Hungarian fluently in just six months.*

Of, till, to—Before a certain hour. *It's ten of/till/to seven in the evening.*

On—Occurring at a certain time, used with specific days and dates. *Call me on Monday. The class begins on September 10th.*

Over—More than a certain period of time. *Melissa and Tom stayed in Hawaii over two weeks.*

Through—From a beginning point until an end point. *Classes are in session from Monday through Thursday.*

Toward—Indicating an approximate time. *The plane landed toward nightfall.*

Within—Inside of a period of time, less than a period of time. *Nora will arrive within the hour.*

D. HOW-TO

It isn't always easy to know for sure when you've received an invitation from an American. Americans sometimes end conversations by saying something like, "Let's get together sometime soon!" But unless a specific date and time have been arranged, this is not usually an invitation. It's frequently just a friendly way of saying good-bye, and indicating that a good time was had. The truth is that although Americans are very casual in many ways, they really often have very tightly scheduled lives. Generally, family needs or work responsibilities come before social events and it isn't always easy to juggle work and family. There's usually very little time left over for socializing, and in order to find time, it has to be carefully planned and organized. That means that you'll know for sure when an American is inviting you somewhere; a specific date and time will be given, and very little will be left vague. Vagueness in social planning often means that the plans haven't really come together yet (or even that there is no intention of making plans), so don't hold your breath if someone says, "Hey, let's get together sometime!"

What do you do if you can't or don't really want to attend a social occasion you've been invited to? An American would never just say, "No, thank you," and leave it at that, because this is considered rude. Instead, Americans always offer an explanation for why they can't make it. For example, someone might say, "I'm sorry. I can't make it to your party Thursday. I have to pick up my brother at the airport that night, and he doesn't get in until late." Giving an explanation is also very important if plans change, so if you accept an invitation, but then find out that you can't make it, it's expected that you'll give a reason. While Americans, like most people, believe that honesty is the best policy, a little white lie is acceptable when turning down an invitation. In fact, most Americans would probably agree that a white lie is more polite than simply saying, "No, I can't make it because I don't feel like coming!" Of course, if you do accept an invitation, it's polite to express your gratitude.

Many Americans like to entertain in their homes, so you may be invited to, for example, a dinner party or a barbeque. But it's just as likely that you'll be invited out to dinner at a restaurant. However, you need to be careful; that doesn't necessarily mean that the person who invited you is planning to pay for your dinner. Americans often "go dutch," so servers may ask if you want separate bills (for each party at the table) for this reason. However, your host could very well be intending to treat you, and he or she may indicate this before the dinner by saying "it's my treat." Or, he or she may simply grab the check when it comes to the table. In this case, many people then insist on paying for at least their portion of the bill, usually knowing that the host will refuse to let them pay. You can also just thank your host very graciously and possibly offer to leave the tip. Your host might accept your offer, or perhaps not. It would then be acceptable for you to say that you'll pick up the tab the next time, and you should be prepared to remember that invitation and make good on it. Of course, it's also possible that your host will take you seriously when you offer to pay your way, so don't feel bad if you end up splitting the bill.

Whether you're going out to dinner or socializing in someone's home, it's very important to know that there are some topics of conversation that you should avoid, and some questions you should never ask unless you know someone very well. Such hot-button issues as gay rights, abortion, capital punishment, and gun control will make many Americans anxious and upset, because most people have very strong opinions one way or the other. Political issues—especially social ones—are best avoided. Religion is also a topic not to discuss. The contemporary social and political environment in the U.S. has been quite divided, often very passionately so. Even so, most Americans prefer to enjoy socializing without getting into arguments, so the best policy is simply to avoid issues that could lead to strong disagreement. There are also some questions you should almost never ask Americans unless you are very close friends. Questions about personal and intimate relationships, age, or finances, such as "How old are you?" or "How much money do you make?" are generally considered rude. So until you get to know Americans very well, keep your conversation topics light, and do not ask very personal questions. Topics like the weather, sports, movies, or occupations are typical light banter. A safe, uncontroversial topic you're sure to know a lot about is yourself, your country, or your culture. You can be relatively certain that this is also a topic that most Americans will find interesting, so don't be embarrassed to talk about yourself a little. Of course, be sure to ask your American friends about themselves as well.

E. ENGLISH IN ACTION

Let's listen as Miyako learns some American social customs.

Brenda: Well, I've got to go to class now, Miyako, but I really enjoyed hanging out with you.

Miyako: Oh, thank you. I enjoyed getting together, too.
Brenda: Yeah. Let's do it again sometime.
Miyako: Oh, yes. I'd like that.
Brenda: Okay, give me a call sometime. See you!
Miyako: Okay. Bye.

A few minutes later . . .

Miyako: Oh, no. I don't have Brenda's phone number.
Steve: Hi, Miyako, what's wrong?
Miyako: Oh, Brenda said we should get together again and that I
          should call her, but I don't have her phone number.
Steve: Oh, I see. Well, don't worry about it. For Americans, that's
          usually just a friendly way to say good-bye.
Miyako: Do you mean that Brenda doesn't want to get together with me?
Steve: No, not necessarily. It usually means she enjoys talking to you
          and that sometime she'd like to talk to you again. It's like when
          Americans say, "Hello, how are you?" but they don't really want
          you to tell them how you are. It's just a friendly greeting.
Miyako: So saying, "Let's get together sometime," is similar to that?
Steve: Yeah, that's right. But how about if I invite you to lunch right
          now? See, I just gave you a specific day and time. That means
          I'm serious.
Miyako: That would be great! I do feel a little hungry.
Steve: Join the club. I'm so hungry I could eat a horse.
Miyako: I'm sorry?
Steve: It's just an American expression. I wouldn't eat a horse, don't
          worry. Hey, we're going to meet up with Phil and Dora for
          lunch at the Casbah. We're gonna split the bill, but I'll pay your
          way because I invited you. You're my guest.
Miyako: Oh, that's very kind of you, but I have money. I can pay my way.
Steve: Nope. You'll have to grab fast to beat me to the check. You
          won't ever even see the bill. Now don't turn me down. That's it.
          I'm paying. So let's get going, okay?
Miyako: Okay.

F.   PRACTICE

Fill in the sentences with the correct form of the following words or
expressions: *come together, make friends, get together, mingle, join the club,
hang out with, pick up the tab, don't hold your breath, meet up with, an outing*

1. Don't be so shy! Get out there and _____ with everyone so you can make
    some new friends at the party.

2. It often seems as if teenagers would much rather _____ each other after class and on the weekends than be at home with their families.

3. We're going to _____ the Smythes at 8:00 p.m. Then we'll all go to that new French restaurant on Broadway for dinner.

4. Whenever the whole family _____ we all end up singing old songs.

5. I think the party's really _____. Everything should be ready by Friday night, so we can relax before the big day on Saturday.

6. —"You think George is going to pay for dinner tonight?"—"_____! He never pays for anything if he can help it."

7. "Hi, Mary. I was just wondering if you were up for going on _____ today. I was thinking maybe we could drive to the beach and have a picnic with some friends."

8. _____ I didn't get an invitation to Rhonda's birthday party either.

9. You seem to _____ easily. You always get along so well with everyone.

10. Let Harry _____. We always pay for dinner, so it's his turn now.

Now fill in the sentences with one of the following prepositions: *during, in, till, before, on, at, by, for, between, through*

1. Derek says he'll be here _____ an hour so we'll be waiting for a while.

2. Can you come in _____ Monday, the 23rd? That's the only day we have open.

3. Your appointment with the dentist is _____ 10:15.

4. Your report is due _____ Wednesday and no later.

5. We have to wait here _____ two more hours.

6. The sculpture exhibit is opening in April and running _____ June. It's already the end of May, so we'd better go soon if we want to see it.

7. Don't get here _____ six. I won't be ready.

8. The dinner party should start sometime _____ 7:00 and 8:00.

9. Some people are so rude. These two women talked _____ the entire movie!

10. The dance club should be open _____ four in the morning. It stays open really late.

G. TASK

If you've been wondering how to make friends in this country, consider hosting a party in your home and serving food from your country. You could invite people from work, school, or anywhere else you have casual acquaintances who you'd like to get to know better. Be sure to tell them that you'll be serving food from your country, and if that tends to be spicy, you might consider a milder version for people who aren't used to it!

H.   REAL LIFE

My name is Christelle, and I moved to the U.S. from France about ten years ago for work. One of the hardest things I found about living in the U.S. was being separated from my friends and family, so I was eager to make new friends in this country. But that wasn't easy! First of all, I realized that even the word "friend" can be confusing, because Americans seem to call everyone they know their friend. To me, a friend is someone very close, maybe someone I've known for years, so I have very few friends, but a lot of acquaintances. Then it hit me that the word "friend" often just means acquaintance, and Americans use the expression "close friend" to mean something very different. Americans have lots of friends, but only a few close friends. So the truth is, it's easy to make friends with Americans, but of course much harder to become a close friend to one. So, how can you make friends with Americans, and maybe, over time, become a close friend? Well, first of all, don't be confused by what might seem like mixed signals that Americans send. Americans love to chat with strangers. They strike up friendly conversations with people in places like elevators, and then, when they get to their floor, they say "it was nice talking to you," and then go on with their lives, never seeing the other person again. This is just considered polite in this country; it's not an invitation to become friends. If you want to make friends, the best way to do it is to be in a situation where you see the same people again and again, maybe at work or in your neighborhood, and just be friendly and open. You could even create this kind of situation for yourself. You could join a club, take a class, volunteer, or take up any activity where you can meet people. You could reach out to your neighbors, too. If new neighbors move in, go over and welcome them by bringing them some small gift, like a cake or cookies. Or just go and introduce yourself. Americans like to have good neighbors, and that can often lead to friendship. Wherever you can regularly see people, just keep talking to them, and see if anything blossoms. The truth is that it's pretty easy to meet people in the U.S., and once you've met someone new, there are many ways to become good friends.

I.   RESOURCES

Cultural behavior:
www.educationusa.state.gov/life/culture/americans.htm
www.educationusa.state.gov/life/culture/customs.htm

www.edupass.org/culture
www.usastudyguide.com/customshabits.htm

Making social connections:
www.myspace.com
www.meetup.com

Books:
In the Know in the USA, Random House

ANSWER KEY

Practice 1: 1. mingle; 2. hang out with; 3. meet up with; 4. gets together; 5. coming together; 6. Don't hold your breath; 7. an outing; 8. Join the club; 9. make friends; 10. pick up the tab

Practice 2: 1. in; 2. on; 3. at; 4. by; 5. for; 6. through; 7. before; 8. between; 9. during; 10. till

CHAPTER 11

Making Friends: Communication Styles

A. ENGLISH CLOSE-UP

> ## Tips on Communicating
>
> - If you are an indirect communicator, you will need to develop a thick skin. Remind yourself not to take it personally when you encounter the more direct style of speaking that is typical in the United States.
>
> - Try to speak honestly and frankly, but don't confuse a direct communication style with rudeness; there is a difference between being frank and being tactless.
>
> - Remember that Americans would rather hear the bad news immediately and directly so that they can change their plans or fix the problem. If you won't be able to meet a deadline, say so and explain why.
>
> - Balance the negative with the positive. A common American lead-in is, "There's good news and there's bad news." The speaker may then go on to say that the good news is that sales are up, and the bad news is that the sales manager quit.
>
> - When dealing with other people's performance or ideas, perface negative comments with positive ones to ensure good morale.
>
> From *In the Know in the U.S.A.*, Random House, 2003

B. VOCABULARY ESSENTIALS

To beat around the bush—To avoid direct communication. *Stop beating around the bush! Just tell me what you need to tell me!*

Easygoing—Calm, not easily bothered. *Marissa is so easygoing; she never gets upset or raises her voice.*

Gestures—Movements of the body, usually with the hands, that communicate meaning. *Bud made a gesture for Rachel to join him at his table.*

To get down to business—To focus on something, to stop making small talk and begin working. *Okay, we don't have much time, so let's get right down to business.*

To get to know—To become acquainted. *I'd like to get to know Robin. She seems like a really interesting person.*

In your face—Very direct and confrontational, at times involving close physical proximity as well. *Suzanne was really in my face about me being just a few minutes late to dinner. I didn't realize it was that big of a deal.*

To intrude—To enter into a place without having been invited. *Americans don't much like having people intrude on their privacy.*

To keep someone at arm's length—To keep someone away, to not want to get acquainted with someone. *Caitlyn always seems to keep Raul at arm's length. I guess she's not really interested in becoming good friends with him.*

To mince words—To speak in an indirect way, to soften an intended message. *Terry is known for not mincing words. He always says exactly what he means, and doesn't seem to worry about other people's reactions.*

Personal space—The distance that people maintain between themselves and others, for comfort and protection. *Alan has no regard for personal space; he stands right next to you when he talks, and he always touches your arm or shoulder.*

To pull punches—To soften a criticism, to avoid saying everything negative that you have to say. *Wow, did you hear Bill's review of the department? He sure didn't pull any punches! He basically said we were all terrible!*

To put off—In certain contexts, to offend or repel someone. *Everyone feels put off by Gene because he always treats his wife with so much disrespect.*

To saunter—To move slowly as if having no concerns. *Keanna and Jean sauntered down the street as though they had all the time in the world.*

Self-esteem—Feeling of worth or value about oneself. *Sometimes it seems as if the average teenager has little self-esteem unless he or she is very popular.*

Shifty-eyed—Describing someone who doesn't maintain eye contact, someone who is untrustworthy or dishonest. *It was difficult for people to trust Joe because he always looked so shifty-eyed.*

To shrug—To raise your shoulders, sometimes with the hands held up with palms out, meaning, "I don't know," "I'm not sure," or sometimes "It was just okay" when referring to a movie, food, etc. Can also be an expression of disinterest. *Don't shrug your shoulders at me as though you don't know what you have to do!*

To spit it out—An informal expression used when asking someone to directly state a point or message clearly and concisely. *What did you want to say to me? Come on, spit it out!*

To stare—To hold your eyes constantly focused on one thing for a long time. *Did you see that guy staring at me? It really gave me the creeps!*

To swagger—To walk with an inflated air of pride or confidence. *When Carl heard that Marie was interested in him, he approached her with a swagger.*

Tactful—Diplomatic and inoffensive in communication style, even when communicating negative criticism. *If you don't like someone's idea, be tactful when you say so.*

To take something personally—To react to a criticism of something such as your work as if it were a criticism of you personally. *Bob, don't take this personally, but I would really like to see a second design proposal. I don't think this one works.*

Thick skin—The ability to take criticism without being too sensitive. *If you're in a creative field, you need to have a thick skin. People will often criticize your work.*

To sugarcoat—To hide a negative message by being insincerely positive. *If you don't like my short story, don't sugarcoat it! Just tell me what you really think.*

Wholehearted—With absolute commitment and complete enthusiasm, with all one's heart. *When choosing a life partner, be sure you are ready to make a wholehearted commitment to him or her.*

Yes-man—A person who insincerely says "yes" to everything and is afraid to tell the truth, especially to a figure of authority such as a boss. *Don't be such a yes-man! When your boss figures out that you've been lying because you're too afraid to stand up to her, she'll be furious.*

GRAMMAR ESSENTIALS: SHORT ANSWERS WITH *SO*, *TOO*, *EITHER*, OR *NEITHER*

You can use *so, too, either,* or *neither* in short answers to show agreement. To show agreement with an affirmative statement, use *so* or *too*. *Too* generally comes at the end of the short answer, and *so* comes at the beginning:

I think urban Americans are less friendly than rural Americans.
I do, too./So do I.

Note that *so* can also be used at the end of a short answer, but in this case it shows strong disagreement. It's only used as an affirmative (disagreeing) response to a negative statement:

New Yorkers are not very kind.
They are so! (They ARE very kind.)

Rob won't like the food from your country.
He will so! (He WILL like it.)

To show agreement with a negative statement, use *neither* or *either*. *Neither* is used with an affirmative short answer, and it comes at the beginning of the sentence. *Either* is used at the end of the short answer, and that answer is in the negative:

I can't understand why Americans call me by my first name.
Neither can I./I can't, either.

We're not sure what that gesture means.
Neither are we./We aren't, either.

Note that you'll also hear *too* and *neither* with *me* and *you*: *Me, too. You, too. Me, neither.* Some speakers may also use these constructions with other pronouns, such as *him, them, us,* etc., but these are less common.

Either and *neither* are also used to mention two or more possibilities. *Either . . . or* links affirmative possibilities, and *neither . . . nor* links negative possibilities:

Either Sara will drive or Nora will.
That gesture means either "hello," "good-bye," or "come here."

Neither Sam nor his brother is coming.
I invited neither Frank, Bob, nor Liliana to my party.

Either and *neither* can also be used on their own:

Either book will do. (One book or the other will do; both are acceptable.)
Neither of those books is mine. (Both books do not belong to me.)

Subject agreement with *either* and *neither* can be confusing. When they're used on their own, use a singular verb:

Either book is a great choice to read.
Neither book is going to be interesting.

With *either . . . or* or *neither . . . nor,* the rule is that the verb should agree with the closest subject:

Either the boy or the girl is leaving now.
Either the boys or the girls are leaving now.

Neither my sisters nor my brother is taking you to the game.
Neither my brother nor my sisters are taking you to the game.

But keep in mind that this more a stylistic rule than anything else, and you'll just as often hear native speakers say, *Neither the students nor the teacher are here yet.* And finally, take note of the pronunciation of *either* and *neither.*

Many Americans generally pronounce both words with a long *ee* sound, as in *see*, or a long *i* sound, as in *eye*, sometimes using both pronunciations interchangeably.

D. HOW-TO

It's sometimes possible to very broadly divide cultures into two types when it comes to communication styles—direct communicators and indirect communicators. Cultures that favor direct communication put a premium on the message that is being communicated. More energy is spent on delivering a concise and clear point than on worrying about nuances. In cultures that favor indirect communication, on the other hand, there is a great deal of value put on showing respect, avoiding offense, and maintaining harmonious relationships. In fact, these aspects of communication are just as essential as the main message. As you might have guessed, the U.S. falls into the category of direct communicators. It's important to keep in mind, though, that it is not the most direct culture, and most Americans do expect some degree of "nuance" in communication. Here are a few general tips and guidelines to help you understand how to communicate with Americans, and how to navigate nonverbal communication tools such as eye contact, physical proximity, handshakes, and so on.

DIRECTNESS

All in all, Americans are a straightforward people, and they tend to say what they mean without mincing words. This can offend people from cultures that value a more subtle approach, but if you're one of those people, it's important to keep in mind that Americans don't mean to be offensive. They just appreciate getting to the point and they're often uncomfortable or frustrated if people take too long to do that. This doesn't mean that Americans blurt out anything they want with complete directness. When Americans are conveying a negative or critical message, they will try to balance it with something positive and favorable. Most Americans recognize and dislike sugarcoating, but they also dislike tactlessness. So, if an American has to communicate some kind of negative criticism, he or she might begin with, "Well, I really liked your ideas and I can see that you put a lot of work into the proposal, but . . ." The negative criticism will then be communicated honestly, but also diplomatically.

Another important thing to keep in mind with direct communication is the ability to say "no." In some cultures, it may not be acceptable to say "no," but this is not the case in the U.S. If you're asked a question to which the answer is "no," say "no," but explain why. "Can you meet next week's deadline?" "I'm sorry, but I don't think that I can. We have another big project, and it's taking more time than we'd anticipated. We'll need another week for this project." To an American, saying "yes" when the answer is really "no" is dishonest and insincere, and it will cause far more problems than answering honestly and directly in the negative. Yes-men are not thought of highly in the U.S.

FORMALITY

Most Americans are not particularly formal, and instead they value a friendly, personable, and laid-back approach. First names are used most often, even in the workplace, and titles are often dropped. The easiest way to navigate through levels of formality is simply to watch the way others in the group are behaving. If they dress very formally, you'll be expected to do the same. If they refer to one another as Mr. or Ms., so should you. But usually, except in very formal settings, Americans take a relaxed attitude. Often when you speak to an American using a title like Ms. or Dr., you'll hear, "Please, call me Sandy."

TOUCHING AND PERSONAL SPACE

Americans like their space, and compared to many other cultures, Americans feel comfortable with a fairly large distance between themselves and others when having conversations. As discussed in Chapter 5, that distance is at least an arm's length, if not more. If you violate that distance by stepping too close, an American will definitely step away from you, uncomfortable or even annoyed, to increase the personal space bubble between himself or herself and you. Take this cue seriously; Americans simply hate to have their personal space violated, and they form unfavorable opinions of people who do this.

In addition, Americans generally do not maintain physical contact while speaking. Occasionally, close friends, particularly women, will touch each other on the forearms, for example, while talking. This is a show of intimacy and affection, and it is usually limited to people who know each other very well and who are very comfortable with each other. Typically, though, physical contact is limited to the first greeting and the good-bye, in the form of a handshake, pat on the back, or hug; otherwise, the personal space bubble is maintained!

THE ALL-IMPORTANT HANDSHAKE

It is still the case, for many Americans, that a person is judged by the quality of his or her handshake. A strong, firm handshake conveys confidence and commands respect, while a limp or uncertain handshake paints a picture of weakness, and perhaps even a lack of trustworthiness. Pay attention to the way that Americans shake your hand when they meet you, and try to imitate it. You'll notice that it's a firm grasp, a locking of just the hands, usually for a single downward motion, but sometimes for several up-and-down pumps. People may briefly nod their heads to each other while shaking hands. The handshake typically isn't accompanied by other contact, such as touching other parts of the arm or patting the shoulder. Sometimes, though, to convey extra warmth or fondness, a person may grasp his or her partner's hand in both hands, one doing the shake, the other placed over the outside of the partner's hand. This behavior is usually restricted to people who have formed some kind of a closer, more personal bond. Along with the handshake, a hearty and warm smile is usually expected, with eye contact maintained during the handshake. We'll come back to eye contact in a moment, as this is very important.

HUGS AND KISSES

As a general rule, Americans do not hug or kiss while greeting or leave-taking, except with very close friends or family. In some parts of the U.S., though, especially in larger cities, it has become increasingly common for friends to hug one another, or even to exchange quick kisses on the cheek. This custom is more common between women, or between a man and a woman, than between two men, although there are of course exceptions. If men want to show close fondness, they may pat each other on the shoulder or back, sometimes while shaking hands, but this is not very common. It's not always easy to tell who is comfortable with a hug, a kiss, or a pat on the back, so it's best to simply observe other people's behavior and imitate. If an American isn't expecting such close physical contact, it can cause a good amount of discomfort.

EYE CONTACT

Along with the strong, confident handshake, eye contact is also very important in American culture. Some Americans take a failure to maintain eye contact as a sign that a person has something to hide. In fact, the expression "shifty-eyed" means just that—someone who is not to be trusted. This doesn't mean that you should stare, though. It's natural and comfortable to look away from time to time during a conversation, but be sure to return your gaze to your partner.

GESTURES

Gestures are very important non-verbal communication tools, and Americans, like people from all cultures, have their own gestural vocabulary. You'll learn about them in the Real Life section of this chapter, so we won't go into detail here. Just keep in mind one general rule: On a scale between extremely emotionally expressive with a lot of gestures and body language on the one hand, and extremely subdued and inexpressive on the other, Americans probably fall somewhere around the middle, but a little bit more toward the inexpressive side. That means that given a choice between the two extremes, Americans are more comfortable with less body language. It's true that Americans talk with their hands a bit, but not too much. Americans appreciate people who are expressive, but not overly effusive. Again, to figure out what, exactly, this comfort zone is, simply observe Americans around you.

TIME

Time isn't necessarily a communication style, but you may be communicating a great deal to Americans through your relationship with time—especially with their time. Americans appreciate, expect, and even demand punctuality, especially for formal meetings and appointments, such as in business. If you show up late for a meeting, most Americans will understand that to mean that you're irresponsible, and that you don't care about wasting other people's time. That's not a good message to give Americans, who value time very greatly. Even in social settings, you're expected to be on time, although there's more of a relaxed window. It's usually acceptable, for example, to show up five to ten minutes late to a social engagement, but you should always apologize and ask your friend if he or she has been waiting long. For parties, it's perfectly acceptable for guests to arrive fifteen or twenty minutes late, and in fact it's often expected. For sit-down dinner parties, punctuality is probably more important. In formal settings, though, even being a few minutes late is not acceptable. If you're on your way to a business meeting and are stuck in traffic, it's really essential that you call ahead and explain your delay. Better yet, leave a little earlier so that you're sure to show up on time.

E. ENGLISH IN ACTION

Rick and Erika are close friends who are meeting for dinner. Listen in on their conversation, and see if you can find the examples of some of the issues you read about in the How-To section.

Rick: Erika, hey! It's great to see you.

Erika: Hi there! (She extends her hand to shake his.)

Rick: A handshake? What are we, in the boardroom? I want a hug! I haven't seen you in so long.

Erika: Oh, a hug . . . Hello! I still have to get used to this. We don't hug much where I'm from and here it seems like everyone always hugs hello.

Rick: Oh, sorry. I didn't realize . . .

Erika: No, no problem. I'm becoming more and more used to it. At first I have to admit it made me really uncomfortable, but I'm warming up to the custom.

Rick: Well, either way, it's great to see you.

Erika: I'm sorry I'm a bit late! Have you been waiting long?

Rick: No, not long at all. I got here about ten minutes ago.

Erika: There was some kind of delay on the subway. I rushed, but . . .

Rick: No problem.

Erika: Hey, where's Susan? I thought you said she was joining us.

Rick: I invited her, but she said she couldn't make it. She's got some big project at work, and she had to stay late at the office.

Erika: Too bad, I was looking forward to seeing her.

Rick: Yeah, but ... Oh, never mind.

Erika: What?

Rick: Oh, it's nothing. I was going to be gossipy. I shouldn't say anything.

Erika: Well, now you have to! Come on, spit it out!

Rick: Oh, okay. But this stays between us! It's just that, well, she was going to bring her boyfriend, and ...

Erika: Aha! Say no more!

Rick: You mean, you don't like him either?

Erika: It's not really that I don't like him. I don't know him very well, so I can't tell if I like him or not. But he's so ... it's just that he's ...

Rick: Exhausting?

Erika: Yes! That's the perfect word.

Rick: He's a nice guy, but he never stops talking.

Erika: And throwing his hands everywhere! I know he's not from this country, and people are more expressive with their hands in his culture, but ...

Rick: But it's exhausting! I swear I never sleep quite as well after I've spent an hour with him! And he gets right up in your face when he talks! I keep stepping away, and he follows me. He once had me in the corner, and I couldn't escape.

Erika: Ha! I've felt awful for feeling this way about him, but I'm glad to see that I'm not alone.

Rick: He's a nice guy and all, but he takes some getting used to. I suppose if you can get used to hugging in a different part of your own country, then I should be able to get used to my friend's boyfriend.

Erika: Well, he's actually not your friend's boyfriend anymore.

Rick: What? They broke up? I thought ...

Erika: No, they didn't break up, they got engaged.

Rick: You're kidding!

Erika: Nope. They're getting married. So you'd better start getting used to your friend's fiancé, because that'll be easier than getting used to her husband!

F. PRACTICE

Fill in the sentences with the correct form of the following words and expressions: *in your face, to sugarcoat, to get to know, to intrude, easygoing, to mince words, to shrug, to put off, to stare, to keep someone at arm's length*

1. Ralph's _____ nature makes it a pleasure to be with him.
2. If you would only take the time to _____ Sarah, I think you would like her.
3. Marjorie was _____ by Billy's rude behavior.
4. If you have bad news for me, don't _____ it! Give it to me straight!
5. Americans often do not _____ when they tell you how they feel about things.
6. Most people feel uncomfortable if others _____ at them for a long time.
7. Nobody likes it when someone _____ into his or her life. It's just so rude.
8. Our neighbor is really pushy. Nobody likes him because he always gets _____.
9. It's probably best to just _____. That way he can't offend you.
10. Meredith just _____ and said she didn't know when I asked her if she was going to see Evan tonight.

Fill in the blanks with both the correct auxiliary verb and *either, neither, too,* or *so.*

1. Americans are friendly people, and _____ _____ you.
2. Americans smile a lot, and I _____ _____.
3. I can't make friends with Americans very easily, and _____ _____ you.
4. We aren't friends with our neighbors yet, and Shiroz _____ _____.
5. Myung Sung Lee doesn't know how to behave around Americans, and _____ _____ her husband.
6. We can try to understand Americans better, and _____ _____ you.
7. They're both beautiful flower bouquets. _____ or both _____ work well on the dinner table tonight.
8. I didn't bring an umbrella today, and _____ _____ Ellen.
9. I can't imagine who left this message.— _____ _____ I.
10. Mitzia really likes to exercise, and her cousin _____ _____.

G. TASK

Go sit in a place where people like to hang out and talk, such as a coffee shop. Sit back and observe people (but don't stare!), and take mental notes of their body language, gestures, directness, physical contact, proximity, and so on. How different are these things from the norms of behavior in your own culture? Then try to take an objective look at your own culture, as if from the perspective of an outsider. What advice would you give Americans who were living in your country?

H.   REAL LIFE

Let's look at some specific gestures and other types of body language, and what they mean in the U.S.

Hand-clapping	Approval; Excitement
Thumbs-down	Bad; "I don't like it"; Rejection
Thumbs-up	Approval; "I like it"; "It's good"
Palm up, fingers pointing away from body, either all fingers or just the index finger pulled several times back toward the body	"Come here"
Holding the hand out in front of you, with the palm facing toward the side, and making a sweeping gesture with the back of the hand, as if chasing away a fly	"Get out of here"; "That's crazy"; "You're being ridiculous"; Dismissal
Thumb held up, pinky held out, other fingers folded over palm, hand held against ear like a phone	"Call me"
Index finger pointed at ear or temple, making small circles over ear	"(He/She) is crazy!"
Middle finger crossed over index finger, hand held up to show crossed fingers	Wishing for good luck; "Let's hope for good luck"
Middle finger crossed over index finger, hand held behind back out of sight	"I'm lying"; "I don't have to tell you the truth"
Two index fingers held in an X in front of body	"Stay away"; "Get back"; "You're/It's bad luck"
Rubbing the thumb against the tips of both the index finger and middle finger of the same hand, making small circular motions	Money; "That's expensive"; Rich
Touching the index finger to the tip of the nose	"That's exactly right"; "That's exactly correct"
Tapping the index finger against the temple, often while tilting the head and raising the eyes	Sarcastically: "That's very smart"; "You have to think before you act!"

Waving motion of hand, fingers wagged downward	Good-bye
Whole hand waves back and forth	Hello; Good-bye
Rolling the eyes	"I don't believe it"; "This is unbelievable"; "This is ridiculous (annoying)"
Shoulders shrugged, hands held out with palms facing upwards and outwards, sometimes accompanied by facial expression of disinterest, dissatisfaction, confusion, etc.	"I don't know"; "Beats me!" "It was just okay"; "I don't care"
Squinting, scratching the side of the head	"I don't know"; "I'm confused"
Wink	"I'm kidding"; "It's our secret"; "Don't tell anyone" (in general, an expression of understanding, shared secrecy, and confidence)
Finger snap	"I got it!" "I understand!"
Turning head from side to side	No
Nodding head up and down	Yes
Wagging finger back and forth	No; "Don't do that"; "That's bad"
Thumb and index finger forming a circle, other fingers held up, hand held up in display	"That's good"; "That's perfect"
Palm held outwards, facing someone	"Stop!" "Don't move!"
Index finger and middle finger held up in V sign	Victory; Peace
Middle finger raised, hand held outward toward someone	&*#@ you! ("the finger," a vulgar expression!)

Even counting is shown differently in different cultures. In the U.S., counting on the fingers is done this way:

One	The index finger held up or out
Two	The index finger and the middle finger held up or out
Three	The index finger, the middle finger, and the ring finger held up or out

Four	All fingers except the thumb held up or out
Five	All fingers and the thumb held up or out
Six	All fingers and the thumb of one hand held up or out, and only the thumb (or index finger) of the second hand held up or out.

It's worth mentioning that in some cultures, it's acceptable to summon someone or get someone's attention by snapping your fingers, for example, at a restaurant when calling the server or in the classroom when getting the teacher's attention. Do not do this in the U.S.; it's considered very rude and obnoxious. Also, some people consider it rude to point at others. To be safe, if you want to get another person's attention in a more formal setting, such as a restaurant, you can try to make eye contact with the person and then raise your hand, holding up your hand and arm slightly, with elbow bent, when eye contact is made. You can wave your hand if you're trying to get a friend's attention. You can also say "excuse me" to servers at a restaurant when they pass by to get their attention. Do not call out to the person whose attention you're trying to attract. Of course, acceptable behavior can vary widely, and, as mentioned before, it's always a good idea to observe and see how other people are behaving around you.

I. RESOURCES

General overview:
www.utmem.edu/international/living.html
www.tripadvisor.com/Travel-g191-c3541/United-States.html

American culture and regional differences:
www.usastudyguide.com/regionaldifferences.htm
usinfo.state.gov/usa/infousa/facts/factover/ch2.htm (and a lot of other helpful and interesting information about the United States)

Personal space:
www.edupass.org/culture/personalspace.phtml

Culture shock:
www.worldwide.edu/travel_planner/culture_shock.html

Books:
In the Know in the USA, Random House

ANSWER KEY
Practice 1: 1. easygoing; 2. get to know; 3. put off; 4. sugarcoat; 5. mince words; 6. stare; 7. intrudes; 8. in your face; 9. keep him at arm's length; 10. shrugged

Practice 2: 1. so are; 2. do too; 3. neither can; 4. isn't either; 5. neither does; 6. so can; 7. Either . . . will; 8. Neither did; 9. Neither can; 10. does too

CHAPTER 12

Making Friends: Visiting People's Homes

A. ENGLISH CLOSE-UP

You are cordially invited
to the Grahams' home
Saturday, September 9th
2525 Canyon View Drive
Cocktails served from 6:30 PM
Dinner served at 8:00 PM
Please RSVP
(505) 555-9129

B. VOCABULARY ESSENTIALS

To burp, to belch—To pass gas loudly from the stomach through the mouth. *Milo, please do not belch in public. It is so embarrassing to hear you burp so loudly.*

BYOB—"Bring your own bottle." This is used for informal parties. It means that if you wish to drink alcohol, you should bring some with you. This term can also apply to restaurants, where it usually means you can bring your own bottle of alcohol for free (or for a small "corkage" fee) and possibly that the restaurant does not sell liquor. *Hey, Jack, do you want to come to my party Friday night? It's BYOB, though.*

To crash a party—To go to a party uninvited. Except perhaps with large college parties, this is usually not considered acceptable behavior. *Can you believe that George crashed our party? He wasn't even invited and he brought two of his friends!*

Doggie bag—A bag or box used to carry leftover food home from a party or a restaurant. "Doggie bag" is a euphemism, because people usually intend the food for themselves, not for their dogs. *Excuse me, this was great but I just can't finish it. May I have a doggie bag?*

To drop in/by—To go somewhere for a visit, usually for a short while, and usually unannounced. Dropping by unannounced at someone's home is often considered bad manners, unless it is a very brief visit to drop something off. *I'm really sorry to drop by uninvited, but I wanted to return the cookbook I borrowed from you.*

Etiquette—Proper manners, expected behavior in a certain setting. *If you're invited to a formal dinner party, you should brush up on your etiquette!*

Faux pas—A social error, literally, "a false step." *It's important to learn about the culture of a country before you visit so you will not commit a faux pas.*

Gracious—Fine or courteous in behavior or manner. *Jacqueline Kennedy was considered by most to be a very gracious lady.*

To light up—In the context of smoking, to light a cigarette. *You can't just light up anywhere anymore. Many states have laws against smoking in public.*

To misconstrue—To misinterpret or misread behavior. *I think you've misconstrued what Ross meant. When he said that Paul spent a lot of time lying around thinking, he didn't mean that Paul was smart, but rather that he was lazy!*

Poise—Holding oneself in a state of balance and composure. *Beauty pageant contestants are judged on poise and talent as well as beauty.*

Polished—Having social refinement and courtesy. *I love seeing a man with such polished manners. He's just so polite and gracious.*

RSVP—"Répondez s'il vous plaît," French for "Please respond." Often placed on invitations to ask invitees to let the person sending the invitations know if invitee will be attending. *Did you RSVP for Germaine's party yet?*

To show off—To make a spectacle of yourself and your accomplishments, to brag or boast. *Mrs. Jones is always showing off how much better her things are than everybody else's.*

Silverware—Forks, knives, spoons, etc., that are made out of silver or stainless steel, but the term is often used to refer to those items in general. Sometimes also called flatware. *Can you get the silverware out and set the table, please?*

To slump—To stand or sit with your shoulders drooping. *Feeling depressed, Sharon sat slumped over in the corner all by herself.*

To slurp—To drink or eat noisily, especially as with soup. *Mind your manners when you're at your grandmother's. And don't slurp when you eat!*

Strict—Strongly disciplined, conforming precisely to the expected way of doing things, or demanding such discipline and conformity. *Children love to visit their grandparents because they usually aren't as strict as their parents.*

Vulgar—Lacking in taste and manners, showing offensive behavior. *I can't believe that you talked about details of your intimate relationships at the dinner party! Did you really think that such a vulgar topic was appropriate?*

C. GRAMMAR ESSENTIALS: GERUNDS

Gerunds are formed by adding *-ing* to verbs, and they function as nouns. They differ from present participles, which are used as adjectives but look exactly like gerunds. Gerunds may be used as the subject, direct object of a verb, object of a preposition, or any other function of nouns. Here are some examples of gerunds used as subjects:

> *Swimming is my favorite sport.*
> *Partying is a way of life for some people.*
> *Belching is vulgar!*

And here are some examples of gerunds used as direct objects of verbs:

> *I like swimming.*
> *Gretchen hates too much partying.*
> *Stop that disgusting belching!*

Gerunds can also be used as indirect objects, objects of prepositions, or predicate nouns:

> *Give hiking a chance; you might like it!*
> *Many people relax by telling jokes and laughing.*
> *Marilyn's favorite form of exercise is swimming.*

Here is a list of some of the most common verbs that take gerunds as objects. The ones marked with an asterisk (*) can take either gerunds or infinitives:

admit	defend	*forget	practice
adore	delay	*hate	*prefer
advise	deny	can't help	propose
anticipate	describe	imagine	put off
appreciate	discuss	keep (on)	quit
avoid	dislike	*like	recall
*begin	enjoy	*love	recollect
complete	escape	mind	recommend
confess	excuse	miss	regret
consider	finish	permit	*remember
*continue	forbid	postpone	resent

resist	*start	*try
resume	stop	understand
risk	suggest	
*can't stand	tolerate	

Bill admitted lying about the money.
I really miss coming over to your place!
They continued dancing and talking into the night.

It's possible to modify a gerund with a possessive like *my, her,* or *John's:*

She hates my asking to borrow money
We really appreciate their coming over early to help.
How can you defend him bringing up that vulgar topic at dinner?

In relaxed speech, you'll often hear the possessives replaced by direct object pronouns (or nouns):

She hates me asking to borrow money.
We really appreciate them coming over early to help.

Here are a few other points to keep in mind about gerunds:

- With many activities and sports, use *go* + gerund. *Do you like to go swimming? Let's go skiing this winter! Ian hates to go bowling.*

- Polite requests with *would/do you mind . . .* are followed by a gerund, as is the response *I don't mind . . . Would you mind coming over early to help me prepare? No, I don't mind coming over early at all!*

- Gerunds are often used on signs and public notices. *No smoking. Hunting is prohibited.*

D. HOW-TO

Americans have a saying, "A man's home is his castle." You could just as easily say, "A woman's home is her castle," too, because both American men and women often think of their homes as personal sanctuaries. This means that if an American says to you, "Why don't you drop by sometime?" you probably shouldn't take that literally. This is an expression Americans often use to be friendly, but it should not be misconstrued as an actual invitation to come visit any time you'd like. If you try dropping in, in fact, you will be made to feel extremely uncomfortable, and your host will be confused, embarrassed, and perhaps more than a bit annoyed. The average American does not appreciate drop-in guests, and instead sees dropping in as an imposition. But don't worry—you'll know for sure when you've received an invitation to an American home, because you will be given a date, a time, an address, and probably directions.

If you receive such an invitation, sometimes you will be asked to RSVP. If you are, make sure you respond. Many people consider it rude to ignore an RSVP request, whether you can make it or not. If you can't make it, say that you're sorry, but you have other plans, or you'll be out of town, or . . . whatever reason you can give. Make sure you give a reason, though. And if you can make it, RSVP to say thank you, and that you'll be coming. Many people expect that if they invite someone to a party, that person will bring a guest— a husband, wife, boyfriend, girlfriend, partner, etc. But it's always good to ask if you can bring someone, and, of course, to say that you'll be bringing someone when you RSVP. Some invitations might even directly tell you that you can invite someone by writing, for example, "John Smith and Guest" on the envelope. Smaller dinner parties might have a more restricted guest list because table space and food will be limited, so unless you're specifically told that you can bring someone, don't.

Time is also a good thing to keep in mind when it comes to parties, dinner parties, and other social occasions. If you come from a culture in which time is viewed in a relaxed manner, remind yourself that your American friends will not be quite so relaxed! Never arrive early unless the host or hostess has specifically asked you to. It's usually acceptable to arrive ten or fifteen minutes late to a dinner party, or perhaps even a half hour late to a very large dinner party. However, don't push it beyond those limits unless you've told the host or hostess that you cannot make it to the party until a later time. If a specific meal time is given, make sure you're there by that time. Formal invitations might say something like, "Cocktails and hors d'oeuvres served at 5:30, dinner at 6:00 p.m." A more casual invitation will be given over the phone or in person, but your host or hostess might say, "Come around 6:00; dinner is at 7:00." Whatever the case, be sure to arrive no later than the dinner hour. Times for some parties, open houses, or housewarmings are much more casual. Guests will come and go as the evening wears on, perhaps just stopping by for a short time as their own schedules permit. In fact, some people try to be "fashionably late" to large parties, which means they try to arrive about a half hour to 45 minutes late, or even later, in order to not be the first one to arrive at the party.

It's always a good idea to bring something for your host or hostess when you've been invited to a party. Flowers are always appreciated. Chocolates or other sweets are also well received. Wine is another good offering; just don't feel bad if the wine you brought is not served with dinner. The host or hostess may already have something specially selected for the occasion. Your hosts will always appreciate it if you bring something from your own country—a variety of wine, candy, etc. Occasionally invitations will say BYOB; if so, bring your favorite beverage, because you will have the opportunity to share it with others, too.

Dining etiquette varies from culture to culture, so if you're invited to an American dinner party, it's a good idea to be aware of some of the more important expectations. On taking your seat at the table, open your napkin and place it in your lap. Occasionally, you may rest your forearms on the edge of the table, but don't put your elbows directly on the table unless the meal is a very casual event with friends. This is usually seen as unrefined. It's also considered rude to start eating before everyone is served. You'll often see people waiting until the host or hostess has served himself or herself, at which point he or she will probably say, "Please!" Typically, Americans use one hand to hold the utensil, and the other hand rests in their lap, rather than on the table next to their food. They usually use one utensil at a time. However, if they need to use both a fork and a knife, Americans usually hold the knife in one hand and the fork in the other. If you're not using a utensil, return it to its place. If you're eating soup, be careful not to slurp it, or any other food or beverage, for that matter. To Americans, eating noisily is highly offensive. Whatever you do, do not talk with your mouth full of food. If someone asks you something and you must talk, cover your mouth with your hand or your napkin when answering, or simply wait until you've swallowed to respond. One last thing about table manners—under no circumstances should you ever burp. While this is seen as a sign of a hearty appetite or appreciation for the food in some cultures, to Americans, belching is rude and vulgar. If you feel a burp coming on, try to suppress it and always excuse yourself if it happens.

Many people enjoy smoking after a meal, but smoking is becoming increasingly unfashionable; in some states it's outlawed in public places. Many Americans forbid smoking in their homes, too. There's a very good chance that your hosts will not appreciate having their guests light up at the dinner table, or probably anywhere in their home. If you smoke, unless you see others smoking around you, assume that you may not smoke in the house. Go outside to the street, the backyard, or the patio, and make sure you're far enough away from the house that the smoke won't drift inside. But you should first ask your host if he or she minds if you go outside to smoke a cigarette.

Americans do love entertaining in their homes. For one thing, it gives them a chance to show off a little. Their homes are usually perceived as an extension of themselves, so having a beautiful, comfortable home is an important goal. Many Americans are very proud of their homes, so once you have received an invitation to an American home that you have never been to before, you are likely to be given a tour on arrival. Americans view their home as a form of self-expression, so you will probably see an individual style of décor on display through plants, art, collectibles, items passed down through the family, and so on. You could also see several TVs, computers, telephones, and all kinds of electronic gadgets and appliances everywhere. You are likely to see a pet or two as well. Americans love their pets and treat them like family, so even if you don't like pets and can't stand the thought of touching an animal, it's a good idea to ask about them. Their owners will appreciate your interest and like you all the more for it. Conversely, if you show open dislike of an American's pet, he or she is likely to take that personally! So enjoy your party, be friendly and social, and you're sure to be invited to more parties.

 ## E. ENGLISH IN ACTION

Most people are surprised when they first encounter the customs and manners of another culture. Listen in on a conversation between Monica and Angelique, a young woman who doesn't have a lot of experience with cultures other than her own.

Angelique: Hello?

Monica: Hello, Angelique? This is Monica. How are you?

Angelique: Oh, Monica, it's you. I'm fine, thanks. How are you today?

Monica: I'm fine. I wanted to ask you if you enjoyed the party at the Grahams' the other night.

Angelique: Oh, yes, I did. Mr. and Mrs. Graham are lovely people.

Monica: Yes, and Mrs. Graham is such a gracious hostess.

Angelique: Yes, you're right. But Monica, do you mind if I ask you about some things I noticed at the party?

Monica: Of course not!

Angelique: Well, the food was delicious. I really enjoyed it, and I think Mrs. Graham is a great cook.

Monica: Well, both Mr. and Mrs. Graham are great cooks. They both cook, and their food is amazing.

Angelique: It is. But I was surprised to see the way the guests were eating.

Monica: What do you mean?

Angelique: Well, why did everyone constantly switch back and forth between using the knife and the fork? It made me dizzy!

Monica: That's just the way that people eat here. It's common to eat that way.

Angelique: And when they weren't using their hand, they put it in their lap. Where I come from, that's considered strange. What were they doing there?

Monica: They weren't doing anything, of course. Here, that's what you usually do with the hand you're not using to eat with.

Angelique: And some people even used their fingers to eat certain foods!

Monica: Well, that depends on the food, but it is considered acceptable to eat some foods with your fingers.

Angelique: Also, when I held out my hand to one man, he nearly broke it, and then he pumped it up and down like a water pump! Do people always do that here?

Monica: Well, some people . . .

Angelique: Oh, and during the dinner, when Mr. Graham offered me more of something, he never offered it again.

Monica: Well, if you said no the first time, he probably thought that . . .

Angelique: And at the end of the party, Mrs. Graham gave me something she called a "doggie bag." I was so confused!

Monica: If you said you liked her cooking, she probably was trying to be nice. If there's a lot of food left over after a dinner, Americans will usually offer it to their guests to bring home, rather than waste it. "Doggie bag" is just an expression that . . .

Angelique: And then . . .

Monica: Angelique! Let me interrupt for a second. All of these things that you're bringing up are interesting cultural differences. I hadn't actually ever thought about them as an outsider; they just seem natural to me, but from your reaction I can tell that they're not natural to everyone.

Angelique: Oh, no, some of this behavior was very strange!

Monica: Strange to you, natural to me. It sounds like we have a great conversation topic! Tell you what, why don't you come over to my place for dinner this Friday, and we can talk more. It could be very interesting for both of us!

Angelique: That's a great idea. I would love to. Thank you for the invitation. But Monica, I have just one more question . . .

F. PRACTICE

Fill in the blanks with the following words and expressions: *BYOB, crash the party, drop by, vulgar, faux pas, RSVP, light up, poise, doggie bag, show off*

1. It's embarrassing to go to another country and commit a social _____.

2. No matter what your new American friend says to you, never _____ his or her home unexpectedly.

3. If you must _____, be sure to go outside where you won't bother anyone.

4. My party is _____, so why don't you bring your favorite beer?

5. Could you please give me a(n) _____? I'd like to share this great food with my husband.

6. I've asked everyone to _____, but so far only a few have called to let me know they're coming.

7. Billy, please don't _____ when Chelsea comes by. I know you want to impress her, but it's embarrassing.

8. Erica has so much _____. She walks so grandly that she could easily be one of those fashion models.

9. Make sure that no one _____. There are to be no uninvited guests.

10. Please don't burp in public. It's so _____.

Use the gerund form of these verbs in the following sentences: *ask, have, call, drive, try, go, pass, take, roller-skate, exercise*

1. If you keep _____ to American parties, you'll make new friends quickly.
2. _____ new foods can be a fun experience.
3. Would you mind _____ to RSVP for the party for the weekend?
4. _____ four or five times a week can keep you in shape.
5. What do you think of my _____ a party next weekend?
6. One American custom is _____ home doggie bags filled with extra food.
7. Would you mind _____ the salt? This dish really needs it.
8. Would you like to go _____ this weekend? There's a rink nearby.
9. Are you okay with my _____ your car to work tomorrow?
10. Please keep _____ me to go to the movies with you. One of these days I'll have time.

G. TASK

Imagine that you're having a dinner party in your country and you're going to invite an American friend who has no idea what's considered rude or acceptable behavior in your culture. Prepare a list of dos and don'ts for him or her. How different is it from what you've seen in this lesson? Which customs from your culture do you think would surprise Americans? Which American customs surprised you when you first learned about them?

H. REAL LIFE

Dear Sammy,

I need your advice! My husband and I recently moved to the United States from India and we were invited to a friend's home for a traditional Fourth of July barbecue. It was so kind of her to think of us! And we are very interested in taking part in a traditional American holiday, but there's one slight problem . . . We're Hindu, and we're vegetarians. I think a "traditional American barbecue" means a lot of meat, doesn't it? Should we simply say no to our friend, and make up an excuse? If we accept, how can we tell her to cook something special just for us? Will she be offended?

Sincerely,
Worried in Winnetka

Dear Worried,

Yes, a traditional American barbecue usually means a lot of hamburgers, hot dogs, sausages . . . and not a lot of tofu! But there's absolutely no reason why you shouldn't accept your friend's invitation, and maybe even add a few flavors to her family's tradition in the process. After all, vegetarianism in the U.S. isn't so alien these days, and just about every supermarket stocks tofu dogs, veggie burgers, and plenty of other options for vegetarians or people who don't want to eat meat every day for a variety of reasons. So, thank your friend, and tell her that you and your husband would love to come, but that you're both vegetarians. Offer to bring something along that the two of you can eat and that you'd love to share with others. Maybe there's a delicious Indian dish that you can prepare, so you'll be offering people a new experience alongside their traditional Fourth of July barbecue. You'll probably find that even if Americans aren't aware of some aspect of your culture or religion, they'll be curious about it, and also respectful of it. And that isn't the case only for vegetarianism. A lot of people observe customs or have beliefs that Americans may not understand, but a little bit of communication goes a long way. You'll experience something new from your American friends, and they'll experience something new from you. It's one of the things that make the U.S. great, and it's a perfect way to celebrate the Fourth of July!

Have a great time!
Sammy

I.   RESOURCES

www.cuisinenet.com/digest/custom/etiquette/manners_intro.shtml
www.bremercommunications.com/Dining_Etiquette.htm
www.usheroff.com/52tips.html
www.emilypost.com

Books
Emily Post's Etiquette by Peggy Post

ANSWER KEY
Practice 1: 1. faux pas; 2. drop by; 3. light up; 4. BYOB; 5. doggie bag; 6. RSVP; 7. show off; 8. poise; 9. crashes the party; 10. vulgar

Practice 2: 1. going; 2. Trying; 3. calling; 4. Exercising; 5. having; 6. taking; 7. passing; 8. roller-skating; 9. driving; 10. asking

CHAPTER 13

Making Friends: Special Occasions

 A. **ENGLISH CLOSE-UP**

"Auld Lang Syne" is a traditional New Year's Eve song based on an old Scottish folk song. It is often played and sung at New Year's Eve parties in the U.S. The Scottish English *auld lang syne* literally translates as "old long since," which essentially means "days long gone by" or "times long ago."

Auld Lang Syne
Should old acquaintance be forgot,
And never brought to mind?
Should old acquaintance be forgot,
and auld lang syne?

For auld lang syne, my dear,
for auld lang syne,
we'll take a cup o' kindness yet,
for auld lang syne.

B. **VOCABULARY ESSENTIALS**

Bachelor party—A party thrown for a man by his male friends before his wedding, sometimes referred to as a "stag party." A bachelorette party is the same thing, but for the bride-to-be instead and thrown by female friends. *Nona was very angry when she found out her fiancé got so drunk at his bachelor party.*

Bridal party—Often the group of people in a wedding who are associated with the bride and groom: the matron/maid of honor, bridesmaids, best man, ushers (groomsmen), flower girl, and ring bearer. However, the meaning can vary widely, and sometimes the bridal party includes the bride and groom, just the bride's attendants, the parents, and so on. Often also used interchangeably with "wedding party." *The photographer wanted to get a shot of just the bridal party.*

Cap and gown—The costume worn by students at their graduation ceremony. The cap is square, with a tassel hanging from the top, and it is usually thrown in the air at the end of the ceremony. *Parents always take plenty of pictures of their kids in cap and gown when they graduate.*

Commencement—A beginning or a start, a term used for the graduation ceremony. *The graduates tossed their caps in the air at the end of the commencement ceremony.*

Condolences—Expressions of sympathy to the family of someone who has died. *You can send your condolences to 3388 Elm Way.*

To cremate—To burn a dead body. In the U.S., cremated remains ("ashes") are sometimes kept in urns in people's homes. *Gladys said that she didn't want to be buried when she died, so we arranged to have her cremated.*

Dearly departed—An expression used to refer to the one or ones that have died. *People often save photographs of their dearly departed to keep their memories alive.*

To embalm—To replace a dead body's vital fluids with chemicals in order to preserve the body for viewing. *They really did a nice job of embalming Harry. He looks great.*

Funeral parlor, funeral home—A place where the dead are cremated or prepared for viewing, and where the viewing or funeral services often take place. Also called a mortuary. *Hank had to make arrangements at the local funeral parlor after his mother died.*

Life passages, milestones—Major events in life, such as birth, graduation, and marriage. *The age of 21 is often considered a milestone for many young people because it is the age at which they can legally drink.*

Long-winded—Using a lot of words, usually poetic or flowery. *John's father is so long-winded. It takes him forever to tell one of his stories.*

To make your mark on the world—To leave an impression or legacy (usually positive) affecting future generations. Implies earning recognition and making a difference in the world. *Charles Darwin left his mark on the world with his theory of evolution.*

Obituary—A newspaper announcement of someone's death. *When we heard that old Jim had died we looked for the obituary in the local paper.*

One last fling—One last party or romantic adventure, usually before settling down to married life. *Angela was very upset and almost broke off her engagement when she found out that Mario had had one last fling.*

To pass away—A euphemism that means "to die." *We were all so sorry to hear that your uncle passed away.*

Pomp and Circumstance—Music composed by Sir Edward Elgar that is widely used for graduation ceremonies in the U.S., also known simply as "the graduation song." *When the tune of Pomp and Circumstance started up, I began to cry.*

To register, to be registered—Often, to enroll in a program (a gift registry) at a store in which the store keeps a listing of items that you want as gifts for your wedding, shower, etc. Guests at your event can then go to the store before the event and select one of the items from the list as their gift. Once they have purchased the gift, the item is removed from the list so that two people cannot buy the same gift. *Many people register for their wedding so that they'll be sure to get exactly the gifts that they want.*

Rite of passage—A special event or action marking a major change in life. *Marriage is an important rite of passage.*

To pop the question—To propose marriage, traditionally by a man. *Hasn't Gary popped the question yet?*

Shower—A party given in honor of a bride (bridal shower) or a mother-to-be (baby shower) in order to give her gifts. Sometimes both parents attend a baby shower, and sometimes a couple may celebrate a "couples shower" before marriage. *Everyone gathered at Pam's house to give the bride-to-be a shower before the big day.*

Tassel—Several thin strands of brightly colored thread or cord bound together. A graduation cap has one hanging from the top center, and it is meant to be moved from the right side to the left side of the cap on graduation. *Kareen has a picture of us at graduation with our tassels hanging in front of our faces.*

Valedictorian—The student, usually with the highest grade point average or academic ranking, who gives a speech during a graduation ceremony. *The valedictorian worked hard on her speech.*

Wedding party—Usually the group of people involved in a wedding from both the bride's and the groom's sides: the bridesmaids, the maid of honor, the flower girl, the best man, the ushers, the ring bearer, and occasionally the parents. Sometimes includes the bride and groom as well. *The wedding party needs to arrive at the rehearsal at 6:00 p.m.*

Wake—A time to view a deceased body, prepared by a funeral home, and to pay respects to the family. A wake may be an almost festive occasion at which food is served. *Old and new friends joined my family for the wake, which was held at the funeral home.*

C. GRAMMAR ESSENTIALS: INFINITIVES

The infinitive is the *to* form of a verb. Like gerunds, infinitives can function as nouns as subjects, direct objects, and predicate nouns. They typically don't function as indirect objects or objects of prepositions. Here are some examples of infinitives used as subjects:

To make friends with Americans is my goal.
To organize a surprise party without Bill finding out will be impossible!

Note that infinitival subjects are often put at the end of a sentence, and the subject *it* is used:

> *It is my goal to make friends with Americans.*
> *It'll be impossible to organize a surprise party without Bill finding out!*

Here are some examples of infinitives used as direct objects of verbs:

> *Did you arrange to have a babysitter for Friday night?*
> *Karl intends to visit his parents this weekend.*

Infinitives can also be used as predicate nouns, or they can function as adjectival or adverbial modifiers as well:

> *Our desire was to observe some American holidays before we left.*
> *You need permission to go in there.*
> *The Lopez family came to learn English.*
> *I'm working hard to find a date when all of Beth's friends can come to the shower.*

Just as some verbs take gerunds as direct objects, there are other verbs that take infinitives as direct objects. Here is a list of the common ones. Verbs that can take both gerunds and infinitives are marked with an asterisk (*).

afford	dare	*like	*can't stand
agree	decide	*love	*start
aim	demand	*manage	swear
appear	deserve	mean	threaten
arrange	expect	need	*try
ask	fail	offer	volunteer
beg	*forget	plan	wait
*begin	have	*prefer	want
care	*hate	pretend	wish
claim	hope	promise	
consent	intend	refuse	
*continue	learn	seem	

> *I can't afford to throw you a big party, but we'll have something nice.*
> *We promised not to stay out late at the graduation parties.*
> *Samantha volunteered to take care of decorations for the bridal shower.*

Here are a few other points to keep in mind about infinitives:

- The immediate future with *going* always takes the infinitive. *Dana is going to visit her mother tomorrow. We're going to be late for the rehearsal dinner!*
- Polite requests with *would like* use the infinitive. *Would you like to come to my party? We would like to bring a guest, if that's okay.*

- You can use the infinitive after *too*, using the pattern *too* + adverb/adjective + infinitive. *It's too hot to wear a suit to the wedding! They left too quickly to remember their coats.*
- You can also use the infinitive after *enough*, using the pattern adverb/adjective + *enough* + infinitive. *The party wasn't big enough to rent a reception hall. We finished the rehearsal dinner early enough to have a drink afterwards.*
- The infinitive of purpose is often used with *in order*, but not always. *You need to turn off the TV in order to finish your homework!*
- You may hear a rule about not splitting infinitives in English, but honestly, this is nothing to worry about. Native speakers do it all the time, and this "rule" was really introduced as a stylistic preference in the 19th century. *Cyril would like to acquaint himself better with American customs. Cyril would like to better acquaint himself with American customs.*

D. HOW-TO

Let's take a close look at certain life passages, how they're celebrated in American culture, and what you need to know if you're invited to participate in a celebration.

BIRTH: BABY SHOWERS

Just prior to the birth of a baby, the occasion is celebrated with a baby shower, where the mother-to-be is "showered" with gifts for the expected baby. Traditionally, baby showers were all-female events, but more recently, men have begun to join in and celebrate their expected babies. With relatives and friends in attendance, the baby shower is a great time for talking, playing games, and eating cake. Toward the end of the party, the mother-to-be opens her gifts, so if you're invited to a baby shower, you should bring a gift. If you have received an invitation to a shower or a birth announcement, that announcement or shower invitation should include a card stating where the parents are registered. Go to that store and select something from the list of requested items. You can often do this online as well. If you have only received an announcement, and you do not know the parents well, you need only send a card of congratulations.

BIRTHDAYS: BIRTHDAY PARTIES

Birthdays are often celebrated in the U.S. with birthday parties. If you have children in school, chances are they'll be invited to several birthday parties each school year. For younger kids, these parties will often be on a weekend afternoon. Young kids play games, eat cake, and generally run around and enjoy one another's company. If your child is invited to a friend's or classmate's birthday party, it's customary to send your child to the party with a little gift for the birthday boy or girl. The gift doesn't have to be very expensive, just something small to wrap up and present at the party. Of course, your child may want to have a birthday party of his or her own, as well. In this case, the child invites friends or classmates to the party, and the parent or parents stock up on cake, ice cream, cookies, pretzels, potato chips, and other party foods that kids enjoy. It's common for other parents to help out, because watching over a large group of small children is a job big enough to require more than one or two adults! Traditional birthday party activities for young children include playing "Pin the Tail on the Donkey" and hitting a piñata. It's also traditional to put small candles on the birthday cake, the same number as the age of the child. The children are gathered together, the lights are turned down, the candles on the cake are lit, "Happy Birthday" is sung, and the cake is brought in and presented to the birthday boy or girl. Then, the child must make a wish (silently!) and try to blow out all of the candles on the cake in one breath. Afterwards, everyone claps.

Of course, teenagers and young adults also often celebrate birthdays, sometimes going out to dinner with a small group of friends or throwing a large party with music and dancing. Teenagers' birthday parties can be organized by parents as well, particularly for a big birthday like a "sweet sixteen." Adults don't all celebrate birthdays, especially as they get older and don't want to be reminded of their age! Still, there are some adult birthday celebrations—perhaps a small gathering at work, complete with cake, or a group of friends getting together for dinner (and treating the person whose birthday it is). It's also possible that a surprise party will be organized by a spouse, partner, or close friend of the birthday "boy" or "girl," who isn't supposed to know the party is going to occur. Surprise parties are a popular choice for almost all ages. Presents are not always necessary at adult birthday parties, and it's probably a good idea not to ask how old the man or woman is!

GRADUATION

The next big event in life is graduation. Although small ceremonies are often held for graduations from elementary school and junior high or middle school, and sometimes even from preschool or kindergarten, the biggest graduation ceremonies are reserved for high school and college. The graduates, usually wearing long flowing robes and flat caps with tassels, march slowly during their commencement ceremony to the music of Pomp and Circumstance. Once seated in front of friends and proud family members, the graduates listen to a series of sometimes long-winded speeches given by various dignitaries exhorting them to leave their mark on the world. When the class valedictorian speaks, he or she shares memories of the class's time together and offers them his or her hopes for their futures. Once the graduates receive their diplomas, the students (or representatives from the school) take their tassels in their hands and move them to the opposite side of their caps, signifying their new status. Afterwards, there is usually some sort of celebration. If you receive an announcement of or an invitation to a graduation, you are not necessarily expected to do anything other than give the graduate a congratulatory card, but if you know the graduate somewhat well it's often a good idea to give the graduate a small sum of money or gift, as well.

MARRIAGE: BRIDAL SHOWERS, BACHELOR/BACHELORETTE PARTIES, AND WEDDINGS

Although the institution of marriage is rapidly undergoing changes in the U.S., most people still choose to marry at some time, and for most couples marriage still retains quite a bit of tradition. In the U.S., couples sometimes date for quite a while before someone "pops the question." Some people find very creative ways to propose marriage. They might have a server at a special restaurant put the engagement ring inside a favorite dessert; some have been known to hire pilots to write the question "Will you marry me?" across the sky. Anyone lacking that kind of imagination will usually ask the question in a more ceremonial way. Bending down on one knee, it is customary to ask, "Will you marry me?" or some variation on that question. If the partner accepts, the engaged couple will usually set a date for their wedding and begin to plan it. About five weeks before the wedding, the invitations are mailed. A few weeks later the bride is given a bridal shower, which is similar to a baby shower, only the gifts are usually housewares and sometimes lingerie or other things. A few days before the wedding, there is a wedding rehearsal, and afterwards the groom's parents traditionally host a rehearsal dinner for the bride's family and the rest of the wedding party. A few nights before the wedding, some grooms and brides are given a bachelor or bachelorette party, respectively, as "one last fling" before the bride and groom are married. The bachelor party is usually thrown by the groom's male friends and the bachelorette party by the bride's female friends.

On the day of the wedding, it is considered bad luck for the groom to see the bride before she walks down the aisle. In a very traditional wedding the bride is dressed in a long, white, satin wedding gown with a veil covering her face, and she is escorted down the aisle, or "given away," by her father. When they reach the officiant, he or she might ask, "Who gives this woman to this man," and the bride's father responds, "Her mother and I do." Of course, less traditional approaches are taken as well. The ceremony itself may consist of the officiant sharing some advice, praying if the ceremony is religious rather than civil, and pronouncing the groom and bride "husband and wife." The officiant might then tell the bride and groom to kiss and present the couple to the audience by the names they will be using in marriage. The bride and groom walk down the aisle and out the door together, and sometimes people attending the wedding throw rice over the newlyweds. Afterwards there is a reception, a (usually) formal dinner and celebration lasting several hours. After all of the ceremonies and festivities, the newlyweds usually go on a honeymoon, a trip to celebrate the beginning of their married life together.

If you are invited to a wedding shower or wedding, a gift should be purchased. The couple has probably registered at a store and will usually include the name of the store in the invitation. If the couple has had a small private wedding, they may send out announcements after their wedding. You may choose to purchase a gift if you feel close to either the bride or the groom, or you might just want to send a card of congratulations.

DEATH: WAKES, FUNERAL SERVICES, AND BURIALS

The last great milestone of life is death. American attitudes and customs surrounding death, like marriage customs, are changing. Until fairly recently, death was a universally gloomy and tragic occasion, but over the past decades, some Americans are gradually beginning to see funerals as a celebration, perhaps not entirely cheerful, but less grim. Traditionally, everyone at a funeral wears black; bodies are embalmed to preserve them for final viewing and then buried in caskets beneath the ground. Services are usually held in a religious center or at a funeral parlor. A wake is a time for people to view the body, cry, and say good-bye. Euphemisms are used in order to soften the feelings surrounding the difficult subject of death and to make it seem less final. The dead are called the "dearly departed," and the act of dying is called "passing away." Although many people still follow the old traditions of having a funeral and a burial service at a cemetery, some Americans are now more likely to celebrate the life of the person who has died. This does not mean that the death is not painful for those left behind. They still need to be comforted with condolences, flowers, or a sympathy card. Cremation, although not a new option, is becoming more and more popular, attendees now occasionally wear more colorful attire than all black, and instead of having traditional funerals, more and more people are requesting memorials during which the deceased's life is reviewed, his or her best qualities are remembered, and favorite music is played.

Deaths are usually announced in the newspapers so the services are open to anyone who wishes to attend. Attendance is appreciated, and nothing more is expected. If you feel especially close to the person who has died or to his or her family, you might wish to send a card or flowers or make a monetary donation to a favorite charity mentioned in the obituary. After the burial, friends and relatives often assemble at the home of the deceased's family, and it's usually the case that people bring food, because the family is not expected to cook or to organize a large gathering at such a time.

E. ENGLISH IN ACTION

Listen in as Ji asks her friend Mark for advice about a birthday party.

Ji: Hi, Mark. How are you?

Mark: Ji! Fine. What about you? How are you doing?

Ji: I'm fine. Oh, Mark, I want to ask you something. My daughter got a birthday invitation from the little boy next door, and I don't know what I should do.

Mark: Oh, that's easy. Just ask his mother or father what he likes, and you can buy him a small gift, wrap it up, and have your daughter bring it to the party.

Ji: Oh, thank you, Mark. What do Americans do on their birthdays?

Mark: Well, they usually have a party. The children usually play games, or maybe they'll do a special art project or go to an amusement park or something.

Ji: Is there any kind of a ceremony? I want to tell my daughter what to expect.

Mark: Well, they usually have a birthday cake and sing "Happy Birthday." Then the birthday boy or girl makes a wish and blows out the candles on the cake, one candle for every year of their lives. They try to blow them all out at once, if they can, since some people think that will help the wish come true. They also can't tell anyone what they wished for, since then it won't come true.

Ji: And does it come true?

Mark: [laughter] Well, if my daughter got everything she wished for on her birthday, our house would probably be overflowing with ice cream and lollipops!

F. PRACTICE

Fill in the sentences with the correct form of the following words or expressions: *valedictorian, bridal shower, to pop the question, dearly departed, to pass away, rite of passage, bridal party, one last fling, long-winded, caps and gowns*

1. Did you hear that Nancy just _____? It's so sad. She was so young!

2. When kids turn 21 in the U.S., they often think it's a(n) _____ to have that first legal drink.

3. The graduates all looked so good in their _____.

4. Because Tracy is _____ of her class, she will be speaking at graduation.

5. We need to take John out for _____ before he gets married.

6. Now let's say a prayer for the _____ and celebrate his life.

7. Did you hear the latest gossip about Dan and Brenda? He finally _____, so they'll be getting married soon.

8. Who's going to throw a(n) _____ for Brenda?

9. I'll be in the _____. I'll be the bridesmaid.

10. I can't stand boring, _____ speeches.

Put the following words in the correct order to form sentences with infinitives. In a few cases, there may be more than one correct answer.

1. acquainted/American/become/important/is/with/holidays/to/.

2. wait/the/movie/don't/see/to/!

3. good/wish/life/is/our/you/for/to/a/have/.

4. tonight/I/stay/am/going/home/to/.

5. cup/like/would/have/a/of/you/to/coffee/?

6. leave/must/in/to/on/get/time/order/back/must/you/now/.

7. to/tired/party/to/too/I'm/the/go/.

8. movies/to/Ben/old/isn't/a/to/the/enough/ask/girl/.

9. in/surprise/party/like/I'd/to/my/to/at/one/life/least/go/.

10. my/broken/I'd/you/car's/offer/home/to/drive/but/.

G. TASK

No matter what time of year it is, prepare an American Thanksgiving dinner. The traditional menu consists of turkey, mashed potatoes, stuffing, gravy, candied yams, cranberry sauce, and pumpkin pie for dessert. Look up recipes on the internet or ask an American friend.

H. REAL LIFE

Here is a list of some of the major holidays celebrated in the U.S.:

New Year's Day—January 1st. Businesses are typically closed on this day, and many people stay in to recover from the parties the night before! But others might be eager to start on their New Year's resolution to learn a language, get in shape, stop smoking, etc.

Martin Luther King Jr. Day—The second Monday in January. This national holiday honors the work of African American civil rights leader Dr. Martin Luther King, Jr.

Groundhog Day—February 2nd. A groundhog (actually, several groundhogs throughout the country!) comes of its hole on this day. If it sees its shadow, there will be six more weeks of winter.

Valentine's Day—February 14th. This is a day for lovers. People go out to dinner with their special someone (their "valentine"), and give chocolates, flowers, and cards, also known as valentines, to one another.

Presidents' Day—Falls on the third Monday in February, around Lincoln's birthday (February 12th) and Washington's birthday (February 22nd).

St. Patrick's Day—March 17th. A day honoring St. Patrick, the Irish saint. Americans celebrate with parades and bagpipe music. Leprechauns and shamrocks will be everywhere. Wear green on this day or you might get pinched!

April Fools' Day—April 1st. A day for playing jokes and pranks on others, and for being careful that others don't play a joke on you! You can let people know that you've just played an April Fools' Day joke on them by saying "April Fools'!"

Passover—A Jewish holiday that commemorates the flight of the Jewish people out of Egypt as told in the Biblical Exodus. The holiday lasts eight days in the spring. Many Jews observe this holiday by not eating any leavened food, such as bread or cake, for the full eight days. Special Passover food is sold in many stores.

Easter—This Christian holiday falls in either March or April, and it is a time when Christians honor the resurrection of Jesus Christ. This is usually a weeklong holiday, beginning with Palm Sunday and ending with Easter Sunday. In addition to religious observances, there is also a more secular side to Easter. For example, many children celebrate Easter by hunting for Easter eggs hidden by the Easter Bunny, and by getting Easter baskets full of candy, such as chocolate bunnies, candy eggs, and so on.

Mother's Day—The second Sunday in May. A day to honor mothers with gifts, cards, flowers, chocolates, or dinner out.

Memorial Day—This national holiday falls on the last Monday in May. This holiday honors those who have sacrificed their lives for their country. Americans observe Memorial Day by visiting the graves of family members who died in military service and by attending parades and family gatherings, such as picnics or barbecues.

Father's Day—The third Sunday in June. A day to honor fathers, usually with gifts and cards.

Independence Day—The Fourth of July. This holiday honors the day when the founding fathers signed the Declaration of Independence in 1776. The Fourth of July is a day when Americans have picnics and barbecues or go to parades and listen to John Philip Sousa marches and the Star Spangled Banner. Most towns and cities have fireworks displays after sunset.

Labor Day—The first Monday in September. It is a national holiday marking the end of the summer. This holiday honoring workers is sometimes the last Monday before school begins, as well. Americans like to celebrate the three-day weekend by having picnics, barbecues, going to the beach, or simply taking one last chance to relax before the summer ends.

Columbus Day—The second Monday in October. This day honors Christopher Columbus's arrival in America in 1492. There are often parades, and banks, post offices, and some schools are closed.

Halloween—October 31st. This is a colorful and carnival-like holiday when children (and many adults!) dress up in scary or amusing costumes. After dark, children usually go trick-or-treating, which involves walking from door to door in costume, ringing the doorbell, and collecting candy. Many people decorate their yards and houses with Jack-o'-lanterns (hollowed-out pumpkins with a face carved in and a glowing candle inside), ghosts, scarecrows, witches, and goblins. Although adults don't go trick-or-treating unless they are accompanying their children, they often dress up, go to parties, or march in parades.

Veterans Day—November 11th. This day honors the retired soldiers who have served in the military, especially those who fought in wars. There are often parades, and flags are flown from many houses.

Thanksgiving—The fourth Thursday in November. It was designated a national holiday by President Abraham Lincoln. According to popular history, this holiday honors the cooperation between the pilgrims, a devout religious sect who had settled in what is today Massachusetts, and the local Native Americans. The story that every American school child learns is that the Native Americans taught the pilgrims how to grow crops indigenous to the region, and how to hunt and fish in their new home. In the fall, food was so plentiful that the pilgrims, to show their appreciation, invited their new friends to a feast where they ate, played games and gave thanks together. The actual history is probably not quite so idealized, but the story is dear to many Americans. Today, Americans celebrate this day by eating foods that are the same as or symbolic of what the pilgrims ate on that first Thanksgiving Day. It is a very important family holiday, and offices and schools tend to be closed on both Thursday and Friday (although many stores are open—and crowded—on that Friday, which is a very popular shopping day).

Hanukkah (Chanukah)—A Jewish festival that honors the rededication of the Jewish Holy Temple after a military victory in ancient Israel. Like Passover, the festival lasts eight days. It is usually celebrated with games, food, and the exchanging of gifts. Hanukkah is often honored in public by displaying a Hanukkah menorah, a type of candlestick with nine candleholders, whose candles are lit each night of the holiday in many Jewish homes.

Christmas—December 25th. The day Christians celebrate the birth of Jesus Christ. Although Christians usually attend church on or near Christmas, and for many people this is primarily a religious holiday, Christmas has also become an important holiday outside of the church as well. Many people put up winter-themed decorations, including Christmas trees, Santa Claus figures, snowmen, and strings of lights. There are also often religious decorations, such as angels and nativity scenes depicting the birth of Christ. Some little children who celebrate the holiday believe that Santa Claus travels the world on Christmas Eve in a flying sleigh filled with presents and pulled by magical reindeer, and pops down chimneys to leave gifts under the Christmas tree.

New Year's Eve—December 31st. On New Year's Eve, Americans celebrate the end of the old year and the beginning of the new year by having parties and watching fireworks. People wear paper or plastic hats, and at the stroke of midnight, they blow horns or noise-makers, throw confetti, drink champagne, and sing Auld Lang Syne. A popular tradition is to watch the New Year's ball drop, counting down from ten to one as the new year begins.

I. RESOURCES

Holidays:
usinfo.state.gov/usa/infousa/facts/factover/holidays.htm
www.usacitiesonline.com/usaholidaylinks.htm

Weddings:
www.brides.com
www.topweddingquestions.com
www.weddingchannel.com
www.theknot.com

Graduation:
parentingteens.about.com/od/graduation
www.jostens.com/graduation/graduation_guide.asp

Funerals:
www.ftc.gov/bcp/conline/pubs/services/funeral.htm
www.lifeintheusa.com/death/funerals.htm
www.funerals.org

ANSWER KEY
Practice 1: 1. passed away; 2. rite of passage; 3. caps and gowns; 4. valedictorian; 5. one last fling; 6. dearly departed; 7. popped the question; 8. bridal shower; 9. bridal party; 10. long-winded

Practice 2: 1. To become acquainted with American holidays is important. 2. Don't wait to see the movie! 3. Our wish is for you to have a good life. 4. I'm going to stay home tonight./Tonight I'm going to stay home. 5. Would you like to have a cup of coffee? 6. In order to get back on time you must leave now./You must leave now in order to get back on time. 7. I'm too tired to go to the party. 8. Ben isn't old enough to ask a girl to the movies. 9. I'd like to go to at least one surprise party in my life. 10. I'd offer to drive you home but my car's broken.

CHAPTER 14

School: Enrolling a Child in School

A. ENGLISH CLOSE-UP

IMMUNIZATION RECORD

Name:	Karina Murcher
Birthdate:	February 5, 2001
Allergies:	Penicillin
Vaccinations:	Polio, DPT/DT, MMR, Varicella, Hib

B. VOCABULARY ESSENTIALS

Adolescent—A teenager, a person at an age between puberty and adulthood. *Adolescents may legally choose to quit school at age sixteen in about half of all states.*

Cutoff—A limit, a final date for doing something. *Every state has its own age cutoff for starting school for the first time.*

To drop out—To quit school before graduation. *Most adults encourage teenagers not to drop out of school, because it's much harder to achieve success without a high school diploma.*

Guardian—A caretaker. *A child's legal guardian is usually his or her parent or parents, but sometimes another adult assumes this responsibility.*

To homeschool—To teach children at home rather than at school. *Caroline homeschooled her children for their first four or five years of school.*

IEP—Individualized Education Program, a legally required educational program for students with disabilities. *School officials and Jessica's parents developed an IEP for her.*

Immunizations (vaccinations)—Medical shots that protect the body against most childhood illnesses. *All school-age children are required to get their immunizations up to date.*

Some types of immunizations and their associated illnesses:

Booster—An additional dose of an immunization that is given to boost the immune system. *Certain vaccines, like tetanus, need boosters to maintain their effectiveness.*

Chicken pox (varicella)—Characterized by a rash, itching, fever, and tiredness. The rash is made up of small blisters. *Until the vaccine for chicken pox became available, some parents used to expose their children to the virus just to get it out of the way.*

Diphtheria—A contagious disease infecting the throat and other respiratory passages, causing difficulty breathing and harm to the heart and central nervous system. *In 1994–95, Russia experienced an epidemic of diphtheria caused by under-immunization.*

DTaP/DPT—Vaccines grouped together as one shot to immunize against diphtheria, pertussis, and tetanus. *Even though DPT vaccines have been very successful overall, there is a risk of side effects.*

German measles—Rubella, or the three-day measles, characterized by a rash of pink dots. It is usually a mild disease but can cause a variety of birth defects in a fetus if a pregnant woman is infected. *German measles was renamed Liberty measles in the U.S. during World War I.*

Hepatitis B (Hep B)—A disease of the liver brought on by a virus, HBV. *All newborns should receive the Hepatitis B vaccine before leaving the hospital.*

Hib—An influenza that can cause a range of invasive diseases, such as bacterial meningitis and pneumonia. *Infants less than six weeks old should not get the Hib vaccine.*

Measles—Rubeola, or red measles, a disease that causes severe symptoms similar to those found in a cold, as well as a high fever and a red rash. Measles lasts about two weeks, and it does not cause permanent damage to infants. *In the 1950s, every child got red measles.*

MMR—An immunization against measles, mumps, and rubella. *Some people do not want their children to have the MMR vaccine because they fear it causes autism.*

Mumps—A viral disease that causes enlargement of the glands in the neck, as well as fever, headache, and sore throat. *Although rare, mumps can cause sterility in men.*

Polio—An abbreviation for poliomyelitis. It can cause disability, brain damage, and even death in its most severe forms. *U.S. president Franklin D. Roosevelt had polio as an adult and consequently used a wheelchair.*

Tetanus—A disease caused by a bacterium usually found in the soil and often associated with rust. Tetanus is characterized by lockjaw and muscle spasms. *If you step on a rusty nail, be sure to get a tetanus shot.*

Whooping cough (pertussis)—An infectious disease that, in its early stages, produces symptoms like those of a mild respiratory infection. The cough then becomes deep and hard to control, ending with a "whooping" sound. *A child with whooping cough can turn red or purple during a coughing spell and may end up vomiting.*

K–8, K–12—Abbreviations meaning "kindergarten through 8th grade" and "kindergarten through 12th grade," respectively, indicating the grades taught in a particular school or district. *This district has a terrible high school, but the K–8 program is really fantastic.*

To skip class, to cut class, to play hooky—To stay away from school or a class without permission. *Let's cut class and go to the beach this afternoon!*

Registrar—The school official or department in charge of maintaining records of enrollment and grades. *If you need a transcript, contact the registrar of your school.*

To sign up (for)—To enroll (in) or register (for). *Have you signed up for the classes you want yet?*

To show up—To arrive for any kind of scheduled appointment. *Has Erica shown up yet? She said she would be here.*

Third-party custody—Custody of a child granted to a third party, anyone other than the child's parents. *If you send your child to live with a friend or relative in the U.S., you need to grant third-party custody to the caretaker.*

Time slot—A designated period of time in which for something to occur. *You can take your math class during the earliest time slot, if you'd like, beginning at 7:30 a.m.*

GRAMMAR ESSENTIALS: COMPARING GERUNDS AND INFINITIVES

In the last two lessons, you saw that some verbs are followed by infinitives, while others are followed by gerunds. There is also a group of verbs that can be followed with either gerunds or infinitives. Usually, there is no difference in meaning, but with some verbs, marked by an asterisk (*) in the chart below, the meaning changes:

*attempt	continue	*mean	start
begin	*forget	neglect	*stop
can't afford	hate	prefer	*try
can't bear	like	propose	
can't stand	love	*regret	
cease	*manage	*remember	

With verbs such as *begin* or *like,* there is no change in meaning whether the infinitive or gerund is used:

> *Many parents like to be involved in their children's education.*
> *Many parents like being involved in their children's education.*

But with several verbs, marked in the table above with an asterisk (*), there is a change in meaning:

> *Did you forget to bring your books?* (Where are your books? Didn't you bring them?)
>
> *Did you forget bringing your books?* (Did you forget the act of bringing your books? Are you losing your memory?)
>
> *Can she manage to get the kids to school?* (Will she get the kids to school on time?)
>
> *Can she manage getting the kids to school?* (Will she be able to handle the responsibility of getting the kids to school?)
>
> *Failing the test means studying even harder.* (The significance of our failing the test is that we'll have to study harder.)
>
> *They mean to study even harder.* (They intend to study harder.)
>
> *I regret to tell you that you won't be Working here anymore.* (I am sorry, but I have to inform you that you've been fired.)
>
> *I regret telling you that you won't be working here anymore.* (I wish I hadn't ever told you that you would be fired.)
>
> *Do you remember visiting your old school?* (Do you have memories of the time that you visited your old school?)
>
> *Did you remember to visit your old school?* (Did you remember that you were supposed to visit your old school, and did you do it?)
>
> *We stopped getting the kids vaccinated because we were afraid of the risks.* (We chose to no longer get the kids vaccinated.)
>
> *We stopped to get the kids vaccinated on our way to school.* (We stopped at the doctor's office in order to get the kids vaccinated.)

The difference between try + gerund and try + infinitive is more subtle. Try + gerund usually expresses an experimental solution to a problem:

> *You have a sore throat? Try drinkingsome tea; that should help.*
> *If you're lonely, you should try joining a club where you can find new friends.*

Try + infinitive usually expresses an actual attempt at the action:

> *I tried to drink some tea, but it was too hot.*
> *I tried to join that club, but they weren't accepting new members.*

Attempt is similar to *try* in this way, but note that it is usually used in official, academic, or literary contexts:

The police attempted setting up a roadblock to apprehend the suspects.
The police attempted to set up a roadblock, but the weather conditions made it too dangerous.

The verbs *allow, permit, advise,* and *forbid* take a gerund if that gerund directly follows the verb. But if any object—noun or pronoun—directly follows the verb, the infinitive is used instead:

Do they allow eating in the library?
Do they allow us to eat in the library?

We advise not being late for this meeting.
We advise people not to be late for this meeting.

The law forbids enrolling children who haven't been immunized.
The law forbids parents to enroll children who haven't been immunized.

Notice that it is common to hear *forbid* + object + *from* + gerund: *The law forbids parents from enrolling children who haven't been immunized.*

Finally, while *like* can take either an infinitive or a gerund, *dislike* can only take the gerund: *Meryl likes to study/studying, but her brother dislikes studying very much.*

D. HOW-TO

In the U.S., public schooling from kindergarten through the last year of high school, roughly from age five through age eighteen, is free and supported by taxpayers. Kindergarten is not required by law, but all children must attend school from age six. Education is then mandatory until American adolescents turn sixteen, but they must stay in school through grade twelve, the final grade of high school, in order to receive a high school diploma. If you would like to register your child for school, you must do so in advance. You can't simply bring him or her to school one day without having first completed the registration process. Because children in public school are typically required to attend school in the district where they reside, you should enroll your child in the K–12 program in your school district. If for some reason you are unhappy with the school in your district for which you are zoned, check with your district to see if there are circumstances under which your children might be permitted to attend a different school within the district or attend school in a different district. Homeless children are also required to attend school, and all school districts should have a plan in place to attend to this need. If you and your family are homeless, check with your local school district to find out about such programs.

In order to register your child, you'll need to have the following information about him or her:

- Proof of birth
- Proof of residency
- A current record of (up-to-date) immunizations
- Proof that he or she meets the age requirement
- A record of physical exam (in most states)
- An official transcript or school record (if your child is transferring from another school)

For proof of birth, your child needs a document such as a birth certificate or a passport. For proof of residency, you may show utility bills, lease agreements, or a deed of purchase for your home. You do not have to be a citizen, nor do you have to prove legal residency status in order for your child to receive a free public education in the U.S. However, the issue of illegal immigration is hotly debated, and it is unclear whether such social services will continue to be available to undocumented immigrants. Each state has its own immunization requirements, but among the required immunizations are diphtheria, tetanus, hepatitis B, whooping cough, polio, mumps, and red and German measles. Most immunizations are given in the early years, but there are a few that should be given during adolescence. For more information about immunizations, consult your doctor or healthcare provider. Note, though, that some parents are wary of immunizations and refuse to give them to their children. If you do not wish to have your child immunized, you may be able to get an exemption. Check with your state for exemption rules for medical or religious reasons.

The age requirement for starting school varies, but generally children can begin kindergarten at the age of five, and first grade at the age of six. There is usually an age cutoff somewhere between September 1st and December 1st. Not all states are the same, though, so if your child was born in September, October, November, or December, you'll need to find out the cutoff date before registering. Schools may begin registration for the coming school year in the spring or early summer. If your state requires a physical examination, this should be recent; check with your school district to set up an appointment for a physical examination if you need to. Finally, if your child is transferring from another school, you will need to have a legal, official transcript of your child's records. You can obtain that from your child's former school.

If your children will be living in the U.S. with friends or family, and you will not be with them, their guardian will need to fill out a custodial statement and agreement, or a third-party custody form. The guardian and the parents usually must both sign this form. Typically, the signed form is enough to allow your children to attend the guardian's neighborhood school, but check with the school district, because there may be some restrictions.

Finally, note that even though education is a requirement in this country, there are alternatives to public schools. Parents who can afford it may choose to send their children to private schools, such as boarding schools, where children live among their peers, or day schools, where they attend class only during the day and return home in the evenings. Parochial schools, such as Catholic schools or Hebrew day schools, offer children an education that includes religion, which is by law not included in the curriculum of public schools. And some parents turn to homeschooling as an alternative to public schools for many different reasons, ranging from religious convictions to dissatisfaction with academic quality in the public system. All alternative options to public schools must meet legal educational requirements, including homeschooling. If you wish to homeschool your children, be sure to check with your school district to learn how you can comply with state law.

E. ENGLISH IN ACTION

Let's listen in as Melina talks to the school registrar about registering her children for school in the fall.

Ms. Kurch: Hello, I'm Ms. Kurch, the school registrar. Can I answer some questions for you?

Melina: Hi, yes. We're new in town . . . Well, actually we're new to this country, and my children need to start school, I think.

Ms. Kurch: Any children under sixteen are required by U.S. law to attend school.

Melina: Okay, well, I do have one older than sixteen, and he'll be attending school, too.

Ms. Kurch: Of course, well, your children will need proof of residency, such as a phone bill, or a rental agreement, or something like that to prove they are residents here. You'll also need to be sure any immunizations are up to date. Here's a list of immunizations required by law. You'll also need to provide proof of birth, you know, a birth certificate or something like that. They should all have a record of a recent physical, within the last six months, and if you have any young children, they need to be age six by November first to attend first grade, and five by November first if you want them to go to kindergarten.

Melina: Okay, so I guess I need get them all physicals, and they haven't had all their required shots yet. We don't have a lot of money, though. Is there a place where we can get their physicals at a reduced cost?

Ms. Kurch: Oh, yes. Here's a list of clinics. Just call to set up an appointment. They should give you a certain time slot to bring

	all your children in. And the physicals will either be free or very low cost to you.
Melina:	Thank you. Oh, um, one of my children—my daughter—is disabled; she's legally blind. Are there any special services for her?
Ms. Kurch:	Yes, of course. Once you get her registered, we'll get her scheduled with the counselor to talk about the services available to her, make out her IEP, you know. Does she read Braille yet?
Melina:	A little. She's pretty young.
Ms. Kurch:	Okay, well, we have a wonderful teacher who teaches Braille, then. You can sign her up for that when you register her.
Melina:	And how much does it cost?
Ms. Kurch:	K–12 public education is free to everyone. You don't have to pay anything, but once they're registered, the children must attend—no cutting classes. Schools get paid according to the number of students that show up.
Melina:	Hmm, wow! That's incredible . . . Oh, I just thought of one more thing . . . When does school start?
Ms. Kurch:	It starts September 6th, so you need to get everything taken care of before then. Okay?
Melina:	All right. Thanks a lot for the info. We'll be seeing you soon.

F. PRACTICE

Complete the following sentences with one of these vocabulary items: *homeschool, drop out, guardian, cut class, showed up, immunizations, sign up for, time slot, registrar, adolescents*

1. It's about time you _____. We've been waiting for you for over an hour.

2. _____ should be in school until at least sixteen years of age.

3. Don't you dare _____ of school! You need to get your high school diploma or you'll never get anywhere.

4. Hey, did you _____ chemistry yet? I'm taking the 10:05 class. You should, too!

5. What is that class's _____? I'd like something in the morning.

6. If your parents hear that you've _____ again, they won't let you go to the party!

7. Unless you have an excuse, your child must have his or her _____ up to date.

8. Please have your parent or _____ sign your permission slip for the field trip.

9. You can contact the _____ about getting a copy of your child's transcript.

10. Some parents _____ their children because they think public schools don't have adequate educational programs.

Circle the correct form of the verb inside the parentheses.

1. Henry can (to speak/speak) three languages.

2. Nona dislikes (to study/studying) for tests.

3. The counselor advised me (to take/taking) a Spanish class.

4. You are allowed (to repeat/repeating) the test several times.

5. If you're coughing all the time, why don't you try (to quit/quitting) smoking?

6. Where's the registration form? Didn't you remember (to pick/picking) it up?

7. Research shows that (to put/putting) your children in preschool is good for them.

8. Did you remember (to fill/filling) out the form? It's due tomorrow.

9. Permit me (to show/showing) you around the school.

10. We advise (to get/getting) your children registered early.

G. TASK

Listed below are links to several different types of schools throughout the U.S.: a public school district in Washington, a country day school in California, an independent school in North Carolina, a Catholic high school in Louisiana, and a Hebrew day school in Ohio. Explore the sites to get a sense of the various types of education available to American children. How are these schools different? How are they similar? Are there differences in costs and application processes? Why do you think American parents choose to send their children to these schools or similar schools?

www.seattleschools.org/area/main/index.dxml
www.ljcds.org
www.communityindependentschool.org
www.catholichigh.org
www.yavneh.org

H. REAL LIFE

The following is a fictitious letter from an invented educational program for children. Both the letter and the program are representative of what currently exists in the U.S.:

Jump Start Public Information Center
11415 17th Street NW
Washington, D.C., 20007

Dear Ms. Ninci,

Thank you for your interest in the Jump Start program. Jump Start is a free program for qualified children, and it is dedicated to enriching the educational experience of low-income applicants. Eligibility for Jump Start is reserved for children of low-income families from birth to age five. You can go to our website, listed on the enclosed brochure, for 2006 income guidelines. Please note that if space is available, children from households with slightly higher incomes are accepted. Ten percent of all spaces are reserved for children with disabilities.

To find the program closest to you, contact your local Jump Start agency, which you can find on our website or by calling us at 1-800-555-2300. If your child does not qualify for Jump Start, you can contact our Child Care Information program at 1-800-555-2396 to find child care in your area.

Once again, thank you for your interest in the Jump Start program.

Sincerely,
Mona Cabeza

I. RESOURCES

U.S. Department of Education:
www.ed.gov or 1-800-USA-LEARN

Immunization schedule:
www.cdc.gov/nip/recs/child-schedule.htm
www.cdc.gov/nip/recs/adult-schedule.htm

Other immunization resources:
www.kidshealth.org/parent/general/body/vaccine.html
www.ncsl.org/programs/health/imschool.htm

Child Care Aware:
www.childcareaware.org or 1-800-424-2246 (to find child care in your area)

Head Start Bureau:
www.acf.hhs.gov/programs/hsb

For additional information on children's services in the U.S., see Lesson 35. Information on IEPs:

www.ldonline.org/indepth/iep
www.ed.gov/parents/needs/speced/iepguide/index.html

Information on school systems in the U.S. (public, private, independent, parochial):
www.schoolmatters.com
nces.ed.gov/ccd/schoolsearch
www.privateschoolreview.com
nces.ed.gov/surveys/pss/privateschoolsearch
www.admissionsquest.com
www.parochial.com
www.nais.org

ANSWER KEY
Practice 1: 1. showed up; 2. Adolescents; 3. drop out; 4. sign up for; 5. time slot; 6. cut class; 7. immunizations; 8. guardian; 9. registrar; 10. homeschool

Practice 2: 1. speak; 2. studying; 3. to take; 4. to repeat; 5. quitting ("to quit" is also correct, but "quitting" expresses more of a suggested solution); 6. to pick; 7. putting; 8. to fill; 9. to show; 10. getting

CHAPTER 15

School: Parent-Teacher Meeting

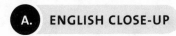

A. ENGLISH CLOSE-UP

KELLER MIDDLE SCHOOL

Quarterly Report Card
for
Oleg Korotkin

Math..A
*Very good understanding of math.

English..B-
*Oleg needs to work a little harder on his English. He struggles with
the grammar, but his spelling is improving.

Science & Health..A

History...A-

**Oleg is an exceptional and very helpful student. He has no tardies and only
two absences this semester.

B. VOCABULARY ESSENTIALS

To check up on—To examine, to review the progress of. *Parents need to check up on their children's progress at school.*

To collaborate—To work together on a project. *Teachers and parents get the best results for children when they collaborate on education.*

Dyslexia—A learning disorder that impairs a person's ability to interpret or sort information, often affecting reading, writing, and spelling. *Nate had so much trouble reading that his teacher suggested he be tested for dyslexia.*

Effective parenting—Parenting methods that positively affect the maturing process of children. *Effective parenting happens when parents are involved in their children's learning process.*

Enrichment activities—Educational activities that go beyond the "core" areas of reading, writing, and arithmetic, in order to develop a well-rounded student. *Our enrichment activities include music, art, and drama.*

Extracurricular activities—Sports or clubs that are organized by schools but that aren't part of the academic curriculum. *Terry is involved in so many extracurricular activities that she never gets home from school until after 7:00 in the evening.*

Feedback—Information about a process or an activity that helps determine its effectiveness. *We value your feedback, so if you wouldn't mind, please fill out this form at the end of the session.*

To jot down—To write down quickly, to take quick notes. *Before your parent-teacher meeting it's a good idea to jot down any questions you might have.*

Learning disabilities, learning disorders—Any chronic problems a person has that interfere with the learning process, especially in regard to math and reading. *I've noticed that your son freezes up during tests, but don't worry; that's a mild learning disorder that we can work with easily.*

To maximize—To take to the utmost extent, to get the greatest benefit possible from something. *Parents can maximize their children's learning by organizing family outings related to what the children are studying.*

Ongoing—Continuous, happening over a period of time. *Learning is an ongoing process. It should never stop.*

To overwhelm—To be too difficult, too upsetting, or too intense for someone to handle. *I think the amount of homework that you assign overwhelms Caleb.*

To prioritize—To put in order of importance, to organize a work load so that the most critical tasks are completed first. *What he needs to do is prioritize his assignments and do the most important tasks first.*

Remedial—Basic, intended to improve rudimentary skills in a specific subject. *Jacinta has very poor reading skills, so her teacher recommended a remedial reading program.*

Standardized tests—Tests given to groups of students in order to evaluate their performance against a standard or norm. *Most colleges rely on standardized tests like the SAT to determine the academic abilities of their applicants.*

To summarize—To describe the main idea. *So, to summarize, Jon needs to get his assignments in on time or his grades are sure to suffer.*

Time frame—A given time period in which something can take place. *You must complete the project within the given time frame, between now and the end of December.*

C. GRAMMAR ESSENTIALS: *IT*

The pronoun *it* can be used referentially, to refer to either an inanimate object or an animal when the gender is either unknown or unimportant:
—"*Where's your book?*"—"*I left it at home. It's in my bedroom.*"
Look at that seal! Isn't it cute?

But there are many non-referential uses of *it* as well, where *it* doesn't actually refer to anything concrete, but is instead used as a kind of filler pronoun:

Weather—*It's cold. It's starting to snow! It's hot today. It's raining.*
Temperature—*It's 82 degrees. It's below zero. It's going to be in the 90s.*
Time—*It's 10:30 a.m. It's morning. It's ten o'clock. It's getting late.*
Date—*It's Friday. It's the 23rd. It was 1982. It was during the 19th century.*
Distance—*It's ten miles from here. It's about six miles from here.*

It is also very commonly used with adjectives, in which case it serves as a "dummy" subject, holding the place of the real subject, which comes later in the sentence. The adjective in these examples is followed by an infinitive, a gerund, a *that* clause, or a *for* infinitive clause, all of which are the actual subjects:

> *It's important to meet with the teacher.* (To meet with the teacher is important.)

> *It's good to exercise every day.* (To exercise every day is good.)

> *It's hard work shoveling all of this snow!* (Shoveling all of this snow is hard work.)

> *It's frustrating listening to their conversation.* (Listening to their conversation is frustrating.)

> *It's funny that you should mention it.* (That you should mention it is funny.)

> *It's likely that he'll call tonight.* (That he'll call tonight is likely.)

> *It's absurd for you to make that accusation!* (For you to make that accusation is absurd!)

Notice that both constructions above are possible in English, but the examples with *it* are much more common and natural.

Sometimes *it* is used with an adjective followed by a prepositional phrase of location. In these cases, *it* stands for the general environment of the place:

> *It's dry in Arizona.*

> *It's comfortable in here!*

It can be the subject of a number of so-called impersonal verbs, which are then followed by infinitives:

It appears to be getting late.
It seems to be a busy time.
It costs too much to send your children to private school.
It looks like he'll need to study harder.
It pays to stay in school.

The verbs *appear* and *seem* can also be followed by *that* clauses:

It seems that we're finished here.
It appears that you are busy.

It can also be used to put focus or emphasis on some element of the sentence. That element is placed at the beginning of the sentence:

It's history that Bobby is having the most trouble with.
It's parents, not teachers, who are ultimately responsible for raising their children.
It's this week, not next week, when we have our parent-teacher meeting.
It was the good school system that made us choose to live in this town.

D. HOW-TO

It is very important for parents to be involved in their children's education. Research has shown that parents' involvement directly correlates with a child's success in school, so it's a good idea to actively engage in parent-teacher conferences at your children's school. Here's what you should know about parent-teacher conferences if you're called into one.

Very simply, a parent-teacher conference (or parent-teacher meeting) is an opportunity for parents and teachers to get to know each other and to discuss any concerns they might have about the student. Parent-teacher conferences usually occur once per semester and last for about thirty minutes. The teacher will contact you to schedule a time for your meeting. Be sure to set a time that is convenient for you, and allow for a little extra time in case the conference lasts longer than expected. You want to make sure you can arrive on time and that you won't feel rushed during the meeting. You might want to bring a notepad to take notes, and don't forget to come prepared with lots of questions. Because there may be time constraints, prioritize your questions and ask the most important ones first. The teacher wants to work with you in educating your child, so you should not hesitate to ask anything. For instance, if you need help handling your child's reaction to homework, don't be afraid to ask for advice. Teachers are trained professionals and are happy to use their knowledge and experience to help you.

In addition to answering your questions, the teacher will tell you about what he or she is teaching in class and how your child is doing. The teacher may even show you class materials, such as completed projects or future assignments. If you do not understand something the teacher tells you, don't be afraid to ask for clarification. Near the end of the session, the teacher will probably want to discuss how best to educate your child. Feel free to engage in the discussion. You are likely to meet with the teacher again sometime during the school year, so you can discuss your child's progress then. The teacher might also encourage you to contact him or her with questions or concerns throughout the year.

Although you might be apprehensive about meeting with your child's teacher, by attending the conference you will gain insights into your child's character and abilities in an environment where you don't normally observe him or her. Furthermore, most teachers enjoy finding the best in children and sharing these observations with parents. Even if your child has a learning disability and struggles with school, most teachers are trained to know how to help children with those or similar difficulties. In fact, you are likely to discover that your child's teacher is very understanding. Few American teachers are hard taskmasters; they prefer to teach with care and by engaging the students, rather than with strict discipline and rote memorization. And most American teachers are delighted and heartened to meet parents who want to actively participate in their children's education.

E. ENGLISH IN ACTION

Now let's listen in on a parent-teacher meeting. Victor Korotkin is meeting with Ms. Sheridan, his son's teacher.

Ms. Sheridan:	Hello, Mr. Korotkin! I'm Oleg's teacher, Ms. Sheridan. How are you?
Victor:	Hello, yes, I'm Victor Korotkin. It's a pleasure to meet you.
Ms. Sheridan:	Let's go over here and sit. It's a little more comfortable.
Victor:	Oh, thank you. How nice. Is this area for the children? I see it looks like a library area.
Ms. Sheridan:	Yes, it is. I like to encourage the children to read as much as possible, so I made a cozy spot for them. Would you like some coffee or tea?
Victor:	Oh, yes. Thank you. Coffee would be wonderful.
Ms. Sheridan:	Here you are. I'd like to start off by saying that it's such a pleasure to have Oleg in my class. He's such a diligent student, and so helpful . . .
Victor:	Really? Oh, I'm so glad to hear that. But can I ask you, how does he get along with the other children?
Ms. Sheridan:	Well, he's a little shy, and he's still struggling a little with the language, I think.
Victor:	Hmm. Yes, well, we try to help him a lot, but he only wants to speak Russian at home.

Ms. Sheridan: Actually, it's a good thing he still wants to speak Russian. So many kids from other countries only want to speak English, even at home. I know it can be frustrating to a lot of parents who want to be sure their children also speak their native languages. But back to your question, he's slowly making friends. I think he'll do fine. Don't worry about him socially.

Victor: Okay, that's good to know. Is he doing okay academically? I mean are there any areas where he needs extra help?

Ms. Sheridan: Well, you probably know he's a whiz in math. He sometimes finds English overwhelming, though, but you probably know that's an ongoing effort for him. He does usually get his work done within the time frame I give them.

Victor: How does he work with the other children?

Ms. Sheridan: You mean, is he a team player? Yes. Well, actually, he could use some work in this area, I think.

Victor: Hmm. Well, he is an only child, so he's not used to sharing or working with others. What do you think, is there anything I can do to help him?

Ms. Sheridan: Yes. As a matter of fact, it's a good idea for you to work with him as much as possible. If you could just check up on his English each evening, I think that would help a lot. I really like parents to be involved in their children's learning process.

Victor: Yes, of course. It's important for me too.

Ms. Sheridan: You can also read to him. You can read in Russian sometimes, but he really needs to have you read to him in English, too.

Victor: Hmm. Okay, well, it's Wednesday, right? So I think I'll take him to the library today and let him pick out some books. We'll start with some stories, in English, of course. How is he doing on his homework?

Ms. Sheridan: Well, during the week, I give my students some pages from their grammar books to work on at home, and, of course, there's a spelling test every Friday. He could really use help with his spelling.

Victor: Okay. This sounds good. We'll get started right away. Well, thank you so much, Ms. Sheridan. This has been so helpful.

Ms. Sheridan: You're welcome. And please call anytime. I always love to talk to parents.

Victor: Of course. Well, we should have lots of stories to share. Oh, and I almost forgot—I'd love to help out in the classroom sometime.

Ms. Sheridan: Mr. Korotkin, that would be wonderful! I love to collaborate with parents. Maybe you could teach them a little Russian. What do you think?

Victor: That would be great! I'm ready whenever you want me to start.

Ms. Sheridan: Okay, well, let's get together . . .

F. PRACTICE

Fill in the sentences with the following words or expressions: *overwhelmed, check up on, collaborate, feedback, jot down, prioritize, ongoing, extracurricular, time frame, maximize*

1. During the meeting, _____ your thoughts or any questions that come up.

2. What is the _____ for this project? What is the schedule for each stage?

3. The students discover that this is a(n) _____ process. Each day, they learn a little more.

4. Surely your son is giving you some sort of _____, even if he's not telling you directly.

5. Parents should _____ their children when they're doing homework to see if they need any help.

6. Your daughter seems to be struggling a bit with her workload because she does a lot of _____ activities in addition to her schoolwork. She might want to cut back a bit.

7. If you spend time helping Monica with her homework it will _____ her learning.

8. It's always a good idea for us to _____ the activities we give our students so that the most important things get done first.

9. Some children get _____ just being around a lot of other children, and they have trouble getting their work done because of all the distractions.

10. If teachers and parents _____, they can help children more as a team.

Now rewrite the following sentences using *it* as the subject.

1. The weather is beautiful today.

2. That you're going to Paris is wonderful.

3. That you told her is interesting.

4. Studying is hard work.

5. To get more sleep would be wonderful.

6. The date is January twelfth.

7. That your child won't be my student anymore is regrettable.

8. The best students are not always the most successful in life.

9. Sometimes nature makes the best classroom.

10. You look like you need a classroom assistant.

G. TASK

If you have children, imagine that you have a parent-teacher conference scheduled for next week, and you have to prepare for it. If you don't have children, imagine that you're Oleg's mother or father. What types of questions would you ask? Are there any aspects of your child's performance, either academically or socially, that you'd like to discuss with his or her teacher? Is there anything you'd like to ask for advice on? Jot down about ten questions or discussion points that you'd like to focus on during your meeting.

H. REAL LIFE

Dear Parents,

Welcome to Keller Middle School. We are very excited about the coming year, and we hope to make your children's semester a successful one. Here are a few tips to help you help your child do well this year:

- Ask your child about the homework he or she might have.
- Sit down with your child and help with any problems.
- Take the time to check over homework before it's due.

Your first parent-teacher conference of the year is coming up, and your child's teacher will be calling to schedule an appointment soon. Before you have your meeting, sit down and make up a list of questions to ask. You'll only have about thirty minutes, so making a list of questions beforehand will help maximize the value of your time with the teacher. Here are some ideas for questions:

- In what areas is my child having difficulty, and how can I help?
- What can I do at home to reinforce what my child is learning at school?
- Are there any special enrichment activities we can do together?
- Are there any after-school activities that would benefit my child?
- How is my child's behavior?
- Have there been any changes in his or her behavior?
- Does he or she get along well with others?
- What kinds of standardized tests is he or she taking?
- Does my child handle tests well?

Remember, your child's teacher wants to form a partnership with you for educating your child, so your questions and comments are appreciated. If you would like to get more involved in your child's class or school, please let us know! We're always happy to have whole families involved.

Good luck!

I. RESOURCES

Information on parent-teacher conferences:
www.nea.org/parents/ptconf.html
specialed.about.com/cs/teacherstrategies/a/conference.htm
www.familyeducation.com/home
www.kidshealth.org/parent/positive

ANSWER KEY
Practice 1: 1. jot down; 2. time frame; 3. ongoing; 4. feedback; 5. check up on; 6. extracurricular; 7. maximize; 8. prioritize; 9. overwhelmed; 10. collaborate

Practice 2: 1. It's beautiful today. 2. It's wonderful that you're going to Paris. 3. It's interesting that you told her. 4. It's hard work studying. 5. It would be wonderful to get more sleep. 6. It's January twelfth. 7. It's regrettable that your child won't be my student anymore. 8. It's not always the best students who are the most successful in life. 9. It's sometimes nature that makes the best classroom. 10. It looks like you need a classroom assistant.

CHAPTER 16

School: Paying for College

A. ENGLISH CLOSE-UP

Financial Aid Package for two selected colleges:

	State University	Regional Private University
Cost to Attend	$14,724	$28,530
Expected Family Contribution (EFC)	4,039	4,039
Total Aid Needed	$10,685	$24,491
Aid Package		
Pell Grant	0	0
State Scholarship	0	5,600
College Grant	3,307	10,109
Work-Study	2,574	2,574
Perkins Loan	0	1,000
Stafford Loan	2625	2625
Total Financial Aid	$8,506	$21,908
Amount not covered (by aid or EFC)	$2,179	$2,583

B. VOCABULARY ESSENTIALS

To break even—To have just enough money to pay bills, but nothing else. *Even though Tom and Marina pooled their incomes, they had just enough to break even.*

College fund—Savings that parents set aside for their children's college education, often begun when the child is born. *To celebrate the birth of their first child, Sarah and Jake started a college fund with $1,000.*

To consolidate debt—To merge two or more distinct debts in order to pay them as one. *Most graduates find that it's easier to make payments if they consolidate their debts.*

To cut corners—To make small adjustments or sacrifices in order to achieve a goal faster or more easily. Often negative, in the sense of sacrificing quality. *By cutting corners wherever they can, college students find ways to have enough money to live on.*

EFC—Expected Family Contribution, the amount of money a family is expected to contribute for a child's college education. It is used to calculate eligibility for financial aid. *The more money and assets your family has, the higher your EFC will be.*

FAFSA—Free Application for Federal Student Aid, an application every student wishing to receive financial aid must fill out. *If you want to apply for grants and scholarships, you have to fill out your FAFSA form.*

Fellowship—Money awarded to a graduate student, providing the means for further study, often in exchange for teaching. *Kiko was awarded a fellowship when she was accepted into a doctoral program in linguistics.*

Financial aid—Monetary assistance through grants, loans, or scholarships. *Many students at American universities rely on some sort of financial aid.*

Financial aid package—The total of all student aid, grants, loans, and scholarships that a university offers an individual student. *You might want to consider going to the university that offers you the best financial aid package.*

To go broke—To use all of your money, to run out of money. *If you don't get a good job right out of college you may go broke just trying to pay off your college loans.*

Grant—A gift of funds to be used for university attendance, often awarded for excellence in certain academic areas, or awarded based on certain types of experience. *Be sure to apply for as many grants as you can, because they are usually free money.*

To keep track of—To have a record of, to remain informed of. *If you want to budget properly, you really need to keep track of your income and your expenses.*

Merit-based—Determined by a student's academic standing, artistic ability, or other accomplishments and skills, not by any sort of financial need. *Not all scholarships are merit-based, but most are.*

Pell Grant—A grant issued by the federal government to undergraduate students who qualify for financial aid. *Congress and the U.S. Department of Education issue a standard formula to determine who qualifies for a Pell Grant.*

ROTC—Reserve Officers' Training Corps (for the army, air force, or navy), a program for students interested in joining the military; students receive tuition assistance and special training during college and then become officers in the armed forces on graduation. *Because Sam wanted to join the army and get a college education as well, the army ROTC made a lot of sense for him.*

To saddle with debt—To encumber with debt, to cause someone to owe a great deal of money. *If you don't want to be saddled with debt, get a job and as many scholarships and grants as you can.*

Sallie Mae—Student Loan Marketing Association, originally owned by the federal government, but now privately owned. Sallie Mae buys student loans from universities and private lenders and is the largest provider of student loans. *Most college students end up owing money to Sallie Mae.*

Scholarship—Money won by students to be used towards a college education. *Apply as early as possible for scholarships, because there's a lot of competition for them.*

To set aside—To save something for future use. *The smartest thing parents can do is to start setting aside money for college tuition the day their children are born.*

Tuition—Fee for getting instruction from an educational institution. It usually does not include books, room and board, and other additional fees. *College tuition gets more expensive every year.*

Work-study—A program that provides guaranteed jobs for students in order to help them pay for their studies. *If work-study is part of your financial aid package, then the school has to try to find a job on campus for you.*

C. GRAMMAR ESSENTIALS: ARTICLES

The use of articles in English can be confusing for some nonnative speakers, especially those whose native language doesn't have articles. Here are some general guidelines to help:

The indefinite article *a* (or *an*) is generally used to talk about something that isn't specific, and it is only used with singular count nouns:
I saw a good movie last night.
Jack is going to a university in the northwest, but I don't know which one.

The definite article *the* is generally used to talk about something specific or particular, usually something that has either been brought up in the conversation already or that is known to both speaker and listener:
The movie was really long, but it was good.
The university where Jack is going is in Oregon, I think.
The states that border the Gulf of Mexico are Texas, Louisiana, Mississippi, Alabama, and Florida.

The definite article can also be used with a singular count noun in a general, non-specific sense:

The bald eagle is a beautiful animal.
The hurricane is one of nature's most destructive forces.

But it's more common to use plural count nouns without any article to speak in a general, non-specific sense:

Bald eagles are beautiful animals.
Hurricanes are one of nature's most destructive forces.

With non-count nouns, generally no articles are used:

Education can be expensive.
Wine and beer will be served at the party tonight.

But it's possible to use a definite article with a non-count noun to make a specific reference:

The education that I got at this college was wonderful.
The wine at the party was great, but the beer was warm.

Here are some other situations in which the definite article is used.

With superlatives:

Which university is considered the best in the world?

With ordering adjectives:

The 49th state to join the union was Alaska. The next one was Hawaii.

With means of transportation:

Do you take the train, the bus, or the ferry to work?

With places of entertainment or performance:

Sometimes we go to the theater or the opera, but more often to the movies.

With places of business, services, government offices, or places where you would run errands:

I went to the post office and the supermarket this morning.
Where's your appointment, at the doctor's, the dentist's, or the chiropractor's?

With the proper names of rivers, mountain ranges, oceans, deserts, or island chains:

The Rockies and the Appalachians are the two major mountain ranges of the continental U.S.
The Antilles are between the Caribbean and the Atlantic.

And here are some other situations in which the indefinite article is used.

When naming occupations:

I'm a teacher, she's a doctor, and he's an electrician.

With nationalities as nouns:
> *Is Jack an American or a Canadian?*

With expressions of time:
> *We have to leave in an hour, so you should start getting ready in a half hour.*

With expressions of quantity or measure:
> *This pitcher only holds a gallon of water.*
> *The recipe calls for a tablespoon of olive oil.*

Finally, here are some situations in which no article is generally used.

With the names of days and months:
> *We leave on Friday and we'll be back in August.*

With certain institutions:
> *Do you go to church or to temple?*
> *Billy goes to high school and Brad goes to college.*

With certain common places:
> *Every day I go to work, then go home, and then go to bed.*

But notice that these expressions can be used with articles in certain circumstances:
> *The Friday before last was hot.*
> *The church across the street is Episcopalian.*

D. HOW-TO

The cost of attending American colleges and universities is very high. Every year the tuition rate goes up much faster than the average rate of inflation. The annual tuition at a private university is often as much as or more than the yearly salary of an entry-level job. In addition, even though a public college's tuition is close to a third of that of a private university, it's still very expensive for the average college applicant and his or her family. Unless the college graduate gets a very high-paying job, it can take twenty years or more for him or her to pay off the debt from student loans racked up in only four or five years.

While it is possible to make the expense of college reasonable, the student needs to be very organized and start early to compete for funding. In truth, the best thing to do is to start saving early. Many parents, in fact, set up a college fund for their children when they are born. Some states even offer the option of prepaying tuition up to eighteen years before a student attends. Although this is one good way to beat inflation, it unfortunately means that parents (and children) have to commit early to attending an in-state public college or university. However, it is often possible to apply the dollar amount in your account towards an out-of-state or private college if necessary. In addition, there is a national plan called the Independent 529 Plan that allows you to prepay tuition for private universities. You can later use the money in your account towards any of the plan's member universities, which number in the hundreds. You can visit their website at www.independent529plan.org.

If relying entirely on savings is not a feasible option, the first thing a student and his or her family should do is check out state-sponsored grants. The federal government sends the states a portion of grant funding. The states add an additional amount from their own treasuries and then determine how much and in what way the grants are offered to students. In many cases, grants cover the entire tuition of a public state university, or a large chunk of a private university's fees. This money is only available to students who choose to attend schools in their state of residence. Grant applicants must also fit income and grade point average (GPA) requirements. In addition, the federal government offers Pell Grants to students who have a low EFC. This grant is for a small amount of money compared to state grants, but it helps fill the gap for families that can't afford to pay for college. The amount received depends on the EFC and the cost of attendance at the college chosen.

In addition to grants, scholarships are also available. In fact, some students who are very talented in academics or athletics, or who are highly gifted in other ways, have their entire tuitions and even some living expenses covered by full scholarships. Of course, not all merit-based scholarships are full scholarships; they often start at $1,000 and go up from there. Also, these types of scholarships are available in a wide range of areas, not just in academics or athletics. You can find merit-based scholarships for everyone from bagpipe players to budding entrepreneurs to those active in community service. While merit-based scholarships are often the easiest to find, they can sometimes be very competitive. However, there is quite a wide variety of other scholarships available. There are scholarships for applicants who are of specific national origins, of specific religions, children of teachers or firefighters—you name it. There are also some need-based (determined by financial need) scholarships available. Some students piece together an entire tuition from many little scholarships. They just have to do the research to see what is out there.

Another option is to apply for student loans to help with any gaps in funding. Many college applicants take out student loans from banks, the federal government, or both to help pay for college. However, it's important to be careful about the amount and type of loans taken on. Some good low-cost loans include federally subsidized Stafford Loans. The government pays the interest on them as long as you are in school. There is also the low interest, unsubsidized, federally funded Stafford Loan, as well as the Parent Plus Loan. Students take out and are responsible for Stafford Loans; parents take out Parent Plus Loans in order to pay for their child's college education. Perkins

Loans, which are very low-interest loans for low-income students, are also available. If a student decides to apply for one or many of these loans, he or she does have the option of consolidating them into one low monthly payment after schooling ends. In addition, there may be tax benefits for both students and their parents to help offset the cost of certain loans. These tax benefits vary from year to year and depend on income. Check with the IRS to determine current tax benefits at www.irs.gov or visit the Federal Student Aid office, a division of the U.S. Department of Education, at http://studentaid.ed.gov.

Finally, there is also a lot of free or low-cost aid available to students from very low-income households, especially if the student's parents are not college graduates. Besides the Pell Grant and the Perkins Loan, there's also the SEOG, or Supplemental Educational Opportunity Grant, which helps to supplement aid for low-income students. In the end, one of the most important things a student can do is fill out the FAFSA. It's necessary to fill out the FAFSA to receive any sort of government aid, including Pell Grants and Stafford Loans. It's possible to find out everything you need to know about this application by doing a simple search online or at the public library.

E.   ENGLISH IN ACTION

Let's listen to An Mei as she talks to her high school counselor about going to college in the U.S.

Mr. Melville:	Hi, An Mei. It's good to see you again. Have a seat.
An Mei:	Thank you for meeting with me.
Mr. Melville:	Well, it's about time to take a look at your plan, right?
An Mei:	Yes. I'm starting to feel a little nervous about going to college. My father says we can't afford it. I know it's very expensive.
Mr. Melville:	It is. But do you know that over 60% of Americans go on to a university after high school?
An Mei:	Wow! How do they afford it?
Mr. Melville:	Well, it's expensive, but there are ways to make it possible for everyone to attend college. So your father is right, you probably can't afford it if you don't get help.
An Mei:	But who wants to give me money to go to college? I don't know any rich people.
Mr. Melville:	Don't worry. You don't have to know rich people. There's money out there just for people like you. An Mei, are you or your parents citizens yet?
An Mei:	No. We aren't. We need at least one more year of residency.
Mr. Melville:	Okay, that's not a problem. Residents qualify too. Here's what you need to do. First you can go to Sallie Mae's website and use their calculator.

An Mei: Sallie Mae? What's that?

Mr. Melville: Oh, that's sort of a nickname for an agency that funds college loans. Okay, so you'll have to estimate some of these things because you have a few years before you're ready for college and, you know, prices go up on everything, right? They don't usually go down.

An Mei: I know. Well, what will this tell me?

Mr. Melville: It's going to help you figure out how much money you'll probably need. You're a good student, I know. What about your family income? Does your family make more than $50,000 per year?

An Mei: I don't think so.

Mr. Melville: Okay, well, that's actually very good for you because you can get more money. Did either of your parents go to college?

An Mei: No, they didn't have the chance.

Mr. Melville: Okay, that's good for you, too.

An Mei: Really? How?

Mr. Melville: Well, a lot of funding is available specifically for people who are at a disadvantage when it comes to going to college—kids from families with limited money, kids whose parents didn't have the same opportunities. So, what you need to do is figure out what kinds of funding you qualify for. Here are some websites for you to check out. You need to do some of the work too, okay?

An Mei: Okay.

Mr. Melville: Then, next January 1st, you need to start filling out this FAFSA form. And make sure that you list the universities you want to attend, in order of preference. In a few weeks, your Student Aid Report, or SAR, will come back with your EFC, your expected family contribution. That will tell you how much financial aid you qualify for, you know, in grants and loans and work-study programs, etc. Once you've done that, bring it in to me and we'll go from there. All right?

An Mei: Wow! I can't believe that I can go to college. Thank you so much, Mr. Melville.

Mr. Melville: Well, believe it. You're definitely college material. Good luck, and you're welcome.

F. PRACTICE

Fill in the blanks with the following words and expressions: *cut corners, break even, FAFSA, go broke, EFC, saddle with debt, tuition, set aside, work-study, keep track of*

1. Try to _____ as much money as you can before you go to college.

2. Before you plan a budget, you have to _____ how much you spend on different things.

3. I don't want to _____ my kids _____ before they graduate from college, so I'll help them out as much as I can.

4. Not going to the movies every weekend and cooking our own meals should help us _____ enough to be able to afford everything we need.

5. The first thing you need to do to get funding is to fill out your _____.

6. A family could very easily _____ if they have more than one child in a university at the same time.

7. After you pay for your books and tuition, you may have just enough money to _____.

8. Once you find out what your _____ is, you'll have some idea of how much you'll have to contribute to your tuition.

9. Some students' financial aid package will include _____ as a way to pay for additional expenses.

10. The _____ is lower at public universities than it is at private universities. However, the cost of instruction at a community college is even lower.

Fill in the blanks with *a*, *an*, or *the*, or leave them blank for no articles. In some cases, there may be more than one possible answer.

1. My father took me to _____ San Francisco.

2. We went to _____ theater while we were there.

3. There is _____ university there that I am especially interested in.

4. I really liked _____ University of California, Berkeley.

5. We drove through _____ Sierra Nevada Mountains on the way home.

6. It took us about ten and _____ half hours to get back.

7. As soon as I graduate, I'll have to go to _____ work to pay off my college loans.

8. I need to drop by _____ office to pick up my paycheck.

9. I need to pick up _____ pound of _____ butter for tonight.

10. Hey, I'm taking _____ vacation before school starts. I'm going to _____ Hawaiian Islands.

G. TASK

Imagine that you or a child of yours is planning on going to college in a few years. Using some of the websites listed in the Resources section, search for loans, scholarships, and grants that you would be eligible for. You could also go to your local library and ask the librarian for help finding information that would be useful to you.

 H. **REAL LIFE**

Dear Sammy,

I am a Swiss high school student, and I would really like to attend an American university. I think I have a good chance of being accepted at one or two universities I applied to, but they're so expensive! What can I do to afford higher education in the U.S.?

Sincerely,
Armand

Dear Armand,

The United States has some of the best universities in the world. Sixty-two of the top two hundred universities are in the United States, and of the top ten, seven are American universities. A degree from an accredited American university is the best investment a college student can make because it can mean the best job offers and highest salaries. The problem is that it is extremely expensive for foreign students to attend American universities. In fact, it is expensive even for Americans and U.S. residents, but more so for foreign students, who pay at least two or three times the price that American students pay.

In order to be accepted into a university in the U.S., you would have to prove that you have at least one year's tuition. As a foreign student, you unfortunately do not qualify for U.S. government funded aid, such as the Pell Grant, the Stafford Loan, etc. (which are only available to U.S. citizens and permanent residents). But there may be funds for you. A good source for researching funds available to foreign students is ww.edupass.org. Another source for funding information is www.foreignborn.com. And by the way, you might want to steer clear of organizations that want you to pay them to look for funding for you. It's always hard to tell whether that's a worthwhile investment!

Good luck!
Sammy

I.   RESOURCES

Federal Student Aid:
www.studentaid.ed.gov (includes information for international students)

University funding information for permanent residents and U.S. citizens:
www.salliemae.com
www.finaid.org
www.collegeispossible.org

You can also check with your bank for information on federal loans as well as private student loans that they offer.

Funding information for foreign students who want to study in the U.S.:
www.edupass.org
www.foreignborn.com

FAFSA:
www.fafsa.ed.gov

Scholarships and grants:
www.fastweb.com
www.findtuition.com

General college information (including financial aid):
www.collegeboard.com

Books:
Paying for College Without Going Broke by The Princeton Review
America's Best Value Colleges by The Princeton Review

ANSWER KEY
Practice 1: 1. set aside; 2. keep track of; 3. saddle . . . with debt; 4. cut corners; 5. FAFSA; 6. go broke; 7. break even; 8. EFC; 9. work-study; 10. tuition

Practice 2:—means the space should be left blank; no article is needed 1. —; 2. the/a; 3. a; 4. the; 5. the; 6. a; 7. —; 8. the; 9. a, —; 10. a/—, the

CHAPTER 17

School: Registering for Classes

A. ENGLISH CLOSE-UP

FAIRMONT COMMUNITY COLLEGE SCHEDULE OF CLASSES

Term: **Fall 2008**
Student Name: **Sofia M. Rinaldi**
Student Number: **0007631**
Major: **Biology**

English	21.101	MWF 10:00–11:00	Newman Hall 201	Sanders
World History	35.190	TTH 9:00–10:30	Quadrangle 511	Beekman
Biology	56.120	MWF 2:00–3:00	Heller 118	Prasada
Biology Lab	56.120.1	T 2:00–3:00	Heller B-11	TBA

B. VOCABULARY ESSENTIALS

Accredited schools—Schools that are given government approval by an official review board made up of educators because they meet certain standards set by the board. *Be sure that your university is accredited before you sign up and pay your fees.*

Add/Drop—Adding classes to or deleting classes from your schedule after registration has been completed. *Don't forget to have your advisor sign your add/drop cards for any classes you add to or drop from your schedule if necessary.*

Advisor—A faculty member of a university, often one who is in the department of the student's major, who is assigned to help a student with such things as selecting courses, planning out his or her overall academic program, and other academic (and sometimes personal) issues. *My advisor says I should wait to take this economics course, but I really feel I'm better off just taking it now.*

Bursar—The department of a college or university that is in charge of receiving tuition. *If you are having problems with your financial aid, talk to the bursar about it.*

Continuing education—Classes offered for adults, usually outside of any degree program. *Many adults take such continuing education classes as photography, cooking, or foreign languages.*

Credit—Unit of study in a university, usually corresponding to the number of class hours per week. You usually need a certain amount of credits in order to graduate from a degree program, and credits are often tied to tuition costs, meaning that each credit that you take costs a certain amount. *I need to pick up an extra hour of credit somewhere in my schedule so that I can be a full time student.*

Deadline—A date when something must be finished and turned in. *Be sure to send in your application before the deadline or you'll need to wait until the following semester.*

Documentation—Official records used as evidence to prove something. *In order for you to attend this school next fall, we need to see documentation that you actually have your high school diploma from your country.*

Elective—A class outside of the requirements of a student's major or minor. *Gary is an engineering student, but he always takes poetry as an elective.*

Major, to major in—The primary area of study of a student at a university, usually officially declared to the college and involving specific courses/credits that must be taken. To specialize in a certain subject at a university. *At first Rob thought he was interested in communications as his major, but he switched to journalism.*

Matriculated students—Students who are registered at a university and have been admitted to and are enrolled in a degree program. *The English writing class is full, so matriculated students will be given preference over nonmatriculated students.*

Minor, to minor in—A secondary field of study at a university, with fewer required credits than a major. To study as a secondary field of interest. *My major in college was French literature, but I took history as a minor.*

Orientation—A meeting or longer series of activities planned to help someone new become acquainted with a program or school. *Incoming freshmen should attend an orientation meeting in room 301 at 10:00 a.m. tomorrow.*

Petition—An official request made to an authority. *You can fill out a petition if there are extenuating circumstances that will keep you from meeting the deadline.*

Prerequisite—Something required prior to something else, for example, a class. *The prerequisite for English 102 is English 101.*

Registrar—The department of a college or university responsible for registering students for classes and for providing official academic transcripts and proof of academic status. *If you're applying to graduate school, you'll need to contact your undergraduate registrar in order to obtain official academic transcripts.*

To reinstate—To allow someone to return at the same level. *After Ted failed to join a Major League baseball team, he asked the college to reinstate him as a full-time student.*

Transcripts—Records of courses taken, as well as grades and credit received. *Before you can register for classes, you need to be sure that the university has your transcript on file.*

Waiting list—A list of students who wish to be in a class that is full and receiving no further students. *If the class is full, get on the waiting list; if anyone drops, you'll be let in.*

To withdraw—To formally drop out of something. *You have too many classes, so you should withdraw from one of them early in the semester.*

GRAMMAR ESSENTIALS: FUTURE EXPRESSIONS USED WITH THE PRESENT TENSE

The following expressions all refer to a future time, but they're used with the present tense in English: *if, when, as soon as, unless, in case, until, before, after, by the time, as long as, on condition that, provided that*

> *As soon as you get your registration materials, you can register.*
> *You will be able to withdraw from class without penalty as long as you withdraw by the deadline.*
> *I have to finish my English literature paper before I start studying for the biology final.*

Let's look more closely at the meanings of these future time expressions:

1. *When* connects two events or conditions in the future that occur at the same time. *When you get your transcripts, you can send them to the university.*

2. *As soon as* is similar to *when*, but the connection is more immediate. *As soon as you get your acceptance letter, you will feel relieved.*

3. *Before* means "prior to." *Before you sign up for the class, you will have to check your schedule to see if that time slot is open.*

4. *By the time* has a similar meaning, but it suggests a longer duration of time. *Orientation is going to take a long time, so by the time you finish, I will be waiting in the parking lot.*

5. *After* means "following" or "subsequent to." *After you fill out your petition, the department chair will look it over.*

6. *Until* means "up to a certain point in time." *You will have to wait to register until your documentation arrives.*

7. *If* refers to a possibility or a condition that must be met in order for something to happen. *If you get on the waiting list, you might get into the class.*

8. *Provided that* and *on condition that* have similar meanings. *You can add this class provided that you pay the late fee. You will get all your money back on condition that you withdraw from the class on time.*

9. *In case* has a similar meaning to *if,* but it suggests a lesser expectation. *In case you want to change your schedule after registration, you will need to fill out an add/drop slip.*

10. *As long as* also has a similar meaning to *if,* but it conveys more of a sense of the necessity of the condition. *We'll let you skip English 101 and go into English 102 as long as you pass the placement test.*

11. *Unless* means one thing will happen only if something else does not happen. *You'll graduate on time unless you fail one of your classes. (You'll graduate on time if you don't fail any of your classes.)*

D. HOW-TO

Once a student has chosen to attend a particular college, he or she needs to start thinking about registering for classes. If you're the parent of a child who is going through this process, you may be curious to know how it works. Or, you may be considering adult or continuing education, in which case you yourself may need to register for classes. In either case, class registration is the process of choosing and signing up for the classes you want to take during a semester. This typically takes place in the weeks or months before the beginning of a semester, but it may also extend a few weeks into the semester. While every school has its own registration process, the following procedures and components are fairly common.

Before a student registers, he or she first gets a course catalog, which shows what classes are offered at the university, when and where they take place, how many credits they're worth, and who they're taught by. Course catalogs are usually online as well. The course description will explain what is covered in the course, and also whether there are any prerequisites or labs. Labs are additional classes that involve hands-on activities and demonstrations that you must participate in if you want to take a certain class. For instance, if you sign up for an astronomy class, you might have to take an astronomy lab as well that meets once a week where you, for example, work with telescopes and chart the paths of planets. Of course, if you're a matriculated student, you may have certain courses required for your major, so these courses should be given priority. After the required courses, students often choose to take other courses for their minors, or perhaps as electives.

If the class has prerequisites, students aren't able to register unless they've taken and passed them. Prerequisites are required because they teach lower-level material that will be assumed as background knowledge in the higher-level classes. For example, if a student wants to take a class on organic chemistry, the university may require that he or she first take a class on basic chemistry; basic chemistry is the prerequisite. If a student has transferred in from another school and has taken a class similar to the prerequisite, it's possible that the department will waive the prerequisite, often after some kind of exam or other proof that the student has mastered the necessary material.

For matriculated students who are taking a number of classes each semester and who need to maintain a certain number of credits, it's probably a good idea to work out a "best case scenario" schedule and also a few alternate schedules if any classes are full or canceled. It's also a good idea to keep in mind the location of the classes, because university campuses may be rather spread out and it may take some time to get from class to class. It may be necessary for students to have their advisor sign off on their schedule, as well.

Naturally, a great deal of paperwork and documentation is usually required in order to register. This could include citizenship or visa documentation for international students, confirmation of loans, previous academic transcripts, or medical records, such as immunization records. It's generally necessary to show all of the necessary documentation before or at the time of registration, and failure to do so may prevent a student from attending classes or even registering at all. Other issues that may keep a student from registering fully include unpaid balances in regard to university fees, academic problems from previous semesters or schools, lack of proper immunizations, or even overdue library books. Therefore, it's a good idea for students to check with the university's registrar and/or bursar to make sure everything is in order and to avoid problems or delays registering.

Actual registration dates vary from school to school. It's also important to note that disabled students and graduate students may have priority registration, and that the newer a student is to the system, the later his or her registration date may be. For instance, most seniors will have earlier registration dates than freshmen, sophomores, or juniors. Therefore, students need to register as soon after their registration date and time as possible in order to get the desired classes. Also, failure to register within the given time period usually results in a late registration fee.

There are usually several ways students register for classes. Most schools now have online registration, but it might also be possible to mail in registration, to register over the phone, or to register in person by what's called a walk-in registration. In the past, before telephone and online registration, all students had to do walk-in registration and were given a time and date to register. All the students would scurry from table to table to try to register for the classes they wanted and needed and then go to the cashier's table and pay the fees. Today walk-in registration usually means that you go in person to the college registrar, often with a completed registration form in hand, and register for classes, although some places still use a variation on the older system. For undergraduate or returning students, some schools may require a walk-in registration for the first semester, or perhaps require that those students meet in person with their advisors.

It's often the case that students aren't able to register for the classes they want or that they register for classes that they're not sure about. This is where the add/drop process comes in. Students are able to add or drop classes from their schedule, usually for a few weeks after classes begin. The exact process varies from school to school, but it can involve an add/drop form or slip and the signature of an advisor or perhaps of the professor teaching the class to be dropped or added. Some schools also allow you to add or drop a class online. Students interested in learning about the add/drop procedure for their school should contact the registrar to find out about the relevant requirements and deadlines. Another possible scenario is that a student isn't able to register for a class he or she wants to take because it's full, so the student is put on a waiting list. In this case, it's important that the student attend all the classes as if he or she were registered, so that if a place opens up, no time or material will have been missed. Also, allowing extra students into a class is often at the discretion of its instructor, and he or she is probably likely to give priority to students on the waiting list who attend each class.

International students in an English language program at a university may have a slightly different registration process. The school may decide which classes are needed, and assign them accordingly. There may be different degrees of flexibility in this, and students will most likely still be able to take one or two electives of their choosing. English language programs for international students are available at many colleges, but the content and structure of these programs can vary widely; see your university of choice for more information.

The registration process for adult or continuing education, technical, or online schools is likely to be much more straightforward. It's important to make sure that technical and online schools are accredited, so students should consider checking with www.ncate.org prior to registration. At technical schools, students are likely to be able to set up schedules with an advisor. For online schools, students usually just need to select the courses they want and pay, and as long as enough students register, the courses will begin as scheduled. Adult or continuing education schools, which provide low-cost or even free classes, have the simplest registration process. Anyone over eighteen is eligible, and sixteen- and seventeen-year-olds can attend with parental permission. The only requirement for registration is a street address. P.O. boxes will not be accepted. It's a good idea for students to check with their school to be sure that they don't need to register in advance. Usually, though, it's possible to sign up, pay if a payment is required, and simply show up for class. As long as enough students are enrolled, the classes will take place as scheduled. Adult education classes are usually open entry/open exit, which means that students can stop or start attending whenever they want. As a result, large classes often end up being much smaller within a month or so.

E. ENGLISH IN ACTION

Let's listen in as Edgar calls his local adult school to ask about ESL classes.

Ms. Tate: Tri-city Adult. This is Ms. Tate. How can I help you?

Edgar: Hello. Yes, this is Edgar Cervantes. I'm calling about your English as a Second Language classes. Can I ask a few questions?

Ms. Tate: Sure. What would you like to know?

Edgar: Yes. Well, someone told me your classes are free. Is that right?

Ms. Tate: Yes, that's right.

Edgar: Well, what's the schedule?

Ms. Tate: We have classes from 7:30 in the morning until 2:30 in the afternoon during the week. We also have evening classes from 6:00 until 9:00 p.m., Monday through Thursday.

Edgar: Wow! Every day, from 7:30–2:30? That's good. Do you have any English classes on Saturday?

Ms. Tate: We have pronunciation and conversation classes, yes. They're from 9:00 a.m. until 12:00 noon.

Edgar: Hmmm. That sounds good, too. Can anyone sign up?

Ms. Tate: As long as you're over eighteen, you can sign up.

Edgar: How can I register?

Ms. Tate: Have you taken English classes here before?

Edgar: No.

Ms. Tate: Okay. Then you need to be evaluated so that you can be put in the right level for you. You should come to the testing office in room 101 between 7:30 and 1:00 during the week. Orientation is on Wednesday afternoons at 1:00.

Edgar: Well, I'm working some days. Do I have to attend every day?

Ms. Tate: No. It's open entry/open exit, so you come when you can, although you need to tell your teacher your schedule so that he or she doesn't drop you from the class if you're absent for more than three days.

Edgar: Okay. No problem. Wow, free English classes. I'm going to sign up on Monday. Thank you so much for the information.

Ms. Tate: You're very welcome. Enjoy your classes, and good luck.

F. PRACTICE

Fill in the blanks with the following words: *minor, prerequisite, drop, elective, orientation, petition, credit, waiting list, withdraw, transcript*

1. I don't know what to take as a(n) _____ this semester, but I know I want a course that's very different from my major.

2. You'll need to send in your high school _____ with your application to the university.

3. The week before school starts there will be a(n) _____ for new students.

4. I only need two more _____ in order to graduate, so hopefully it'll be a quick and easy semester.

5. If you don't think that you're ready for this class, you should _____ it.

6. I've decided to _____ in French. That way I can study the language while still focusing my studies on biology.

7. If you _____ from the class before September 28th, there will be no penalties.

8. There aren't many students on the _____, so you might be able to get into the class.

9. The only way to be waived from taking this class is to _____ the dean.

10. You can't take this class, because you haven't taken the _____.

Put the following words in the correct order to make sentences with future expressions.

1. you/skip/You/talk/instructor/to/unless/can't/this/class/the

2. we'll/lunch/After/finish/you/go/orientation/have

3. arrives/deadline/sure/your/Make/application/mailed/before/is/the

4. you/credits/will/If/class/you/a/some/lose/drop

5. financial/aid/bursar's/your/contacts/office/When/they/talk/the/you/will/about

6. register/we/leave/As soon as/can/you

7. class/halfway/it/By the time/drop/you/will/through/the/be/you

8. you/As long as/waiting/list/are/might/class/in/on/the/you/want/to/the/on/sit

9. will/101/In case/for/sign up/English/you/you/book/need/this

10. you/through/you/feel/will/go/registration/nervous/it/about/Until

TASK

Select a local school—a four year college or university, a community college, a technical school, or a school that offers adult or continuing education programs. Go to their website and find out about the registration process. When does registration open? What sort of documentation do new students need? Can students register for classes online? Are there special requirements for international students?

H. REAL LIFE

Hi, my name's Cathy, and I'm an adult education ESL instructor. I thought you might like some information about English classes. Most ESL—English as a Second Language—classes can be found through your local school district. Sometimes adult ESL classes are a part of the local community college offerings in your area. You should be able to find free classes close to your home by checking with the local K–12 school district or community college. Most ESL classes are offered in K–12 classrooms or churches. Community colleges may have the classes at their own schools or offer classes on other college campuses. Once you find a school near you, you'll need to go there and get registered. You'll probably take some kind of a test to see what your level is, and then you will be assigned to a class or classes. Some schools offer extras like pronunciation, conversation, writing, and computer labs. Most schools offer classes to fit your schedule, so you should be able to find classes in the morning, afternoon, or evening. You will find that ESL classes are different from other classes you have taken because they are designed to be low pressure so that you will feel comfortable. Studies have found that people learn a new language better when they feel very comfortable with the teacher, the work, and their classmates. You will probably work with a partner or in a group more often than you work alone, because ESL teachers believe that students learn best when they help each other. Many ESL students will tell you that their ESL classes are among the best classes they've ever taken because they feel comfortable and make many new and sometimes lifelong friends from different countries.

I. RESOURCES

Information about colleges, universities, and research institutions in the USA:
www.educationusa.state.gov/scholars.htm
www.ed.gov/students/landing.jhtml
www.usnews.com

ESL programs:
www.esl.com

International students in the U.S.:
survival.abroadplanet.com
www.uscis.gov (U.S. Immigration Department, for information on student visas)

Testing information:
www.ets.org (TOEFL, or the Test of English as a Foreign Language, GRE, etc.)
www.collegeboard.com (SAT and SAT subject tests, APs, CLEP)

Technical and vocational schools:
www.ftc.gov/bcp/conline/pubs/services/votech.htm
www.technicalschools.org
www.rwm.org/rwm

Community colleges:
www.aacc.nche.edu

Online colleges:
www.elearners.com/colleges

ANSWER KEY
Practice 1: 1. elective; 2. transcript; 3. orientation; 4. credits; 5. drop; 6. minor; 7. withdraw; 8. waiting list; 9. petition; 10. prerequisite

Practice 2: 1. You can't skip this class unless you talk to the instructor. 2. After you finish orientation, we'll go have lunch. 3. Make sure your application is mailed before the deadline arrives. 4. If you drop a class, you will lose some credits. 5. When the bursar's office contacts you, they will talk about your financial aid. 6. As soon as you register, we can leave. 7. By the time you drop the class, you will be halfway through it. 8. As long as you are on the waiting list, you might want to sit in on the class. 9. In case you sign up for English 101, you will need this book. 10. Until you go through registration, you will feel nervous about it.

CHAPTER 18

Health and Emergencies: Health Insurance

A. ENGLISH CLOSE-UP

HEALTH INSURANCE CLAIMS

1. MEDICARE MEDICAID GROUP HEALTH PLAN ☐ ☐ ☐		Insured's ID number
2. Patient Name (Last, First, MI)	3. Patient's Birth Date _____mm/dd/yy Sex ☐ M ☐ F	4. Insured's Name (Last, First, MI)
5. Patient's Address (No., Street)	6. Patient's relationship to insured self spouse child other ☐☐ ☐ ☐	7. Insured's Address (No., Street)
City State	Patient Status	City State
Zip Code	Single Married Other ☐ ☐ ☐	Zip Code

B. VOCABULARY ESSENTIALS

To be covered—To be protected, as by insurance. Can be in regard to medical care in general or to specific services. *Not everyone is covered by health insurance, and even if people have insurance, not every type of medical care is covered by their policies.*

Benefit period—The annual period of time insurance is active, often from January 1st to December 31st of the same year. *Why have my premiums gone up during the present benefit period?*

Cap—A limit set on how much an insured person must pay for medical bills each year. Also called a "stop loss" or coinsurance cap. *If you meet the $5,000 annual cap, all you need to pay after that is the monthly premium.*

Co-payment (co-pay)—A small fee paid by the insured to the doctor or dentist for a visit or service, a portion not covered by insurance. *Your co-payment is $25.00. Will that be cash, check, or charge?*

Covered expenses—Products or services an insurance plan will pay for. *Check to see if well-baby care is a covered expense.*

Deductible—The annual amount of money an insured person must pay before insurance applies. *Daniel chose a high deductible so that his monthly insurance premiums would be low.*

Dependent—Children or relatives who are financially supported by you and qualify for coverage by your insurance plan (as a "qualifying child" or "qualifying relative") based on IRS regulations. *You must list all dependents when applying for an insurance policy.*

Disability—A physical or mental difficulty or disorder that interferes with a person's ability to work, move around, etc. Also, a type of insurance payment made to a person suffering from a disability. *Ever since breaking his ankle at work, Troy has been out on disability.*

Domestic partner benefits—Insurance benefits extended to the unmarried partner of an employee. *Anthony's company offers domestic partner benefits, so his partner is also covered by his health insurance.*

Double coverage (duplication of coverage or dual coverage)—When an individual is covered by two or more health plans. *Trina doesn't need to make any co-payments because she has double coverage, so her other insurance plan picks up the co-pay.*

Exclusions—Services that are not covered by health insurance. *Check the exclusions in your insurance booklet to see what's not covered.*

Generic—Refers to the chemical rather than the brand name of a medication. The generic version of a brand-name drug (a medication with a specific brand name used to market the medication to the public) contains the same active ingredients as the brand-name version but is sold at a lower cost. Not all brand-name drugs currently have generic counterparts. *Insurance plans may charge a lower co-pay for generic drugs than for brand-name drugs.*

Group insurance—Insurance for a group of people paid for through work or an organization. *Does your company offer a group insurance plan to its employees?*

Hospice—Care for terminally ill patients who are expected to live no more than six months. Many insurance plans cover hospice care. *We knew that our dad didn't have much time when the doctors suggested starting hospice care.*

Long-term care insurance—Insurance to be used in the event that the insured individual needs to have long term-care in a medical facility, most often used by the elderly. *Ana purchased long-term care insurance at a young age, so her premiums are very low.*

Managed care—A way of providing health care where an insurance company asks the doctors to accept a lower payment for care and the policyholders agree to use only a certain group or network of doctors. *My doctor complains about all the paperwork she has to do for managed care.*

Out-of-network—Indicating a medical professional who does not participate in a particular managed care insurance policy. With such policies, a policyholder must usually go to "in-network" doctors, dentists, etc. *If you go to an out-of-network doctor, your insurance company will not necessarily cover your expenses.*

Over-the-counter—Medicines that can be purchased without a prescription. *You can buy aspirin and cough medicine over the counter.*

Policy—The specific type of agreement an individual has with an insurance company. *I pay higher premiums, but my policy allows me to go out-of-network.*

Preexisting condition—A health problem a person had before his or her insurance policy became active. *If you already have diabetes or heart problems, those are preexisting conditions that might make your new insurance policy more expensive.*

Premiums—Monthly insurance payments. *To keep your premium low, you need a high deductible.*

Preventive care—Medical care that helps prevent health problems. This includes visits to the doctor, well-baby care, immunizations, and mammograms. *It's a good idea to follow preventive care and have a physical at least once a year.*

Primary care physician—The major medical care provider chosen by a person who participates in a managed care plan. Usually, the primary care physician is the general practitioner who sees a patient for regular visits, and who refers the patient to (in-network) specialists when needed. *If you want to go to a specialist for any problem, you first need to get a referral from your primary care physician.*

Provider—The person by whom or place where your health problems are taken care of. *You need to select a provider. That could be a doctor, a hospital, or a clinic.*

C. GRAMMAR ESSENTIALS: NON-PROGRESSIVE VERBS

There are several verbs in English that are typically not used in progressive tenses. They tend to indicate states or conditions, including psychological or emotional ones. These verbs can be divided into several different categories:

Description	*be, appear, look, seem, look like, resemble, sound, sound like*
Knowledge & Belief	*believe, guess, hope, feel, know, think, doubt, wonder*
Emotion & Attitude	*dislike, fear, hate, like, love, despise, care, mind, want, desire, need, prefer, appreciate, doubt, feel, wish*
Possession	*have, possess, belong, own, owe*
Sense & Sensation	*smell, see, hear, taste, ache, burn, feel, hurt, itch, sting*
Relationship	*depend on, consist of, include, contain, entail*
Measurement	*cost, equal, measure, weigh*

These verbs are most often used in simple tenses or perfect tenses.

> *The sky is blue. The dog has a sad face. We hated living there. He weighed 165 lbs. They've owned three houses.*

A few of these verbs can be used in progressive tenses, but only with a change in meaning:

He appears tired.	*He's appearing in a new movie.* (acting)
I see you over there.	*Nat is seeing a new woman.* (dating)
Rhea weighs 110 pounds.	*Jeremy is weighing some apples.* (using a scale to measure)
Nadia has a new car.	*We're having dinner at 8:00.* (idiomatic, eating)

It's possible to use many of the other verbs listed above in a progressive tense, not with a change in meaning, but with a different nuance. This is, in fact, a rather common feature of conversational English. For example, verbs of description can be used progressively to emphasize a temporary behavior or characteristic, most often a negative one:

> *You're appearing very foolish right now.*
> *He was being such a jerk at the meeting!*
> *You're sounding like your father!*

Verbs of knowledge and belief can be used progressively to show an ongoing thought process:

> *We were hoping you'd say that!*
> *I'm thinking that we need to change the color of this wall before we look at a new carpet.*
> *I'm guessing that we're going to need another fifty dollars for this . . .*

Verbs of emotion or attitude can be used progressively to show an intense feeling of the moment or a general trend:

> *I'm loving this new song I downloaded!*
> *I was feeling really good right after I started going to the gym.*
> *We were really hating the movie until the middle.*

Verbs of sense and sensation can be used progressively to stress that the act of perception is occurring at the moment, over a short period of time:

> *What am I smelling?*
> *Okay, I'm hearing a lot of resistance to the new proposal . . .*
> *What you're seeing right here is a small tumor.*

You may also hear some of these verbs used in progressive tenses when the speaker wants to be polite, wants to engage the listener, or wants to put some distance between himself or herself and a question or suggestion:

> *Are you needing to be alone right now?*
> *Are you thinking what I'm thinking?*
> *What are you feeling right now?*
> *I was wondering, maybe you'd like to go out to dinner with me sometime?*

In conversational English, it's also common to use these verbs in progressive tenses when telling a story:

So I'm thinking she's going to yell at me, because she's looking really upset. I was really feeling bad about what happened, and I was doubting myself, when . . .

D. HOW-TO

Health insurance in the United States can be very confusing. There are so many choices that it can often be hard to understand which insurance plan will work best for you. Whether your workplace provides insurance or you have to get it on your own, you will most likely have more than one plan to choose from. In order to make the best decision, you need to know more about some of the most typical insurance plans available, including HMOs, Fee-for-Service, and PPO plans.

Health Maintenance Organizations (HMOs) offer prepaid health plans where your medical care is paid for in return for a monthly premium. In addition to the monthly premium, you will also need to make a co-payment each time you visit a doctor, hospital, or other health care provider. As a result, it is easy to manage your medical expenses within an HMO, because the expenses are very predictable. HMOs also help simplify the insurance process by not requiring that you fill out claim forms after you visit a doctor in order to get reimbursed. You only need to show your insurance card and pay the co-payment each time you visit a provider.

In addition to providing insurance, an HMO also provides medical care through a network of health care providers. In an HMO, you must visit doctors or other health care providers that are "in-network," or contracted with by the HMO. Because your choice of providers is therefore limited, it can be difficult to get immediate appointments. The HMO will, however, cover the cost of doctors, hospitals, or clinics outside the HMO network if you have a medical emergency. Nevertheless, not all HMOs offer the same coverage. Some plans may not cover services such as mental health, home, or chiropractic care, so make sure you know exactly what is and what isn't covered.

A Fee-for-Service plan is a traditional insurance plan. With this type of insurance, the insured pays a monthly premium and has a deductible. A deductible, which renews at the end of the benefit period, is the amount paid for out-of-pocket by the insured for medical expenses. "Out-of-pocket" simply means paying for something yourself. Only costs covered under the insurance policy will count towards the deductible. Once the amount of the deductible has been met for the benefit period, the insurance company will share medical expenses with the insured. They will typically pay 80% of medical fees, while you pay the remaining 20%. In order to receive payment for the insurance company's portion, you may need to fill out forms and send them to the insurer. However, many doctors' offices will take care of this paperwork for you. Unfortunately, one drawback of this type of insurance is that if your doctor charges more for a particular service than is customary, you must pay the difference unless you can negotiate with your doctor to accept the insurance company's lower fee.

Although a Fee-for-Service plan will only share medical fees with you after the deductible has been paid, there is usually a cap of several thousand dollars on annual medical expenses. This means that once that amount has been met, you no longer have to pay anything for that year except the monthly premium. In the end, if you end up choosing a Fee-for-Service plan, check to be sure that your policy is a "comprehensive plan." A comprehensive plan will give you major medical insurance in addition to basic protection.

A PPO, or Preferred Provider Organization, is a combination of Fee-for-Service and HMO. Like HMOs, you have to choose from a limited network of health care providers to get full coverage. Also similar to an HMO, you only need to show an insurance card and make a co-payment for an in-network doctor's visit. You do not need to fill out any claim forms in this case. However, unlike an HMO, it is often possible to visit a doctor who is not part of the network. You will simply have to pay more and fill out claim forms. Finally, there will be deductibles with PPOs, too.

In addition to PPOs, Fee-for-Service plans, and HMOs, there are other options. For instance, Health Savings Accounts (HSAs) allow you to purchase a health insurance plan that has a high deductible but a very low monthly premium. In other words, you pay most of your medical expenses out-of-pocket while only paying a small amount to insurance. HSAs also allow you to invest an annual amount in a type of retirement account. You can withdraw money from the account for medical expenses without paying taxes on the money you've taken out. If you need to, you can take money out for other things, but you have to pay taxes on the amount withdrawn and there's a penalty you must pay. When you turn 65, you can withdraw your funds penalty-free so that the money invested becomes an addition to your retirement account. HSA accounts are opened at a bank or a credit union, but you must also find an insurance company with which to set up your high deductible insurance, so check first with your insurance company to see if they offer HSAs. If you want to find out more information about HSAs, you can visit the websites in the Resources section.

Once you turn 65, you also qualify for Medicare. Medicare is government health insurance that is paid for by mandatory payroll deductions. In addition to those over 65, Medicare may be available to people who meet specific criteria, such as certain disabilities. Medicare has two parts. Part A requires no monthly premium payments, but can have expensive co-payments. Part A only covers hospitalization, hospice care, nursing at home, in-home care, and hospital psychiatric care. However, you can choose to get Part B as well, which does have monthly payments but covers more general medical care, such as basic medical services or physical therapy. If you have another type of insurance, you might want to opt out of Part B. In fact, while Medicare is a safety net for those who can no longer work and pay for insurance, it's a good idea to have some sort of health investment account or additional insurance to help with the expenses incurred by someone who is advancing in age and therefore needs more health care.

Finally, Flexible Spending Accounts (FSAs) provide pretax money that can only be used towards medical expenses. FSAs, which are set up through your employer, withdraw a sum of money from your salary, before taxes, and place it in some sort of investment fund. The money can then be withdrawn to pay for medical services, such as dental care, therapy, or medical deductibles. The major drawback is that if the money is not used by March 15 of the following year, you may lose the funds and the money goes back to the employer, so it's important to do careful calculations when considering an FSA.

In the end, it is a good idea to do a significant amount of research before choosing a medical insurance plan. You need to make sure you have first figured out what is best for you and your family, taking into consideration issues such as current medical health, whether you have dependents, and both immediate and long-term financial concerns. With some planning and a decent understanding of the health insurance systems in the U.S., it's possible to have both medical coverage and peace of mind.

E. ENGLISH IN ACTION

Let's listen to Marta and Juan discussing their insurance needs as they look over the health insurance material they have received from their benefits office at work.

Marta: Juan, this is all so confusing. How do we know what kind of health insurance is best for us?

Juan: Well, I'm thinking we need to ask ourselves what's important. We need to see what the covered expenses are in each plan.

Marta: You mean, like if we want to have kids?

Juan: Yeah, well, that's a big one for us, since we haven't started our family yet. So we need to see how maternity care is covered, and I think we also need to look at well-baby care, where the child immunizations are paid for, you know. That's important since we want to be sure our kids grow up healthy. But I was thinking about things like, can we choose our own doctor, is it easy to see a specialist if we need to, does the insurance cover regular screenings for things like, you know, different kinds of cancer?

Marta: Yes, well, I think it's more expensive to choose our own doctor, and we can probably find a good doctor in the group of doctors we're offered. It looks like maternity is covered in all these plans, too. Oh, and well-baby care is for sure. But what about you? I mean, you have diabetes, and I think they call that a preexisting condition. We need to be sure that your treatment will be covered.

Juan: Oh, yeah, you're right. I have to take so much medicine, we'd better be sure our prescription plan isn't too expensive, too. I can't just get along on over-the-counter medicine.

Marta: Since I'm going to have the babies in this family, I want to know which hospitals we can go to and if emergency care coverage is good.

Juan: Well, let's make a chart and see which has the best plan for the best price for us. Oh, and I think we need to see the—what are they called?—the exclusions.

Marta: You know what? Ana told me that she and her husband have dual coverage. I think we qualify for that. Since we're married and we both have insurance at work, maybe we should choose two different plans and make sure most of our expenses are covered that way.

Juan: That's brilliant!

Marta: Oh, Juan, I'm just being economical . . . Now, could you pass me that brochure over there about the prescription plans?

F. PRACTICE

Fill in the blanks with the following terms: *provider, pre-existing condition, long-term care insurance, hospice care, dependents, preventive care, covered expenses, be covered, cap, double coverage*

1. Do you have any _____ other than your young children?

2. Our _____ is Tri-City hospital. We get pretty good care there.

3. The _____ my father received before he died made his last months easier for him and for us.

4. This insurance company has a(n) _____ of $3,500. That's better than a lot of companies!

5. This plan's _____ include chiropractic care. That's important to me.

6. If you don't have insurance, you won't _____ if you become seriously ill.

7. When our aunt couldn't take care of herself any more, everyone was so glad that she'd purchased _____.

8. What happens if someone has a(n) _____ like arthritis? Is it covered?

9. This HMO has _____ as well as other kinds of coverage, so hopefully we can stay healthy longer.

10. If we have _____, which of our policies pays for our health care, my husband's or mine?

Circle the correct verb form in the following sentences.

1. Maria (appears/is appearing) in a new Broadway musical.
2. So I (think/was thinking), how would you feel about buying a new TV?
3. Tahera (weighs/is weighing) a little more than she wants to.
4. We usually (have/are having) dinner in the evening.
5. Do you smell that? I think something (burns/is burning).
6. Whatever it is, it (smells/is smelling) awful.
7. This soup (tastes/is tasting) awful, too.
8. Did you know that Joe (sees/is seeing) someone from work now? And so soon after he broke up with Kate!
9. I (have/am having) a hard time understanding you right now.
10. You always (look/are looking) so beautiful.

G. TASK

Go to an online service that compares health insurance plans, such as www.healthinsurance.org or www.healthinsurancefinders.com. Research two or three different plans available to you and make a table to compare the plans and determine which one would be better suited to your needs. Some points you may consider comparing them on are: How much are the premiums? Co-payments? Deductibles? Caps? Is your current doctor in the network? How many doctors are there in the network locally? What other services are covered?

H. REAL LIFE

Good evening, ladies and gentlemen, and welcome to the presentation. Tonight we'll be speaking about the importance of long-term care. You'll have the opportunity to meet with long-term care insurance providers to decide if you want this type of coverage and which company you think is best. You'll also be hearing from hospice care representatives, and you'll be able to attend a variety of workshops on end-of-life issues, as well. But before we break up and go to the various workshops, I'm going to give you a little overview of what long-term care means, as well as what hospice care entails.

First, let's take a look at what kinds of things long-term care insurance provides, to help you decide if you think you might want to go in that direction. Long-term coverage is really for those folks who have degenerative conditions or some sort of cognitive disorder. Basically, long-term care insurance primarily covers support services, rather than medical services. For medical services, you need your own health insurance or Medicare. "Support services" means things like helping people with their day-to-day activities when they are unable to do them on their own and their families are too busy, too exhausted, or perhaps too far away to do these things for them. For instance, when people get to the point where they can no longer dress themselves or feed themselves and they need someone to help them out, long-term care insurance will help cover the expense. The only problem is the uncertainty. None of us knows who will need this kind of long-term care, so you don't really know now whether you will eventually need this insurance, when you're still young enough to purchase it cheaply. You can still purchase it later, but the price goes up the older you get. I'm guessing that a lot of you may be thinking that you want to go in this direction, so take a look at what's available to you.

Hospice care is for those who are approaching the end of their lives. The purpose of hospice care is to help make the patient as comfortable as possible and to provide quality time with family and friends to make the final months the best they can be given the circumstances. Hospice care offers a whole host of professionals and volunteers to help make this possible. Along with the primary care doctor, who will continue to provide treatment, a hospice doctor who specializes in end-of-life care will offer treatment guidance. There will be a nurse available to travel to the patient's home or care location, which could be a hospice center. Hospice care providers also have home health aids available and spiritual counselors of all faiths ready to assist; there are social workers and bereavement counselors, as well. Usually, hospice care doesn't begin until the doctor has determined that the patient only has six months of life left. It's covered under many insurance plans as well as Medicaid and Medicare. Hospice care never turns anyone down just because he or she has no insurance, because hospice care providers also can rely on donations they already have in place. It's a really good thing to know about, so I'm hoping you'll check that out as well.

Okay, well, my time is up. Enjoy your workshops and don't forget there are plenty of refreshments left, so help yourselves. We'll see you back here tomorrow. Thank you.

I. RESOURCES

For information on health insurance for low-income families, see Lesson 35.

Medicare:
www.medicare.gov

HSAs:
www.health—savings—accounts.com
www.treasury.gov/offices/public-affairs/hsa

To compare health plans:
www.healthchoices.org
www.ehealthinsurance.com

Consumer information on health insurance coverage:
www.ahrq.gov/CONSUMER/insuranc.htm#head4
www.healthinsuranceinfo.net
www.iii.org/individuals/health

Hospice care:
www.nhpco.org/templates/1/homepage.cfm

FSAs:
www.fsafeds.com/fsafeds/index.asp

Information on generic drugs:
www.fda.gov/Cder/consumerinfo/generics_q&a.htm

ANSWER KEY
Practice 1: 1. dependents; 2. provider; 3. hospice care; 4. cap; 5. covered expenses; 6. be covered; 7. long-term care insurance; 8. preexisting condition; 9. preventive care; 10. double coverage

Practice 2: 1. is appearing; 2. was thinking; 3. weighs; 4. have; 5. is burning; 6. smells; 7. tastes; 8. is seeing; 9. am having; 10. look

CHAPTER 19

Health and Emergencies: Doctors

A. ENGLISH CLOSE-UP

Medical Reference Information				
Previous Surgeries		Medical Illnesses		
Allergies to Medication		Present Medication		
Referring Physician and Address		Family Doctor and Address		
Is this illness or injury employment related?	Date of injury	Is condition related to an auto accident?	Date	If so, name of Auto Insurance Company
Insurance Information				
Name and address of Insurance Company	ID number	Group number	Subscriber's name number	Soc. Sec. number

B. VOCABULARY ESSENTIALS

Alternative medicine—Health care remedies that do not fall within the bounds of traditional Western medicine, such as acupuncture, aromatherapy, homeopathy, herbal medicine, and naturopathic medicine. *Although Lisa trusted that her prescriptions were working, she preferred to supplement them with some form of alternative medicine.*

AMA—American Medical Association. An association of medical doctors in the U.S. that works to further the interests of medical doctors and is involved with national health issues. *The AMA is also involved in programs that help to enhance public health.*

Battery of tests—A number or range of tests. *They ran a battery of tests on Ken to find out what the problem was, but they still don't know what's causing the fatigue.*

Board certified—Describing a doctor who has completed residency and passed the medical exam for a specialty field. *Most American doctors are board certified.*

Checkup—Routine physical examination involving an array of tests. *I think I need to call my primary care physician and schedule my annual checkup. I hope my blood pressure and cholesterol are okay.*

Chiropractic care—Treatment that involves manipulating the spine. *If you have chronic back or neck pain, you might want to consider chiropractic care.*

Diagnosis—A health evaluation based on a patient's symptoms. *My diagnosis is that you have arthritis.*

To draw blood—To take blood from a vein for medical tests. *Doctors have to draw blood in order to test for a wide variety of diseases.*

Family medicine (family practice)—A medical practice that treats all ages and can involve the whole family. *We use a family practice so that our family can be treated as a unit.*

GP (General practitioner)—A doctor who doesn't specialize but takes care of general medical needs, also called a family doctor. *First see your GP, and then ask her for a referral to a specialist.*

Internist—A doctor who practices internal medicine, which involves diagnosing and treating diseases that affect the internal organs. *When you reach middle age, it's probably better to see an internist than a GP.*

Remedy—A therapy or treatment to relieve pain or cure disease. *You can ask your doctor what remedies are available to you.*

Second opinion—A diagnosis sought from a second doctor. *A patient has the right to ask for a second opinion to verify or disagree with the first doctor's opinion.*

Syringe—Needle, used for injections. *Little Samantha hates getting shots, so when she saw the nurse take out a syringe, she started to cry.*

Treatment—The method of caring for a health problem, the administering of remedies. *You can't take any aspirin prior to or during treatment.*

To be up-front—To be direct and not hide information. *A good doctor should be up-front about your medical condition.*

C. GRAMMAR ESSENTIALS: NEGATIVES

As you know, the negative adverb in English is *not,* which can occur in its full form or as a contraction. Contractions are generally used in spoken English, and use of the full form *not* typically adds emphasis:

> *I haven't gone to the doctor's since last July, so I should make an appointment.*
> *I have not gone to the doctor's since last July, so stop saying I'm a hypochondriac!*

Not (or *-n't*) follows forms of *be,* auxiliaries, or modals. But in the simple present, *do* or *does* is used, and in the simple past, *did* is used:

> *Karen Waters isn't a good doctor.*
> *They won't make an appointment for next week.*
> *The nurse hasn't drawn blood yet.*
> *We don't go to have checkups yearly.*
> *They didn't take an X ray.*

There are a few general points to keep in mind about negation in English. Double negatives (such as "you don't do nothing" or "I can't see no doctor") are not grammatically correct in standard English. With negatives, *any* is used instead:

> *You don't do anything.*
> *I can't see any doctor here.*
> *Don't do anything at all!*
> *There aren't any appointments available.*

Certain negatives, such as *never, rarely, seldom, not once, not a single,* and so on, can come at the beginning of a sentence, in which case they cause the subject and verb to invert:

> *Never have we waited so long for an appointment!*
> *Rarely will that doctor answer his own phone.*

If the sentence has a simple tense, then a form of *do* is used as an auxiliary:

> *Seldom do I trust a first opinion.*
> *Not a single question did he ask me.*

When asking negative questions, the word order changes depending on whether the full form *not* or the contraction is used. With a contraction, the order is *do/does/did + n't +* subject, and with a full form *not,* the order is *do/does/did +* subject *+ not.* There is also a slight difference in meaning. A negative question with a contraction suggests that the questioner expects a positive answer, but a negative question with a full form negative carries more of a sense of surprise or disbelief:

> *Don't you go for annual checkups? I thought you told me you did.*
> *Do you not go for annual checkups? I'm surprised! I thought everyone did!*

Don't forget that tag questions after an affirmative statement are in the negative, whereas tag questions after a negative statement are in the affirmative:

> *You're calling about a prescription refill, aren't you?*
> *You aren't feeling worse, are you?*

Negatives can often be used to soften speech. Take a look at the following examples:

> *Won't you please sit down?*
> *You haven't ignored your doctor's advice, have you?*
> *Your cholesterol level isn't as good as it should be.*

Not is the negative that you'll use with verbs, but there are plenty of negative prefixes that you should be aware of: *un-, in-, im-, il-, ir-, dis-, a-,* and *non-.* Some examples are *unfamiliar, insensitive, impatient, illiterate, irreverent, dishonest, atypical,* and *nonsense.*

D. HOW-TO

It is very important to have a good doctor. The outcome of any future health problems can depend on the care and skill of your doctor. Therefore, if you're new to a community, you don't want to just look in the yellow pages to find a doctor. Instead, find out all you can about the local doctors. Of course, you may already be limited by your insurance, but even within that smaller pool of doctors, some will be more suitable than others. A great way to start looking for a good doctor is to ask your neighbors, friends, coworkers, or family for recommendations. You can also ask any other health care providers you know for suggestions. You'll want to ask such questions as whether the doctor gives good advice, practices preventive medicine, listens to the patient, explains everything clearly, or treats the patient with respect. And, of course, you'll want to know the practical information, such as what types of insurance the doctor accepts, what types of hours he or she keeps for appointments, and how far the office is from your home. Once you've got a few names that sound like good potentials, you'll probably want to know where they went to school, what they specialize in, what other languages they speak, and so on. As a potential patient, you have the right to all of that information, and doctors' offices will usually be happy to give it out. You could also check with the American Board of Medical Specialties or the AMA (see Resources below) about a particular doctor, as well. Finally, you'll want to meet with the doctor to get a sense of his or her treatment methods, the friendliness and efficiency of the staff, rates, and so on. If your insurance allows you to do this with a short list of potential doctors, it's a great idea to schedule appointments with each of the doctors you are considering. Only after meeting a doctor in person will you be sure that he or she is right for you and your family.

As you can probably imagine, because there are so many different doctors in the U.S., there are also many different kinds of practices available. Beginning with the youngest among us, children have pediatricians, doctors who specialize in children's health care. There are even adolescent medicine specialists for teenagers. They deal with specific problems that teens might have, like acne, diet, eating disorders, and depression. You can also choose a doctor who specializes in family practice. These doctors are a little like the family doctor of the past. They care for all the family members from birth to old age and can refer patients to specialists. As an adult you might prefer an internist, a doctor who specializes in internal care or problems with the heart, digestive system, or other internal organs, as your primary care doctor.

Internists might also refer you to a specialist, such as an oncologist, urologist, cardiologist, dermatologist, gynecologist, or immunologist, for specific health problems. Besides hospitals and doctors' offices, there are also clinics, which are more low cost than doctors' offices, and free clinics for those who do not have insurance. Clinics provide outpatient services, services for people who get treatment but don't have to stay overnight. If you have an emergency that is not serious enough for you to be admitted to the hospital, it might be better to go to a walk-in urgent care center. Emergency rooms are often very busy, and if your emergency is not too serious, you could wait many hours to be seen. Urgent care centers are usually not as busy as the emergency room. They're for walk-ins, so you don't have to have an appointment, and they are often open longer hours than a doctor's office or clinic.

No matter where you go to meet with your doctor, there are a few practical pieces of information you should know about making and going to doctors' appointments. If you need to make an appointment with your primary care doctor, you can just call the office to make an appointment. If it's just a routine appointment, you may have to wait a few weeks or even months, but if you need to be seen right away, they will usually either squeeze you in to see your doctor or give you an appointment with an available doctor. If you need to see a specialist, your primary care doctor or internist can give you a referral. In fact, sometimes your insurance might require that you get a referral in order to see almost any sort of specialist. Sometimes your primary care doctor's receptionist will schedule appointments with specialists, or the receptionist might give you the phone number and possibly ask you to wait a few days for the referral to go through before you can call to make an appointment. Be sure to schedule any appointments for a time that is convenient for you. If something comes up and you cannot make your appointment, you should always call as early as you can to change your appointment. You could be charged for an office visit if you do not cancel within a day or two of your appointment. In case you have an urgent need to see your doctor, the doctor's office will give you an emergency phone number to call. It might be your own doctor or an emergency care doctor service. You can also call the emergency room and ask for the "doctor on call" for urgent medical advice. You should carry your insurance cards with you at all times. You could have several different insurance cards, including a special one for pharmaceutical care, which you show your pharmacy when you go there to buy medicine so that your pharmaceutical insurance will help cover the cost of the medicine. Your doctor's office will ask to see your insurance cards, sometimes even each time you go to see your doctor. If your visit to the doctor is your first, you can expect to fill out a medical history and a medical consent form along with information about allergies to medicines or latex. If you have insurance, you most likely will need to have a co-pay ready. Be sure you know how much that is. Your insurance cards should have the current co-pay information. It is also usually possible to be billed for your co-pay should you forget to bring cash or a check.

A very important thing to keep in mind about health care is that you should always remain actively engaged. That means scheduling regular visits for checkups and not being afraid to ask questions that you may have, whether about a simple illness or a more important problem. Make sure you understand what your doctor tells you, from advice on diet to diagnosis of a disease. If your doctor recommends a particular treatment or medication, don't be afraid to ask about side effects or possible drug interactions. If your doctor says you need surgery, ask about the benefits and risks, the recovery time, and other options. Finally, don't be afraid to get a second opinion, especially with diagnoses that involve risky or invasive treatment. Ask another doctor for his or her diagnosis. You can also do research on your own to help you better understand what the doctor tells you, but in this age of information, it's always a good idea to keep in mind that not everything you find on the internet is trustworthy, and not everyone has a license to practice medicine!

E. ENGLISH IN ACTION

Let's listen in as Ivan and Dr. Sing discuss Ivan's health.

Dr. Singh: Well, Ivan, overall, your health picture looks good, but I'm a little worried because your cholesterol levels are not as low as they should be. However, at this point I think we should just watch it. I'd like you to get tested again in a few months.

Ivan: Should I be concerned if my test results are the same next time?

Dr. Singh: Well, your LDL needs to come down. If it remains the same, we can just continue watching it, or you can change your lifestyle to bring it down. If it goes up, then that would be a little worrisome. It's one of the risk factors for heart disease.

Ivan: Hmm. What are the other risk factors?

Dr. Singh: Smoking. Do you smoke?

Ivan: I used to. I smoked for about twenty years, but since I came to America I stopped.

Dr. Singh: Okay, well, it's good that you stopped. Your blood pressure's high-normal, but if that changes, we'll need to do something about that, too.

Ivan: Hmm. My father died of a heart attack. Should I worry?

Dr. Singh: You're a little overweight. Are you physically active?

Ivan: No, not really. Would that help?

Dr. Singh: Yes, it would. It will help you lose weight, bring down your LDL, and reduce your blood pressure. It helps in a lot of ways. That takes away some of your risk factors. If and when you need it, I could give you a prescription to help you with your blood pressure and another one for your cholesterol.

Ivan: I'd rather not take anything for it. Would it help if I changed my diet some?

Dr. Singh: Absolutely! Eat lots of fresh fruits and vegetables. Cut down on red meat consumption as much possible. Many heart patients have found it helpful to cut out meat altogether. A good diet will help prevent diabetes, too. Looking at your chart, I see that your parents have diabetes. I'd try changing your diet and exercising, for starters.

Ivan: That sounds like work, but I think I'd like to try that.

Dr. Singh: Ivan, prevention is much better than a cure any day. I like the idea that you want to get ahold of this before it becomes a problem, and you know that that'll take a little bit of work on your part.

Ivan: But it'll be worth it.

Dr. Singh: Absolutely. Okay, well, I'm going to write you up for a cholesterol blood draw in three months. That'll give you a chance to get started on your new program. Call me when you've had the blood test and we'll see where we are.

Ivan: Thank you, Doctor.

Dr. Singh: You're welcome. See you next time.

F. PRACTICE

Fill in the blanks with the following words: *battery of tests, upfront, remedy, second opinion, diagnosis, alternative medicine, chiropractic care, preventive care, internist, blood drawn*

1. _____ might be the best thing to help you with your back problem.

2. I'd like to have some _____ in order to check the level of iron in your blood.

3. Now that you're older, you might to consider seeing a(n) _____ instead of just a general practitioner.

4. _____ can make a difference in controlling diseases before they become a problem.

5. Some people turn to _____ to supplement their treatment through traditional Western medicine.

6. They ran a(n) _____ to figure out what the problem was.

7. What's the best _____ for a sore throat?

8. So, after all of those tests, what's the _____, doctor?

9. Please be _____ about my condition. I'm not afraid to hear the truth.

10. You're welcome to get a(n) _____, but I suspect that most doctors will agree with my diagnosis.

Decide whether each of the following sentences is written correctly. If it isn't, rewrite it. There may be more than one correct answer.

1. You need to do your homework to find not only a good doctor but also one that suits your needs.
2. You must be not afraid to ask questions.
3. It used to be that patients didn't ask no questions.
4. Looking for a doctor in the yellow pages is not the best way to find a good doctor.
5. I'd rather not take nothing for it.
6. The doctor isn't in, isn't he?
7. I can't take no medicine for three days.
8. You can't take any aspirin prior to or during treatment.
9. Seldom eats he vegetables.
10. Your cholesterol levels are not as low as they should be.

G. TASK

Fill out as much as you can of the sample patient information form that you saw in the English Close-Up section.

Medical Reference Information				
Previous Surgeries		Medical Illnesses		
Allergies to Medication		Present Medication		
Referring Physician and Address		Family Doctor and Address		
Is this illness or injury employment related?	Date of injury	Is condition related to an auto accident?	Date	If so, name of Auto Insurance Company
Insurance Information				
Name and address of Insurance Company	ID number	Group number	Subscriber's name number	Soc. Sec. number

H. REAL LIFE

Dear Sammy,

My uncle Michael just moved to the United States from Russia and his English is not so good. He's diabetic, so he needs to see the doctor on a regular basis. We were wondering how we could find a doctor that speaks Russian. We've taken him to the Clinic for Adult Specialties and it seems like most of the doctors are from other countries too, but so far no Russian doctors. With his poor English and some of the doctors' heavy accents, he's finding it very difficult to explain things to them and it's even harder for him to understand them. Please don't say that we should send a family member with him. We all try to go with him whenever we can, but we can't always be there. What do you suggest?

Thank you,
Michael's Niece

Dear Niece,

You are right. There are more and more foreign doctors in American clinics and hospitals. Their English is good, but they do often have accents, and this can cause problems for all patients, not just the foreign born. Actually, your uncle's problem is a common one. If there's no one to translate for him, he could try asking the doctor to speak more slowly, but all you really have to do is tell the receptionist that your uncle needs an interpreter when you call to make your appointment. The clinic will arrange for an interpreter to come in. Sometimes a nurse or a receptionist might speak the language needed. If not, the clinic will hire an interpreter to come in and interpret for your uncle. There is no need to be concerned about misinterpretations; interpreters must go through very rigorous training and become state certified before they can work as interpreters for doctors' offices, hospitals, or clinics. They have to be familiar with all the idioms in both languages and know all the subtle little nuances of both English and the second language. For example, I know an interpreter who is originally from Colombia. Because she works in California, she often interprets for Mexicans and Central Americans, so she had to learn the idioms of other countries as well as English idioms. So don't worry, your uncle will be well cared for at no extra cost to him.

Good luck!
Sammy

I. RESOURCES

How to choose a good health care provider:
www.nlm.nih.gov/medlineplus/choosingadoctororhealthcareservice.html

Agency for Healthcare Research and Quality (part of the U.S. Department of Health and Human Services):
www.ahcpr.gov/CONSUMER

U.S. Department of Health and Human Services at www.hhs.gov or 1-877-696-6775

Locate a doctor:
webapps.ama-assn.org/doctorfinder/home.html
doctor.webmd.com/physician_finder
www.docboard.org

The American Board of Medical Specialties at www.ambs.org or 1-800-733-2267

The American Medical Association (AMA) at www.ama-assn.org or 1-800-621-8335

ANSWER KEY
Practice 1: 1. Chiropractic care; 2. blood drawn; 3. internist; 4. preventive medicine; 5. alternative medicine; 6. battery of tests; 7. remedy; 8. diagnosis; 9. upfront; 10. second opinion

Practice 2: 1. Correct. 2. You must not be afraid to ask questions. 3. It used to be that patients didn't ask any questions. / It used to be that patients asked no questions. 4. Correct. 5. I'd rather not take anything for it. / I'd rather take nothing for it. 6. The doctor isn't in, is he? / The doctor is in, isn't he? 7. I can't take any medicine for three days. / I can take no medicine for three days. 8. Correct. 9. Seldom does he eat vegetables. / He seldom eats vegetables. 10. Correct.

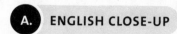
Health and Emergencies: Dentists

A. ENGLISH CLOSE-UP

> **Are You Interested in a Career as a Dental Hygienist?**
> Do you enjoy helping others and working closely with
> people from all walks of life to keep them healthy and happy?
> Then you'd be a great dental hygienist!
>
> The skill and care of a dental hygienist is an essential part of any dentist's
> office. Dental hygienists assist the dentist in caring for patients in a number
> of procedures, but they also act as motivators and instructors for patients,
> explaining how to maintain oral health and how to get the most out of their
> regular visits to the dentist. A career in dental hygiene is both rewarding
> and interesting. If you see a future for yourself in dental hygiene, call
> Underhill School of Dentistry to find out more about our dental hygienist
> training program. We're waiting to hear from you! **1-800-555-3800**.

B. VOCABULARY ESSENTIALS

Amalgam—A mixture of metals, especially mercury, silver, tin, and copper, used as a tooth filling. *Dentists used to always use amalgam for fillings, but now they may use composite resin instead.*

Braces—A dental appliance made with wires and bands used to straighten teeth. *Many children hate the idea of having to wear braces.*

Bridge—A false tooth connected to two artificial crowns, used to replace a tooth that has been pulled or has fallen out. *After I had to have my tooth pulled, the dentist recommended that I get a bridge.*

Cavity (dental caries)—A hole in the tooth caused by decay. *If you don't get your teeth checked, you'll never know if you have any cavities until you get a toothache.*

Cleaning—A regularly scheduled dental appointment where the hygienist cleans and polishes the teeth, often followed by X rays checking for cavities. *It's been six months since my last cleaning, so I'd better schedule another one.*

Composite resin dental fillings—Tooth fillings made of plastic resin that are colored like natural teeth. *If we use composite resin to fill your tooth, you won't even be able to tell you have a filling.*

Crown—A natural crown is the part of the tooth covered by enamel. An artificial crown is one made to replace a natural crown that has decayed too much for simple fillings. *Many people start needing crowns on their teeth when they hit middle age.*

Dental floss—A thread used to clean between the teeth. *Use dental floss every night to clean between your teeth and to help keep your gums strong.*

Dental hygienist—A trained professional who assists the dentist, especially with cleaning and polishing patients' teeth. *The dental hygienist offered me a new toothbrush after she cleaned and flossed my teeth.*

Dental plaque—A film, composed mostly of bacteria, that builds up on teeth and that needs to be cleaned off regularly. *Brushing, flossing, and gargling with mouthwash can all help remove plaque.*

Enamel—The white outer layer of the teeth. *Brushing too hard can damage your enamel.*

Fluoride—A chemical element that helps prevent tooth decay. *In some places, fluoride is added to drinking water to help prevent cavities.*

Gingivitis—An inflammation of the gums that can lead to periodontal disease. *Gums infected with gingivitis are red and swollen.*

Gums—The pink flesh around the teeth. *Bleeding gums are often a sign of dental problems.*

Orthodontics (orthodontia)—The practice of straightening the teeth and aligning the jaw, often by using braces. An orthodontist is a dentist who specializes in orthodontics. *All of our children will need orthodontic treatment because they all have crooked teeth.*

Pediatric dentist—A dentist who specializes in the care and treatment of children's teeth. *Dr. Lewis is one of the best pediatric dentists around.*

Periodontal disease—An infection in the gums and the bones that hold your teeth in place. *Massaging your gums can help you fight periodontal disease in the early stages.*

Retainer—A dental appliance used to hold teeth in place after braces have been removed. *The orthodontist said I had to wear my retainer every night to keep my teeth straight.*

Receding gums—A condition in which the gums move away from the teeth. *Receding gums may be a sign that you're not brushing correctly.*

Root canal—A dental surgical procedure in which the inner part (pulp) of the tooth is replaced with filling, used when decay or infection is advanced. *"Root canal" is often the last thing a patient wants to hear from the dentist.*

Sealant—A thin layer of resin applied to children's molars to help prevent decay. *Sealant can save you a lot of money and your children a lot of tooth decay.*

Sweet tooth—A desire to eat sweets often. *You have a real sweet tooth, judging by the amount of candy on your desk!*

Tooth decay—The rotting of teeth caused by bacteria. *Brush and floss your teeth to help prevent tooth decay.*

Tooth extraction—The act of pulling a tooth out of the mouth. *Can you come in on Wednesday at 3:10 for your tooth extraction?*

Wisdom teeth—The four backmost molars, which are the last to appear as a child approaches early adulthood. *Many people have to have some or all of their wisdom teeth taken out because they grow in the wrong direction and displace other teeth.*

 ## GRAMMAR ESSENTIALS: *LIE/LAY, SIT/SET, RISE/RAISE*

The verbs *lie* and *lay, sit* and *set,* and *rise* and *raise* are confusing to both native and nonnative speakers of English. In each of these three pairs, the first is intransitive and the second is transitive. So only the transitive verbs *lay, set,* and *raise* take direct objects. The intransitive verbs *lie, sit,* and *rise* cannot take direct objects.

Of the three pairs, *lie* and *lay* are the most confusing and most often mixed up, in fact, very commonly, even by native speakers. This may be due to the past tense of *lie* being the same as the present tense of *lay. Lie* (lie, lying, lay, lain) means "to recline, to put oneself in a horizontal position." *Lay* (lay, laying, laid, laid) means "to place something down in a horizontal position":

> *Every Saturday we lie on the beach.*
> *We always lay a towel out on the sand.*
> *Your father is lying down right now.*
> *They're laying out the food for the party.*
> *After I got home I lay right down.*
> *He laid his cards on the table.*
> *You've lain around all day! Get up!*
> *Have they laid down the new flooring yet?*

Keep in mind that with *lie,* the subject is the one that's reclining, while with *lay,* the subject is placing something else in a reclining position. (Think of the vowels to help you remember: *lie* = to recline, *lay* = to place.) But also remember that it's possible to lay oneself down, as a reflexive verb, and the meaning is the same as *lie*. An example in the past tense would be:

> *I lay down for a couple of minutes.*
> *I laid myself down for a couple of minutes.*

There are just two more points to remember. The verb *lay* is also used with chickens, as in "chickens lay eggs." And don't confuse either of these verbs with *to lie*, meaning "to fail to tell the truth." That's a regular verb with the forms *lie, lying, lied,* and *lied*.

The verbs *sit* and *set* are confused much less commonly than *lie* and *lay*. *Sit* (sit, sitting, sat, sat) means "to take a seat," and *set* (set, setting, set, set) means "to place an object down, either vertically or horizontally":

> *We sit on the porch in the evenings.*
> *Before I go to bed I set my reading glasses down on the nightstand.*
> *I'm sitting up in the front row.*
> *The hygienist is setting out the dentist's instruments.*
> *They sat in the waiting room for hours.*
> *I set all of the name tags on the desk.*
> *Have you ever sat on a boat at sunrise?*
> *Pam hasn't set those files down all day.*

There are a lot of idiomatic uses of and phrasal or prepositional verbs constructed with *set*:

> *The sun sets in the west.*
> *Set the clock.*
> *Who sets the table?*
> *Have you set a date for the wedding?*
> *Who set the record for the Tour de France?*
> *I set about learning French.*
> *The receptionist set aside my folder and picked up the phone.*
> *This problem will set us back two weeks.*
> *The cold weather set in last week.*
> *We set off fireworks for the Fourth of July.*
> *They set out on their hike at 8:00.*
> *Could you set up the conference room for the presentation?*

Rise (rise, rising, rose, risen) means "to move from a lower to a higher position," and *raise* (raise, raising, raised, raised) means "to lift something up":

> *The sun rises in the sky each morning.*
> *They raise the flag every day.*
> *The temperatures are really rising today!*
> *The construction crane is raising steel girders up to the roof.*
> *The smoke rose high into the sky.*
> *The children all raised their hands.*
> *Have you ever risen so early in the morning?*
> *He's never raised his voice to yell at his kids.*

The verb *raise* has a few other common meanings:
   Parents raise their children.
   Farmers raise cows, chickens, corn, and wheat.
   The Girl Scout troop raised enough money to take a trip to Catalina.

D. HOW-TO

Today's dentists have many tools at their disposal to make a visit to their office as effective and painless as possible. In fact, dentists in the United States hope to prevent as many painful procedures as they can. A good dentist promotes optimum oral health, hoping to prevent dental problems instead of waiting for them to occur. As a result, U.S. dentistry encourages cleanings and checkups at least once if not twice a year. But before you can schedule any appointments, you need to find a dentist that you trust. The first step is very similar to finding a doctor—ask your friends, family members, colleagues, and neighbors. There are also some great resources for finding dentists listed in the Resources section of this lesson. Of course, you also want to make sure that any dentist you visit participates in your dental plan. Dental plans are similar to health care plans, and your employer can help you. If you're not sure whether the dentist accepts your insurance, always ask before you schedule an appointment.

Here's what you can expect during a standard cleaning and checkup. First, the dental hygienist will thoroughly clean your teeth of any plaque that has built up since your last cleaning. The hygienist will also use a probe to check for abnormally deep crevices between your teeth and gum line and might encourage you to massage your gums to decrease any pockets you might have. You will also get your teeth polished and flossed. Once your cleaning is finished, the dentist will come in and check your teeth for cavities. The dentist will also check your gums for any signs of gingivitis or other periodontal diseases. He or she will then probably inspect the inside of your mouth for other irregularities that may indicate medical or dental problems. Throughout this process, both the dentist and the hygienist will chart everything they have done and found in order to establish a history of your dental health.

If the dentist finds any problems, he or she will let you know and will recommend treatments. If you need to have some cavities filled, the dentist may suggest that you choose composite resin over amalgam in order to keep your teeth looking as attractive as possible. A composite filling is the color of teeth and thus will blend in well, unlike the silver color of amalgam. If your dentist doesn't give you this choice, you should speak up, and if you have questions about the benefits of one type or the other, don't be afraid to ask. Also, your dental plan may not cover as much of the cost of the filling if you choose to use a composite filling in certain teeth rather than amalgam, so make sure you're aware of your insurance coverage before choosing a type of filling. If you routinely have cavities, the dentist might suggest a fluoride treatment and will probably encourage you to keep your sweet tooth in check. These suggestions will help prevent more serious problems from developing, such as the need for a root canal, a crown, or a tooth extraction. If one or more of your teeth have to be pulled, the dentist might suggest an implant, a bridge, or both to help fill in for the lost tooth or teeth.

If you have children, you will most likely deal with childhood dental problems. Americans usually have their children's teeth checked for the need for braces early on. With a little preventive care your child might even be able to avoid braces by having certain molars pulled early enough to preclude crowding. But most American children (and some adults) do get braces. It's sort of an American rite of passage. After the braces come off, the dentist will supply retainers. Retainers may be worn for a few years or even at night for the rest of one's life. Most Americans' wisdom teeth are also checked as they begin to grow in, which is usually in adolescence. If there is not enough space or if the wisdom teeth are not growing in properly, the dentist will advise having them removed. Otherwise, they could crowd the mouth and cause teeth to become crooked.

Because many people go for regular checkups and cleanings at their dentist's every six months, they may see more of their dentist than their doctor. It is therefore important to find a dentist that you're comfortable with, and who is good with your kids, if you have any. Even though a lot of people fear the dentist, going for dental appointments doesn't have to be difficult, or awful!

E. ENGLISH IN ACTION

Children are encouraged to have good dental health habits from a young age in the U.S. Let's listen in as Mylo gets his teeth checked. Then we'll hear his pediatric dentist talk to him and his mother about his dental condition.

Dr. Rutgers: Hey, Mylo. Good to see you again. Why don't you just set your dinosaurs on this chair right here? Then, how about if you sit in this chair for me? Good. Now lie back, and I'll lay this chair back so I can look at your teeth.

Mylo: Okay.

Dr. Rutgers: Raise your right hand if it hurts at any time, okay?

Mylo: All right.

Dr. Rutgers: Okay, Mylo, all done. I'm going to raise this chair up, okay? Oh, good, Ms. Feltman, there you are, just in time.

Ms. Feltman: Hello, Dr. Rutgers.

Dr. Rutgers: He's looking good.

Ms. Feltman: Fantastic!

Dr. Rutgers: Well, Mylo, your teeth look pretty good this time. It looks like you've been brushing and flossing better since the last time I saw you.

Mylo: Uh-huh.

Ms. Feltman: So, no cavities?

Dr. Rutgers: Not this time, I'm happy to say.

Mylo: Yeah!

Ms. Feltman: Yes. He's been working very hard to keep his teeth clean. It really helps when the hygienist gives him such cute toothbrushes, too.

Mylo: Yeah, I like the ones with the dinosaurs.

Dr. Rutgers: I recommend that we keep him on the fluoride treatment, and I'd encourage you to think about maybe putting sealants on his teeth.

Ms. Feltman: Sealants?

Mylo: Yeah, what's that?

Dr. Rutgers: Well, Mylo, sealants are stuff we paint on your molars—your back teeth—to help prevent them from getting any decay.

Mylo: Oh.

Ms. Feltman: Well, we'll have to think about it. What about orthodontics?

Dr. Rutgers: Well, he's still a little young for braces, but we'll watch how his teeth grow in. His bite looks pretty good. We might be able to get away with pulling a few teeth and putting him in a retainer for a while.

Ms. Feltman: Really? Wow. Well, keep me posted on that.

Dr. Rutgers: Oh, I definitely will. We want Mylo to keep his nice smile, don't we?

Ms. Feltman: Of course.

Mylo: Yeah.

Dr. Rutgers: Okay, Mylo. I'll see you again in about six months.

Ms. Feltman: Okay. Thank you, Doctor.

Mylo: Okay, bye. Thank you for the balloon!

Dr. Rutgers: You're welcome, Mylo.

F. PRACTICE

Fill in the blanks with the correct forms of the following words: *braces, cavity, crown, to decay, dental floss, orthodontist, sweet tooth, tooth extraction, plaque, retainer*

Mindy Chang went to the dentist because she had a toothache, and she thought she might have a(n) (1) _____. The dentist told her that her tooth had (2) _____ too much, so he couldn't just fill it. She needed a(n) (3) _____. He told her that she was lucky she would be able to keep her tooth, and that there was no need for a(n) (4) _____. The dentist also told her she should use (5) _____ to clean her teeth, because she had a lot of (6) _____ between her teeth. Mindy laughed and said the real problem was that she had a(n) (7) _____ and couldn't stop eating chocolate. The dentist also suggested she see a(n) (8) _____ about getting (9) _____, because her teeth were a little crooked. But Mindy wasn't sure she wanted to wear a(n) (10) _____ every night for the rest of her life.

Fill in the blanks with the correct forms of *lie, lay, sit, set, rise,* or *raise.* There may be more than one correct answer.

1. I saw a beautiful orange tabby cat _____ in the sun.
2. What time does the sun _____ in the morning?
3. There's a chair for you. Go _____ down and relax.
4. If you feel any pain at all, _____ your hand.
5. I need to get up. I've _____ on the couch all morning!
6. _____ the instruments down on this tray so the doctor can easily get to them.
7. Why don't you _____ down and take a nap?
8. If you're standing, you'd better _____ down to hear this story.
9. If you leave the food _____ around out of the fridge, it will spoil!
10. Take the dishes out of the dishwasher and _____ them out on a paper towel to dry.

G. TASK

Talk to your friends or your employers or use one of the resources listed in this lesson to find two or three dentists in your area. Find out whether they accept your insurance plan, are members of the American Dental Association (ADA), speak any other languages, have flexible hours for appointments, and so on. Think of a few other questions that are important to you and your family as well and try to find answers.

H. REAL LIFE

Dear Sammy,

I came to this country more than fifteen years ago with my husband. We've raised three children here, and now our oldest daughter is in high school. She's a very sweet girl, and while she's very much an American teenager, she tries to stay involved with the culture of her parents and her relatives overseas. But lately she's been pushing my husband and me to pay to have her teeth whitened. For some reason, she's ashamed of her smile. She has a lovely smile! But I don't seem to be able to change her mind. She's convinced that she needs cosmetic dentistry to be as pretty as the other girls in her high school. What should I do?

Signed,
All Smiles

Dear All Smiles,

You're certainly not the only parent who doesn't see cosmetic alteration in quite the same way as your child. Many Americans put a lot of emphasis on beauty by having face-lifts, liposuction, hair implants, and so on. Now cosmetic dentistry is rising in popularity, too. Among the many popular cosmetic dental products are veneers, implants, fixed bridges, bonding, gum lifts, and yes, teeth whitening.

Many people who have stained or discolored teeth are choosing to have their teeth whitened using bleaching products. There are several types of teeth whitening techniques. The ones that last the longest can be quite expensive, but none of these offer permanent solutions. Those who want permanently white teeth may opt for veneers, which are custom-made laminates that are affixed directly onto the teeth. The procedure can be rather expensive, anywhere from $250 to $2,500 per tooth, depending on the type of veneer.

None of this answers your question, of course. What should you do? Well, that's really up to you. Some people think it's extravagant to spend a lot of money on cosmetic dentistry, and other people ask how you can put a price on a beautiful smile. Your daughter may grow out of her need to have the brightest smile around, or if she's really ashamed of her smile, she may develop other problems as she matures. I can't answer your question for you, but I can tell you that your daughter is not the only kid in America who wants a perfect smile. The best thing to do is to find out about the options—including costs—and sit down and talk to her about them.

Good luck!
Sammy

I. **RESOURCES**

How to choose a dentist:
www.qualitydentistry.com/consumer.html

Find a dentist:
www.ada.org/public/directory/index.asp
www.1800dentist.com or 1-800-DEN-TIST
www.dentists.com

American Dental Association:
www.ada.org or 1-312-440-2500

Dental insurance information and plan comparisons:
www.ada.org/public/topics/insurance_faq.asp
www.dentalplans.com
www.dentalinsurance.com

Cosmetic dentistry:
www.nlm.nih.gov/medlineplus/cosmeticdentistry.html

ANSWER KEY
Practice 1: 1. cavity; 2. decayed; 3. crown; 4. tooth extraction; 5. dental floss; 6. plaque; 7. sweet tooth; 8. orthodontist; 9. braces; 10. retainer

Practice 2: 1. lying; 2. rise; 3. sit; 4. raise; 5. lain/been lying; 6. Set/Lay; 7. lie; 8. sit; 9. lying; 10. lay

CHAPTER 21

Health and Emergencies: 911, Emergency

A. ENGLISH CLOSE-UP

Emergencies: 911

Police: 419-555-6300

Fire: 419-555-4900

Crestview Memorial Hospital: 419-555-6000

Laurel Ridge Emergency Medical Center: 419-555-3232

Poison Control: 1-800-555-1222

Animal Control: 419-555-9035

Dr. Heller: 419-555-8282

Eastlake Dental Associates: 419-555-9700

ABC Veterinary Hospital: 419-555-6324

Emergency Preparedness Kit:

2 gallons water, 2 boxes granola bars, 2 boxes instant oatmeal, 2 boxes instant soup, 1 bag dried fruit, 16 oz. apple juice, 1 radio, 6 AA batteries, 2 flashlights, 4 C batteries, first aid kit, 8 oz. disinfectant

B. VOCABULARY ESSENTIALS

Baby-proof—Made safe for a baby or toddler. *Could you put some baby-proof fasteners on the cabinets? I've already moved the knives and other sharp things.*

Blizzard—A long and heavy snowstorm, often with a lot of wind, that results in very hazardous conditions. *You should never get in your car if you know a blizzard is coming.*

Blackout—A period when there is no electricity over a large area. *Remember that blackout a couple of years ago? I had to walk for four hours just to get home and then I had to walk up twenty-five flights of stairs because nothing was working without electricity.*

To black out—To lose consciousness. *I must have blacked out during the accident, because I don't remember anything after skidding off the road.*

Cardiac arrest—Heart attack. *The victim was in cardiac arrest when the ambulance arrived.*

Coma—A state of deep unconsciousness that can last for a long time, caused by a serious injury or illness, or by a drug or poison. *Troy survived the car accident, but he was in a coma for several weeks.*

Common sense—Natural good judgment, knowing what is best to do in any situation. *During any emergency, using your common sense can save you and your loved ones.*

Concussion (of the brain)—A bad head injury that can lead to altered brain function, such as loss of consciousness, confusion, etc. *If you hit your head hard enough, it's possible to get a concussion.*

CPR (cardiopulmonary resuscitation)—A combination of cardiac (heart) massage, artificial respiration, and drugs, used to restart a heart that has stopped beating. *The paramedics used CPR to get Mr. Ruiz's heart beating normally and saved his life.*

Defibrillator—A device used to give an electric shock to the heart muscle to restore normal beating. *Many public places now carry portable defibrillators.*

Earthquake—Violent shaking of the earth caused by natural movements in the Earth's crust. *California, Japan, Turkey, Iran, and Indonesia are just some of the places that experience many earthquakes.*

Emergency dispatch operator (911 operator)—A person who answers 911 calls. *When Eddie called 911, the emergency dispatch operator asked for his address and details about the emergency.*

EMS (Emergency Medical Services)—The group of people medically trained to respond to emergencies, including paramedics and emergency medical technicians (EMTs), among others. *EMS arrived at the scene of the accident minutes after it happened.*

To evacuate, an evacuation—To leave a building or area during an emergency or before a disaster. *Have an evacuation plan in place in case you need to evacuate your home in a hurry.*

First responders—People who are the first to arrive at the scene of an emergency, such as police, paramedics, and firefighters. *First responders often put their lives on the line to help rescue others.*

Hazard—A danger, something that can cause accidents or injury. *If your home is flooded, all electrical appliances become hazards.*

Hurricane—A huge and powerful tropical storm involving very high winds, torrential rain, and coastal flooding, centered around an "eye," which is an area of very low pressure. Called typhoons or cyclones in other parts of the world. *Residents of Florida, the Gulf Coast, Georgia, and the Carolinas deal with hurricanes every year.*

Hygiene—Practices that promote cleanliness and sanitary conditions. *Don't forget to teach your children good hygiene to help prevent any unnecessary health problems.*

Hypothermia—Body temperature below normal. *If you're exposed to cold water for long enough, you'll begin to suffer from hypothermia.*

Leak—A break or tear that allows a liquid or gas to escape. *Do you think there's a leak in the pipes?*

On hand—Easy to find, nearby, available. *Most people keep canned food on hand in case of an emergency.*

Overdose—The physical reaction to taking too much of something, such as a medication or drug. *Many young people die each year from drug or alcohol overdoses.*

Paramedic—A person trained to provide emergency medical care, those at the most advanced level of training for emergency medical technicians. *When Mike fell from the tree, the paramedics warned us not to try to move him in case he had injured his spine.*

Poison Control Center—An emergency call center that people contact in case of accidental exposure to a poison. Experts guide callers on what to do, including calling an ambulance or going to the hospital if necessary. *After Mindy walked into the kitchen and saw that her toddler had gotten into the cleaning supply cabinet, she frantically called the Poison Control Center.*

Potable—Drinkable. *There's often a lack of potable water after disasters, so it's essential that individual families keep their own emergency supplies.*

Shock—Medically, a very serious and potentially fatal physical response to trauma or severe illness, involving loss of blood pressure, lower rate of circulation, and decreased blood flow. *Danny was talking for a while after the accident, but suddenly he went into shock.*

Smoke inhalation—A serious condition resulting from breathing in smoke, characterized by difficulty breathing, choking, coughing, upset stomach or vomiting, confusion, or even death. *Experts estimate that 50–80% of all deaths during fires are caused by smoke inhalation.*

Storm surge—An increase in sea level from a few feet to thirty feet or more, caused when a landfalling hurricane pushes up the ocean surface ahead of it. *Even though the winds of a hurricane are terrible, most deaths and destruction are the result of storm surges.*

Twister—Another name for a tornado, a very destructive funnel-shaped column of winds moving as quickly as two hundred miles per hour or more. *There were reports of twisters all throughout Texas and Oklahoma.*

Toxic—Poisonous, able to cause death or serious injury. *Carbon monoxide is a highly toxic gas that is colorless and odorless.*

C. GRAMMAR ESSENTIALS: COMMANDS

Emergencies are a good example of a situation in which you're likely to hear commands. As you know, a command is the basic form of the verb:

> *Shut all doors during a fire.*
> *Call 911 right away if you see an accident!*

Negative commands are formed with *do not* or *don't* plus the bare verb. *Don't* is more common, but *do not* is used when *not* is given special emphasis:

> *Don't leave now—we're supposed to have a blizzard!*
> *If you think he has injured his neck or back, do not try to move him!*

Commands are usually addressed to one or more other people, in other words, in the second person singular or plural, or *you*. However, it's also possible to give a command or make a suggestion in the first person (*we*) or third person (*he, she*). For first-person commands or suggestions, use *let's* or *let us* in the affirmative, or *let's not* or *let us not* in the negative:

> *A twister's coming! Let's get out of here!*
> *Let's not be caught unaware by an emergency; let's prepare.*

Third person commands or suggestions in English are possible with *let* as well. The negative, *let . . . not*, has the meaning of a (strong) wish or plea:

> *If he can't drive in this weather, let him walk home.*
> *After we called the paramedics, we kept thinking, let there not be any traffic!*

In emergency situations, simple commands are to be expected. But in everyday situations, commands are usually softened in English with *please, could you, would you mind, try to, don't forget to,* etc.:

> *Please pass me the butter.*
> *Could you open the window? It's getting warm in here.*
> *Would you mind helping me with these dishes?*
> *Try to be home on time!*
> *Don't forget to pick up your sister on your way home.*

Commands can be made more emphatic or personal with the use of *you*:

> *You keep his legs steady, and you help me lift this off of him.*

It's also possible to address commands to names or pronouns like *nobody, somebody,* etc.:

> *Ray, keep her from blacking out!*
> *Nobody go on the ice—it's too thin!*
> *Somebody help, please!*

D. HOW-TO

Although you cannot always prevent emergencies, you can minimize their effects by being prepared. One of the first things you can do is follow general safety guidelines. You should have smoke and carbon monoxide detectors as well as fire extinguishers in your home. Make sure you are aware of potential hazards (falling objects, fire, or gas leaks) and that you keep important family documents in fireproof and waterproof containers, have first aid kits, and have one or more people in your house who know CPR. You can find CPR classes at www.redcross.org/services/hss/courses.

It's also important to have emergency numbers on hand and know when to call 911. The 911 operator is available 24 hours a day to take emergency phone calls and will direct your call to the appropriate emergency response system. Sometimes the emergency response system is very busy, but don't hang up if it is. Stay on the line until you are connected to an operator, and be sure your situation is truly an emergency. 911 is a phone line dedicated to emergencies only, so do not call if you do not have a life-threatening emergency. However, if you think you truly have a life-threatening emergency, don't hesitate to call 911. Emergency paramedic services are taxpayer supported. Paramedics are trained in emergency assistance and will be able to determine whether you should be transported to the hospital or not. For more information on calling 911, see the Real Life section of this lesson.

As mentioned in Lesson 19, the emergency room is not the only place to go in the event of a sudden medical problem. You can also go to urgent care if your emergency is not life-threatening, for example, a small dog bite, a broken arm, or a bad cut that might need stitches but isn't too serious. Urgent care hours often go beyond the normal office hours of most doctors' offices, usually 10:00 a.m.–10:00 p.m., and occasionally urgent care centers are even open 24 hours. As long as you don't have a serious medical condition, urgent care centers can be a better choice than the emergency room. Although insurance covers emergency care, you may have to pay a large co-pay if you are admitted to the hospital, while urgent care will only require your minimum co-pay. The wait in the emergency room could take several hours just to see the doctor, but you are likely to be seen and treated within an hour or so at an urgent care center. But for anything life-threatening, the emergency room is much better equipped to handle serious emergencies. If you do need to go to the emergency room, you will first fill out the necessary medical consent and insurance forms (provided you are able) and then you will be triaged, or sorted into a level of priority based on your symptoms. The more serious your health emergency, the more quickly you will be seen by a doctor, because emergency rooms operate on a patient-need basis rather than a first come, first served basis.

Besides medical emergencies, another reason to call 911 is if you are the victim of or have witnessed criminal acts. Again, 911 should only be called if you think there is a threat to life—for example, if you know that a thief has a weapon. If it's something like seeing your neighbors' house being burglarized when you know they are not at home, call the local police. (Every neighborhood has a precinct that should be relatively close to your home.) It can sometimes be difficult to assess the level of danger, so if you are uncertain, call 911. Whichever you do, you will need to supply the address where the emergency need exists. You will also need to describe the emergency by telling the 911 operator, whether, for example, someone has had a heart attack or been attacked or if there was a car accident involving serious injury. Once the police arrive, you will need to supply a statement about what you have witnessed. The officer will give you his or her name, badge number, and a phone number where he or she can be reached in case you have more information or need an update. If you yourself are the victim of a crime, in certain situations you may need to think about contacting your insurance provider. If someone has stolen something from your home and/or broken into your house (and also if there has been a fire in your home), you can contact your homeowner's or renter's insurance agency to file a report. If your car has been stolen, you will need to contact your auto insurance company to place a claim. However, if something of value has been stolen from your car, your homeowner's or renter's insurance company may also be called to see if you can get more complete insurance coverage. You will need to file a claim in either case if you have lost something valuable and you want to be compensated for it. Try asking for the claims department or wait for the prompt for filing a claim. The agent will ask you some questions and fill out the claim for you by phone. The insurance company may mail or fax paperwork to you for your records or signature. You will be given a claim number, which you should copy down and keep handy because you will need it whenever you call about your claim.

In addition to medical and criminal emergencies, fire, smoke, and carbon monoxide (CO) are also safety concerns. Your home should have smoke detectors in or near every room, and they should be tested once a month. One way to do this is to push the "test" button to see if the alarm goes off. Better yet, light a match, blow it out, and hold it up to the smoke alarm. If the alarm sounds, you'll know it's working. It might be a good idea to purchase a carbon monoxide detector as well, and in some areas, it is the law to have one. Carbon monoxide is a potentially fatal, colorless and odorless gas that comes from equipment that burns fuels, such as fireplaces, furnaces, cars, gas stoves, etc. You can usually find both types of alarms (and alarms that detect both smoke and carbon monoxide) at a hardware store. Smoke alarms should be installed on the ceiling, and CO detectors based on the manufacturer's instructions. Batteries should be replaced annually. For more information on carbon monoxide and smoke detector requirements and guidelines, check with your local fire department. Smoke detectors go off when there's smoke in the home, and CO detectors sound an alarm when too much CO is in the air. When you hear a smoke detector, be sure that it isn't just excess smoke from cooking. If something in your house has caught fire, you should call 911 even if you have put the fire out. The fire department needs to check your home to be sure there are no burning cinders anywhere that you are unaware of. If your CO alarm goes off, you need to open the windows and get everyone out into the fresh air. If anyone in your home has symptoms of carbon monoxide poisoning, which are flu-like symptoms, call 911. You should have a qualified technician come out to check for any leaks. In addition to a CO leak, another similar and serious danger is a natural gas leak. Like CO, natural gas is odorless, colorless, and highly explosive. Because there's no odor, an unappealing scent that smells like rotten eggs is added to gas so that you can smell it when it leaks. Again, open all the windows, leave the house, and call both 911 and your gas and electric company, because an untended gas leak is a serious issue.

Carbon monoxide detectors and smoke alarms help prevent many potential disasters. Similarly, the effects of such large-scale disasters as natural disasters or epidemics are minimized by warning systems that many communities have in place. If there is a natural disaster or other large-scale emergency, you will probably hear warning sirens. If you hear a loud siren, turn on your radio or TV for information about what to do and where to go.

There will always be emergencies, but the threat to life can be mitigated through proper emergency and disaster preparedness. The most important thing you can do in any disaster situation is to have a plan in place and to prepare a disaster supply kit. To prepare a kit yourself, see www.ready.gov/america/index.html, or you can purchase one already prepared for you at an organization dedicated to disaster assistance like the Red Cross, which you can visit at www.redcross.org. Regardless of the emergency, your disaster supply kit should be all-purpose. Water is essential, one gallon a day per person for 72 hours, or three days. A can opener and enough canned food for 72 hours, disinfectants, a first aid kit, a flashlight with extra batteries, a portable radio, blankets, clothing, shoes, and cash are the other most important items. In addition to a kit, you should have an emergency plan in place. Think about where you and your family members will meet if you get separated. Find addresses of two or three places you can go in case of an emergency, for example, a motel or a friend or family member's house. Figure out what will be your best escape routes. Practice escape drills. It's always a good idea to know what types of disasters are the most likely to occur in your part of the country, because what you do will probably vary depending on the type of emergency. However, we're going to provide a general overview of various disasters and how best to prepare for them.

If your area is prone to earthquakes, know how to shut off gas, water, and electricity at the source. Check to be sure your house is bolted to the foundation. Secure the water heater, large appliances, and large furniture to the wall. During an earthquake, the greatest danger is from falling objects, so if you are indoors, stay indoors and try to get under a heavy table or desk or stand close to interior walls. Do not stand near windows, mirrors, hanging objects, fireplaces, or tall, unanchored furniture. If you are outdoors, go to an open area away from trees or electrical lines. If you are driving, stop your car and pull over. Stay in your car, and stay away from overpasses. After the earthquake, check for cracks, gas leaks, and water leaks. Turn on your radio and wait for instructions. Additionally, if you live in an area that tends to have a good amount of earthquakes, you might want to consider buying earthquake insurance.

If you live in an area where flash flooding can occur, it is important to listen to your local radio station during rainstorms to know whether you're in danger. If you live in a flood zone, move to higher ground when there's a possibility of flooding. Otherwise, use your common sense, secure your home, and move essentials to a higher level. If instructed to do so, turn off your utilities at the main valve. Disconnect any electrical appliances, being careful not to touch them if you are wet. If you feel you must leave home, do not walk in moving water, and do not drive into flooded areas. If you do, get out of your car and move to higher ground. After the flooding has stopped, be sure to avoid drinking the water until you know it's safe. If you live in a flood zone, you might want to get flood insurance. In some places, flood insurance is not optional; you have to buy it when you live in a flood zone.

During a hurricane, unless you live in a coastal or low area, you may not be asked to evacuate. Therefore, it is important to secure your house as much as possible from wind entry, focusing on the roof, roof straps, shutters, doors, and garage doors. Decide which areas of your house are safest, usually interior rooms away from windows and glass doors. Do not go outside, and have your disaster supply kit with you during a hurricane. After the hurricane, listen to the radio for instructions about going outside and community shelter openings, if necessary.

If you're at home when a tornado strikes, either move to a shelter nearby or go into your basement if you have one. Otherwise, go into an interior hallway or room on the lowest floor and get under some very sturdy furniture. Stay away from windows. If you are in a car, get out and try to find shelter in a building nearby. Don't try to outrun a tornado with your car, and if you live in a mobile home, get out. Mobile homes offer no protection from tornadoes. Turn on your radio to listen for further instructions.

If you are preparing for or recovering from large-scale emergencies such as these, you may want to think about contacting or learning more about existing public emergency programs and organizations. Emergency organizations include the Red Cross, the Salvation Army, and Habitat for Humanity. Every community has plans for epidemics, floods, and evacuations. To find out what they are, look up the information on your city's website or at your local library. To find your community's public health plans in case of an epidemic or other public health emergency, go to www.apha.org/public_health/state.htm and find your own community's health department. If you need a support group or want to contact an organization for victims of criminal acts, the Office for Victims of Crime; www.ojp.usdoj.gov/ovc/help/welcome.html will direct you to victim support groups in your area. Also, don't forget about the federal government's agency for disaster assistance, FEMA, or Federal Emergency Management Agency.

E. ENGLISH IN ACTION

Samantha and George have been listening to the news about the big hurricanes that have hit the country. Let's listen in as they talk about being prepared for emergencies.

Samantha: George, with all these hurricanes this country's been getting, it makes me think that we should prepare ourselves for any emergencies. Do you think I'm overreacting?

George: No, absolutely not. My mother always said you should be prepared for anything.

Samantha: Well, of course. Your mother's right. After all, she was the one who told us about baby-proofing our house when the kids were little, and I'm so glad we took her advice. Joey was always trying to get into the cabinet where we kept all our cleaning supplies. It's a good thing we put locks on all the cabinets where we kept anything toxic. And thank goodness she reminded us to put the kitchen knives way out of reach. I still shudder to think what could have happened. . . .
Whew . . . Okay, so where should we start?

George: Well, let's just see what the Red Cross or some other emergency organization recommends. I'll check online. Hmm. It says here that we should have an emergency kit filled with food, water, blankets, etc. And we need to keep a supply of bottled water on hand.

Samantha: This website says we should get smoke detectors, which we have, and check them annually. It looks like we need to get some CO detectors, as well. It says they shouldn't be within five feet of anything that burns fuel, like a fireplace.

George: You know, I should check our fire extinguishers, too. They might need refilling.

Samantha: And we do get tornadoes occasionally in our area, so maybe we should think of a plan so we know exactly what to do in case one comes.

George: Yeah, that's definitely a good idea. You know, we do have that bathroom in the basement. It's away from windows and down below the house. Maybe that could be our tornado "safe room," and we could keep a disaster supplies kit there.

Samantha: That sounds like a good plan to me! Hey, maybe I should take a CPR course. Isn't that a good idea? I bet your mom would agree with me. Why don't we take one together?

George: Isn't one of us enough?

Samantha: Well, what if I need CPR? Besides, we could practice on each other rather than have to do mouth-to-mouth on a dummy or another classmate.

George: Oh, I hadn't thought of that. You know, sign me up, too.

Samantha: Okay, I'll sign us up right now. How's next Tuesday around 7:30?

F. PRACTICE

Fill in the blanks with the following words: *common sense, paramedics, emergency dispatch operator, evacuate, hazards, hygiene, on hand, concussion, toxic, blackout*

1. You'll have to give an address to the _____ when you call 911.

2. That was a terrible _____. The whole city didn't have electricity for three full days.

3. When the _____ arrived at the accident, they began to give CPR and treat the wounded.

4. There are many unknown _____ during a flood, like potential for electrical shock, rushing water, and sinkholes.

5. When Gordon was thrown from his bike, he hit his head on a tree and got a(n) _____.

6. One of the easiest ways to help prevent infectious diseases from spreading is through proper _____.

7. Your best protection during emergencies and natural disasters is not to panic and to use _____.

8. When powerful hurricanes are coming, many coastal residents are told to _____.

9. House fires generate _____ gases, as well as fire and smoke dangers.

10. It's a good idea to have canned foods and bottled water _____ in case of emergencies.

Let's see how well you remember earthquake preparedness. Match the two parts of the commands below by writing the corresponding letter to each number in the blank.

1. Know how to _____	a. interior walls.
2. Be sure _____	b. an open area away from trees and electrical lines.
3. Do not _____	c. shut off the gas, water, and electricity at the source.
4. Turn on _____	d. stand near windows, mirrors or heavy furniture.
5. Check for _____	e. your house is bolted to the foundation.
6. Go to _____	f. your car.
7. Stay in _____	g. a heavy table or desk.
8. Stay away from _____	h. your radio and wait for instructions.
9. Get under _____	i. cracks, gas leaks, and water leaks.
10. Stand close to _____	j. overpasses.

G. TASK

Make an Emergency List similar to the one that you saw in the English Close-Up section.

Emergencies: 911
Police:
Fire:
Hospital:
Emergency Medical Center:
Poison Control:
Animal Control:
Doctor:
Dentist:
Veterinary Hospital:
Emergency Supplies Kit:

H. REAL LIFE

Hi, I'm Pauline, a 911 operator. The 911 operator service is very important to the safety of this country and its citizens, so it's important that everyone living in the U.S. understand when and when not to use it. 911 should only be used for life-threatening emergencies, such as fires, health emergencies like heart attacks, strokes, etc., and police emergencies that involve dangerous weapons or explosives. While it's true that you may not know whether something is life-threatening or not, when it comes to these types of emergencies, it's usually best to call 911. If you know that a situation is not a life-threatening emergency, call your local police operator instead of 911. You can find that number in the front of your telephone book. The reason we ask people to do this is because 911 emergency lines can get so busy that people may have to wait several minutes to get through to an operator. In the time it takes to get connected to an operator, lives can be lost.

Of course, sometimes people mistakenly dial 911 when they don't mean to. This could happen if an area code is similar to 911, or even when children are playing with telephones. If this ever happens to you, you should apologize and explain to the operator that it was a mistake. Otherwise, an officer may be sent to your location to make sure there's no emergency. There are also things called phantom 911 calls, like when a cell phone is bumped, and the number 9 is pressed, and then 911 is automatically dialed. This is a serious problem across the country that diverts 911 resources. And believe it or not, some people even intentionally call 911 as a prank, or as a way to divert police attention from another area where they want to commit a crime. Of course, we're working to address all of these problems to cut down on the volume of unnecessary 911 calls, but please help us by doing your part. Only dial 911 for a true emergency situation.

I. RESOURCES

Information on 911 for kids:
www.kidshealth.org/kid/watch/er/911.html

Information about home medical emergencies:
www.health.harvard.edu/fhg/firstaid/firstaid.shtml

Office for Victims of Crime:
www.ojp.usdoj.gov/ovc/ovcres/welcome.html or 1-800-851-3420

Federal Emergency Management Agency:
www.fema.org or 1-800-621-3362

Emergency preparedness:
www.bt.cdc.gov (from the Centers for Disease Control and Prevention)
www.hhs.gov/disasters (from the U.S. Department of Health and Human Services)

Red Cross:
www.redcross.org

Habitat for Humanity:
www.habitat.org

Natural disasters:
www.spc.noaa.gov/faq/tornado (tornadoes)
www.nhc.noaa.gov (hurricanes)
earthquake.usgs.gov/regional/neic (earthquakes)
www.fema.gov/areyouready/flood.shtm (floods)
www.spc.noaa.gov (National Weather Service, for general storm tracking and information)

Worker safety:
www.osha.gov/SLTC/emergencypreparedness

Poison Control:
www.poison.org (for information) and 1-800-222-1222 (for poison emergencies)

Local health departments:
www.apha.org/public_health/state.htm

National Response Center, Toxic Chemical and Oil Spills:
1-800-424-8802

ANSWER KEY
Practice 1: 1. emergency dispatch operator; 2. blackout; 3. paramedics; 4. hazards; 5. concussion; 6. hygiene; 7. common sense; 8. evacuate; 9. toxic; 10. on hand

Practice 2: 1. c; 2. e; 3. d; 4. h; 5. i; 6. b; 7. f; 8. j; 9. g; 10. a

CHAPTER 22

Everyday Life: Buying Groceries

A. ENGLISH CLOSE-UP

Nutrition Facts		
Serving Size: 1 cup (245g)		
Servings Per Container: about 2		

Amount Per Serving		
Calories 170	Calories from Fat 10	

		% Daily value*
Total Fat	1g	**1%**
Saturated Fat	0g	0%
Cholesterol	0mg	**0%**
Sodium	550mg	**23%**
Total Carbohydrate	30g	**10%**
Dietary Fiber	8g	31%
Sugars	6g	
Protein	11g	

Vitamin A 45%	• Vitamin C 4%	
Calcium 8%	• Iron 20%	

*Percent Daily Values are based on a 2,000 calorie diet

B. VOCABULARY ESSENTIALS

Aisle—A pathway or walkway; the areas in a grocery store between the shelves. *You can find paper goods on aisle 10.*

Bar code—A series of varying lines, each representing a single digit number, placed on most consumer product containers. Laser scanners read bar codes to help locate information on the product, such as price. They are often used for checkout at grocery stores, among other things. *Look for the bar code on the bottom or back of the box. Then scan it into the register.*

To be out of something—To not have something that is usually available or kept on hand. *Are we out of eggs again? It looks like I won't be able to make an omelet for breakfast.*

Bulk—A large quantity of something, such as food. There are some discount grocery stores that specialize in selling food and other products in bulk. *You* can buy beans, rice, and canned products in bulk and store the extras in your garage.

Chain—A series of grocery stores, theaters, restaurants, etc., owned and often standardized by the same company. *We have a store in every major city, so if you join you can get the same discount anytime you go to any one of the stores in our chain.*

Checkout—The counter or area where purchases are paid for. *I'll meet you in the checkout line when I've finished shopping.*

Cold cuts—Cold, sliced, precooked meats. *A lot of people like cold cuts for sandwiches.*

Deli section—The section of the store where cold cuts, cheeses, salads, and other cold specialty items are kept. *The potato salad is in the deli section next to the macaroni salad.*

Discount/Club card—Cards offered by many stores providing discounts to people that continually shop there. At some stores, registration for the discount card is free, but at discount club stores, you usually have to pay a fee to become a member and receive the card. *Let's go to the Pet Company first. I have a discount card for that store.*

Express lane (or line)—A fast checkout counter that permits a limited number of items per person and occasionally doesn't allow personal checks or only allows cash, so that checkout is faster. *If you have fewer than ten items, you can go through the express lane.*

Food pyramid—A pyramid-shaped representation of the food types we need and the daily amounts that should be consumed. The different food types included are grains, fruits, vegetables, milk, meat and beans, and oils (fats). *The USDA recently introduced a new food pyramid to make its recommendations more accurate and individualized.*

Goods—Products. *You'll find frozen goods in the freezer section at the back of the store.*

Instant—Of a dish or snack, able to be produced in a few minutes with little or no cooking, for example, instant cereal, instant macaroni and cheese, or instant pudding. *Nobody has time to cook breakfast anymore, so I usually just have cold cereal or instant oatmeal or something.*

Mom-and-pop stores—Small stores that are owned and run by a family rather than a corporation. *There used to be a great mom-and-pop store here where I bought lunch every day, but now it's closed.*

Organic—Food made without hormones, fertilizers, or pesticides that are not natural, or synthetic. To be labeled organic by the USDA, goods must meet specific criteria. *Organic food has become more and more popular in the U.S. as some Americans have become wary of the impact of artificial foods and additives on health.*

Preservatives—Something added to a product to prevent it from spoiling. Most preservatives are synthetic chemicals. *If you buy organic products, you can usually avoid eating food with synthetic preservatives in it.*

Processed—Altered in some way for human use. With the exception of fresh fruits and vegetables, most food is processed in some way—flour is ground, foods are canned and frozen, and natural or chemical additives are used. *Although some people try to stay away from "processed" food because they consider anything not organic to be "processed," processing means more than just putting in chemical additives.*

RDA—Recommended Daily/Dietary Allowance. The daily amount of a vitamin, mineral, or nutrient considered by the Food and Nutrition Board of the National Academy of Sciences to be 100% of what is needed by the human body. *According to the RDA, a healthy adult needs 5,000 IUs of vitamin A, 400 IUs of vitamin D, and 1,000 mgs of calcium daily.*

To run out of—To be without a product. *I'm sorry. We've run out of red leaf lettuce, but we have romaine.*

To ring up—To enter prices into a cash register or to scan bar codes at checkout. *I can ring up your groceries over here.*

Rip-off—A price that is too high. *Avocadoes are $4.00 each? What a rip-off!*

Special (special offer, on special, on promotion)—Products being sold at a price that is lower than usual, often for a limited time. *There's a special on corn today. It's four for a dollar.*

To spoil—To rot, to go bad. *If the expiration date on the milk is close to the date of purchase, it'll spoil pretty quickly.*

Staples—Foods that are kept on hand and used often, such as potatoes, rice, or beans. *Are we out of any staples like pinto beans or white beans?*

Stock, to carry or stock—Inventory, available merchandise. To stock/carry means to regularly reorder for sale in a store, to keep in supply. In a grocery store, stock can also refer to a type of broth used as a soup base.—*"Do you carry the Five Star brand of vegetables?"*—*"No, but we stock their dried fruit."*

USDA—The United States Department of Agriculture. This government department works with farmers and ranchers and is involved in hunger campaigns, conservation efforts, nutrition research and promotions, setting certain food safety guidelines, and so on. *The USDA sets the nutrition labeling guidelines for poultry, meat, and egg products.*

Wide selection—A large variety of products available. *I like to go to Food Mart because they really have a wide selection of products.*

C. GRAMMAR ESSENTIALS: TALKING ABOUT THE FUTURE

There are several different ways to talk about the future in English. The simple future tense, which is formed with *will* plus the bare verb, often conveys a sense of determination or (near) certainty, or it makes a strong prediction:
> *Julie will stop by the store to get some milk on her way home from work.*
> *You will clean up your room or you won't go to the movies tonight.*

It can also be used to talk about expected future habitual actions:
> *Beginning next week, Food Mart will carry a variety of Super products.*

Will can also be used to convey a present or general sense when making predictions about habits. The following example isn't a prediction about a specific future event, but rather a statement of general habit:
> *Marla is so predictable. She'll stop by the store without a shopping list. She'll inevitably forget something and will have to go back the next day.*

In addition, *will* is used in the result clause of future real conditionals. In these constructions, note that the *if* clause is in the present tense:
> *If you hurry, you'll get to the store before it closes.*
> *If you show them your discount card, you'll pay less for those groceries.*

Another common way of expressing the future is to use *am/are/is going to.* This is sometimes called the "immediate future" because it's often used to speak about near-future events:
> *We need to get a few groceries because we're going to have a party.*
> *I haven't gotten milk yet, but I'm going to go shopping this afternoon.*
> *They're going to open up a new Food Mart in town soon.*

But it's important to note that *going to* can be used with expected events further in the future, and *will* can be used with immediately expected events:
> *With that new supermarket in town, I bet the mom-and-pop store is going to close in a few years.*
> *I said I'll go shopping tonight!*

The main difference between *going to* and *will* is really that *will* carries more of a sense of determination and a greater degree of certainty than *going to.* Use *will* when you're expressing strong expectations, determinations, and firm decisions, and use *going to* when you're expressing more neutral future expectations or casual plans. Many times, though, *going to* and *will* are interchangeable.

Also note that it's possible to express future actions or expectations with the simple present or present continuous (present progressive) tense:

Your order comes in this Friday.

This weekend I'm shopping, cooking, and cleaning my house.

D. HOW-TO

American grocery stores are often huge, and many of them carry just about everything. From lettuce to toothpaste to prepared meals, and plenty of nonfood items, many of the things you need for everyday life can be found in the aisles of a grocery store. As a result, the stores can sometimes be overwhelming. Fortunately, there will usually be signs to help point you toward whatever you are looking for, and products tend to be stocked in logical groups. Paper goods are usually all in one aisle, canned goods in another, kitchenware will usually be in the same aisle as baking products, and so on. You may even be able to find things like stationery, greeting cards, oil for your car, and other home care products such as flashlights, extension cords, or lightbulbs. And naturally, if all else fails, don't be afraid to ask for help.

There are a few things you should know about the checkout at a grocery store. First of all, there will often be an express line for people with fewer items, usually ten to twelve items or fewer, so look for the express line if you're not buying that many things. Also, the employees at a grocery store will usually bag your groceries for you. You can often let them know how you want your groceries to be bagged. You can get paper or plastic bags, or both, or ask for your groceries to be double-bagged, which is a good idea if you have heavy groceries. Some stores might also have a policy of giving you a discount or money back if you bring in used store bags or your own cloth bags. You might also want to use coupons to get discounts on food and give them to the cashier when you check out. You can usually find food coupons in the newspaper or mail. Grocery store chains will often offer discount cards to members. Show this card to the clerk on checkout also. You might also find that your store has a home delivery program (there are many websites that specialize in the home delivery of groceries as well). Just call in your order or send it in online and your food will be delivered to your door. You might also be able to shop in the store, buy your groceries there, and then ask to have them delivered instead of having to take them home yourself. If you have problems, questions, or concerns about a product or your shopping experience—for example, if you need information on home delivery or discount cards—you can go to the courtesy counter for help.

As you are looking for the products you need in a grocery store, you might notice that some seasonal products are available year-round in many U.S. grocery stores. For example, you can often buy cherries any time of year, but they will be very expensive until they come into season in the summer, because they're shipped from very far away. If you're looking for purely seasonal food, you might want to visit a local farmer's market if possible. Farmer's markets are where local farmers bring whatever they have available at the time to a school, a park, or even a parking lot in town. You'll find fresh vegetables, fruit, herbs, cheese, and milk. You can also usually find all kinds of specialized products, such as cookies, breads, sauces, and flowers.

In addition to farmer's markets, you can look for specialty items at a health food or organic grocery store. Health food stores are stores that carry natural foods and other products believed to enhance overall health, such as dietary supplements, while organic grocery stores naturally carry mostly organic foods. If you're a vegetarian, a health food store or organic grocery store might be a good place for you to look first for food that fits your diet. On the other hand, more and more general grocery stores are now carrying health food and organic items.

One more type of grocery store you should know about is the discount warehouse store. From food to appliances, discount warehouses have most everything you need. However, you have to buy almost every product in bulk, which means in large quantities. If you have a big freezer or storage space in your garage, or if you just like to keep lots of staples on hand, then it might be a good idea to check out these warehouse stores, because buying in bulk is often cheaper than buying one item at a time. Some discount warehouses, such as wholesale clubs, might ask you to become a member (for a fee) before allowing you to shop there, so you should check out the policy of the discount warehouse in your neighborhood before or when you go.

Finally, the U.S. also has large drugstores that don't just carry pharmaceuticals. Many Americans go to drugstores to find beauty products, household cleaning items, paper products, greeting cards, shampoos, moisturizers, dental and eye care products, some foods, and more.

E. ENGLISH IN ACTION

Emma's in her local grocery store looking for a few items, but she's surprised to learn that even basic items may not mean quite the same thing from culture to culture.

Emma: Hmm. Cheese, where's the cheese? Let's see. Shouldn't it be in the dairy section? Why isn't it with the milk?

Jimmy: Can I help you find something, ma'am?

Emma: Oh! Oh, sure. I was just looking for the cheese. But I don't see it here in the dairy section.

Jimmy: There's cheese right here.

Emma: That's cheese?

Jimmy: Sure. That's just slices of cheese. You can put them on sandwiches, or make grilled cheese, or . . .

Emma: I don't mean the little slices wrapped in plastic. I mean real cheese, you know, that comes in wedges or wheels?

Jimmy: Oh, sure. That'll be in the deli section, you know, next to the cold cuts.

Emma: The deli section? Oh, you're right. There it is. Thank you. And that's where I can get olives, too, right? I mean, not the kind in a can.

Jimmy: Yes, sure. We have canned black and green olives in the canned food aisle, but we also have lots of types of olives in the deli section. Is there anything else I can help you find?

Emma: Umm . . . Yes. Actually, I'm looking for bread.

Jimmy: There's a big aisle with bread, over near the produce.

Emma: Yes, but I mean fresh bread. You have lots of loaves of soft slices of bread in plastic bags, but I mean, you know . . . bread, fresh bread!

Jimmy: Oh, okay. I see what you mean. That's in the bakery section. We do have quite a lot of bread like that, Italian bread or French baguettes.

Emma: Thank you. That's great. I was worried that I'd have to go somewhere else. I actually have one more question. I saw that you have lettuce, but it's only the big iceberg kind, you know, the big pale green round kind. Is that the only kind of lettuce you have?

Jimmy: No, there are plenty of other kinds—red leaf, Boston, romaine. There are also mixed greens and other kinds of greens.

Emma: Oh, thank you so much for your help.

Jimmy: No problem! Have a good day.

F. PRACTICE

Fill in the blanks with the following words or expressions: *be out, carry, goods, on hand, run out of, rip-off, ring up, spoiled, stock, wide selection*

1. Oh, no. We've _____ milk. We'll have to pick up some more.

2. Sir, if you're paying cash I can _____ your groceries over here.

3. If you don't see an item on the shelf, ask someone if the store has any left in _____

4. Many American grocery stores carry a very _____ of breakfast cereals.

5. How can you _____ of Sandylane margarine? I saw it here this morning!

6. We _____ the best and freshest tasting vegetables in town. You'll find them all in the produce section.

7. It's always a good idea to keep flour _____, because you can use it so often.

8. This milk has _____. I'm going to throw it out.

9. I looked in the paper _____ section, but I couldn't find the paper towels.

10. What a _____! These cookies cost double what they cost in other stores!

Fill in the blanks with the best verb form expressing the future, using *will, be going to,* or the present progressive or simple present. There may be more than one correct answer.

1. Has anyone heard what kind of a store that new shop on the corner _____ (be)?

2. I know that he _____ (stop off) at the coffee shop, because he does every day.

3. We _____ (have) a special on canned goods this weekend.

4. We _____ (be) home in a few minutes. Then we _____ (have) dinner and relax.

5. Let's leave now so that we _____ (get) back in time to watch the news.

6. From now on we _____ (have) dinner together on Fridays.

7. Be home by 6:00, because we _____ (see) a show tonight.

8. I _____ (lose) ten pounds by next month no matter what!

9. The delivery truck _____ (arrive) here in an hour.

10. If you wait long enough, eventually they _____ (go) on sale.

G. TASK

One of the things that people often miss when they move to a new country is the food that they're used to. Many items don't taste quite the same and some items just simply aren't available. Thankfully, that's changing now, because supermarkets stock more and more international items, specialty stores are opening just about everywhere, and many food items can be bought online and shipped all around the world. For this task, think of your favorite dish from your country and make a list of all the ingredients you would need in order to prepare it. Which items can you find at your local supermarket? (You may be surprised to see how many are stocked there!) Which items can you only find in a specialty store? And which items would you have to order online?

H. REAL LIFE

FOOD MART EXPRESS

Reading Labels and Expiration Dates
The labels and expiration dates are on our food products for a reason.
There are four different types of dates you'll see.

*Expiration date—Tells you when the product is no longer good. By law, all baby products have expiration dates.

*Freshness date—The manufacturer expects the product to be of the best quality until this date.

*Pack date—The date the product was packed. Check to see which package has the most recent date. That's the one you're going to want to purchase. It will be the freshest.

*Sell by date / Pull date—The product must be sold by this date or store will pull it off the shelves. The product will remain fresh in your home for about a week beyond this date.

Food labels provide important information for the consumer. Required information includes the company name and the ingredients (in order from greatest amount to least). Any health claims are voluntary.

Each package must state the net contents in both metric units and English units. The food must be identified, and, if applicable, the label must indicate that the food does not have natural flavoring. Processed or packaged foods must declare information about nutritional value.

Foods labeled "organic" have met USDA organic standards.

I. RESOURCES

USDA:
www.usda.gov

For food safety questions regarding meat, poultry, and egg products:
www.fsis.usda.gov/Food_Safety_Education/usda_meat_&_poultry_hotline or
1-888-MPHotline (1-888-674-6854)

Information on food labeling:
www.fsis.usda.gov/Fact_Sheets/Food_Product_Dating/index.asp
www.cfsan.fda.gov/~dms/flg-toc.html

Information on organic foods:
www.ams.usda.gov/nop/Consumers/brochure.html

Food pyramid:
www.mypyramid.gov

Information on types of grocery stores:
www.fmi.org/facts_figs/superfact.htm

General grocery store information:
www.bls.gov/oco/cg/cgs024.htm
couponing.about.com/od/groceryzone

ANSWER KEY
Practice 1: 1. run out of; 2. ring up; 3. stock; 4. wide selection; 5. be out; 6. carry; 7. on hand; 8. spoiled; 9. goods; 10. rip-off

Practice 2: 1. is going to/will be; 2. will stop off; 3. are having; 4. are going to be/will be, will have; 5. will get; 6. are going to have/will have; 7. are going to see/are seeing; 8. will lose; 9. arrives; 10. will go

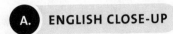

CHAPTER 23

Everyday Life: Getting Things Fixed at Home

A. ENGLISH CLOSE-UP

Home Maintenance Classes

Brought to you by your Local
Hardware and Home Supply Store

Painting Techniques	Saturday, October 15th
Wood Floor Installation	Sunday, October 16th
Deadbolt Locks	Saturday, October 22nd
Faucet Installation	Sunday, October 23rd

Classes held from 9–Noon

B. VOCABULARY ESSENTIALS

To blow a fuse—To draw too much electrical current through a fuse, causing it to open the circuit. *If you turn on too many appliances at once, you can blow a fuse!*

Cabinet refacing—The replacing of doors, handles, and the outer surfaces of cabinets, leaving the inside unchanged. *If you can't afford to have new cabinets put in your kitchen, how about refacing them?*

Clogged drain—Blockage of the pipe that empties a sink or bathtub by food items or other material. *Don't throw all that food in the sink or you'll have a clogged drain!*

Coat—A layer of paint, varnish, or some other liquid product that is applied to a large surface. *It'll take at least three coats of varnish to protect this floor.*

Contractor—Electrician, plumber, painter, carpenter, or other trained professional hired to perform work and provide supplies. *Repainting the whole house is too big of a job for me. Let's hire a contractor.*

Crawl space—A narrow space or passageway under the house or below the roof, often used for access to plumbing or electrical wiring. *I need a ladder so I can get into the crawl space and check your heater.*

Dead bolt—A lock with a heavy bolt (separate from the doorknob) that slides into the wall at the turn of a key or a latch. *If you add a dead bolt to the door, the occupants will feel safer.*

Drywall—A sheet of prefabricated material nailed over studs to form interior walls, also called sheetrock or wallboard. *The best way to fix this wall is to take it out and just put up new drywall.*

Engineered (wood) flooring—Wood flooring made up of hardwood, plywood, and a top layer of hardwood veneer, made to withstand moisture and heat-related problems. *What do you think? Should we replace this floor with a laminate or engineered flooring?*

To fall apart—To be in very poor condition, to break into pieces. *The furnace in this place is so old that it is falling apart.*

Fuse—An electrical safety device consisting of a tiny piece of metal that melts when too much electricity is drawn through it, thereby opening the electrical circuit and shutting down the flow of electricity. *The fuse blew again, so I have to go down to the fuse box.*

Flooded—Filled with water. *It looks like the basement got flooded again during the storm.*

To give someone a hand—To help or assist. *I can't reach the screwdriver. Can you give me a hand?*

Installation—The action of putting something into place and making any necessary electrical or piping connections. *When would you like to schedule an appointment for the installation of your new washer?*

Laminate—A type of flooring made to look like real wood, tile, or stone, but consisting of synthetic material. *Let's get the laminate flooring. It will last a long time and it's easy to maintain.*

Model—A company's style or design of a product, such as that of a car or appliance. *We have several dishwasher models.*

Mold—A fungus that can grow in damp areas inside houses and be dangerous to the health of the occupants. *How do we get rid of the mold once it starts? Will bleach do it?*

Primer—A first coat, applied before repainting walls, to help prepare the wall for painting. *If the wall you want to paint is a dark color, you'll probably need to apply a primer first.*

Running—Working, particularly when referring to equipment. *Can you hear the refrigerator running? It's so quiet.* (Note: A "running toilet" is a toilet that doesn't function properly because water continues to run through the bowl.)

Siding—Sheets that cover the outside of houses in place of paint, usually made of aluminum or vinyl. *That's it! No more exterior paint. Next time we get aluminum siding for this house!*

Snake—A tool used by plumbers to clean out clogged drains. *The clog is so bad that I'm going to have to use a snake.*

Spackle—A dry powder that is mixed with water and used as a paste to fill holes in walls. It can be bought as either the powder or the paste. *After you hang drywall, you need to fill in the nail holes with spackle.*

Spare—A replacement or extra product that is set aside for when it is needed. *The lightbulb just blew. Do we have any 100-watt spares?*

Stud—The wood or metal frame inside a wall or ceiling, beneath the drywall. *If you want to hang a heavy mirror or picture, you need to hammer the nail into a stud, not the drywall.*

Stud finder—A small device that indicates where studs are located beneath drywall by the movement of a magnet passing over nails. *Don't just start hammering anywhere on the wall! Use a stud finder!*

Varnish—A thin, clear liquid applied to wood that dries to a glossy sheen. *If you want to protect the wood, put a varnish on it. It'll also give it a great shine.*

C. GRAMMAR ESSENTIALS: THE PASSIVE VOICE

The passive voice is used when the doer of an action is either unimportant or unknown. To form the passive, use a form of *be* and the past participle of the main verb:

> *The first coat of varnish should be applied and allowed to dry for eight hours before the second coat is applied.*
> *Then the house was painted.*
> *New copper pipes were put in.*
> *Fresh wallpaper was hung.*
> *The floors were sanded and varnished.*
> *The kitchen tile was replaced with granite, and modern new cabinets were installed.*

There are as many passive tenses in English as there are active tenses. They are formed by using *be* in the correct tense, along with the (unchanging) past participle:

The house is painted. The house has been painted. The house is being painted. The house would be painted. The house was painted. The house would have been painted. The house was being painted. The house is going to be painted. The house will have been painted ...

Certain progressive tenses are awkward in the passive because they require stringing together too many forms of *be*. But they are still grammatical, and appropriate in certain contexts.

The house will be being painted when you get back.

By the time you get back, the house will have been being painted for two months!

When I got back, the house had been being painted for far too long.

It's possible to express the doer of the action in a passive construction with a *by* phrase:

The house was painted by professionals.

The wiring was put in by an unlicensed electrician, so you'd better have it checked.

Notice that in spoken English, *get* is often used instead of *be* in passives:

The basement got flooded again!

The roof got damaged during last year's storms and it still hasn't gotten fixed.

D. HOW-TO

Unfortunately, like many things, homes age. They need to be maintained, and this means making occasional repairs and installing replacement parts before problems become more serious. One way to make sure you're aware of any potential problems is to look your house over carefully every year or so. You can look for cracks and leaks in walls and pipes as well as peeling paint, check the shingles and flashing on the roof for wear, and check for unwanted pests like roaches, rodents, termites, or bats. It is also common to hire a trained professional to inspect your heating and cooling systems every year, and you can hire an exterminator if you have any problems with rodents or other pests.

If you discover any problems or if any problems arise, you should take care of them as soon as possible. Make a list of what needs to be done and figure out what you can do yourself and what you might need someone else to do. If you decide to do some or all of the repairs yourself and need some additional information or help, you have several options. You can get a home maintenance book or magazine from a bookstore or library. You can also go online. There are many websites that give advice on things like fixing clogged drains, eliminating mold, or choosing between solid wood, laminate, and engineered wood flooring. If you'd like more personal or intensive help, you can go to a home maintenance or hardware store and get advice from someone who works there. The store might also offer some classes on things like floor installation, repairing and varnishing old wood floors, interior and exterior painting, cabinet refacing, and plumbing.

If you decide that some tasks are just too big or complicated for you to handle on your own, you can always hire a professional. In fact, if you're dealing with electricity, gas, or plumbing, it's probably best to hire a professional unless you really know what you're doing. Making incorrect repairs to plumbing can create far greater problems than a few little leaky faucets and cost you much more in the end. And making incorrect repairs to gas lines or electrical wiring is hazardous and can even be fatal. Don't try to save money by doing things yourself that only knowledgeable professionals should do.

When looking for a contractor, it's best to do your homework. Otherwise, you may hire someone who is too expensive, untrustworthy, unreliable, or simply bad at his or her job. There are lots of stories of contractors who cause more heartache for their customers than the problems they were called to fix. The best way to find a good, reliable, and reasonably priced professional is to ask your friends if they can recommend someone. If you have a real estate agent, he or she might also be able to give you a good referral. Additionally, you can check with the Better Business Bureau or a prescreening agency like Angie's List. The Better Business Bureau is a private, nonprofit organization that monitors businesses to ensure honesty and quality work. You can find their website in the Resources section of this lesson. Whenever possible, try to hire someone who is licensed, bonded, and insured. You can find this information out by checking with the Better Business Bureau in your state, county, or city. A prescreening agency is an organization that has a list of plumbers, painters, electricians, and other contractors that have been prequalified by individuals who have used them. These agencies can also tell you when someone has not been recommended and they will usually charge you a fee to use their list. Another option is to hire the services of a home maintenance or hardware store when you buy its products. They will usually install products for a fee that they add on to the purchase price of your product; they may not make repairs, but they might offer to train you to make the repairs instead. Once you've gathered a list of multiple contractors, get several bids before making a choice. And no matter what you decide, make sure you sign a contract that specifically states what will be done, along with an estimate of costs. After the work is completed to your satisfaction, the contractor should give you a written bill listing all work performed and materials used. Finally, make sure you get a receipt for all your payments.

Of course, you may not be able to catch a minor problem before it becomes a major problem in need of immediate repair. If there is a serious problem in need of quick repair, it'll be much easier if you have the name and phone number of a good repairman on hand and at the ready. So even if you don't think you need to research the names of good professionals, it's a good idea to do it anyway. It'll make your life much easier!

An additional thing to keep in mind is that when you purchase a new appliance or hire a contractor to fix or replace something, the product will most likely come with a warranty and, depending on the situation, the contractor might provide a warranty for his or her labor as well. The labor might be under warranty for 30 days, while the appliance could have a warranty for 90 days or longer, and you could have the option of extending the warranty. If the product is still under warranty and breaks, call the manufacturer and they'll replace or repair it for free. If it's a labor warranty, contact the contractor. So, when you purchase a new appliance, such as a refrigerator or furnace, or hire a contractor, check to see what the available warranty is. Also, keep in mind that in order to maintain the warranty, you need to keep a receipt of your purchase. If you are purchasing or selling your home, you may be interested in a home warranty, which covers most appliances and home equipment under one warranty. Speak to your real estate agent for further information.

If you rent rather than own, you should talk to your superintendent or landlord about any repairs that need to be made around the house. A homeowner is responsible for his or her own repairs, but renters are not unless they have caused the problem. So unless the renter is responsible, he or she will need to rely on the owner or superintendent ("super") to make the necessary repairs. It's important to contact the landlord or super promptly. Sometimes they don't get back to you immediately, so you may need to call again. Don't be shy about it. It's their job and their responsibility. Making repairs sooner is better for them than if they have to make the repairs later. The landlord is not obligated to make cosmetic repairs, but he or she is obligated to keep the apartment habitable. If you have trouble getting your landlord to get back to you, write him or her a letter describing the problem; you should also remind the landlord that keeping the apartment in good repair is to his or her advantage and/or remind the landlord about the importance of keeping the apartment safe. Be sure to keep a copy of the letter. If the problem is ignored, then depending on the problem you may be able to contact the health department or the city or county housing department (you can find them in your local phone book). When you call, someone should be able to tell you whether your problem is a violation or not and force the landlord to repair it. Finally, you may be able to sue your landlord in small claims court. If you can prove that the problem decreases the value of the property, the judge may award you a small sum to recompense you for your trouble. But hopefully, you have developed a good relationship with your landlord or super and he or she will be amenable to making all the necessary repairs you request. For additional information regarding repairs in rentals, see Lesson 28.

E. ENGLISH IN ACTION

Illiana's kitchen sink is clogged, so she's calling her super to see if he can come and fix it.

Mr. Benson: Hello.

Illiana: Hello, Mr. Benson? It's Illiana in apartment 403B.

Mr. Benson: Oh, yes. Hello.

Illiana: I'm sorry for calling so late, but my kitchen sink is stopped up. I've been using the plunger, but it won't go down.

Mr. Benson: Is it the side with the disposal or the other side?

Illiana: It's the side with the disposal.

Mr. Benson: Have you turned on the disposal?

Illiana: Yes, of course, but then the other sink fills up, too. It goes down after a while, but it's been like this since yesterday.

Mr. Benson: Since yesterday? Why didn't you call me earlier instead of waiting till bedtime?

Illiana: Oh, I don't know. I didn't want to bother you, I guess. We could wait until morning.

Mr. Benson: Does the bathroom sink work?

Illiana: Yes.

Mr. Benson: Okay, run all your water from there, and I'll be there first thing in the morning.

Illiana: Oh, thank you, and I am sorry.

Mr. Benson: It's okay. These things happen, just next time, don't wait until 9:30 at night to call me. I could have taken care of it earlier if you'd called.

Illiana: I know.

Mr. Benson: Well, what's done is done. Just remember, stuff like clogged drains needs to be taken care of as soon as possible, because it could affect the bathroom sink and toilet, too. Then you'd really be in trouble.

Illiana: Okay. Next time I'll call you right away. Thank you, Mr. Benson. And good night.

Mr. Benson: Don't worry about it. Good-bye.

F. PRACTICE

Fill in the blanks with the correct forms of the following words: *drywall, be running, fall apart, primer, spackle, give me a hand, clogged drain, installation, mold, model*

1. With a couple of sheets of _____ and a coat of paint, that wall will be as good as new.

2. We must have a(n) _____, because the sink is full of water.

3. We've gotten a new stove, but we don't know what _____ refrigerator we want yet.

4. Could you _____? I'm too short; I can't reach that light to replace the bulb.

5. The plaster on these walls is so old that it just _____ if you touch it.

6. The toilet _____ all night last night. We'd better get it fixed.

7. If you've got to fix a small hole in the wall, you'll need some _____.

8. I wanted to paint the living room last night but forgot to buy the _____.

9. _____ in a house is especially bad for people with allergies.

10. When would you like to schedule the _____ of your dishwasher?

Rewrite the following sentences in the passive voice. Don't use a *by* phrase.

1. The carpenter hammered the nails into the wall.

2. We will screw the ceiling fan into the ceiling with four large screws.

3. Someone has blown a fuse in the next apartment.

4. The workers clean up the site at the end of the day.

5. They deduct taxes from your mortgage payment every month.

6. The former owner planted a new garden just last spring.

7. The landlord had added a second story before we moved in.

8. The decorator will purchase new curtains next week.

9. One of my former workers broke my good drill.

10. The janitor will be cleaning the floor when you leave tonight.

G. TASK

Find a home maintenance checklist online or in a home maintenance book or magazine and use it to go through your house to check for things that might need maintenance. If you don't have the names of reliable plumbers, electricians, carpenters, or other professionals, ask your friends, neighbors, or colleagues for referrals. You never know when they'll come in handy!

H. REAL LIFE

Hi, my name is Lee, and I bought a small house in Oak Park. It needed lots of repairs. That's why I was able to buy it, because it was pretty cheap. Well, some guy came by my house and said he could fix my roof for me and I wouldn't have to pay much money. Then he gave me some names to call to check on his work. I checked and everyone said he was good. So I said okay, and I thought he did a great job on my roof. Anyway, I have this deck in my backyard that was starting to rot and fall apart. My wife even fell through one of the boards because it was so bad. I was really happy with my roof, so I asked this guy to fix my deck too. He said fine, he wrote me an estimate that was pretty cheap, and I felt very happy about that. He asked me for $1,500 to buy some supplies. He and his crew came by and delivered the supplies and worked for a little while, but it started to rain, so they left. It rained for several days. Then finally the sun came out, and his crew came by and sat in their car, but he never showed up. Then they left. I waited a week, then two weeks, and finally I called, but nobody answered. I called and I called every day. Then I remembered that I had his address, so I went to his house. His wife came to the door and said he wasn't home. I told her that I'd paid him $1,500 but he didn't do much work. I told her everything. She said she'd tell him to call me. He did call, and he told me he would come the next day. This happened over and over. I'd call; he'd say he was coming, but he didn't. Finally, I just wrote him this letter and told him I was going to take him to small claims court, because that's what my neighbor said to do. Well, that scared him, so he came over and talked to me. He told me he was having a really hard time. He was sorry. He would try to pay me. I agreed to take less money because he'd bought the supplies for me. You know, I needed to get something. Well, it took him about a month but he finally paid me back about $1,000. I hired someone else to finish the work, so it was okay, but I will never hire someone I don't know or that a friend hasn't referred. It took too much work to just finally get all the money back. Well, I think I was lucky, because he could have just never come back.

I. RESOURCES

Help and information on fixing things and other home improvement issues:
www.doityourself.com
www.diynetwork.com/diy/home_improvement
www.bobvila.com/FixItClub
www.homedepot.com
www.lowes.com
www.mrsfixit.com/Fixits/index.asp
www.servicemagic.com/resources.Home-Maintenance.36.html

About hiring a contractor:
www.bbb.org/alerts/article.asp?ID=521

Find contractors and check references and reliability:
Better Business Bureau www.bbb.org
www.angieslist.com

www.contractors.com
www.servicemagic.com
www.reliableremodeler.com

ANSWER KEY
Practice 1: 1. drywall; 2. clogged drain; 3. model; 4. give me a hand; 5. falls apart; 6. was running; 7. spackle; 8. primer; 9. Mold; 10. installation

Practice 2: 1. The nails were hammered into the wall. 2. The ceiling fan will be screwed into the ceiling with four large screws. 3. A fuse has been blown in the next apartment. 4. The site is cleaned up at the end of the day. 5. Taxes are deducted from your mortgage payment every month. 6. A new garden was planted just last spring. 7. A second story had been added before we moved in. 8. New curtains will be purchased next week. 9. My good drill was broken. 10. The floors will be being cleaned when you leave tonight.

CHAPTER 24

Everyday Life: Problems with a Neighbor

A. ENGLISH CLOSE-UP

Noise Ordinance for the City of Oceanview:

The City of Oceanview has deemed the following noises a public nuisance and an unlawful noise disturbance regardless of the time of day.

- Frequent, repetitive, or continuous noise made by any animal, which unreasonably disturbs residents.

- Frequent, repetitive, or continuous sounding of horns or sirens, except as a warning.

- The creation of frequent, repetitive, or continuous noise in connection with the starting, operating, repair, rebuilding, or testing of any motor vehicle, motorcycle, or off-highway vehicle so as to unreasonably disturb residents.

- The creation of frequent, repetitive, or continuous noise by use of a musical instrument, whistle, sound amplifier, stereo, radio, television, or other device capable of reproducing sound so as to unreasonably disturb residents.

B. VOCABULARY ESSENTIALS

Abatement—Moderation, decreasing, or lessening, especially in reference to noise. *Many municipalities have noise abatement programs to reduce unnecessary noise pollution.*

Arbitration—The process by which an impartial individual or panel judges a dispute between individuals or groups. The judgment may or may not be binding. *If you and your neighbor can't agree on a resolution, you might need to go into arbitration.*

To ban—To prohibit, often by law. *There is a ban on smoking in public places.*

To be hard on—To treat severely, to meet with unnecessary force. *Don't be so hard on the neighbors! It's the first time they've had a party in years, and it wasn't very loud.*

Boisterous—Especially loud and noisy. *The crowd was particularly boisterous in our neighbor's yard last night.*

To cause someone grief—To make someone unhappy. *Our new neighbors seem nice and quiet, so I doubt they'll cause us any grief.*

Code—A group of laws and standards, used, for example, to regulate building construction. *The neighbors tried to build a room that was not up to code. They were told to fix it or pay a fine.*

To come to your senses—To return to rational behavior. *Morris has finally come to his senses and stopped leaving his dog outside at night.*

To comply—To obey and follow a request or command to do something. *During arbitration, the arbitrator forced the offending party to comply with the other's request.*

To encroach—To gradually violate a boundary or take possession of a space. *Little by little your garden has been encroaching on my lawn, so please cut it back.*

To evict—To legally remove a person from property, such as a tenant from a rental property. *Did you hear that the next-door neighbor got evicted because he wouldn't pay his rent?*

Noise pollution—Sound that annoys others or pollutes the atmosphere. *Noise pollution is a very common problem in overdeveloped parts of the U.S.*

Permit—Legal consent, authorization. *Did you get permits before adding on that second story?*

Police precinct—An area patrolled by a certain unit of police officers. *Starting next month, there will be an additional ten officers on patrol in this precinct.*

Property line—The boundary between the land owned by one person or group and the land owned by another. *We have a fence that runs all along our property line.*

To put up with—To accept or endure (something that is unpleasant). *Don't put up with the next-door neighbor's barking dog.*

Run-in—A conflict or disagreement. *Nobody enjoys having run-ins with others, but they are often a fact of life.*

To see eye to eye—To agree, to be of the same opinion. *Lydia and her husband see eye to eye on everything but allowing their daughter to stay out late.*

Setback—The distance allowed between a house or other structure and the street, a neighbor's property line, or some other boundary line. *Isn't the setback for a fence about six feet from the street?*

Zoning—The division of land into areas regulated for specific uses, such as commercial, residential, agricultural, etc. *If you want to have a home-based business, you'll need to check the zoning laws to see what is permitted in your area.*

C. **GRAMMAR ESSENTIALS: REPORTED SPEECH**

Reported speech is used to paraphrase what another person has said. It is not the same thing as a direct quote, which is exactly what someone else has said. In reported speech, the conjunction *that* is usually optional, pronouns are changed to the third person, time references or demonstratives may change, and the verb tense is different. Compare the following pairs:

Direct Quote	Reported Speech
John said, "I am tired of the noise!"	*John said that he was tired of the noise.*
Paula said, "I will take them to court."	*Paula said she would take them to court.*
They said, "We arrived here yesterday."	*They said they had arrived there the previous day.*

The most notable characteristic of reported speech is the tense shift. Notice in the above examples that *am* became *was, will* became *would,* and *arrived* became *had arrived.* The following chart summarizes how the tenses shift "back" in reported speech:

simple present → past	"Your music is too loud."	*He said that our music was too loud.*
simple past → past perfect	"I called the police."	*She said that she had called the police.*
simple future → conditional	"I will take you to court!"	*He said he would take us to court.*
present progressive → past progressive	"My neighbors are making too much noise."	*She said that her neighbors were making too much noise.*
past progressive → past perfect progressive	"They were singing all night long!"	*He said that they had been singing all night long.*
future progressive → conditional progressive	"You will be paying for this damage for a long time!"	*She said that I would be paying for that damage for a long time.*
present perfect → past perfect	"We've just moved here from out of state."	*They said that they had just moved here from out of state.*

past perfect → remains past perfect	"We had never been here before."	*They said that they had never been there before.*
future perfect → perfect conditional	"I will already have called the police."	*He said that he would already have called the police.*
present perfect progressive → past perfect progressive	"I have been waiting for three hours."	*She said that she had been waiting for three hours.*
past perfect progressive → remains past perfect progressive	"We had been sleeping when we heard the noise."	*They said that they had been sleeping when they heard the noise.*
can → could	"We can hear your party all the way down the block!"	*They said they could hear our party all the way down the block.*
may → might	"I may take you to court."	*He said that he might take us to court.*
must → had to	"You must turn it down."	*He said I had to turn it down.*
commands → *tell* + infinitive	"Turn down your music!"	*She told us to turn down our music.*
requests → *ask* + infinitive	"Could you turn down your music?"	*She asked us to turn down our music.*

Notice that the reporting verb *said* is in the past tense in all the above examples. If the reporting verb is in the present, present perfect, or future tense, then the reported verb does not shift to a past tense:

"The dog barks all night."	*He says the dog barks all night.*
"The dog barks all night."	*He has said the dog barks all night.*
"The dog barks all night."	*He will say that the dog barks all night.*

To report yes/no questions, use *if* instead of *that*, and follow the same rules for verb tense shift:

"Do you always play your music so loud?"	*He asked if we always played our music so loud.*
	Every day he asks if we always play our music so loud.
"Did you report this problem to the police?"	*She asked if we had reported this problem to the police.*
	Every time we complain she asks if we reported the problem to the police.

Finally, note that *say* is just one verb that can be used for reporting speech. Other possibilities are *report, suggest, exclaim, hiss, shout, yell, whisper,* etc.:

"They've been making noise all   *He reported that they had been making*
night!"   *noise all night.*

"You will regret this!"   *She hissed that we would regret it.*

Other verbs, apart from *ask* and *tell*, that can be used to report commands or
requests are *suggest, recommend, insist, command, order, urge, beg, compel,
persuade, convince*, and so on. Note that *suggest, recommend*, and *insist* are all
followed by *that* + a clause, while *command, order, urge, beg, compel,
persuade*, and *convince* are followed by a *to* infinitive:

"You should call the police."   *He suggested that we call the police. He
                                         persuaded us to call the police.*

"Could you please stop making so   *He begged us to stop making so much
much noise?"   noise. He urged us to stop making so
                                         much noise.*

"Go in the house!"   *He insisted that we go in the house. He
                                         ordered us to go into the house.*

D. HOW-TO

Almost everyone has had a run-in with a neighbor at one time or another.
After all, even the best neighbors can sometimes cause a problem. People
living close to each other are bound to disagree and intrude on each other's
lives at some point. However, it's often difficult to know what to do in these
situations, because you will most likely still have to live near your neighbor
after a problem has been resolved. So, you'll need to handle any issues firmly,
yet delicately. Hopefully, some of the tips below, which discuss some of the
most common problems, will help guide you and let you know what's
expected, allowed, and illegal in the U.S.

Noise pollution is probably the number one problem most people have
with their neighbors. Late night parties, TVs running all day, loud music, and
lawn mowers going at 8:00 on a Sunday morning are just a few of the
possible offensive noises you might encounter. Whatever the cause, you can
do something about it. Your first action should be to politely explain the
problem to your neighbor. If nothing changes after asking once, then find a
copy of your local noise ordinance. An ordinance is a local law established by
a municipal governing body, and these ordinances typically deal with such
issues as construction, zoning, trash removal, and noise. Check the link in the
Resources section for your community's ordinances and codes. If you can't
find the ordinances there, you can find a copy of local ordinances at your
city's website. After looking it over, you may find that some noises are actually
banned. If your problem noise is banned or restricted in any way, send a copy
of the ordinance along with a letter or note to your neighbor. Don't make any
threats of legal action, because that could only make things worse, and
simply citing the law is an obvious enough message. The neighbor will know
what your rights—and his or her responsibilities—are by reading the

ordinance. Also, remember to retain a copy of the letter and ordinance so that you have a record of what you sent. If sending the ordinance doesn't work, start documenting how and when offending noises occur to use in mediation or any other conflict resolution procedures. Mediation involves using a neutral third party to help negotiate a resolution between two conflicting parties. You can try mediation by contacting local/neighborhood mediation services, which should be free and can be found in your local phone book. If mediation doesn't work, you can contact the police in your local precinct or noise abatement, which is the city or neighborhood code compliance department. You might also want to consider arbitration. As a last resort, you can take your neighbor to small claims court.

If you rent and the offender is in another unit owned by the same landlord, talk to the building's superintendent or turn the problem directly over to the landlord. Because the landlord has the power to evict, that should be able to get some results. If you live in a community that has a homeowners' association (an organization of neighbors concerned with managing the common property in their community), it's a matter for the association. Homeowners' associations have board meetings once a month. You can either attend the meeting and bring up problems there, or send a letter asking them to address the issue at the next meeting. In some cases, if the issue is something that is already violating the rules, you can just call the association office and report the problem to them. Whatever the case, the law is on your side. You have a right to a quiet environment.

Dogs can also fall into the category of noise pollution, but they cause additional problems and so merit their own category. Remember, dog owners are responsible for their pets' behavior. In most neighborhoods, leash laws require that dogs be kept on a leash at all times when they are out of their yards or in dog parks. When a dog soils a neighbor's yard or a sidewalk, the owner usually must clean up after the dog. Owners are also often required to pick up any trash strewn about by their dogs. Dog owners can additionally be liable for their dog's behavior if the dog gets into a neighbor's yard and digs it up, destroys other parts of the neighbor's property, or bites someone. If you have any of these problems, follow the same procedures mentioned above regarding noise pollution. If these suggestions fail, you may be able to contact your local animal control authorities. For more information on pets and their owners' responsibilities, see Chapter 25.

Fences are another source of dispute between neighbors. There are often fights over maintaining fences and where they are placed. If you have a problem with a fence, check your local fence ordinance. You can check with your city's planning or zoning department or the city attorney's office to find out what the laws are in your area. Property line fences may be owned and used by both neighbors, and thus both parties may have to share maintenance expenses. If the fence crosses into your yard rather than staying on the property line, check to see how long it has been there. Depending on local law, after a certain period of time the encroachment may become the legal boundary line. If the fence is new, now is the time to say something. Fences can be a complicated issue, so it's best to inform yourself by reading your local laws.

Trees and other plants can also constitute a legal issue between neighbors. If your neighbor's tree hangs over into your yard, you usually have the right to cut it back up to the property line. However, the tree's upkeep is the owner's obligation. Grass and weeds may also be an issue. Depending on your neighborhood, you may or may not be able to do anything about yards that are not being mowed or otherwise maintained. If your neighbor's yard bothers you, check your local ordinances to see what can be done about it. Some neighborhoods do have strict laws regarding the upkeep of their residents' yards.

Construction is another noise issue, but there's not a whole lot you can do about it. Fortunately, it's only a temporary annoyance. Each city has its own construction hours, dictating when construction can occur in the city, often beginning at 7:00 a.m., with construction forbidden on Sundays and national holidays. But for construction of any kind, the county must grant a permit. Along with an application for a building permit, copies of site plans, building plans, and a fee might need to be included. The fees vary according to location. Keep in mind that usually any home additions, such as a garage, a porch, or additional rooms, need approval. Once the permit is granted, building may begin, but the building permit must be posted at the building site for all to see. If the building impacts the neighbors, there may be a public discussion before the plans are approved. This includes any additions and remodeling in high-rise condos or apartment buildings that might block the other residents' views.

Trash and general unsanitary conditions are also regulated by law. Your city may have a designated type of trash container to use, which they may sell to residents. Trash cans or bags and recycling bins or bags usually have specific times of day when they can be placed out on the curb and when they must be taken in. Where you place your trash can is also usually up to the city. The way trash and garbage is wrapped is also regulated by your city; trash is usually to be bagged in either plastic bags or brown paper. Recycling must also usually be placed in specific bags. Trash cans are to be kept clean and as odor free as possible. Any violation of the city's rules might prohibit your trash from being collected. You can find this information by checking with your real estate agent or a neighbor, or by checking the city ordinances. For additional information on waste services, see Chapter 30.

In closing, you probably noticed that many of the above issues were written with the expectation that your neighbor would be the offending party. Don't forget, you have legal responsibilities to your neighbors, and you could be the cause of a problem, rather than the victim. Make sure you're aware of the relevant laws in your community, and make sure you comply with them. Of course, simple courtesy is probably the safest rule of thumb, not to mention the Golden Rule—do unto others as you would have others do unto you!

E. ENGLISH IN ACTION

The McClellens' dog is barking again and Ian and Magda can't sleep. Let's listen in to see how they resolve the problem.

> Ian: It's that dog again!
>
> Magda: I wonder if the McClellens are aware that their dog is keeping people awake at night.
>
> Ian: I don't know, maybe not. But somebody has to tell them.
>
> Magda: Yes. Why don't you go over there tomorrow morning first thing? You know something about dogs. Maybe you can give them some advice.
>
> Ian: I think you should be the one. You're so much more tactful than I am. And you know as much about dogs as I do.
>
> Magda: Hmm. Maybe so. . . . Okay, I'll do it. Where are you going? I thought you wanted me to go over there.
>
> Ian: Oh, I'm not going over there. I'm just getting some earplugs. You want some?
>
> Magda: Sure, that sounds like a good idea.

Later the next morning Magda goes over to talk to Mr. McClellen about his dog.

> Mr. McClellan: Oh, hello Magda. What can I do for you?
>
> Magda: Well, we were wondering if you knew that your dog barks at night.
>
> Mr. McClellan: Really? Bessie's been barking? I didn't know that.
>
> Magda: Hmm. You must be a very sound sleeper.
>
> Mr. McClellan: Yeah. Well, I'd bring her in, but my wife won't allow it.
>
> Magda: Um-hum. I know a little about dogs. Maybe I can give you some ideas.
>
> Mr. McClellan: I'm open to anything except getting rid of her. Bessie's like a part of my family. But I don't want her to be bothering my neighbors.
>
> Magda: Oh, we don't want you to get rid of her either. Do you think she might be barking because she's lonely? If that's the case, bringing her in at night might be the only option. Maybe you could put her in the laundry room or some other room where she can feel that she's close to you. You also might want to check to see if she has enough water or if she might be hungry.

Mr. McClellan: That's easy. I'll check, but I don't think that's the problem.

Magda: Maybe she needed exercise. You might want to take her out for a long walk right before bedtime to help her get rid of any excess or boisterous energy. She probably needs to run. If you run with her she would probably sleep most of the night.

Mr. McClellan: Yeah. That might do it. And then I'd probably sleep soundly through the night myself. But I try to take her out; I just can't always do it at night.

Magda: Hmm. This isn't sounding too good. I have a few other ideas. For example, you could spray her with water whenever she barks inappropriately.

Mr. McClellan: Yeah, but I don't hear her barking at night.

Magda: I know. Well, there's one last hope. You could get her one of those collars filled with citronella.

Mr. McClellan: What would that do?

Magda: Well, to us citronella has a mildly pleasant smell, but dogs hate it. So each time she barks, it'll spray citronella. Eventually she'll figure out that her barking causes the citronella smell.

Mr. McClellan: Well, maybe that would work. Where can I find them?

Magda: Oh, just about any good pet store . . .

F. PRACTICE

Fill in the blanks with the following words: *ban, be hard on, cause grief, property line, run-in, setback, comply, zoning, see eye to eye, evicted*

1. The _____ law says that you can't build anything within three feet of the street.

2. The Hendrixes and the Garcias maintain a fence that runs along their _____ .

3. There's a(n) _____ on smoking in public places here.

4. We had a(n) _____ with the neighbor, and now he won't speak to us at all.

5. If any other tenants complain about you, you're going to be _____ !

6. I'm really sorry about the noise. I don't want to _____ you any _____ !

7. I don't _____ with my neighbor on what good music is.

8. You need to _____ with the law.

9. Don't _____ the neighbors for not trimming the grass; their kid has been very sick.

10. You can't run a business out of your garage here. The _____ laws forbid it.

Change the following sentences to reported speech.

1. Bill said, "I'm going to trim the tree."
2. The city has said, "You must tear down that building."
3. Our neighbor asked, "Can you keep your cats in your house?"
4. The man next door said, "I put your dog inside your gate."
5. My husband said, "I will lock the gate after I put the dog in."

Now change the following five sentences from reported speech to quoted speech.

1. He said you should build a new fence. (He said,)
2. The city told us we had to move the fence back two feet. (The city said,)
3. He told us to stop mowing our lawn at 7:30 in the morning. (He said,)
4. They said they thought our car was too noisy. (They said,)
5. They asked me if I could move my old cars off the street. (They asked,)

G. TASK

Get a copy of your local noise ordinances. You can probably find them online on your town or city's website, or you can get one by calling up the municipal or city offices and requesting a copy. What are the local laws that residents must comply with?

H. REAL LIFE

August 19
Dear Mr. Crouch and Ms. Lampton,

We noticed that you are building on the back of your property next to the fence. We are concerned because not only does the large bay window look right onto our backyard, but also, the roof actually comes down over our property. We have checked with the city, and they told us that your building appears to be in code violation. According to the county, all structures should have at least a three-foot setback. There should not be a window that looks directly into our yard, and in fact our neighborhood zoning does not permit a separate building of that size. We also know that you have not as yet applied for a permit with the city. We are currently preparing to put our house on the market, and our real estate agent has advised us that our property may be devalued as a consequence of your adding this building so close to our property line. We understand that you have probably put a significant amount of money into this building and do not expect you to have to tear it down unless there is no other option. We are willing to go into some sort of mediation or arbitration with you in order to resolve this issue.

We are enclosing a copy of the city ordinance for your information. We hope that we can come to an agreeable solution to this matter.

Sincerely,
Bill and Mary Albertson

I. RESOURCES

Pet behavior:
www.purina.com/cats/behavior/GoodNeighbor.aspx (cats)
www.purina.com/dogs/behavior/BeingAGoodPetNeighbor.aspx (dogs)
www.larimerhumane.org/protection/neighbors.cfm (dogs)

Noise pollution:
www.nonoise.org
www.noiseabatementsociety.com

Zoning laws:
real-estate-law.freeadvice.com/zoning

Local ordinances:
www.naco.org/Template.cfm?Section=About_Counties (click on "Codes and Ordinances")

Home additions (permits and other information):
www.doityourself.com/scat/homeadditions

Books:
Neighbor Law: Fences, Trees, Boundaries & Noise by attorney Cora Jordan

ANSWER KEY
Practice 1: 1. setback; 2. property line; 3. ban; 4. run-in; 5. evicted; 6. cause . . . grief; 7. see eye to eye; 8. comply; 9. be hard on; 10. zoning

Practice 2: 1. Bill said he was going to trim the tree. 2. The city has said I/we had to tear down that building. 3. Our neighbor asked us if we could keep our cats in the house. 4. The man next door said that he had put our dog inside the gate. 5. My husband said that he would lock the gate after he put the dog in.

Practice 3: 1. He said, "You should build a new fence." 2. The city said, "You have to move the fence back two feet." 3. He said, "Stop mowing your lawn at 7:30 in the morning." 4. They said, "We think your car is too noisy." 5. They asked, "Can/Could you move your old cars off the street?"

CHAPTER 25

Everyday Life: Pets

A. ENGLISH CLOSE-UP

License No.		Chk. Code	
Date Issued	Expiration Date		
Dog Breed		Code	
Dog Color		Code	
Other ID	Year of Birth		
Markings	Dog Name		

Dog License

Original   Renewal
Transfer of ownership

Rabies Certificate Required
Rabies Vaccine:
Manufacturer_____
Serial Number_____
   1 yr. vacc.   3 yr. vacc.
Date Vaccinated_____
Veterinarian_____

Owner Identification (Last, First, Middle Initial)   Area Code

Mailing Address   Phone Number

B. VOCABULARY ESSENTIALS

ASPCA—American Society for the Prevention of Cruelty to Animals. An organization dedicated to preventing mistreatment of animals. *We make monthly donations to the ASPCA.*

Alley cat—A homeless cat. *There were some alley cats yowling out back last night.*

Breeder—A professional who raises breeds of animals for sale. *We got our new pug from a breeder.*

Feral—Wild or untamed, or returning to the wild after domestication. *There are organizations that send volunteers out to find and spay or neuter feral cats.*

To get fixed—To spay or neuter, to remove the reproductive organs of an animal. *Getting your pets fixed can help limit the number of unwanted and homeless animals.*

To lavish—To give extravagantly. *The Whitleys lavish their dog with toys and affection.*

Litter box—A box inside which cats or other pets urinate and defecate. The box usually contains cat litter, which is a material—often sand or dirt—that absorbs the moisture. *Don't forget to clean the litter box!*

Litter—The group of offspring born at the same time, as from a cat or dog. *My cat just had a litter of kittens.*

To housebreak—To train pets to use a litter box or go outside to urinate or defecate. *You'll be happier if you get a dog that's already housebroken.*

Humane Society—An organization dedicated to the protection of animals. *The Humane Society website offers great tips for keeping your pets safe.*

Inhumane—Cruel, lacking compassion. *Many people believe that it's sinful or unethical to treat animals inhumanely.*

Mutt—A mixed breed dog. *Because mutts are not interbred, they are often healthier than purebred dogs.*

To neuter—To castrate, to remove a male animal's reproductive organs. *Most dog and cat owners neuter their pets.*

Pedigree—A recorded list of an animal's known ancestors. *Pedigree dogs can be very expensive.*

Puppy mill—A place that or person who breeds dogs for sale in unsanitary and inhumane conditions. *You should never buy a dog that comes from a puppy mill.*

Purebred—Bred from a specific lineage or family group of animals. *That's a beautiful purebred racehorse, isn't it?*

To put to sleep—To cause the death of, usually in a humane way. *We all cried when we had to put our beloved dog to sleep, but she was in too much pain to keep her alive.*

To spay—To remove the ovaries of a female animal. *It'd be a good idea to spay your cat, or you'll have lots of kittens soon.*

Stray—A pet that does not seem to have an owner, or a domestic pet that has wandered away from its home. *Our neighbors have been feeding a stray cat regularly, and I think they want to adopt it.*

Treats—Foods that pets enjoy eating, often used for training purposes. *Baby carrots make good treats for dogs, because they're not fattening, and many dogs love them.*

Veterinarian (vet)—A doctor trained to medically treat animals. *I found an avian veterinarian, or a vet who specializes in birds, so I think I'm going to take my parrot to her.*

To wean—To stop nursing, to stop drinking a mother's milk. *Kittens usually wean at about seven or eight weeks.*

C. GRAMMAR ESSENTIALS: *WOULD* VS. *COULD*

Would and *could* are both conditional modals, but they have different uses.
Let's focus on them now. The following are the main uses of *would*:

1. To show the conditional. *If I had a dog, I would feel safer. I would never buy from a puppy mill!*

2. To report speech with *will*. *You said you would take my dog to the vet. Who told you they would give you a kitten?*

3. To express a future in the past. *I never thought you would buy me a horse! We believed a dog would be a great addition to the family.*

4. To express a habitual past action, similar to *used to. I would take my dog for a walk every day after school before I went off to college. We would always go horseback riding.*

5. To make polite requests. *Would you take the dog for a walk? Would you mind feeding my cat?*

6. To show a degree of certainty. *It would seem that you like cats. Yes, that would be the case.*

7. To show presumption. *It's 6:00, so they would just be getting home now. It's late, so they would probably be asleep.*

8. To make a suggestion. *It would be a good idea to get your cat spayed. It would be better if you adopted a pet from a shelter.*

The following are the main uses of *could*:

1. To show the conditional of *can. If you had brought your dog in, I could have examined him. If we had the money, we could buy a horse.*

2. To report speech with *can. He said he could see us tomorrow. Who told you that you could bring home a stray animal?*

3. To make polite requests. *Could you show me your new fish? Could I please have a kitten?*

4. To express past ability, often used with frequency adverbs. *I could never have pets when I was a child because I had allergies. We could see all the way across the bay on a clear day.*

5. To show possibility or probability. *Your cat could have a virus. The dog could be pregnant.*

6. To show surprise. *That dog couldn't be a terrier! My dog couldn't have bitten you!*

7. To show timidity or uncertainty in making suggestions. *I could help you find your bird. We could keep the puppies.*

8. To make wishes with *if* and *only. If only we could get another dog! If they could only be here earlier!*

D. HOW-TO

Many Americans love their pets. Well over half of all American households have pets, and if all apartment dwellers were allowed to have pets, that number would probably rise significantly. The most common pets are cats and dogs, but birds, turtles, fish, hamsters, gerbils, and rabbits are also popular. More exotic pets include lizards, snakes, and even tarantulas! Because pets are often lavished with affection, toys, and treats, a full-fledged industry of pet-oriented businesses has sprung up in the U.S. You can find everything from sprawling pet stores to dog spas and pet clothing stores.

There are laws in every state regarding the maintenance and care of pets. Each state, or even town or city, has specific laws on this subject, so you should contact your county department of animal welfare to find out which laws are in effect where you live. Nevertheless, there are some common laws in all states. For example, both dogs and cats are required to have rabies shots, but in most states only dogs need to be licensed. In order to maintain a dog license, most states require that each dog have an up-to-date rabies shot when the license is renewed, and in many cases the license fee is lower for a spayed or neutered dog. Also, dogs should be kept on the owners' property and not allowed to roam. Stray dogs as well as cats are routinely picked up by the local pound, and if the owners are not available within a reasonable period of time, they may be put to sleep. If your pet has a place outside, it should probably be fenced. Some dog owners prefer an electric fence, which is an underground line that runs around an area where the owner wishes his or her dog to stay. The dog wears a collar with a receiver on it, and if the dog gets too close to the electric fence, he or she gets a mild shock. Dogs are usually not allowed out of their yard without being held on a leash at all times. However, there are some areas designated as leash-free zones that permit dogs to run freely as long as they remain inside the area. Additionally, some communities will fine dog owners if they do not pick up after their pet has defecated. Furthermore, pet owners can be held liable if they abandon their pets, do not provide adequate shelter, food, or water, or otherwise treat them inhumanely. Dog owners are also held responsible if their dogs are caught disturbing the peace or if they bite anyone (see Chapter 24). Finally, a pet owner who wishes to breed sometimes needs a license to do so.

If you have a pet, it's a good idea to have a veterinarian you and your pet like. Vet bills can add up quickly, and there are two things a pet owner can do to ensure that money paid to the vet is well spent. One is to find a good and trustworthy vet; the other is to get pet insurance. One way to find a good veterinarian is to ask your friends. You can also get the names of reputable vets from your local AVMA, American Veterinary Medical Association (see Resources). Getting veterinary insurance will also help reduce and control the cost of how much you spend on veterinarian bills each year. Veterinary insurance is similar to human insurance policies, involving deductibles, coverage plans, and so on. Once you have found a vet, ask him or her about when to spay or neuter your pet. The vet will also vaccinate your pet for rabies, heartworm, and other health concerns specific to your pet and provide flea and tick medication. A veterinarian may also provide dentistry, grooming services, boarding services while you are away on vacation, and behavior training courses for both your pet and you.

If you live in an apartment or condominium community and want a pet, you should be aware of what the pet restrictions are in your apartment building or community. Many apartment buildings do not allow pets or will only allow small animals, such as cats, small dogs, or birds. Condo communities are less restrictive, but you may be expected to keep a dog quiet or else you could be asked to get rid of it.

Some areas have restrictions on certain types of exotic pets. Exotic animals like alligators, large cats, certain large birds, and hedgehogs may not be permitted in certain cities and states. In addition, some states and communities do not allow certain breeds, and more than half of the states in the U.S. have laws against dangerous dogs. As a result, you may want to do your homework in your state before selecting a pet for your home and family.

If you do decide to get a pet, you can adopt a pet from a local animal shelter, rescue group, or other adoption center. However, if you are interested in purebreds, breeding purebred animals yourself, or a pet you can enter into shows, you will probably want to purchase your pet from a reputable breeder. You can also purchase a pet from a pet store, but you should first confirm that the store treats animals humanely and acquires them from legitimate sources.

E. ENGLISH IN ACTION

Kyle and his mother are at the local animal shelter preparing for a pet adoption.

Ms. Dasai:	Hello, Mrs. Grainger. I'm Lila Dasai, one of the pet counselors here at the shelter. How are you?
Mrs. Grainger:	Fine. Oh, and this is my son, Kyle.
Ms. Dasai:	Hello, Kyle. It's nice to meet you.
Kyle:	Thank you. You, too.
Ms. Dasai:	So you would be here to adopt a cat, is that right?
Kyle:	Well, actually, I'd like a kitten.
Ms. Dasai:	Okay, well, we don't have a lot of kittens here right now. They get adopted much faster than the adult cats do.
Mrs. Grainger:	I see.
Ms. Dasai:	Well, let's talk about your home environment. Are there any other cats, or do you have a dog?
Kyle:	No. It's just my mom, my dad, and my baby brother, and me. Why?

Ms. Dasai:	Well, kittens especially like a companion. Dogs don't always make the best companion, but another cat would.
Mrs. Grainger:	Oh, I hadn't thought about two cats.
Ms. Dasai:	Well, it's just that kittens feel more secure if there's another cat around. You could have an adult cat, too. Adult cats often prefer not to have any competition. Okay, well, we can come back to that. I just need to talk to you a little about cat care. You'll need to change the litter box at least once a week, and if you have two cats you should have two boxes. All of our cats have had their shots, and they've been neutered. We also include a microchip.
Kyle:	What's that for?
Ms. Dasai:	If they get lost you can call us and we'll track your cat for you so you can find it again.
Kyle:	Oh.
Ms. Dasai:	All the cats have been examined by the vet already, and you'll get all those records. You also get a free visit with the vet if you come in within two weeks. You should keep your cat inside your house.
Mrs. Grainger:	But cats like to be outside, don't they? Aren't they naturally comfortable outdoors?
Ms. Dasai:	Well, some of our cats are feral or alley cats that we have taken in and tamed, so yes, they are accustomed to being outside, but there are lots of dangers outside, like other animals, cars, and even people. Your cat could get lost or hurt outside, so we recommend that you keep them indoors.
Mrs. Grainger:	Hmm.
Ms. Dasai:	Would you have a problem with that?
Mrs. Grainger:	Well . . .
Kyle:	Mom! You promised.
Mrs. Grainger:	Yes, I did. Well, when can we look at the cats?
Kyle:	Yay!
Ms. Dasai:	Come with me. Over here you'll see Mitzi. Mitzi was born . . .

F. PRACTICE

Fill in the blanks with the following words: *lavish, get fixed, housebreak, litter, put to sleep, weaned, treat, mutt, stray, pedigree*

1. Reward your dog with a(n) _____ for good behavior.

2. Many American pet owners _____ gifts and affection on their pets.

3. It takes time and patience to _____ a cat or a dog, but it's well worth the effort.

4. Many cat owners do not want to risk their cats having kittens, and so they _____ their cats _____.

5. Don't take a kitten or puppy away from its other until it has been _____.

6. There are six puppies in the _____.

7. Hank isn't purebred, he's just a(n) _____, but we love him.

8. Ms. Hobbs takes in every _____ cat she finds in the neighborhood.

9. To some pet owners, _____ is important because they like to know their pet's lineage.

10. Ben was so sad when his parents decided to _____ their dog _____, but the dog was very old and sick.

Fill in the blanks with *could* or *would*.

1. She _____ already ride a horse when she was eight years old.

2. I wish you _____ take your dog for a walk. He really needs to get out of the house.

3. When I was a child, my family _____ always take in strays.

4. It _____ appear that your cat is male, not female!

5. My dog _____ easily jump over this gate if she wanted to.

6. You promised me you _____ give me a kitten.

7. You're not serious. You _____n't have a boa constrictor as a pet!

8. _____ your cat be sick?

9. I thought you _____ enjoy having a little hamster as a pet, so I got you one.

10. I _____ take care of your pets while you're gone, if you'd like.

G. TASK

Get a copy of your local ordinances regarding pets. You can probably find them online on your town or city's website, or you can get one by calling up the municipal or city offices and requesting a copy. What are the local laws that pet owners must comply with?

H. REAL LIFE

American Pet Insurance
Dear Ms. Grainger,

Every year Americans spend billions of dollars on pet care. Veterinary bills can be staggering, and when you add up office visits, tests, and medications, you could be paying hundreds or even thousands of dollars to care for your pet.

More and more Americans are opting for pet insurance to cover those bills. Our prices can be as low as $10.00 a month with a $50.00 deductible, and that covers routine appointments as long as your pet doesn't have any preexisting or hereditary conditions. You can get coverage for up to $2,500 per accident or injury. This could add up to huge savings for your wallet at just pennies a day. Here's how it works. You can go to any authorized vet worldwide, pay for the visit at time of service, have an authorized veterinary staff member fill out our claim form, sign and send it to American Pet Insurance, and we will reimburse you.

We know you love your pet, so give us a call at 1-800-555-5980 or go to our website for more information or to enroll.

Very sincerely,
Rhonda Appleby

I. RESOURCES

Find a vet:
State Veterinary Medical Associations at www.avma.org/statevma and select your state.
American College of Veterinary Surgeons at
www.acvs.org/AnimalOwners/FindaSurgeoninYourArea for board certified veterinary surgeons

Information for pet owners:
www.avma.org/care4pets (general information on pet health, finding a vet, selecting a pet, etc.)
www.fema.gov/plan/prepare/animals.shtm (what to do with pets in event of emergency)

Pets in the U.S.:
www.lifeintheusa.com/community/pets.htm

Restrictions on bringing pets into the U.S.:
www.cdc.gov/ncidod/dq/animal.htm (U.S. Customs and Border Protection)

The Humane Society www.hsus.org
The ASPCA www.aspca.org

Adopt a pet:
www.petfinder.com
www.pets911.com
www.1-800-save-a-pet.com or 1-800-728-3273

ANSWER KEY

Practice 1: 1. treat; 2. lavish; 3. housebreak; 4. get . . . fixed; 5. weaned; 6. litter; 7. mutt; 8. stray; 9. pedigree; 10. put . . . to sleep

Practice 2: 1. could; 2. would; 3. would; 4. would; 5. could; 6. would; 7. could; 8. could; 9. would; 10. could

CHAPTER 26

Everyday Life: Following a Recipe

A. ENGLISH CLOSE-UP

American Cooking Measurements			
Unit	Abbreviation	Defined as	Milliliters
Pinch		Amount held by two fingers	
Drop		One drop from liquid dropper	.05 ml
Dash	tsp. or t	1/6 of a fl. oz.	4.93 ml
Tablespoon	Tbsp. or T	1/2 fl. oz.	14.79 ml
Fluid Ounce	oz.	1 fl. oz.	29.57 ml
Cup	C	1/2 pint	236.59 ml
Pint	pt.	2 cups	473.18 ml
Quart	qt.	2 pints	946.35 ml
Gallon	gal.	4 quarts	3,785.41 ml

B. VOCABULARY ESSENTIALS

Batter—A semi-liquid mixture usually composed of flour and water or milk plus other ingredients. *You'll need to thin the pancake batter a little before frying.*

To beat—To mix quickly with a spoon or other device, such as an electric beater. *Beat the eggs to a thick froth before adding them to the batter.*

Comfort foods—Rich, filling, and often starchy and/or sugary dishes that are simple to make, comforting, and can remind people of their childhoods. *I think my favorite comfort food is macaroni and cheese.*

Corn on the cob—An ear of fresh corn that is cooked and eaten whole. *Some people like corn on the cob best when it's grilled.*

To cream—To beat into a soft, creamy mixture. *The recipe says to cream the butter and sugar together then add the vanilla.*

Double boiler—Two cooking pans, one nested inside the other. Water is boiled in the bottom pan, and the top pan is used for slow cooking or melting. *Melt the chocolate in a double boiler.*

To drain—To let liquid run off. *Wash and then drain the lettuce leaves and dry them with a paper towel.*

Dry ingredients—Flour, sugar, salt, baking powder or soda, etc. *Mix all the dry ingredients together.*

To dust—To lightly cover with flour, sugar, cocoa, or some other very fine ingredient. *Dust the pan with flour and then pour the batter in.*

To fold—To mix by carefully drawing one edge over the other a few times. *Gently fold the dry ingredients into the beaten egg whites.*

Fudge—A very rich, soft, chocolate candy made on top of the stove. *Mr. Finch always makes the most wonderful fudge for Christmas.*

To grate—To cut into small pieces by rubbing against a board with small holes. *Top the casserole with grated cheese.*

Heaping spoonful—A spoon filled to overflowing. *Add one heaping spoonful of cocoa.*

To grease—To rub oil or grease in a pan prior to putting batter in it. *Grease two cake pans, and then lightly dust with flour before pouring in the cake batter.*

Leavening—An agent, usually yeast or baking powder, that causes a batter or dough to rise. *Brownies are usually made without any leavening so they end up very dense and chewy.*

Lumpy—Containing small pieces of denser or harder substance. *Pancake batter is best if it is a little lumpy.*

To poach—To cook at a slow simmer in liquid. *Would you like your eggs poached this morning?*

Rustic—Not elegant, coarse, typical of country living. *Rustic food can very delicious and satisfying.*

Saucepan—A small but deep cooking pan that has a handle. *Use a saucepan to melt the butter.*

To scatter—To throw and distribute loosely. *Scatter nuts over the top and bake for 30 minutes.*

To skim—To remove what has floated to the top, usually cream or grease. *Cool the soup and then skim the grease off the top before warming to serve.*

Wet ingredients—All liquid ingredients, such as milk, eggs, juice, or water. *Mix the wet ingredients thoroughly before adding the dry ingredients.*

To whisk—To mix with quick, light movements with a fork or a wire utensil called a whisk. *Add the vanilla to the eggs and whisk quickly several times.*

C. GRAMMAR ESSENTIALS: QUANTIFIERS

Quantifiers describe an amount or quantity, and they answer the questions *how much* or *how many.* They operate as adjectives, describing the amount or quantity of the noun that follows. Numbers and measurements are exact quantifiers; numbers are simply used directly before the noun they quantify, and measurements are typically used with the preposition *of.* However, in recipes, *of* is often omitted:

> *I bought two cans of tea.*
> *We need three cups of flour. The recipe says to add three cups flour.*

The quantifiers *no, none of,* and *not any* indicate a quantity of zero:

> *I used no butter in the recipe.*
> *None of the recipes is low-fat.*
> *I didn't add any sugar.*

There are also many common quantifiers that are not specific or exact. Some are used with noncount nouns, answering the question *how much,* and some are used with count nouns, answering the question *how many.* Still others can be used with both. The following table summarizes approximate quantifiers, with quantities increasing toward the bottom of the table:

how much?	how many?	how much? / how many?
a bit of / a little	*(a) few*	
	several	*some / any*
much	*many*	
a great deal of	*a (large) number of*	*a lot of*
a large amount of	*a great amount of*	*plenty of*
		lots of
		all of

> *Add a little salt to almost all recipes.*
> *To make ice cream, use a great deal of cream.*
> *You'll need a large amount of ice and rock salt to put in the ice cream maker.*
> *You'll need a few overripe bananas to make banana bread.*
> *To make a deep red frosting, use several drops of food coloring.*

A large number of cookies were baked for the party.
It takes a great amount of carrots to make a little carrot juice.
Add some nuts, if you'd like.
We have a lot of bananas that you can use for the bread.
We have plenty of milk.
There's lots of sugar.

The following quantifiers work like degrees of adjectives, with a comparative and a superlative degree as well as the basic form:

plural count, increasing quantity	*many*	*more*	*most*
noncount, increasing quantity	*much*	*more*	*most*
plural count, decreasing quantity	*(a) few*	*fewer*	*fewest*
noncount, decreasing quantity	*(a) little*	*less*	*least*

We still have many apples, more bananas, and the most grapes.
Do these cookies have much sugar? They have more sugar. These have the most sugar.
I'll just have a few pancakes. He'll have fewer pancakes. He ate the fewest pancakes.
You only need a little salt! Use less salt than that. This recipe calls for the least salt.

Let's focus now on some of the quantifiers that are sometimes problematic for non-native speakers:

A few and *few* are countable. *A little* and *little* are not countable. Use *a few* and *a little* to talk about a small quantity:
I think there are a few more potatoes. Would you like them?
Yes, there's a little cole slaw left in the refrigerator.

Use *some* to express an indefinite amount that is not a large quantity. *Some* is typically used in affirmative statements, while *any* is used in negative statements and questions:
This recipe uses some orange juice.
This recipe doesn't call for any butter.
Do we have any milk on hand?

Use *some* in requests:
> *Could you pick up some rice?*
> *Could I please have some sugar?*

To make offers, use *some* or *any*:
> *Would you like some more coffee? / Would you like any more coffee?*

All means the total amount or sum, and is used with either count or noncount nouns:
> *All of the cake is gone.*
> *All of the cookies are gone.*

Each and *every* are singular, and they mean "all, individually." They're only used with count nouns:
> *Each dish was different and delicious.*
> *Every recipe is a little different.*

Both means "each of two," so it's only used with count nouns. It can be followed with a plural noun, a definite article plus plural noun, or *of* and a definite article plus plural noun:
> *I ate both apples. I ate both the apples. I ate both of the apples.*

Another is singular, and it adds a second, third, fourth, etc., of something:
> *Would you like another cup of coffee?*
> *I've already eaten three cookies; I couldn't eat another!*

Neither and *either* are singular and suggest a choice. *Either* is affirmative, while *neither* is negative:
> *I didn't make either one of these cakes.*
> *Neither one tastes better than the other.*

D. HOW-TO

American cuisine is probably most well known for foods like hot dogs, hamburgers, and French fries. While these are certainly foods commonly eaten in the U.S., they are not all the country has to offer. In fact, many different regional and fusion cuisines have developed out of the wide range of cultures and customs in the United States and the use of foods that are native to the Americas.

If you travel across the country, you will find a wide variety of local or regional cuisines. Many have sprung out of the fusion of a specific area's cooking style and ingredients with those of another country or countries. For example, Tex-Mex is a popular fusion cuisine often found in many restaurants in the U.S. Its name derives from the combination of "Texas" and "Mexico" and is thus, not surprisingly, a mixture of Mexican and Texan cooking styles and ingredients. Beef enchiladas, for example, might appear on a Tex-Mex menu, as well as salsa, chili peppers, burritos, chili con carne, and more. Another example of a fusion cuisine is Louisiana Creole. Creole is a fusion of Spanish, French, African, Caribbean, and Native American styles of cooking. Some common ingredients in Creole cooking are sweet potatoes, squash, cayenne pepper, okra, beans, corn, shrimp, and crawfish. Other fusion cuisines include Cajun, Italian-American, Pennsylvania Dutch, and many others. In addition, there are many other regional cuisines (which can also be fusion cuisines) in the U.S., such as New England cuisine, Hawaiian cuisine, and so on. In truth, almost every major city and region has a cuisine or dish that is particular to that area. Chicago, for instance, is known for its deep-dish pizza, Philadelphia for its cheese steak, and New York for its bagels and cheesecake.

However, there are some popular dishes that you will most likely see in many restaurants across the U.S., regardless of where you are. Typical American "classic" menu items include macaroni and cheese, club sandwiches, grilled cheese sandwiches, BLTs (bacon, lettuce, and tomato sandwiches), steak, meatloaf, fried chicken, pancakes, chocolate chip cookies, apple pie, and, of course, hot dogs, hamburgers, and french fries. Diners, which are family-style restaurants that serve a wide range of dishes, will typically offer all of these foods, plus much more. There are also common cooking methods, such as barbeque, that appear across the United States. Barbeque (or barbecue), often abbreviated as BBQ, is a style of slow cooking with open fire, usually with an open fire on a grill and usually using a seasoned, often spicy and tomato-based sauce (a barbeque sauce). Barbeque can also refer to a get-together where barbecuing takes place. There are many different styles of barbeque. Typically, meat is the primary object of a barbeque, with vegetables, such as corn, tomatoes, and even potatoes barbequed along with the meat. Some BBQ cooks marinate the meat, while others cook the meat so long that it shreds with the fingers. These styles are called strip, shredded, or pulled barbeque. Whatever the method, barbeque is a popular style of cooking in restaurants and homes and is often used for family events.

Many family events in the U.S. are also structured around brunch, a type of meal. Brunch, a combination of the words "breakfast" and "lunch," is usually served mid to late morning and even into the early afternoon. Foods commonly served at brunches include bagels and toast, eggs, bacon or fried ham, pancakes, waffles, fried potatoes, fruits, orange juice, sometimes mimosas (orange juice and champagne), and, of course, coffee and tea. There are also many restaurants throughout the U.S. that serve brunch on the weekends, sometimes as a buffet.

E. ENGLISH IN ACTION

Let's listen in as popular cooking instructor Daisy James and her son, Mylo, share how to make an all-American meal with her radio audience on "American Cuisine."

Daisy James: Today we're going to make some popular American dishes: scalloped potatoes, Caesar salad, and chocolate brownies.

Mylo: Mmmm. Sounds good!

Daisy: Yes, it does, doesn't it? Especially on a cool, rainy day like today. Scalloped potatoes are one of those all-time favorite comfort foods. Let's start with that, since it takes the longest to bake. First, we'll make a cream sauce. Melt about four tablespoons of butter in a saucepan over a low flame, then add four tablespoons of flour and stir together until it's a thick and creamy mixture. Now, gradually add two cups of milk. Pour a little of the milk in at a time while mixing slowly so that the sauce doesn't get any lumps. Once it gets lumpy, it's pretty hard to get it smooth again. Once you've poured and mixed in all the milk, add some salt, about a quarter of a teaspoon, and add a bit of pepper, about an eighth of a teaspoon, and mix them in. There, now it's nice and thick. If your sauce doesn't thicken very quickly, turn the heat up a little. Now slowly sprinkle in about three quarters of a cup of your favorite grated cheese. Mine is cheddar, because it has such a nice tang to it. Now peel and thinly slice five large Russet potatoes and one large onion. Layer the potatoes, onions and cream sauce in an 8 × 10 baking dish, sprinkling a little more cheese on the top layer if you like. Some people like to top this casserole with a few breadcrumbs. If you want to do that, scatter two heaping tablespoonfuls on top. Bake at 350 degrees for about 60 minutes or until a fork sinks into the potatoes and the top is bubbly. Now Mylo is going to tell us a little about the origin of Caesar salad. Mylo?

Mylo: Yes, thank you. Most people think of Caesar salad as a very typical American dish, but did you know that the first Caesar salad was actually tossed in Mexico in the 1920s? Its inventor, Caesar Cardini, was an Italian immigrant to the U.S. He lived in San Diego, but he operated a restaurant in Tijuana, Mexico, rather than San Diego, in order to avoid the laws prohibiting alcohol that existed in the U.S. during that time. The story goes that he developed the famous salad for his restaurant in Tijuana.

Daisy: Hmm. That's really interesting. One of my favorite salads. It sounds like a real international joint effort!

Mylo: Yes, definitely—an Italian American who worked in Mexico!

Daisy: So how do you make it?

Mylo: Okay, well you start with a large head of Romaine lettuce, wash, drain, and cut it into one-and-a-half-inch pieces. Pat it dry and put into the refrigerator for 30 minutes while you make the dressing. In order to make the dressing, you'll need . . .

F. PRACTICE

Fill in the blanks with the following words: *batter, comfort foods, drain, dust, grate, grease, leavening, lumpy, poach, skim*

1. You'll need to _____ off all the liquid before adding the olives to the casserole.

2. What ingredients do you mix together to make brownie _____?

3. If the mixture is too _____, try mixing it more thoroughly and adding a bit of water.

4. I'd prefer to _____ the salmon, instead of grilling it.

5. You'll need to _____ the cream off the top of the milk and set it aside.

6. Be sure to _____ the carrots before mixing them with the mayonnaise.

7. I think you forgot the _____. The cake is very flat and dense.

8. _____ remind people of their parents' cooking.

9. Lay a doily on top of the cake and _____ lightly with confectioners' sugar.

10. Don't forget to _____ the pan, or the cake will stick to the bottom.

Some, but not all, of the underlined quantifiers in the following paragraph are used incorrectly. Find the mistakes and correct them.

Another delicious American dish is apple pie. Choose (1) <u>a little</u> of your favorite apples. Try (2) <u>any</u> green ones if you like a tangy touch and add some yellow or golden apples if you like a sweeter pie. Slice the apples in a bowl and then mix in (3) <u>a little</u> or (4) <u>much</u> of sugar depending on your taste. You may not need (5) <u>some</u> sugar if the apples are sweet enough. Add (6) <u>more</u> teaspoons of cinnamon and a couple of tablespoons of flour. (7) <u>A little bit</u> of ginger adds a nice touch, but don't use too (8) <u>many</u> or your pie will taste bitter. Mix (9) <u>all</u> the ingredients together and put the apple mixture in a piecrust. Next, make a mixture of nuts, sugar, flour, cinnamon, and butter. Top the pie with just (10) <u>enough</u> to cover it. Bake for about one hour at 350 degrees.

G. TASK

After reading about brunch in the How-To section, buy or borrow an American cookbook or go online to find some recipes for typical American food that you'd have for brunch.

H. REAL LIFE

Do you know what brownies are? They are rich, fudge- or cake-like bar cookies that are very popular all over the United States. Nobody knows their origins for sure, but they might be an American original, dating back at least to the 1890s. They might have been discovered by accident by some American housewife who forgot to put the leavening in her cake batter. But that may be a myth, because most brownies have twice as much sugar as flour, while cakes have more flour than sugar. Whatever the case, mistake or not, Americans are very happy that the brownie was invented. If you like a rich, chocolaty dessert, try these brownies. You're guaranteed to love them!

DAISY JAMES'S FAVORITE BROWNIES
4 oz. or squares of baking chocolate
½ cup butter or margarine
4 eggs
½ tsp. salt
2 cups granulated sugar
1 tsp. vanilla
1 cup flour
1 cup nuts, preferably walnuts (optional)

Melt the chocolate squares and butter or margarine either in a microwave or a double boiler. Check and stir often so as not to burn. Allow to cool. Whisk eggs, sugar, and salt until light and fluffy. Add the melted butter and chocolate to the eggs and quickly fold together. Add the vanilla but do not overmix. Fold in the flour, and before the flour is thoroughly mixed in fold in the nuts. Pour the batter into a 13" × 9" greased pan dusted with flour or chocolate powder. Spread the batter evenly with a spatula. Bake in a 350-degree oven for 25 minutes. Do not overbake; brownies should be moist. Frost with your favorite frosting if you'd like, or top with chocolate chips that melt onto the hot brownies, and/or serve with vanilla ice cream. Brownies are delicious plain as well.

I. RESOURCES

Food in the U.S.:
www.ers.usda.gov/publications/foodreview/Archives
www.usatourist.com/english/inside/cooking.html
www.keyingredients.org
www.carnegielibrary.org/subject/food/american.html (regional American cooking)

American recipes:
www.foodbooks.com/recipes.htm (classic American)
www.foodtimeline.org/foodmexican.html (Mexican and Tex-Mex)
www.gumbopages.com/recipe-page.html (Cajun and Creole)
www.barbecuen.com (barbeque)
brunch.allrecipes.com/default.asp (brunch)
Miscellaneous recipes and food information at www.foodtv.com and
www.epicurious.com

American diners:
www.dinermuseum.org/index.php

Classic American cookbooks:
Joy of Cooking by Irma S. Rombauer and Marion Rombauer Becker
The Fannie Farmer Cookbook by Marion Cunningham

ANSWER KEY

Practice 1: 1. drain; 2. batter; 3. lumpy; 4. poach; 5. skim; 6. grate; 7. leavening; 8. Comfort foods; 9. dust; 10. grease

Practice 2: 1. some; 2. a few; 3. correct; 4. a lot; 5. any; 6. a few; 7. correct; 8. much; 9. correct; 10. correct

CHAPTER 27

Finding a Home: Looking for a Home

A. ENGLISH CLOSE-UP

**Relax in your large, secluded
2 bedroom, 1 bath apartment in Kenton Heights.**

Apartment faces the river. Near hospital and all major freeways.
Award-winning schools in the area.
Very low rent!
Pets okay. Application and credit check fee.
Available Mar. 1st.
Open house Monday, 10 a.m.–3 p.m.
Call Jim at **555-7901** for more information.

B. VOCABULARY ESSENTIALS

Amenities—Extras, special attributes that add to the attractiveness of a place. *Among the many amenities the condo has, there's a pool, an exercise room, and a clubhouse.*

Bay window—A window that projects out beyond the exterior wall. *This apartment has a nice bay window with a window seat overlooking the river.*

To up—To raise, to increase. *Our rent was upped again! To be honest, I don't know if we can afford to continue to rent this apartment.*

To check out—To look something over. *Check out the prices of these apartments. They're almost reasonable.*

Complex—A group of buildings, often owned or operated by the same person, company, or organization. Examples include an apartment complex or a condo complex. *My apartment complex is right here on the left.*

Condo (condominium)—A type of ownership where the units, such as apartments, in a building or group of buildings are owned by individuals but common areas are owned by all. A maintenance fee must often be paid for upkeep of the common areas. Condo can also refer to the unit itself. *They're putting in new condos next to the strip mall.*

Co-op (cooperative)—A building or group of buildings owned by a corporation that sells shares of ownership to buyers, who are purchasing the rights to live in one of the units, such as an apartment. Maintenance fees must usually be paid to the corporation for building upkeep, share of taxes, etc. There may be tax deductions. *I'm meeting with the co-op board next week. I'm really nervous and I hope they approve my application!*

Droppings—Waste left by insects and small rodents. *Check the house carefully for any droppings. We don't want to have to call the exterminator the first week.*

Duplex—A duplex house is a house made up of two separate apartments. A duplex apartment is an apartment with two floors. *I really liked the duplex we looked at, but I'd want to meet the people in the other half before I decided to rent it.*

To exterminate—To eliminate permanently, such as insects or rodents. *We have to call someone to come and exterminate the roaches in the basement.*

Leads—Information or tips. *I have a few leads on some nice apartments in the city.*

To look over—To review, to examine. *You'll need to look over the contract carefully before signing it.*

Mantel (mantelpiece)—A shelf that comes out of a chimney above the fireplace. *There are a lot of family pictures on top of the mantel.*

National Association of Realtors® (NAR)—An organization of real estate professionals. A Realtor® is a professional who works in real estate, is a member of NAR, and follows NAR's code of ethics. *The term Realtor® is often used synonymously with real estate agent or broker, but not all agents and brokers are necessarily Realtors® as well.*

Open house—A scheduled time when a home is open for prospective renters or buyers to see. *If you're interested in that apartment, there's an open house this Saturday from 10:00 until 5:00.*

Real estate agents and brokers—Agents and brokers act as intermediaries between a property owner and a renter or buyer. They negotiate for either or both parties for a fee and both must usually have a license in order to do business. Although the terms "real estate agent" and "real estate broker" are sometimes used interchangeably, they are not the same thing. A broker usually has additional experience and can own his or her own real estate company with agents working for him or her. Often, when someone says they have a real estate broker, they actually have a real estate agent. *In some cities, you have to hire a real estate broker if you want to find a nice place.*

Run-down—Uncared for, needing repair, in bad condition. *If you notice the apartment is run-down, don't rent it. It may mean a lot of appliances and other things will break soon.*

Seedy—Dirty, old, run-down, disreputable. *I'd prefer not to live in this seedy area.*

Square footage—The area of a property in square feet, which is the area of a square with sides each one foot in length. *How many square feet do you think this living room is? What's the square footage?*

Studio—An apartment that has no bedroom. One large room serves as the living room and bedroom, although there could be a sleeping loft or alcove for more privacy. *If you don't mind sleeping in the living room, you could get a studio for less money.*

To sublet—To rent an apartment from the current tenant, whose name is on the lease. Also, to be a renter who then rents out his or her apartment. *If you decide to move out before your lease is up, you'll need to sublet the apartment yourself.*

Super (superintendent)—The person in charge of taking care of an apartment building, and who sometimes shows apartments to prospective renters. *Buzz number 1 if you want to see if the super is available.*

Tenement—An apartment building, traditionally cheap and poorly maintained. *Many immigrant families lived in tenements on New York's Lower East Side, and some of these apartments are very expensive now.*

Townhouse—A home with two or more stories that is attached to one or more other townhouses. The owner owns not only the townhouse, but the property it sits on as well. *If you like having an attractive home in the city that might have a small yard and a balcony, a townhouse might be the best choice for you.*

C. GRAMMAR ESSENTIALS: PREPOSITIONS OF LOCATION

Earlier in this course we looked at prepositions of motion and direction, and prepositions of time. Now let's focus on prepositions that describe the location of something. Many prepositions in English can express both motion or direction and location. In this section, we'll only focus on the meanings that refer to stationary location or position:

Alongside—Next to something else, beside, or by the side of. *There's a row of trees alongside the apartment building.*

At—Within the boundaries of something, or inside a designated space. *There's a pool at Twenty-Nine Palms Apartments.*

Behind—In back of, in the rear of, beyond the backside of something. *Keana and Bob live in a little apartment behind the owners' home.*

Below—Under, beneath, lower than something else. *I live on the fourth floor and my best friend lives on the third floor. She lives right below me.*

Beside—Next to, at the side of. *There are several large pine trees beside the apartment building.*

Between—Occupying the space in the middle of two things. *Jeremy lives in building C. It's between building B and the swimming pool.*

In—Within the boundaries of. *Do you live in a condo or in a house?*

In front of—Directly beside the front of something. *There's a bus stop right in front of our apartment building.*

Inside—Within boundaries, on the inner side. *The exterior may not be that attractive, but it's really beautiful inside that building.*

Near—Close to. *The laundry room is near the pool.*

Next to—Beside, at the side of. *Oh, look. There's a bathroom next to each bedroom.*

On—Positioned above and resting on something. *There's a nice shine on the wood floor.*

On top of—Positioned above and resting on the upper surface of something, often stressing height. *Can you believe it? There are some shoes on top of the roof.*

Outside (of)—On the other side, external to something. *There's a deck right outside the kitchen.*

Over—Above or higher than something. *There is a lovely alcove over the fireplace.*

Under—Resting below or lower than something. *There's a nice closet under the stairs.*

Underneath—Immediately under something, covered by something. *What's the floor like underneath the carpet? Is it wood?*

D. HOW-TO

There's an old joke about the three most important things to look for when trying to find a home—location, location, location. In other words, the area where your house or apartment is located is the most important thing about it. Even if that's a bit of an exaggeration—you might be a little concerned about the home itself, too!—location is an easy place to start your hunt for a new home. You probably want to live in the nicest area possible for what you can afford, and the nicer the area, the more likely it is that you'll find a clean, safe, and well-kept place to live. So, if you can afford to pick which area you want to live in, you might want to start your hunt by simply deciding on two or three areas or neighborhoods where you'd like to live based on your needs and desires. Think of schools, public transportation, access to parks or water, medical facilities, cleanliness, safety, and so on. If you're buying a home, you might also want to think about property values—is the value of your home going to increase after purchasing it? If the city or town where you're looking is new or unfamiliar to you, the first thing you need to do is find out more about the communities and neighborhoods in it. The best way to do this is to go there and look for yourself, and to talk to people who live there if you can. A broker might be able to help you find a suitable area, too. But it's always a good idea to see the area yourself and speak to people who live there, as well.

Once you have chosen two or three areas where you'd like to live, you can start thinking about what kind of place you want to live in. What do you need in terms of square footage and rooms? Do you need a two- or a three-bedroom place? Do you like lots of light? What amenities do you wish to have? Do you want a furnished or an unfurnished home? Do you want to buy a home in mint condition (in excellent shape) or a home that is a fixer-upper? A fixer-upper is a place that needs a lot of work, but some people prefer this because it means they can design more of the house themselves. Most people have a pretty good idea of what they need before they sit down and think about it, but it's still a good idea to put it all on paper, especially if you plan to hire a broker to help you. So make a list of must-haves and wishes for your new home.

The next question is how to find the right place for you. For some people, the answer is simply to go to a real estate broker or agent and tell him or her want you want. If you can't look on your own—for example, if you are too busy or you live in another city or country—you will probably need someone else to do the legwork for you. In some large cities in the U.S., it can be very difficult to find a place to live without hiring a broker. Unless you are willing to do a lot of work and probably be pretty aggressive, you might not find a very good home, or even a place to live at all, in a big city. So a broker can be the "one-stop shopping" solution for finding a home. However, brokers almost always charge a fee. A rental broker's fee is often a commission, usually a percentage of the yearly rent. For example, if the rent of the apartment you get through the broker is $1,000 a month and the broker charges 12%, then the fee for your broker's services is $1,440. For more information on finding and paying for a broker, see Lesson 29.

If you don't use a broker and prefer to find a place yourself, you're going to have to do your homework to find the best deals that are out there. Many people also like to use brokers as well as look on their own at the same time. Homes for rent and for sale are listed in newspapers, online at websites like Craigslist.com or apartments.com and at the websites of real estate management companies, in rental or real estate magazines, and on bulletin boards you can find outside supermarkets or at shopping centers or community centers. If you're in school, your school might also have listings or provide off-campus housing help of some kind. Real estate agencies will have plenty of listings as well (homes can be listed through multiple agencies), but to get to those homes you will most likely have to use one of their brokers. Also, keep in mind that just because you're not working directly with a real estate broker does not mean that there might not be some sort of fee involved. Some websites, management companies, and others might charge fees for using their services, although they will often be less than those of an agent or broker.

If you can easily get to the community where you'd like to live, another way to find a place is to go to the neighborhoods you are interested in and drive or walk around looking for signs. Some landlords don't like to post ads in newspapers or online, and they like the personal touch of someone seeing a sign in the window and inquiring. You can find some great deals this way, including small apartments or houses in the back of the owner's home, duplexes where the landlord lives in one unit, rooms for rent, and so on. And if the owners live on the property, they are more likely to take very good care of it, because it is their home as well, after all.

The next step is to start looking at the places you've found, and that means scheduling appointments with the owners, landlords, brokers, or supers. Some places may also have open houses, which will be listed in any ads. When you visit a place, you have to be ready to take in a lot of details, often in a short period of time. A lot of this means checking for problems or potential problems, even before you get into the apartment or home. Is the exterior clean? Does it seem safe and well lit? What do the neighbors' places look like? Is there anything that's going to make a lot of noise, such as certain types of businesses, highways or freeways, or train tracks? Once you're inside, take a good general look around you. Does the place look clean or run-down? Is there fresh paint? A new carpet? Enough storage? Are the appliances new, or at least in good shape? Is the refrigerator noisy? Check the plumbing for leaks and water pressure. How large is the water heater, and do you have to share the water heater with other tenants? Are there smoke detectors? Check the ceiling for any signs of leaks. Check in several rooms to see if there are enough outlets and phone jacks for your needs. Is the place cable-ready, i.e., is it wired for cable TV and/or internet service? Do the windows open and close properly? Do other windows in the neighborhood have security bars, and if so, do the windows in the places you're looking at have them as well? Check the locks to be sure they are secure. Does the door have a deadbolt lock on it? How does the place smell? Some smells can be removed, but some smells, like cigarette smoke or mold, are not so easy to remove, and could cause you health problems if you were to live there for a while. Check to be sure the building has good insulation and ventilation. Also check for rodent or insect droppings or walls that are too thin. Ask about who pays the utility bills and find out about any maintenance fees and what the property taxes are, if applicable, as well as what any other additional expenses might be and how much your expenses are. You might also want to find out if there are any financing restrictions and if there are any credit check or application fees. Finally, if you're a renter, try to find out as much as you can about the landlord. You'll be asked for references as a renter, but did you ever think about asking the landlord for references? Having a good landlord can make the value of your rental worth a lot more than just getting a nice apartment. A good landlord will take care of any problems that come up in a timely manner, and he or she will also be fair.

We'll cover the next steps for both buyers and renters in the next lessons, but for now, happy home hunting!

E. ENGLISH IN ACTION

Rita and Ed have been looking for a new apartment. They are just about to look at an apartment Rita found while driving around the neighborhood.

Ed:	I can't believe you found this place just driving around!
Rita:	I know. It looks really nice, doesn't it?
Ed:	Yeah! Especially considering all the seedy places we've had to look at so far!
Rita:	I hope it's as nice inside as it is outside.
Ed:	Honey, like I said, it's got to be better than what we've looked at so far. That duplex was awful!
Rita:	Oh, this must be Mr. Kendall now.
Mr. Kendall:	Hi, I'm Jim Kendall.
Rita:	Hi, I'm Rita and this is Ed.
Ed:	Nice to meet you.
Mr. Kendall:	You've probably seen enough of the yard. Let me show you inside.
Rita:	Ohhh. It looks nice. It's so quaint. Are these real wood floors? They are, aren't they? Oh, look, honey. A bay window! And a fireplace with a mantel! How many square feet is it?
Mr. Kendall:	Yes, they're real wood. It's just under 1,100 square feet. Here's the kitchen.
Rita:	Ed, what are you doing?
Ed:	I'm checking for mice or rat droppings, you know.
Mr. Kendall:	Even if you find droppings, we just had it fumigated.
Ed:	Good to know.
Rita:	Hmm. Let's check out the bathrooms. Ed, Ed? What are you doing under there?
Ed:	Just checking the pipes, dear.
Rita:	Oh. Do you see anything?

Mr. Kendall: He shouldn't. I've had everything checked over. It's worth it to me to keep everything in good repair. It just costs too much to let things get run-down.

Ed: You ought to tell that to some of the other landlords in this town.

Rita: Ed!

Mr. Kendall: Ha! No, that's okay. He's right. But I live here on this property. I don't want to look out at an old shack, you know.

Ed: I suppose that's true. Well, you have a pretty nice place here. Rita and I are going to be looking at a couple of other places. We'll try to get back to you later today.

Rita: Ed, I really like this place!

Ed: Right, well, we have a few things to discuss before we decide. Thanks, Mr. Kendall.

Mr. Kendall: You're welcome, Ed, Rita. Nice to meet you both!

F. PRACTICE

Fill in the blanks using the following words: *check out, droppings, leads, upping your rent, run-down, seedy, exterminate, amenities, broker, studio*

1. We aren't having much luck finding a place, so we'd better hire a(n) _____.

2. Everything in this neighborhood is so _____! Nothing's been repaired in a long time.

3. There's an apartment on 5th I think we should _____; I think we'll like it.

4. Wow, they're _____ by a lot! Are you thinking of moving elsewhere?

5. This area looks a little too _____ for me. I'd be scared to live here.

6. It looks like nobody has been here to _____ for a long time. There are roaches everywhere!

7. Are those mouse _____ in the corner?

8. This _____ is really nice, but it's so small, and I could never have guests!

9. The _____ in this apartment building are really amazing—patio, fireplace, new washer and dryer . . .

10. We have to be out of this apartment in two weeks and we still don't have any _____ on a new apartment.

Fill in the blanks with the following prepositions: *underneath, outside, on top of, near, beside, in, on, at, inside, alongside.*

1. Can you place the napkins _____ the table, please? We're going to be having dinner soon.

2. There's a nightstand _____ my bed so I can easily reach my glasses if I need them.

3. There's a lot of dust on the floor _____ the coffee table. We obviously don't think about cleaning under there very often.

4. I left my keys _____ the house. I'll run and get them.

5. You can't miss it. It's a big yellow house with a small stream running right _____ it.

6. The house is green outside and a soft yellow _____.

7. There's a large picture sitting _____ the mantel.

8. If you look _____ the bedroom window, you can see a rose garden.

9. Is your house _____ the old bowling alley? I thought I remembered passing it on the way here once.

10. We live _____ 3452 Bowling Green Road.

G. TASK

Imagine that you need to find a new place to live. (If you really do, then this will be especially helpful!) Make a list of what you would like in a new apartment or house, and write down how much you can afford to spend. Then choose one or two neighborhoods you would like to live in, and look in your local newspaper, rental magazine, or online house finder for something that fits your needs and price range. If you can, walk or drive around the neighborhoods you're interested in to see if there are any signs posted.

H. REAL LIFE

Hi, I'm Rae Anne Bennett, a rental broker. For the last twenty years or so I've been helping people find suitable housing. One of the things I've noticed is that people aren't always sure whether they want to rent an apartment, a house, or townhouse. The problem is that this takes time away from actually finding what you really want. You could miss out on the perfect place while trying to decide which type of home is best suited to your lifestyle. Choosing a place to live can be as important and time consuming as finding a job. One way to help you make a decision is to look at the options available to you and understand the differences.

Let's start with houses. A majority of people would like to live in a house. A house offers privacy, probably a yard, and a homeyness you just can't find anywhere else. A house is probably the best place for young families or those who are about to start a new family. But a house also has extra responsibilities. Many houses have good-sized front yards and backyards. That means maintenance, unless you've negotiated with your landlord to have someone come in and do the yard work. Furthermore, you will most likely have to commute to work unless you work for yourself.

Then there are apartments. An apartment probably does not have a yard. You might have a balcony where you can put a few flowerpots, but there's no extra maintenance. You have less privacy, but apartments are usually less expensive and more convenient than houses because they can be closer to town, so you probably won't have to commute.

Finally, there are townhouses. A townhouse is a nice compromise between an apartment and a house. You can usually find townhouses in the city, so there's probably no commute. They can be attractive and fairly private. There's sometimes a small yard that you'll need to maintain, but that means that you have your own little piece of nature where you can read or barbecue and entertain. However, townhouses in big cities can sometimes be very expensive to rent (or to own!), so keep that in mind if you're looking to rent a whole townhouse or even an apartment in one.

I hope this information helps you make a very important decision and saves you time. Good luck!

I. RESOURCES

National Association of Realtors®:
www.realtor.com (for listings, sales, and rentals, and for information on finding a home)

Finding a home:
www.move.com
www.craigslist.org
www.apartments.com
www.mls.com (Multiple Listing Service, for more information see Lesson 29)
www.nytimes.com/pages/realestate
www.apartmentguide.com
www.forrent.com
www.homelistings-usa.com/realestate.html
www.offcampusnetwork.com
www.sublet.com

Information on finding a home:
www.vidaamericana.com/english/apartment.html
www.soyouwanna.com/site/categories/apartments.html

Information on brokers and agents:
www.bls.gov/oco/ocos120.htm

ANSWER KEY

Practice 1: 1. broker; 2. run-down; 3. check out; 4. upping your rent; 5. seedy; 6. exterminate; 7. droppings; 8. studio; 9. amenities; 10. leads

Practice 2: 1. on; 2. beside; 3. underneath; 4. in; 5. alongside; 6. inside; 7. on top of; 8. outside; 9. near; 10. at

CHAPTER 28

Finding a Home: Renting an Apartment

A. ENGLISH CLOSE-UP

RENTAL AGREEMENT

Property owner _____ hereafter known as the landlord agrees to rent _____ (address) to tenant _____ for one year, beginning _____ and ending on _____, unless both parties agree to terminate this agreement. Rent of $_____ will be paid for one year (twelve months) for the dwelling at _____ _____.

B. VOCABULARY ESSENTIALS

Breach—A violation. *Check for smoke detectors. If there are none then that could be a safety breach.*

To break a lease—To move out before a lease is up. *If we break the lease we'll lose our deposit, but because we found a nicer, cheaper apartment, it might be worth it.*

Cleaning deposit—An amount paid to the landlord that will be paid back when you move out, provided the apartment is in the condition it was in when you moved in. Can sometimes refer to a nonrefundable cleaning fee, charged by the landlord in order to pay for cleaning after you move out. Sometimes synonymous with *security deposit. It looks like there's a cleaning deposit of $550. I guess we can handle that.*

Dwelling—A place to live in. *This area isn't zoned for residential dwellings.*

To feel at home—To feel comfortable. *So, do you like your new place? Do you feel at home yet?*

Furnished—Equipped with furniture. *The apartment comes furnished for an extra $75.00 a month.*

To give notice—To officially notify your landlord you will be moving, usually 30 days before the move-out date, often in writing. *We have to give written notice at least one month before we want to move out.*

Guarantor—A person who legally ensures that the tenant will fulfill his or her rental obligations, including paying rent, usually if the tenant does not meet a landlord's qualifications for renting the property. A guarantor often must meet higher qualifications, such as a higher salary, than a potential tenant. *If you have bad credit or a low salary, you may need to get a guarantor in order to rent certain apartments.*

HUD—U.S. Department of Housing and Urban Development. A government agency that deals with improving housing for the public. *If you believe your housing rights have been violated, you can go to your local HUD office to file a complaint.*

Lessee—The one who rents a property, usually the tenant. *The lessee must pay the lessor the sum of $1,500 on the first of each month.*

Lessor—The person who rents a property to another, usually the landlord or owner. *The Bowman Company will be the lessor on this property.*

Liability—Legal responsibility or debt. *Many renters purchase renters' insurance to help cover theft, fire damage, and other potential damages, as well as to protect them from any liability in case someone gets hurt in their home.*

Low-income housing—Housing that is designated for families with low incomes and is made affordable through government subsidies, tax credits, funding, etc. *Check the HUD database to find low-income housing. If you qualify, you'll be able to get a nice place for a lot less money.*

To make ends meet—To have enough money to live on. *With such an expensive apartment, I'm not sure we'd be able to make ends meet.*

Middle-income housing—Affordable housing for middle-income people; only available in certain parts of the U.S. *Did you know that you can get middle-income housing assistance in New York City?*

Mother-in-law cottage—A small house built in the back of a house, often to accommodate an aging parent or in-law. They often become rental properties. *Did you see the cute mother-in-law cottage on Wilkes Road? It's tiny but really cozy.*

To negotiate—To discuss something, usually a price, in order to come to an agreement, to bargain. *Chances are not good that you'll be able to negotiate a lower price, but you might be able to negotiate for some additional options.*

Public housing projects—Government owned, administered, and funded housing for low-income or elderly people or people with disabilities. Rent

(Total Tenant Payment, or TTP) is based on family income, minus any deductions. *If your income is considered low-income by the government, you can get on the waiting list for the neighborhood housing project.*

Rent control—A means of limiting the cost of rental properties in a city or town by placing a cap on how much a renter can be charged in rent. *I found a great apartment on the West Side, and it's even rent controlled.*

Rider—An amendment or addition that is added to a contract that both parties agree to and sign for. *So if you want to get an additional garage, you might be able to ask the landlord to add a rider to your lease agreement allowing you an extra garage. It'll cost you a little extra, but at least you'll be able to get one.*

Security deposit—An amount of money paid to the landlord to insure that you will fulfill your rental obligations as well as to cover any damage done to the apartment during your stay. It is fully refundable unless damage is done or the obligations are not met, for example, if you break the lease. *It looks like the security deposit is one month's rent.*

To sign on the dotted line—To make a formal agreement with someone, to sign a contract. *Make sure you read the contract carefully before you sign on the dotted line.*

Subsidized housing—An arrangement whereby the tenants pay less than the going rate while the government subsidizes or provides funding to the owner of the property. *If you make below a certain amount of money, you can get subsidized housing.*

Tenants' association—A group of tenants in a building that organize to advocate for the improvement of conditions in their apartment building, and strategize ways to deal with their landlords. *If you're having trouble getting the landlord to make repairs on your property, you can take your concerns to the tenants' association if there is one. Better yet, join the association.*

Termination notice—A notice that a person must move by a certain date, usually 30 days after receiving notice. *The landlord is selling the building to a condo association, so all the tenants just got a termination notice.*

 C. GRAMMAR ESSENTIALS: CONFUSING WORD PAIRS

There are a number of word pairs that look or sound very similar, but have different uses or entirely different meanings. Let's see if we can sort out the differences:

Accept vs. *Except*

Accept—A verb meaning "to agree to receive something." *If you <u>accept</u> the terms of the contract, you can sign it.*

Except—Usually a conjunction meaning "excluding," but also a verb meaning "to exclude." *I agree with everything <u>except</u> the "no pets" rule.*

Affect vs. Effect

Affect—To cause someone to feel something, to influence someone or something, to create a result. *The crime statistics from this neighborhood have really <u>affected</u> real estate.*

Effect—A result or consequence. *The <u>effects</u> of all of the negative publicity were immediately felt.*

All ready vs. Already

All ready—Completely or in all ways prepared. *I was <u>all ready</u> to tell them we wouldn't be taking the apartment.*

Already—At a prior time. *I've <u>already</u> signed the lease.*

All together vs. Altogether

All together—As a unit, as a whole, as a group. *The neighbors decided to make a complaint <u>all together</u> rather than individually.*

Altogether—Completely. *They told the landlord there was <u>altogether</u> too much noise coming out of apartment 3C.*

Besides vs. Beside

Besides—An adverb or preposition that means "more," "in addition," and sometimes "moreover." *<u>Besides</u> three bedrooms, this place has two bathrooms.*

Beside—A preposition that means "next to." *There's a bathroom <u>beside</u> the master bedroom.*

Between vs. Among

Between—In the middle of two things or people. *I prefer the small house <u>between</u> the two trees.* A common idiomatic expression is "Between you and me ...," meaning, "No one else knows but the two of us," or, "It's our secret."

Among—In the company of more than two things or people, surrounded by. *This is only one house <u>among</u> many.*

Capitol vs. Capital

Capitol—A building that is the seat of government of a city, state, or country. The building where the U.S. legislature meets. *Have you ever been to the <u>Capitol</u>?*

Capital—The city that holds the state or national government. *Have you studied your state <u>capitals</u> yet? Capital* can also mean "uppercase letter," "very important," or "money gathered for a project."

Complement vs. Compliment

Complement—Something that goes along with or completes something; to go along with or complete something. *The color of the sofa <u>complements</u> the color of the walls.*

Compliment—Praise or kind words of approval, to give praise or kind words of approval. *I'd like to compliment you on how beautifully you've decorated this place.*

Hard vs. *Hardly*

Hard—An adjective that means "strong" or "durable," and an adverb that means "difficult." *It is often hard to find the perfect place to live.*

Hardly—An adverb that means "not much" or "almost nothing at all." *This place is hardly big enough for all of us to live in.* A common joke in the U.S. entails asking a person, "Working hard or hardly working?" The meanings are quite different—"Are you putting forth a lot of effort to work, or are you doing so little work that you're almost not working at all?"

Personal vs. *Personnel*

Personal—Private, individual, face-to-face. *If you go to the manager personally, he won't be able to refuse your request.*

Personnel—Employees, the human resources department. *If you go to the personnel office you'll be able to apply for a job with the company.*

Principle vs. *Principal*

Principle—Moral standard of behavior. *There are principles that tenants should follow and principles that landlords should follow.*

Principal—Most important, chief, or primary, the most important, chief, or primary participant in a given situation. *The landlord and the tenant are the two principals involved in the contractual relationship of property rental.*

Stationary vs. *Stationery*

Stationary—Remaining in one place, not moving. *The garden has many stationary objects, like a birdbath and a fountain.*

Stationery—Paper used for writing letters. *Mr. Wilkes sent us a letter on his business stationery.*

D. HOW-TO

Finding a place that you like and can afford is probably the most difficult part of the process of renting an apartment. But there are a few things you should know about renting an apartment, and there's just a little more work to do before you can move in and start to decorate.

Some landlords will rent on a month-to-month basis, without any lease. The benefit for renters in this situation is that they can move out whenever they want, sometimes simply giving thirty days notice. There's no long-term lease that they have to worry about breaking. But the risk is that there aren't the same guarantees and protections in place that a lease offers. You could be asked to leave before you're ready, or rent can be increased at any time. With a long-term lease, the problem of rising rent doesn't exist, at least not for the duration of the lease. A lease is a contract between the lessor and lessee, so all the rights and duties of both the landlord and the tenant are spelled out clearly—who pays for what repairs, whether the tenant can have pets or not, additional storage, how clean the apartment must be kept, etc. A lease also covers all the fees involved (such as rent, as well as security and possibly cleaning deposits) and is usually set up for one or two years, which means that the rent stays the same for the entire length of the lease. This is a plus for the lessee because apartment rents generally go higher, not lower, and they usually don't stay the same after a year. A lease should outline whether or not subletting is allowed, and how to sublet if allowed. It discusses the condition of the property at the time of contract signing, any repair issues that may come up, and who's responsible for what. The lease will also include the rights and duties of any guarantors, who will also need to sign the lease. It's very important that the lessee read over the contract very carefully before signing. Because a lease is a contract, it is a legal document that can be upheld in court should it be violated in any way by either party.

There are a few laws regarding rentals that are important for you to know if you're planning on renting, both when you're signing a lease and once you've moved into a place. First of all, according to the Fair Housing Act, no landlord is allowed to discriminate because of your sex, race, color, disability, nationality, disability, or family status. This act is enforced by HUD, the U.S. Department of Housing and Urban Development. Other laws regulate the amount of money you pay for rent. In some areas, rental properties may be regulated by rent control, meaning that there is a cap on the amount of money that can be charged as rent. Not all properties are covered by these laws, so check with any local rent control boards for specific information. In addition, the health department sets laws which are meant to control the condition of the rental property. This usually means that you should not have to contend with rodents or insects and the landlord must take action if your dwelling has an infestation. You have the right to a certain amount of privacy, so the landlord should call to inform you if he or she needs to get inside your apartment, except in case of an emergency, such as a gas leak. Eviction laws vary from state to state, so you should educate yourself about yours.

Low-rent government-subsidized housing, as well as public housing, is available for individuals or families that are eligible, i.e. low-income households (50% of the median income for the area for very low-income and 80% for low-income), people with disabilities, and senior citizens. Low-income families may qualify for the Housing Choice Voucher Program, in which families pay 30% of their income for a rental in the housing of their choice and the government pays the balance directly to the property owner.

These programs are all administered by HUD. The only problem with any of these programs is that the waiting lists can be very long, sometimes even years long. To apply and get on the waiting list for public housing and the voucher program, contact your local Public Housing Agency or PHA. See www.hud.gov/offices/pih/pha/contacts to find your local agency. To search for low-rent subsidized housing, and for more information on all of these programs, go to www.hud.gov/renting. In addition, in some areas, such as New York, subsidized middle-income housing exists, although these programs are not nearly as widespread as subsidized or otherwise funded low-income housing. To find out about subsidized housing in your area, check the "planning" section of your city's website.

E. ENGLISH IN ACTION

Let's get back to Rita and Ed, who were looking at a rental property in the last lesson. They've decided to take it, so let's listen in as Ed and the new landlord speak.

Mr. Kendall: Hello?

Ed: Hello, Mr. Kendall, this is Ed Miller. Rita and I have already talked it over and would like to rent your house.

Mr. Kendall: Okay. Great.

Ed: So, do we need to fill out an application?

Mr. Kendall: Yes, I'm sure you folks would be great tenants, but we've got to dot all our i's and cross all our t's.

Ed: I understand. We have great credit, and I can get references from our last landlord if you'd like.

Mr. Kendall: Sure, that would be wonderful.

Ed: What's the deposit, by the way?

Mr. Kendall: I'll need first and last months' rent upon signing of the lease. Oh, and you pay the utilities, except heat, sewer, and water. And there's a $500 cleaning deposit. You'll get it all back if you leave the place in pretty much the same condition as when you move in. I expect there to be normal wear and tear.

Ed: So, no security deposit?

Mr. Kendall: Sorry, I forgot to mention that. There is a security deposit and it's the amount of one month's rent.

Ed: What if we want to do anything or fix anything?

Mr. Kendall: I'd appreciate it if you asked me first. It depends upon what it is, too. Paint and stuff like that's okay. But if something breaks, tell me and I'll take care of it.

Ed: Is this a one-year lease or a two-year?

Mr. Kendall: We could do either.

Ed: Well, I think Rita and I would like to stay for a few years, so we probably prefer the two-year.

Mr. Kendall: That's great. So, the next step is just that you'll need to fill out the application, and my lawyer will make me run a credit check on you, ha ha . . .

Ed: Like I said, I understand. You can't be too careful. Shall I leave you something to hold the apartment?

Mr. Kendall: Yes, I'll take a $500 deposit, plus $50 for your credit check. If everything checks out, the deposit will go toward your rent. But if you change your mind or something pops up on the credit check, you'll get it all back, except for the credit check fee. Otherwise, I'll draw up the lease for you to look over and sign. Okay?

Ed: Sounds good to me.

Mr. Kendall: All right, so when do you want to stop by to fill out the application?

Ed: Why don't we stop by tomorrow? Rita and I would love to do another walk-through. We might have some more questions. But I'll send the deposit right away.

Mr. Kendall: Okay, sounds great. I'll see you tomorrow, then.

F. PRACTICE

Fill in the blanks with the following words: *negotiate, break the lease, sign on the dotted line, give notice, rider, feel at home, furnished, termination notice, make ends meet, dwelling*

1. If you _____, you usually lose your deposit.

2. The neighbors who haven't paid their rent for months just got a(n) _____ in the mail.

3. I don't have any furniture, so I'd prefer to rent a(n) _____ apartment if possible.

4. Do you _____ in the new place yet, or do you miss your old house?

5. What kind of _____ do you reside in?

6. Okay, here's the contract, just _____ and I'll give you the keys to your new home.

7. If you want to move out, you need to _____ at least two months before you plan to leave.

8. I wonder if we could _____ with the landlord. Maybe if we sign a two-year lease she'll lower our rent a little.

9. Do you think we'll have enough money to _____, or should we find some place cheaper?

10. The lease says no pets, but the landlord added a(n) _____ that said I could have a cat.

Choose the correct word from each of the following pairs.

1. Everyone has moved in (accept/except) the Busbys.
2. Moving to a new town will (affect/effect) the whole family in some way or other.
3. I heard that they had (already/all ready) moved in.
4. The tenants are acting (altogether/all together) to pressure the landlord to make repairs.
5. Haven't you found anything else (beside/besides) that one place that's small and dark?
6. Some people like to have lots of friends in their apartment building and to live (between/among) friends.
7. (Hard/Hardly) anybody can afford the rent on those new townhouses.
8. I hope you'll (accept/except) these cookies as a way to welcome you to the neighborhood.
9. Are we (already/all ready) for the movers to move us?
10. What (affect/effect) will the new ecological report have on our neighborhood?

G. TASK

Are you a well-informed renter? Take a look at www.hud.gov/renting and read about renters' rights and the tips for tenants. You might be surprised by what you learn, and you could find information that will save you a lot of time and trouble.

H. REAL LIFE

Dear Sammy,

I recently moved out of my old apartment and into a new (and better!) one. I would like to get my security deposit back to help pay for buying new furniture and other things for my new apartment, but I still haven't gotten it back from my former landlord. When he came by before I moved out and inspected the apartment, he said that it was in great condition and that I would be getting my deposit back. However, it's been over a month and I still haven't received it! What should I do?

Sincerely,
Frustrated

Dear Frustrated,

First, I would like you to keep in mind that laws governing security deposits vary from state to state and leases certainly vary as well, so you should check out your lease and the laws in your state. But as a general overview, here are a few things to keep in mind regarding the return of security deposits.

Did you get a written confirmation from your landlord regarding the condition of the apartment? If at all possible, you should try to secure a written statement from your landlord confirming the apartment's condition. Take pictures of the apartment before you move out if you can. Also, your landlord probably should have asked you for a written statement containing instructions for where to send the deposit. If you did not send him or her such a statement, preferably by certified mail, try to get in touch with the landlord to see how to fix that situation and/or get that information to him or her as soon as possible. You should also make sure you have returned all of your keys and that you have fulfilled any other moving out and deposit return requirements detailed in your lease. If you have, then your landlord should return your deposit to you (with an itemized list of any deductions) in a reasonable amount of time. Some states have laws that note exactly how much time landlords can take to return the deposit, but not all do, so check the laws in your state. If your landlord has exceeded the allotted amount of time, or a reasonable amount of time, and has not sent you any letters explaining any deductions, then you'll probably want to write a letter, sent by certified mail, requesting the return of your deposit. Keep a copy of the letter for yourself. If the landlord still doesn't respond, you may want to consult a lawyer or consider suing the landlord in small claims court.

Sincerely,
Sammy

I. RESOURCES

HUD:
www.hud.gov or 1-800-569-4287
www.hud.gov/renting (for low-income rentals and general tenants' rights information)

Housing discrimination:
www.hud.gov/complaints/housediscrim.cfm or 1-800-669-9777 (to file a complaint)
www.usdoj.gov/crt/housing/faq.htm

www.apartmentratings.com/rate/fairhousing
www.fairhousinglaw.org

Rent control:
realestate.findlaw.com/tenant/tenant-rent/tenant-rent-control.html

Income limits to qualify as low-income:
www.huduser.org/datasets/il.html

Tenants' rights and tips for renting:
realestate.findlaw.com/tenant/tenant-overview
offcampusnetwork.com/movelearn.asp
www.apartmentratings.com/rate/TipsForRenters.html

Books:
Every Tenant's Legal Guide by attorney Janet Portman and Marcia Stewart

ANSWER KEY
Practice 1: 1. break the lease; 2. termination notice; 3. furnished; 4. feel at home; 5. dwelling; 6. sign on the dotted line; 7. give notice; 8. negotiate; 9. make ends meet; 10. rider

Practice 2: 1. except; 2. affect; 3. already; 4. all together; 5. besides; 6. among; 7. Hardly; 8. accept; 9. all ready; 10. effect

CHAPTER 29

Finding a Home: Buying a House

A. ENGLISH CLOSE-UP

Today's Mortgage Rates

	Today	Last Week
30 year fixed	6.35%	6.49%
15 year fixed	5.59%	5.66%
5/1 ARM	5.79%	5.99%
30 year fixed jumbo	6.48%	6.57%
5/1 jumbo ARM	5.98%	6.01%

B. VOCABULARY ESSENTIALS

Appraisal—The estimated value of property made by a trained specialist. *This appraisal shows your property to be valued at $700,000! That's $75,000 more than you paid for it.*

To appreciate—To increase in value either by upgrading the quality or through rising property values in general. *If kept in good condition, a house normally appreciates annually.*

ARM—Adjustable rate mortgage. The total interest rate equals the index rate (which changes) plus a usually fixed margin (percentage points that are essentially the lender's profit) that is determined by the lender. *It can be easier to afford a house with an ARM, but you need to be sure you can afford to pay a higher rate at a later date if the index rate your ARM is tied to rises.*

Buyer's market—When there are more houses for sale than there are people to buy them, meaning that buyers can get a lower price for a house. *Maybe now's the time for us to buy a house; it's a buyer's market and prices have dropped quite a bit.*

Buyer's remorse—A feeling of fear or regret at having made a purchase. *Buyer's remorse is just part of the experience, especially if it's your first house. You'll get past it.*

Closing—When escrow closes, the sale is completed and the property transfers to the new owner. *Your closing date will be June 30th. That's about 30 days from today.*

Deed—The legal document confirming your ownership of the house. *I'm so excited. The sale closed and I finally have the deed to my new house!*

To depreciate—To decrease in value. *Homes rarely depreciate except during economic downturns or if the home is not properly maintained.*

Down payment—A percentage of the sale price that the buyer must pay at the closing in addition to any money borrowed. The down payment plus mortgage amount equals the purchase price of the home, so the higher the down payment, the lower the amount of money you need to borrow. Lenders generally require a down payment in order to get a loan on a property. *It's a good idea to make at least a 20% down payment on a house so that you don't have to pay PMI (private mortgage insurance), insurance to cover the risk to the lender that you might default on the loan.*

Escrow—When a third party holds the money, property, and deed during the process of completing the sale, which usually takes about 30 days. *Your escrow company will be First Title and Trust.*

To fall out of escrow—For a sale to fail, because, for example, the buyer or seller changes his or her mind, or the buyer doesn't have enough money. *The agent just called to say we fell out of escrow. What are we going to do? I loved that house.*

Fixed rate mortgage—When the interest rate is set at the beginning of the mortgage process and never changes throughout the duration of the loan. *I can give you a fixed rate mortgage of 6.75%. That's still a very low interest rate.*

Foreclosure—When a property owner cannot make payments to the bank for many months, the property goes into foreclosure and the lender takes legal possession of it. *Whatever you do, don't let your house go into foreclosure. You might never be able to buy another one.*

Home equity—The difference between the mortgage and the value of the property. *We may not have much money in the bank, but on paper we're rich because we have a lot of equity in our house.*

Index rate—An established interest rate used by lenders to help determine the interest rate on loans. Common index rates used are those from Treasury securities, the Cost of Funds Index, and the prime rate. *If you're thinking of using an ARM to purchase your home, you should check with your lender to see what index rate they use and how often the interest rate will change on the loan.*

Listing—A property that is for sale through a licensed real estate agent or broker. When you look at a listing on the MLS or elsewhere, you will see information on the seller's terms, the price, and a description of the property. *After we sign a contract with a real estate agent, our apartment will be listed.*

MLS (Multiple Listing Service)—A database of all the properties for sale in the U.S., searchable by area, through licensed real estate agents or brokers. Having your house on the MLS insures that the most people possible will know that your house is for sale. *I'll run a list of properties in your price range on the MLS.*

Mortgage—The name given to a bank loan used to purchase a property. The property owner makes payments on a sum of money the lender has loaned him or her plus the interest on that money. *I'm going to be 90 years old before I pay off this mortgage!*

Mortgage broker—A loan officer. A licensed professional who draws up, gathers, and processes documents for the sale of a real estate property and who interfaces between the lender and the buyer. *One of the first steps in buying a home is talking to a mortgage broker to see what you can afford.*

Real estate market—The current sales market of real estate property, i.e., the number of properties available, the number of buyers, and how quickly properties are selling. *The market seems to be slowing down a little, but it's only a matter of time before it heats up again.*

To pay down—To make payments that gradually lower the amount left on a loan. *Once the interest gets paid down, the amount paid on the principal starts going up until all you're paying on your home loan is principal.*

Prepayment penalty—A feature of some loans wherein a fee is added if the loan is paid off early. *If Mom refinances her house before the third year of the loan, she will have to pay the prepayment penalty, which is six months' interest.*

Prequalification—A process in which a lender looks at how much money a buyer is able to borrow before the buyer has bought a home. *Before you can even think about buying a house, you might need to go through prequalification.*

Prime rate—The interest rate that banks charge their preferred customers. *The rate on our ARM is linked to the prime rate.*

Principal—The total amount owed on a property at any given time. *Your house payment includes principal and interest, and for many years, the interest is much higher than the principal.*

To refinance—To obtain of a new loan on a property that already has a loan, in order to get a lower interest rate or to take cash out of one's equity. *Let's refinance and get a little extra cash to fix up the house.*

Seller's market—When there are more buyers than there are properties for sale, meaning that sellers can get more money for their property. *Now that it's a seller's market we can sell our house, buy something cheaper, and live off our equity!*

Walk-through—The final property inspection the buyer takes before the property sale is closed. *We'll need to schedule your walk-through for this weekend so that the house will be yours early next week.*

C. GRAMMAR ESSENTIALS: *HAVE*

In Lesson 8, we looked at *have*, meaning "to partake" (as of food or drink), as compared to the verb *take*. But you probably know that *have* has many, many meanings and uses in English. In this lesson, we will focus on the verb *have*. Let's start with its grammatical function as an auxiliary. *Have* is used as the auxiliary in all perfect tenses in English:

> *Have you ever seen such high prices in real estate?*
> *We had been working with another agent, but after a year we thought we needed a change.*
> *By the time you make up your mind, the buyers will have lost interest!*

As we discussed in Lesson 3, *have to* is a modal, with a meaning similar to *must*. It's different from *must* in the negative; *must not* means "it's required that you not . . . ," whereas *don't have to* means "it's not required that you . . ."

> *We have to take out a second mortgage to pay for college!*
> *You don't have to apply for a mortgage in person.*

Have can also be used in the causative. This will be discussed more in Lesson 30:

> *Have the broker give me a call when she gets in.*
> *The bank had us fill out many forms for the loan application.*

Now let's look at some of the different meanings of *have* as a main verb, apart from its use discussed in Lesson 8:

1. To possess something concrete, to own. *Jill has a condo in the city, and she also has a house in the country.*

2. To possess as a characteristic or emotional quality. *Linda has a great fondness for old houses. You don't have enough patience to find a house!*

3. To possess body parts. *Linda has blue eyes. You have really long legs!*

4. To be in relation to family members. *I have two sisters. We have a lot of cousins.*

5. To possess something abstract, such as knowledge. *Your agent will have all the answers for you. We don't have enough time for this!*

6. To possess as a part, to include, to be partially made up of. *Jill's condo has a fireplace and her house in the country has a wood stove.*

7. To hold in one's mind. *I have my doubts that we'll be approved. She has some suspicions about this new real estate agent.*

8. To experience. *We had a really hard time finding this place! Who's ever had trouble getting a mortgage?*

9. To undergo a disease or physical ailment. *You'll have a heart attack when you see the prices. My aunt has diabetes, and this house is close to her doctor's office.*

10. To engage in some act. *We had a long talk about our finances. They had a fight and aren't speaking.*

11. To get, obtain, receive, or take. *Have you had any news from the agent?*

12. To permit, to allow. *I won't have you making all this noise! Our agent wouldn't have us waiting any longer, so we left.*

13. To put in a certain situation. *This mortgage application has me really confused! The monthly payments have me concerned that we'll go broke.*

14. To give birth to. *Jessica had a baby right after she moved. She's had three daughters.*

There are also several common idioms using *have*:

To have at it—To attack vigorously, to fight. *Wow, they really had at it!*
To have had it—To be unable to endure any more, to be spent, tired, or drained. *I've had it! No more walking around looking at houses today!*
To have it coming—To be deserving of some punishment. *Well, you lied first, so you really had it coming.*
To have it in for—To desire for something bad to happen to another person. *I think the new boss really has it in for me.*
To have it out—To argue, to openly fight about some previously unspoken problem. *They weren't speaking for weeks, but they finally had it out the other day, and now they're friends.*
To have to do with—To be related to, to be connected to. *The cost of this house has nothing to do with your refusal to live in this neighborhood!*
Let's have it—An invitation to share something, to speak, etc. *Come on, let's have it. Why are you upset?*

Finally, *have* can also be a noun, referring to a person who possesses wealth of some kind, often contrasted with *have-not*. *As long as it is divided between haves and have-nots, the world will be filled with conflicts.*

D. HOW-TO

So you think you might want to buy a house in the U.S. This is a long and complicated process, one that you can read entire books about and take entire seminars on. In this short section on buying a house, we certainly can't cover all the details, but we'll lay out the process in broad steps so you have some idea of what's involved. We'll also point you in the right direction for finding more information or other resources.

1. How do you qualify to buy a home and get a mortgage in the U.S.?

    Besides American citizens, anyone with a social security number can also buy a home in the U.S. Those who are not legal residents can buy a home also, but because they don't have a social security number they need an ITIN, or Individual Tax Identification Number. To learn more about ITINs, go to the IRS's website at www.irs.gov. A buyer must also have good credit to buy a home. To find out what your credit is like, you could go to the website mentioned in Chapter 7, www.annualcreditreport.com, or to sites like www.experian.com and www.equifax.com (which are also accessed on annualcreditreport.com), and request a credit report. They will produce a credit report for you, along with a credit score if you request it. The higher the credit score, the better. A lender can also check your credit for you. In addition, lenders look at your debt-to-income ratio, which is the ratio of all of your debt, including credit cards, car loans, etc., to all of your income, such as salary, interest, dividends, etc. A ratio of 20% is considered good. If your debt-to-income ratio is higher, you may still be able to get a mortgage, but you will not get the best interest rates. And finally, of course, you have to be able to afford the home you want to buy. Your monthly income needs to be high enough to cover your mortgage as well as your other expenses. Most experts agree that your mortgage payment should be about 20% of your gross monthly income, although that can depend on your situation. Keep in mind that loans may require a down payment of up to 20% or more of the selling price before you can borrow the money to pay for the house, so you'll also need some kind of savings to put toward your down payment. There are loans that allow you to make a smaller down payment, but they usually require PMI (private mortgage insurance). Without PMI, the bank could lose money on what they lend you if they have to foreclose on the property.

2. How do I choose a real estate agent or broker?

    Once you have decided that you are ready and eligible to buy, you can start looking for an agent or broker you feel comfortable with. A real estate agent or broker is a professional trained to guide you through the home buying process as smoothly as possible. This includes discussing how much you can afford as well as where and what type of property you want to buy, showing you listings, taking you to visit homes, and making offers and negotiating on your behalf once a suitable place has been found. A good agent will be patient with you, will encourage you, will help you find exactly what you want, and will negotiate to get you the lowest price possible. An agent's input can also serve as a good "reality check," to help you know what is reasonable and what is impossible.

    To find a good agent, you can ask your friends for recommendations. Are any of your friends agents? You can also walk into to any real estate agency and get acquainted with the agents they employ, go online, or check the yellow pages. Because you may not want to divulge up front that you are actually looking for an agent, try going to open houses. That way you can get acquainted with a number of agents. Watch them as they interact with people. Listen to what they say. Do you feel comfortable with any of them? Which ones come across as the most honest, hardworking, and competent? Are you comfortable and relaxed with any? Once you've answered these questions, you've probably narrowed your list down to one or two. Then, if you can, interview them and make your choice (all of the above also applies to finding a rental broker or agent).

As an additional note, you should be aware of how agents get paid. Your agent only makes money on the purchase of a property, usually 3% of the purchase price after splitting the commission with the seller's broker (although the percentages might not be divided evenly). His or her income depends on how much you pay for the house. The more expensive the house, the more the agent makes. But you should also be aware that the agent's percentage is deducted from the selling price and reduces the amount the seller receives. The buyer usually doesn't have to set any money aside to pay for the commission.

3. How do I choose a lender and get a mortgage?

Once you feel confident that you qualify and can afford to make house payments, you'll need to find the lender who can offer you the best loan. There are a lot of lenders available. This step can come before or after you find an agent; however, an agent you trust can usually give you a good recommendation for a lender. Shop around to several banks and savings and loan associations for the best rates and terms. Try talking to a mortgage broker, because he or she will have access to more loan packages than a bank lender. Again, ask your friends for a recommendation. Who really helped them find the best loan and saved them the most money? Go to your own bank and ask to meet with a lender. Go online to find a lender. You can also check your newspaper for lending rates. Look for a good loan, then call that bank.

The lender makes money by selling you the loan. It's to his or her advantage to sell you the loan that makes him or her the most money. This does not necessarily mean the loan with the highest interest rate. For example, you can sometimes pay "points," or fees where each point is 1% of the loan amount, in order to get a lower interest rate. However, you might end up paying more over the life of the mortgage once the points are included. To see what the "effective interest rates" are, or the interest rate offered with any points added in, and to figure out your mortgage payments, look for mortgage calculators online or ask your real estate agent. The points that banks charge are sometimes called "origination fees."

4. How do I know what I want to buy and where I want to buy it?

Read the home or real estate section in your local newspaper. You'll learn a lot about the market, loans, housing prices, and what's available in your area. As discussed in Chapter 27, you can also go to open houses. These are free and open to the public. At an open house, the seller shows off his or her house, hoping to attract a buyer. This is one way to find out what's available. It takes time, but it can also be fun. You can check online newspapers as well as real estate agency websites. More and more agents are featuring their listings online. If you have an agent, he or she can also run a list of homes from the MLS based on what you want and what you can afford. Then you and the agent will decide which homes to look at, and he or she will chauffeur you around to look at potential homes. It can take several months to find a home, so don't be discouraged if you don't find what you want right away. It's a long process, which is good, because there's so much money involved.

5. How do I make an offer?

Once you've found something you like and can afford, you're ready to make an offer. The sellers have placed a price on their house, but if they are serious about selling, the price will always be negotiable. Your agent will help you determine the lowest possible price the market will bear. You may be asked to put up a small sum of money, often called earnest money or deposit, to show your serious intention to buy the property. You, your agent, the sellers, and the sellers' agent will negotiate with offers and counter-offers until you or the sellers decide to end the negotiation by either accepting a price or walking away because the price isn't right. If your negotiation fails, then you start over with another home you think you'd like to buy until you have an accepted offer.

6. What's escrow?

When your offer is accepted and all the legal paperwork has been drawn up and negotiated, i.e., the purchase agreement and any additional documents required by the state in which the purchase is made, your future home goes into escrow. Lawyers are used in many states because there are so many legalities and a whole lot of money involved. Escrow means that the deed for the home is temporarily put into the hands of a neutral third party, possibly a bank but more often an independent escrow company, and held until the transaction is completed. During escrow, several things happen, and with each one you come closer and closer to becoming the owner of your new home. The seller's obligation is to make sure the house is in good shape, unless you buy it in "as is" condition. "As is" condition means the owner is exempt from making necessary repairs. This usually yields a much lower price than if the house is purchased with all repairs having been made by the seller. Your obligation toward closing escrow is to get homeowners' insurance and make sure you get your loan. To get insurance you can check with your car insurance and/or renters' insurance company. You can also ask your agent for suggestions. But this is your obligation. Neither your agent, nor your lawyer, nor the lender can get an insurance policy for you. But making sure that your loan goes through is a cooperative effort between you and your lender. The lender needs to tell you what steps you need to take, for example, if you need a larger down payment, or if you need to pay off your credit cards, or if you will have to also purchase PMI, etc. If you really want this house, do whatever the lender asks you to do in a timely manner, because the process of getting a loan can be difficult if your debt-to-income ratio is very close and you aren't willing to make adjustments. If all of these steps are accomplished, you won't fall out of escrow.

7. What are inspection, title search, and final walk-through?

Although not always required by law, the buyer should always hire an inspector to do a thorough inspection of the home. You can also make the purchase of the house contingent on a good inspection, but this must be done during negotiations. A good inspector checks absolutely everything— windows, doors, plumbing, vents, roof, foundation, termites, etc. The best inspectors charge more, but it's usually worthwhile to the buyer to pay for the best. Your agent should know which inspectors are better than others. If you're buying without an agent or you want to look around yourself, you can check the phone book or such websites as Homeinspection.com. Home inspectors should be certified, have a lot of experience in the field, and belong to a professional organization. After the inspection, you can request that the sellers make any repairs that might be needed, or if serious problems are uncovered, you can cancel the deal if you have negotiated the inspection contingency discussed above. During escrow your potential home will also have a title search, to ensure that the deed or title has passed correctly from owner to owner. At the very end of this process, you will have what's called a final walk-through, which is one last chance for the buyer to inspect the property before closing on it. The final walk-through happens only after the former owners have moved out, and within days of the final closing. Before you purchase, you want to be sure that the property is left in the condition you expect, so the buyer and the buyer's agent walk through the house and property to check whether all necessary repairs have been made, that items agreed to remain are there, and that all the former owner's things have been removed.

8. What's a closing and what are the costs?

The closing is simply the final signing of the legal documents, and the actual moment when ownership of the home is transferred. The closing happens once the condition of the property is approved and all necessary loans and insurance are in place. In states or cities where attorneys are used during the process of buying a home, they may be present at the closing itself, along with the buyer, seller, and real estate agents. But this varies from place to place, so make sure you understand what your local laws and expectations are. When in doubt, consult one of the resources listed in this lesson, or simply ask your agent or someone who's been through the process. The closing may take place at the escrow office, title company, or attorney's office, but this may vary from state to state as well. Your attorney, agent, or escrow officer will let you know. During the closing, both parties sign their respective legal documents, the money is transferred, and the home is yours. There are some costs associated with a closing that you should know about, and these can vary from state to state and transaction to transaction also. But usually there are the lender's fees, i.e., loan origination fee, appraisal fee, credit report, etc., and title insurance, notary fees, recording fees, and inspection fees may be included. It's the end of a long and sometimes grueling process, but now you can hopefully say . . . Home Sweet Home!

E. ENGLISH IN ACTION

Martin and Irma's real estate agent said that Janet Pizner was the best mortgage broker to be had, and that they should talk to her about getting qualified and finding the best loan options.

Janet: Good morning, I'm Janet.

Martin: Hi, I'm Martin, and this is my wife Irma.

Irma: Hello.

Janet: Have a seat. Well, let's see. We've run a credit report on you, and your credit looks clean. You have a few credit cards you should pay off, though. I recommend you pay off these two here, on the report.

Irma: You mean we won't be able to buy a house until we do that?

Janet: You'll get a better interest rate and you'll be able to afford more if you pay these off. Lenders look at these extra expenses as a negative to your credit.

Irma: Oh, okay. We'll see what we can do.

Janet: Okay, I can get you a "no cost" loan if you'd like. That means all the closing costs will be rolled into your loan so you won't have to pay anything up front.

Martin: Does that mean the mortgage will be higher?

Janet: Well, yes, but your monthly payment won't be affected that much. It'll just be easier on your budget this way.

Martin: But that means we pay interest on those closing costs, right?

Janet: That's right, because they get folded into the loan. But if you put more down, you can probably get a better rate.

Martin: Well, we have $15,000 right now. Isn't that enough for both?

Janet: Okay, well, you probably don't have enough to put 20% down, so you're going to have to pay PMI anyway. If you buy a house at $150,000, your down payment will be 10%. If you use some of that money to pay closing costs, you won't have 10% to put down, so that doesn't help you get the best interest rate. Do you see what I mean?

Martin: Maybe...

Irma: I think I understand. You're saying we'll be able to lower the cost of the loan by getting a no cost loan and by putting all our money into the down payment.

Janet: That's right. You could also pay the closing costs and put, say, 3% down and use whatever's left for fixing up your new place. But you'd have to get an ARM, or adjustable rate mortgage. You wouldn't be able to get a fixed rate.

Irma: But that means our payment could go up.

Janet: That's right, but that doesn't happen until after a certain amount of time passes, which can be anywhere from one month to years depending on the mortgage. Then it could only go up a quarter of a percent a month, depending upon the type of mortgage and the interest rate at that time. It could also go down. And once you've built up some equity, you can refinance if you want and get a lower interest rate on the money you've borrowed.

Irma: Probably.

Janet: Yes, probably. Of course that depends on the market. In six months you might be making more money, too.

Martin: Or less.

Irma: Oh, Martin. Don't say that. We don't want to go into foreclosure...

Janet: Don't worry. You guys look like good credit risks. You won't go into foreclosure.

Martin: Thanks very much for the information. Irma and I will talk it over and get back to you.

Janet: Okay. Whatever you decide to do, you'll have the loan that you want.

F. PRACTICE

Fill in the blanks with the following words: *buyer's market, seller's market, walk through, listing, falls out of escrow, refinance, foreclosure, mortgage, agent, equity*

1. Our agent has already taken a(n) _____ for our house, and you should be able to find it on the MLS very soon.

2. We were able to get a good price on our house because the previous owner was about to go into _____.

3. Everyone's saying it's a(n) _____, but the prices still seem pretty high!

4. We got in on an adjustable rate mortgage, but as soon as the rates go down we'll need to _____ so we can get a good fixed rate.

5. It's a good idea to shop around for a(n) _____ to make sure you find one you trust.
6. Now that we have some _____, we can refinance to get a little cash out of our house.
7. If you're thinking of selling your home, you should do it now—it's a(n) _____.
8. You'll know that your escrow is about to close when the agents call you to set up your final _____.
9. If you become very attached to a house and then it _____, it can be very difficult.
10. It may not always be wise to pay off your _____, because it can be a good tax write-off.

Place the letter corresponding to the meaning of *have* in each sentence in the blank: a. to be in possession of; b. to possess as a part; c. to experience; d. to possess knowledge; e. to be at one's disposal; f. causative

1. _____ Have these documents signed by Wednesdays.
2. _____ We always have the MLS to help you find the home you're looking for.
3. _____ This is one of the nicest lots to have.
4. _____ I had a lot of fun looking at houses, but it was exhausting!
5. _____ The house has air conditioning.
6. _____ My agent has an idea of the kind of place I want.

Match the *have* idiom with the sentence that best corresponds to its meaning: a. have it out; b. let's have it; c. have it coming; d. have had it

1. _____ Okay, you can tell me the bad news. I can take it.
2. _____ Sara and Tom had the biggest fight of their lives, but they actually resolved a lot of issues afterward.
3. _____ I'm really tired of this town and all its gossip. I'm moving!
4. _____ Okay, I deserved that. I haven't always treated you as well as you deserve.

G. TASK

Even if you're not in the market for a new house, imagine that you are and that you need to figure out financing. Figure out how much money you'd have for a down payment, check your credit report, and look up mortgage interest rates. Try and figure out about how much your monthly payments would be with your down payment and different mortgages.

 ## H. REAL LIFE

Hi, my name is Margaret McWhorter, and I've been an agent for more than 40 years. I've got some suggestions for those of you who may be wondering whether you should hire an agent or do it yourselves to save money. If you think you don't want to hire an agent, then you really have to educate yourselves about the area you're thinking about looking in, learn everything you can about real estate law, and know the property you're interested in. Then, if you feel qualified to do so, you'll need to make up a checklist to be sure you do everything that is necessary. Of course, as a real estate agent myself, I can't really encourage people to be "do it yourself" buyers or sellers. I believe agents have knowledge of the real estate market in their area that you need in order to find the best home for you. I believe agents can save you money and make the deal work for you.

However, it's important to be aware that, as in every profession, there are unethical agents out there. Agents should be licensed by the state. If they are a member of the Board of Realtors®, the organization will carefully police them. If one of their Realtors® behaves unethically with his or her clients, the board will revoke his or her license. I suggest that, if you want to find a good agent, you ask your friends who you know have gone through the process successfully and with few problems for a recommendation. You might also want to interview two or three agents. Hear what each of them has to say. Remember, you'll be spending a lot of hours with your agent. You'll want to know that you are in good hands and you'll want to feel comfortable being with him or her for long periods of time. I wish you the best in your hunt for your home—an investment of time well worth the expense!

I. RESOURCES

Helpful information on buying a home:
www.hud.gov/buying
www.ourfamilyplace.com/homebuyer/checklist.html
www.realestate.com/learning-center/finding-a-home
homebuying.about.com/cs/howtobuy/a/buying_home.htm

Property research (foreclosures, title history, sales data, etc.):
www.propertyshark.com

Information on ARMs:
www.federalreserve.gov/pubs/arms/arms_english.htm

General mortgage help and information (including mortgage calculators):
www.federalreserve.gov/pubs/mortgage/mortb_1.htm
www.mortgage101.com
www.bankrate.com/brm/rate/mtg_home.asp
www.hsh.com
www.aarp.org/money/revmort (reverse mortgages)

About escrow:
www.escrowhelp.com

ANSWER KEY
Practice 1: 1. listing; 2. foreclosure; 3. buyer's market; 4. refinance; 5. agent; 6. equity; 7. seller's market; 8. walk-through; 9. falls out of escrow; 10. mortgage

Practice 2: 1. f; 2. e; 3. a; 4. c; 5. b; 6. d

Practice 3: 1. b; 2. a; 3. d; 4. c

CHAPTER 30

Finding a Home: Utilities and Other Household Essentials

A. **ENGLISH CLOSE-UP**

CHANGE OF ADDRESS FORM

Name_____

Former Address_____

_____

New Address_____

_____

Effective Date_____

B. **VOCABULARY ESSENTIALS**

Broadband—A way of transmitting data at very high speeds. *Cable, satellite, and DSL are all broadband internet services.*

Brownout—A reduction of energy due to a shortage of power or overuse of power by customers. *Brownouts are common during energy crises.*

To burst—To explode open, as in a pipe or tire. *A water main burst over on 50th and there's a fountain of water coming out of the ground.*

Connection—A link. *What kind of internet connection do you have? DSL, wireless, cable, or dial-up?*

Contaminated—Unclean or dangerous because of something added. *The contaminated water was harming the fish and plants living in the lake.*

Current—A flow of electrical energy. *I think this outlet is dead. There doesn't seem to be an electrical current running through it.*

Dial tone—The sound on a phone line indicating that calls can be made or received. *The electricity's out, but thankfully we still have a dial tone.*

Dial-up—Internet access through phone lines using a modem that dials the number of the service provider. Typically, a lot slower than high-speed options like cable and DSL, and you cannot use the telephone while you're using dial-up on the same phone line. *My friends keep telling me that I should stop using dial-up to access the internet, but isn't cable or DSL a lot more expensive?*

DSL—Digital subscriber line (or loop). A type of high-speed internet connection using existing phone lines. *Most people choose either cable or DSL for internet service because they're so much faster than dial-up.*

To flow—To run smoothly and continuously, like a liquid or gas. *The water wasn't flowing well because there was a clog in the water line.*

Gas line—A pipe that transports gas. *New gas lines are added whenever new homes are constructed.*

Generator—A machine that takes mechanical energy and converts it into electrical energy. Some people use generators during power outages in order to have electricity in their homes. *There's no electrical line to the cabin on top of the mountain, so we have a generator up there.*

To get through to—To be successful in contacting someone. *Did you ever get through to your boss to let her know you were sick?*

Grid—A network of power lines and facilities that distributes electricity to an area or region. *There's a power outage on the grid. It's going to take a while to repair it.*

Hard water, soft water—Hard water contains calcium and magnesium salts and other minerals. It interferes with soap lather and can build up deposits. Soft water does not have much calcium or magnesium salt content; these salts and minerals may have been removed. *We had a soft water system installed, but I prefer hard water because soft water feels soapy.*

High-speed internet—An internet connection that delivers information at a very high speed. *Once you've tried high-speed internet, you'll never be able to go back to a dial-up service.*

To hook up—To connect with wires. *We moved in yesterday, and we still haven't had our cable or internet hooked up.*

Landfill—A place where waste is disposed of. *The city council is voting on where to open up a new landfill, but nobody wants it in his or her own neighborhood.*

Meter—A device that measures usage of water, gas, electricity, etc. *The meter reader comes by to check your utility usage and record it on a handheld computer.*

Modem—Electronic device used to convert computer signals so they can be transmitted over a phone line. A cable modem does the same thing but uses cable TV lines instead of phone lines. Modems can be internal or external to the computer. *If you want dial-up service, you need a modem.*

Phone line—A line that transmits telephone signals. *If your phone line is down, you'll need to call your phone service to get it repaired.*

Power outage—A failure in the power supply system. *There was a power outage last night, so my alarm clock isn't working.*

Reception—The quality of radio or television waves received. *We need cable TV, because reception is awful here.*

Recyclable—Able to be processed for reuse. *Glass, paper, metal, and some plastics are usually recyclable.*

Renewable resource—Any resource that can renew itself, such as wood, wind, or solar energy. *Some utility companies allow you to sign up to purchase energy from them that is derived from renewable resources.*

Router—A device that links networks and connects them to the internet. It makes sure information goes where it's supposed to go. *If you want a wireless network at home, you'll need to get a wireless router.*

Septic tank—A tank where sewage is processed and disposed of. *If you want to dig up the backyard, you need to know where the septic tank is first.*

Snow—White flashing dots on a television screen that are a result of poor reception. *What happened to our reception? All the TV's getting is snow!*

Utilities—Essential services and products, like water, electricity, gas, and sewage. *Public utilities* can refer to the government-regulated companies that provide these services. *The apartment's rent is pretty low, but utilities aren't included, so I hope they're not too expensive.*

Waste—Garbage, trash, or sewage. *Some apartment buildings have a policy of recycling as much waste as possible.*

Water main—A primary pipe for the movement of a water supply. *There was a water main break downtown, and four blocks are flooded.*

Water pressure—The force of the weight of water in a given area. *The water pressure here is too low for anyone to take a shower while the washing machine is running.*

C. GRAMMAR ESSENTIALS: CAUSATIVES AND PERMISSIVES

Causatives are verb forms used to show that someone has caused someone else to do something rather than doing something him- or herself. There are three main verbs that express causation: *make, have,* and *get.*

Make shows that someone requires, compels, or forces another person to do something. The construction is *make* + object + bare infinitive:

The cable company made us pay for a new router when we lost the old one.
The post office makes you go pick up larger packages.

Have expresses less force, and it shows more of a cooperative relationship or agreement:

Don't install the phone line yourself. Have the phone company do it. It's
their job.
My boss had me distribute all of the reports.

Get is similar to *have*, but it involves persuasion or coercion. The construction is *get* + object + *to* infinitive:

She got him to put in another jack, even though it wasn't part of the job.
Somehow we managed to get the company to give us a month free, but it
wasn't easy.

There's also a passive form of the causatives, formed with *get* or *have* + object + past participle. *Make* is not used in the passive causative. *Get* implies that there is some sort of effort involved in bringing about the action, while *have* sounds more routine:

He got the phone line fixed only after several complaints.
We had the water heater replaced and new acoustic tiles put up in the
basement.

Permissives are verbs that are similar to causatives, but they imply giving permission or making it possible for someone else to do something. *Let* and *allow* are used in permissive constructions. *Let* is more neutral, and *allow* has a slight connotation of power, either through strength or rules, although in practice these verbs mean virtually the same thing. The constructions are *let* + object + bare verb, and *allow* + object + *to* infinitive:

The police didn't let anyone into the neighborhood until the gas main leak
was contained.
The phone company allowed us to keep our old number when we moved.

D. HOW-TO

Here's a list of a few things that you'll most likely need to do when you move into a new place.

CHANGE OF ADDRESS

Whenever you move, you'll probably want to make sure that you get any mail from your old home sent to your new address. The first step you should take is to pick up a change of address form from your local post office, fill it out, and send it in. You can also fill out and submit the form online. In addition, you'll find information on the U.S. Postal Service website explaining how your mail—and which mail—will be forwarded from your old address to your new address after you complete the form. The U.S. Postal Service will then send you a verification letter, along with information about how to notify businesses and creditors of your change of address. You'll probably also want to notify friends and family of your new address. Some people send out a notice announcing their change of address, and others wait until the holidays and send the new address with their greeting cards. You also should notify all of the businesses that need to communicate with you—your employer, insurance, credit card companies, banks, charities you may contribute to, and so on. You can either call them or save an old bill that has "how to change your address" information and follow the instructions given once you've moved. Although the IRS updates its address information through the U.S. Postal Service's files, it's usually a good idea to fill out and send in the IRS's change of address form as well. You can download it from the IRS's website at www.irs.gov. Additionally, if you are not a U.S. citizen you may be required to report any moves to the USCIS. Go to www.uscis.gov/graphics/howdoi/address.htm for more information and to download the form.

TELEPHONE

There are numerous options for landline phone service, and your choice will be determined by how many phone calls you make on a landline as well as how many local, long-distance, and international calls you make. Some people are choosing not to have a landline at all if they already have a cell phone. And many people who opt to have landlines are choosing digital phone service, provided over the internet, instead of analog, provided over phone lines. With analog service, you typically have to purchase long-distance service as well as local, but digital service usually allows you to call anywhere in the U.S. and Canada for a monthly flat fee. The prices are often cheaper than analog, and you get a long-distance package as well. There are some complications, though. Some digital companies don't have the same sound quality as analog, and currently digital service does not always have backup power during power outages, which means your 911 emergency service could also be cut off. Watch for low rates as companies vie for customers. Phone companies also have special package deals that may make more sense for you if you make most of your phone calls in the evenings, or on weekends, or if you typically make long distance or international calls to the same place. Be sure to ask about special packages that might fit your needs.

CABLE VS. SATELLITE TV

Not everyone in the U.S. pays for television service. There are several broadcast networks that do not require additional, paid service in order to be viewed; all you need is a television and antenna of some sort. However, reception of these networks varies widely depending on your location. Paid TV services like cable and satellite provide much more consistent television reception, in addition to tens if not hundreds more channels than broadcast (the broadcast networks are also provided through these services). If you do opt for some kind of TV service, you can choose among the various types, such as cable service via cable TV lines or satellite service via a satellite dish. You can compare services through a website like moveutilities.com to see which one makes the most sense for you and what their relative strengths and weaknesses are (as well as what is available in your area). To give you a brief overview, many houses and apartments already have the cable hookups, and TVs are all cable ready, so often all you need is a cable box or boxes, cable, and service to be all set. In other words, installation is usually fairly easy. For satellite service, you need a satellite dish installed and a receiver for each TV in the house.

There are advantages and disadvantages to each option. Cable service offers a variety of basic channels, and premium packages include certain movie channels like HBO, Cinemax, and Showtime, as well as other specialty programming. Satellite also offers basic, midrange, and premium packages, but if you like sports, the satellite premium package often includes a good number of sports channels. For those of you who like to use your television to watch a lot of local programming, cable television might be better for you. Satellite TV is subject to weather-related disruptions that can be brief, while cable wires can be accidentally cut, interrupting cable service for periods of time while being repaired. Once the cable wires are repaired, you will usually have to reset the cable box to get the TV to unscramble for reception. Cable cannot reach out-of-the-way places until the cable line is brought into the area, but satellite can usually work anywhere, even remote locations. In fact, for those who live in remote areas where cable is not yet available, satellite TV may be the only choice. Although the prices are competitive, and the equipment from both types of service can be rented, cable can often be a little cheaper, especially if you bundle together cable TV, telephone, and internet services. However, it may also be possible to bundle together your satellite TV with other services as well. In addition, some satellite companies ask you to sign a contract, forcing you to keep the service for a certain amount of time, while cable companies do not ask you to sign a contract. Cable can also be more convenient if you live in an area where cable service already exists. Apartment and condo dwellers might be better off with cable because the placement of the dish required for satellite reception might need to be negotiated with others in the building. Currently, cable companies are usually assigned areas, giving cable customers no choice among cable service providers.

GAS AND ELECTRICITY

You should contact your gas and electric provider several weeks before you move to arrange for your gas and electricity to be turned on. You can find the contact information in your phone book or online, or ask your landlord or real estate agent for help. If you are a new customer, you might need to pay a security deposit if you don't have a credit history yet. But don't worry; you'll get your money back when you move out as long as you maintain good credit by paying your bills on time. To sign up for services, you can call, go online or visit your utility office. If you are on a fixed income, there are a few ways to make your gas and electric bills easier to manage. One way is to get on a level pay plan. Because usage varies throughout the year, some months can be very high while others are lower. On a level pay plan, your usage will be projected for one year, and that cost is divided into twelve equal payments. You will probably have to pay more some months, but it won't be a big difference. There is also a special plan for low-income customers called the low-income home energy assistance program. For more information, visit www.acf.hhs.gov/programs/liheap. Your savings under this program could be helpful.

INTERNET

Among the top Internet Service Providers (ISPs) in the U.S. are AOL, Comcast, AT&T, Verizon, Roadrunner, and EarthLink. Each company offers different packages and different types of internet access, from dial-up to DSL, and your choice of ISP really depends on your budget, your internet usage habits, and the number of computers you have. You can also choose independent companies, such as Net Zero, Juno, and People PC, and pay less money, although certain services are limited. If you are accustomed to high-speed internet or simply don't have the patience for dial-up, you might want to pay more for high-speed service. DSL, cable, and satellite services might be more expensive, but your internet speed will be lightning fast compared to dial-up. Another option is wireless, which can be very convenient if you're using a laptop, but you may have to buy a wireless router for your computer. Your internet service can usually be bundled with your phone service for either dial-up or DSL, or, as discussed above, through your cable or satellite TV service. You can also have a separate provider, but it is likely to be cheaper if you get two or three services bundled together on one bill for one monthly price.

WATER AND SEWER

If you are a renter, this is one bill (along with heat) you probably won't have to pay, because your landlord is most likely responsible for it. But if you are a homeowner, you need to find out who services your water and sewer. There are not multiple providers, or these services are provided through the local government, so find out about your provider from your real estate agent or the former tenant or owner. If you have a septic tank, you can find out about any permits or other payments you may need to make for it from your agent or the former tenant/owner as well. Your bill for sewage and water may come monthly, every other month, or even quarterly.

TRASH

In most places, especially cities and suburban areas, trash service is selected or administered by the local government, so you don't have a choice among service providers for trash removal. In many cases, the city will pay the cost of removing your trash, which of course is passed onto you in the form of local taxes. But in some areas you will be billed personally, or you may need to select a trash removal service, especially in rural areas. Typically, trash is removed on particular days of the week when garbage trucks follow routes and empty the trash cans or take the trash bags left at the side of the street by residents. In some cases your trash cans will be provided for you, but you may also need to buy them yourself at a home goods center or from the trash removal service. Recyclables are picked up separately from trash, from specially marked receptacles and/or bags. Each community differs in what it recycles and how recyclables are picked up, so check with your municipal offices, your landlord, your new neighbors, or your real estate agent for help. Some cities have a once or twice yearly bulk trash removal service when some large objects like building materials can be collected. Whether refrigerators are allowed to be included in bulk trash removal or not, remember that for the safety of the neighborhood children and small pets, you need to remove refrigerator doors when preparing to dispose of them. Check with your city to see if they offer bulk removal service, what the pickup schedule is, and what materials can be collected. Household toxic waste also needs special handling for disposal. Your city should have a program for disposal of toxic chemicals such as paint, aerosols, automotive fluids, batteries, etc. You can find out locations, times of pickup, and what kind of disposal or removal is available to you by calling city hall or checking your city's website under waste, toxic chemical, and bulk trash removal.

AUTO REGISTRATION

If you are bringing a vehicle with you when you move, you will need to register it in your new state. Your local Department of Motor Vehicles is the place to register your auto. To find your local DMV, you can check your phone book or look it up online. The site www.dmv.org also offers a lot of information on DMV offices and other information relevant to drivers.

DRIVER'S LICENSE

If you are moving to a different state, you will need to get a new driver's license. If your move is temporary, or if you are visiting for a short time, your driver's license may be valid. But if your move is permanent or semipermanent, you'll need to get a driver's license for your new state of residence. To find out what you need to do, contact your local DMV.

E. ENGLISH IN ACTION

Let's listen in as Deb talks with Western Cable to help her decide whether she wants cable internet service or not.

Western Cable:	Western Cable, this is Tony. How may I help you?
Deb:	Hello, my name's Deb Austin, and I've just moved into 4229 South Mission Road. I'd like to get cable service.
Western Cable:	Let me check . . . Yes, it looks like service is available in your area. Would you like to sign up for our cable television service, internet, digital telephone, or all three?
Deb:	Well, right now I want to sign up for cable TV, but I'm just gathering information about internet service. I'm not sure whether I want to go with cable or DSL. I didn't know you offered phone service as well.
Western Cable:	All right, well, I can help you with that. Right now we have a special going on if you want to bundle television, internet, and digital phone service together. Basic cable is $39.95, our high-speed Internet service is $49.95, and you can add digital telephone for only $19.95 more.
Deb:	Oh, well, how much is that?
Western Cable:	It's about $110.00
Deb:	Wow, that's a lot.
Western Cable:	Well, our digital phone is a flat-fee long-distance plan throughout the entire U.S. and Canada, so you don't pay any more for long-distance service, ma'am.
Deb:	Okay, let me think about how much I'm used to paying for each of these services individually. Hmm. Yeah, I guess that is pretty cheap, since I've been paying about $26 for my phone service and an additional $15 or so for my long-distance service.
Western Cable:	Would you like to add premium cable service for only $9.95 more?
Deb:	I don't know . . . Not right now, I don't think so. And I'm not sure whether I want DSL or cable internet, so I need to do some price comparisons. Can you give me that info?
Western Cable:	Absolutely. And then we should probably talk about scheduling your installation, as well . . .

F. PRACTICE

Fill in the blanks with the following words: *reception, flow, brownouts, burst, get through to, hook up, dial tone, grid, landfill, power outage*

1. It's important that you _____ your gas and electricity company as soon as possible to tell them to turn off your gas and electricity when you move out.

2. I swear, every time there's the tiniest bit of wind, there's a(n) _____ in this area. I hope the electricity isn't out for too long.

3. They need to put in a new _____, because there's too much garbage for the old one.

4. If you don't hear a(n) _____ when you pick up your phone, the line is probably dead.

5. The water pressure is low because a water main _____ over on 54th Street.

6. We really get terrible _____ out here. You can't get any channels at all without cable.

7. Let the water _____ for a while before using it if it's sat in the pipes for a long time.

8. I'm trying to _____ all my services today so I can watch TV and use the phone and Internet.

9. The blackout is huge. The entire _____ is shut down.

10. Expect a lot of _____ this summer, because with the heat, they'll need to control the flow of power.

Fill in the following with the correct causative or permissive. There may be more than one correct answer.

1. We _____ them install cable instead of DSL or satellite.

2. Jeremy really needed cable and was very happy when he _____ them to install his cable earlier than expected.

3. The Willets _____ their car reregistered when they moved to Alabama.

4. I hope they _____ us to change our service so soon after getting it installed.

5. The U.S. _____ visitors to use international driver's licenses when they come to the U.S.

6. The gas and electric companies _____ people with low incomes pay less for their service.

7. We _____ the cable company bundle our TV, Internet, and phone service together.

8. We _____ the city to bill us online, just like we wanted.

9. The bank sent our checks with the wrong address, so we _____ them send us new ones.

10. We didn't know who to call about our water and sewer service, so we _____ our agent find out for us.

G.   TASK

Imagine that you need to change your ISP. Compare dial-up, cable, DSL, and satellite internet services for price, quality, and speed.

H. REAL LIFE

Western Star Cable
3451 Main Street
Lubbock, Texas

Dear Ms. Austin,

Thank you for choosing Western Star Cable as your cable television provider. Please be aware that we also offer high-speed internet and digital telephone service. As a new customer, you can take advantage of our low bundled rates. Just call 1-800-555-2300 for rate information.

Because you are a new customer with no credit history, you may need to pay a fully refundable deposit for our services. Our billing department will contact you to discuss this. We make paying your bills to Western Star Cable as simple and convenient as possible. You will receive your bills in the mail, online, or both, if you choose. You have the option of paying by check, credit card, or ATM card, but you can also pay your bill online through Western Star Cable or by direct withdrawal from your bank account. You may also pay by phone. Paying by phone is the same as direct withdrawal, but you have more control over when your account is debited. Another option is to pay your bills through your bank's bill pay program. And of course you can always pay in person at 3451 Main Street, right here in Lubbock.

You will receive a call regarding installation within the week to have your new cable installed. Once again, thank you for choosing Western Star Cable.

Sincerely,
Robert Mews

I. RESOURCES

To find, compare, and order services online, such as phone, TV, internet, electricity, natural gas, change of address form, moving quotes, renters' insurance, newspapers, etc.:
www.moveutilities.com
www.WhiteFence.com

Post office change of address:
moversguide.usps.com

Immigration change of address:
www.uscis.gov/graphics/howdoi/address.htm

Information on broadband internet:
www.fcc.gov/cgb/broadband.html
www.broadbandinfo.com

DMV information:
www.dmv.org

ANSWER KEY
Practice 1: 1. get through to; 2. power outage; 3. landfill; 4. dial tone; 5. burst; 6. reception; 7. flow; 8. hook up; 9. grid; 10. brownouts

Practice 2: 1. had; 2. got; 3. got/had; 4. allow; 5. allows; 6. let; 7. had; 8. got; 9. had/made; 10. had

CHAPTER 31

Government and Immigration: Taxes

A. **ENGLISH CLOSE-UP**

TAXES (DEDUCTIONS)				EXEMPTIONS		
Description	YTD	Current	Tax. Gross	M/S	No	Add'l Amt.
Federal Taxes	$3,987.19	$366.77	$5,011.77	M	04	
State of Calif. Tax	$735.02	$70.57	$5,011.77			
Fed. FICA Medicare H	$4073.63					

B. **VOCABULARY ESSENTIALS**

Adjusted gross income (AGI)—The amount of taxable income left after certain adjustments, such as deductible retirement contributions, have been taken out. These adjustments do not include standard or itemized deductions. *After you've calculated your AGI, you can reduce your taxable income even more by taking out deductions and exemptions.*

Audit, to be audited—An examination of your financial records and tax returns by the IRS in order to see if they match and are accurate. To get your financial records and tax returns examined by the IRS. *It's always a good idea to keep sound records of your finances just in case you're audited by the IRS.*

Deductions—The money that may be subtracted from income before taxes are calculated. *Paying a mortgage on a house may be one of the best deductions you can have, because you can deduct the interest and taxes.*

Disability insurance—Part of Social Security insurance that pays benefits if someone becomes disabled and unable to work. *Disability insurance is rarely enough to pay all the bills, but it helps.*

To do your taxes—To complete your tax return by April 15th. *Minnie always pays an accountant to do her taxes and she usually gets money back from the government.*

Excise tax—Taxes on luxury or nonessential items that are not paid directly to the government, but are paid to the merchant, who then pays them to the government. *Excise taxes are sometimes levied on such items as cigarettes and alcohol as a way to discourage their purchase.*

Exemption—A deduction in your amount of taxable income. You can usually get exemptions for yourself, a spouse, and any dependents. Also called "allowance." *You need to calculate your exemptions on the W-4 form.*

FICA (Federal Insurance Contributions Act)—Social Security, which is money paid into a government insurance fund that is used for retirement income, disability, and Medicare. *If you look on your paycheck and see FICA deductions, those are your Social Security deductions.*

To file (taxes)—To fill out and mail in or electronically submit federal income tax forms prior to April 15th each year. *A lot of people need help filing their taxes each year, because the process can be very confusing.*

Fiscal year—A twelve-month period used for the accounting of funds. In contrast, January to December is a "calendar year." *The U.S. government fiscal year is October 1st to September 30th.*

Gross income—Total income before any taxes or deductions are taken. *The average American's gross income seems high until you see how much money is taken out in taxes.*

Head of household—A married or single person who has at least one dependent living with him or her. *You can't file as head of household because you don't have any dependents.*

In the black—Taking in more money than you are spending, profitable. *After many years of losses, the company was finally back on track and in the black.*

In the red—Spending more money than you are making, unprofitable. *A business can only operate in the red for so long before going into bankruptcy.*

IRS—The Internal Revenue Service, the part of the U.S. government that collects taxes. *Count yourself lucky if you never get audited by the IRS.*

Net income—The amount left in a paycheck after all deductions have been taken, also called "take-home pay." *Net income is the amount of money you actually take home each pay period.*

Payroll taxes—All taxes taken out of your paycheck each month. *Many Americans complain about the amount of payroll taxes taken out of their checks.*

Pension—Retirement income, paid in monthly increments. *For many Americans, Social Security is the only pension they receive.*

Progressive tax, regressive tax—A progressive tax is a system of taxation in which the more money you make, the higher your tax rate is. A regressive tax is a system of taxation in which the more money you make, the lower your tax rate is. *A progressive tax system is designed to benefit low-income people.*

Revenue—The money a government takes in from taxes. *Government revenue increased because the economy improved.*

Taxable income—The amount of income that is taxed. On the tax return, it is equal to your gross income minus any adjustments, deductions (itemized or standard), and exemptions. *Once you figure out your taxable income on your return, you look at the tax tables provided to see how much tax is owed on that level of taxable income.*

Tax rate—The percentage that is paid in taxes. *You'll have a high federal income tax rate if you have a high taxable income.*

Tax return—The forms used to file your income tax with the IRS. *The most common tax return form is the 1040 Individual Income Tax Return.*

W-2—A form that employers must send to their employees each year in order for them to file taxes. The W-2 summarizes all income from the employer and taxes taken out on that income. *Check your W-2 if you're not sure of your exact income, including salary, bonus, and so on.*

W-4—A form that employees must fill out for their employers in order for the correct amount of taxes to be withheld. *As a new employee, I need to fill out a W-4 in order to get paid.*

W-8—A form that foreigners who receive U.S. income must use to calculate tax. There are variations on the W-8 form, including the W-8BEN and W-8ECI. *Jin isn't a U.S. citizen, so make sure he fills out a W-8 if he does work for us.*

W-9—A form that an employer uses to request a taxpayer ID for a U.S. citizen or resident alien whom he or she will pay. *If you do any freelance work for this company, you'll need to fill out this W-9 so we can send it to the IRS.*

Withholding—Income tax that is deducted or withheld from your paycheck during the year. *If your withholding is too high, you'll receive a refund with your tax return.*

Write-off—A tax deduction through depreciation, expense, or loss. *If you donate your car to charity you can take the loss as a write-off on your income taxes.*

C. GRAMMAR ESSENTIALS: MORE PREPOSITIONS

So far we've looked at prepositions of motion or direction, prepositions of time, and prepositions of location. There are many other prepositions that describe other types of relationships, such as purpose, intention, and so on. Let's look at them now:

About—Referencing. *Here's a good book about tax reductions.*

Against—Not in support of, contrary to. *We're against regressive taxes because the poor have to pay a disproportionate amount of their income.*

At—Because of. *I feel sick at the thought of paying out so much in taxes each year.*

Besides—In addition to, apart from, or other than. *Besides federal taxes, there are also state taxes.*

But—Similar to *except,* something separated or excluded. *We got all but $350 of our federal taxes back.*

By—With an agent or performer. *Our taxes were prepared by an accountant this year.*

Except—Excluding something. *We've done everything with our taxes except send them in.*

For—In place of, as compensation. *I'll take good schools, a safe community, and a great library for a few taxes.* In favor of. *Some people are for big government and some are for small government.*

From—Caused by. *The high cost of cigarettes in some states is from taxes.* Source. *We got a letter from the IRS.* Differentiated. *I couldn't tell state taxes from local taxes. Who knows the difference?*

In spite of—Despite, in defiance of. *In spite of the high cost of cigarettes in some places, plenty of people still buy them.*

Instead of—In the place of. *Many people prefer to make donations instead of paying more in taxes.*

Of—About. *Have you heard of online tax preparers?* Relation. *You can pay a part of your taxes now and a part of them later.* Possession, belonging to. *Here are a few pieces of the puzzle.* Reference. *This is Marilyn Beyer of B&B Financial Services.*

To—Comparison. *I believe this online tax program is comparable to using an accountant to help you do your taxes.* Concerning. *If you call this number you can get answers to your tax questions.* In alignment with, following. *To my satisfaction, we finished our taxes on time.*

With—Together, as in accompaniment. *Ralph went with his wife to see a tax preparer.* On the same side as. *Mary thinks we need more deductions and I'm with her on that.* Manner. *I was met with excitement when I returned home last night because our tax return had arrived.*

Without—An absence of. *We've lived without ever having someone to do our taxes until now.*

Through—Processing. *It takes a while for all the paperwork to go through, but once it does you'll get your check right away.* Means. *We found out about online tax filing through a friend.*

D.   HOW-TO

Let's focus on some of the main taxes that people pay in the U.S. We'll start with federal, state, and local income tax, which is a tax that's taken out of your paycheck, and which can cause a lot of headaches and last-minute rushing right around April 15th each year. We'll also look at FICA, which is also taken out of your paycheck, as well as sales tax, excise tax, and property tax, which are paid either when purchases are made or by certain due dates.

INCOME TAX
Income tax is an annual federal, state, and sometimes local tax on either the personal or business income you earn. If you do not own your own business, your employer takes income tax directly from your paycheck. How much is taken out is determined by how much you earn and by the information you entered on your W-4 form, i.e., whether you are single or married, how many dependents you claimed, and whether you requested an additional amount withheld or not. The basic formula is: the fewer exemptions you claim on your W-4, the more tax is withheld from each payment, and, in turn, the more you're likely to get back come tax time. Once all of the exemptions, filing status, and other tax issues are determined, your taxes will be deducted from your paycheck. However, that's not the end of it. Each taxpayer must also file a tax return every year, due by April 15th. The purpose of this process is essentially to give individual taxpayers a chance to correctly calculate whether the government has taken out too much tax and owes the taxpayer a refund, or has taken out too little tax, in which case the taxpayer must pay more to the government. Correct taxes for each year are calculated based on such things as income adjusted for interest received on bank accounts, income not reported to the IRS during the tax year, and so on. Deductions (and credits) are calculated based on any number of factors, such as mortgages, childcare, medical care, business expenses, etc. All of these calculations are done on worksheets and forms available at your local post office, through the IRS, or online. The process is not a simple one, but online services such as the ones listed in the Resources section have made it much simpler over the past few years. Let's walk through the major steps in the process now.

The very first part of the tax process is selecting your filing status, which you had to select on your W-4 as well. There are four different types of status—single, married, married filing separately, and head of household— and which one you choose helps determine your tax rate and how you file, e.g. whether to file separately from or together (jointly) with your spouse if you are married. Next, you start figuring out your gross income. Your gross income includes your annual salary, any bonuses you've received, and any other income reported on your W-2. You also need to include any additional income not reported on your W-2, such as interest, dividends, lottery winnings, business income, etc. There are several possibilities for additional income listed right on the 1040 IRS Individual Income Tax Return form, so be sure to look over the different sources of income possible. Next, adjustments are calculated. Adjustments include payments to certain retirement plans, alimony payments, moving expenses, paid student loan interest, and so on. Once these adjustments have been subtracted, you're left with your adjusted gross income (AGI).

Next, deductions are taken out of your AGI. Deductions include local and state taxes, interest paid on your mortgage, charitable donations, health insurance, and medical expenses, to name just a few. If you list and calculate each one of your deductions, then you are doing what is known as itemizing your deductions. However, to make the process simpler than this, the IRS also offers several other options apart from itemizing your deductions. Rather than adding up each deduction separately, you may choose to take a standard deduction, which is often higher but more straightforward. Additionally, the IRS offers the option of filling out a very simple form called the 1040EZ. You must meet certain qualifications to use it, such as not claiming any dependents and having an income below a certain limit. You can find additional information about this form on the IRS's website. However, if you think you may have large deductions or are not eligible for the standard deduction based on IRS regulations, then you might want to consider itemizing your deductions. But you can't take both the standard deduction and itemized deductions—just the larger of the two.

After you have figured in all your deductions, whether standard or itemized, you then subtract exemptions, and once you have subtracted exemptions, the figure you have is your taxable income. You can claim exemptions for yourself, your spouse, and any dependents. So, if you are married and have two qualifying children, you can usually claim four exemptions, one for each person. And let's suppose your adjusted gross income minus deductions is, for example, $52,000, and this year the IRS allows you to deduct $3,000 per person. With four exemptions, you will deduct $12,000, bringing your taxable income to $40,000. From your taxable income, what you owe in taxes is determined by looking at the tax tables provided to see how much tax is owed on that level of taxable income for your filing status. You may subtract any credits from that tax amount owed, such as childcare payments, if applicable, to get your total tax owed. From the total tax owed, you can determine whether you've paid too much (more than the total taxes owed) for the year, or too little. If you've paid too much, you'll be happy to know that you get a refund check from the IRS. If you've paid too little, you must pay what you still owe. If you file your W-4 correctly, you can be assured of a refund each year, or at least not a huge amount of tax owed.

The filing deadline for tax returns is April 15th the following year for the previous year's taxes. For example, you would file a tax return on April 15th,

2009, for your income in 2008. If you cannot file by April 15th, you can file an extension if necessary. You should get your W-2s by the end of January. You can get your tax return forms from the post office or from the IRS. Dial 1-800-829-3676 to order your forms from the IRS or go online to www.irs.gov/formspubs/index.html and print out the forms and publications you need. You can use a tax-preparing program such as TurboTax if you want to do your own taxes, but preparing federal taxes can be complicated, so you have the option of hiring someone to take care of your taxes for you. There are also free online tax preparation websites and local volunteer organizations that may be able to help you prepare and file your taxes.

In most cases, you will need to file your state taxes and your federal taxes at the same time. There are deductions with state taxes as well. Your state taxes are likely to be much less complicated and quite a bit lower than federal taxes, and you can file them with your federal taxes whether you use an accountant, do them yourself, or file them online. Keep in mind, however, that although you may be able to file your federal taxes for free online, the site you are using to file may charge you a fee to file your state taxes through the site as well. How your taxes are structured, what percentage of your income you pay for state taxes, and whether you pay state taxes or not all vary according to your state. A handful of states do not charge state taxes. A couple of states limit their taxes to dividends and interest income only. You can find out whether your state charges income tax and if so, what percentage by going to your state's tax department website, which can be found by searching online or through www.taxsites.com/state.html.

After you've filled out all the forms and made all the calculations, you'll see how much you owe or how much the federal and state government owes you. If the former, you need to send in a check and perhaps a payment voucher along with the tax return to the address indicated. For more information, visit the IRS's website at www.irs.gov. If the latter, you'll receive a refund check in the mail, or the amount that you're owed will be deposited in your bank account if you've chosen the direct deposit method of payment. It may take a while for you to get the money owed you, because the IRS has a lot of forms to process. As a result, if you turn your forms in early (earlier than most people file) and opt for direct deposit, you'll most likely get your refund much faster.

Now that we've covered income tax, let's highlight a few other categories of taxes that you're likely to encounter on a pretty regular basis.

FICA

FICA is a tax that's taken out of your paycheck to cover Social Security and Medicare. Social Security is a pension that you receive when you retire or if you become disabled. Medicare covers health insurance for those over 65 and for some disabled former workers. Although FICA is really an insurance plan, it is thought of and treated as a tax.

Every worker in the U.S. should have a Social Security number, and children are assigned a number shortly after birth. Although most jobs require that you pay into Social Security, some do not. For example, employees with certain types of state pensions don't pay into Social Security because retirees with state pensions may only collect a very small percentage of Social Security. However, everyone pays into Medicare. For those who do pay into both Social Security and Medicare, these taxes can amount to about 10% of wages. Workers who pay into a different retirement program and don't pay Social Security still can pay around 1.45% of wages for Medicare. Whatever the employee pays, the employer pays a matching amount into FICA.

SALES TAX

When you make a purchase, you are probably paying sales tax for it. The revenue from sales tax pays for a whole host of state and local services. Sales tax varies from state to state, ranging from nothing to more than 8%, and even food and prescription medication may be taxed. For example, if your local sales tax is 5% and you buy a couch for $800, your total bill will be $840. If you order something through the mail, you are generally charged the sales tax for the state you live in rather than the state you order from. At the time of this printing, you only pay sales tax on internet purchases if the company you buy from has an office in your state.

EXCISE TAXES

Excise taxes are levied on products like gasoline, alcohol, cigarettes, and other tobacco products, and they vary in price from state to state and from product to product. Unlike sales taxes, excise taxes are added into the final cost before purchase, so people often don't know how much they are paying in taxes. Some excise taxes go toward supporting infrastructure. For example, taxes on gasoline are used for highway maintenance, bridges, and transportation systems. Other excise taxes are levied as a deterrent to purchasing a particular product, such as cigarettes and alcohol. Often these taxes are used to address issues or concerns associated with the product taxed. For example, an excise tax on alcohol is used to pay for treatment of alcohol related diseases.

PROPERTY TAX

Property taxes are state and local taxes paid on real estate, and they are determined by the value of the property and the tax rates that apply, which vary from state to state. Property taxes are only paid by property owners, so if you rent, you do not pay them. The revenue pays for such things as police forces, fire departments, municipal salaries, schools, libraries, and other local or state services. One major benefit of property taxes is that they can be "written off" of your federal taxes. Property tax payments are often included in your mortgage. Talk with your lender about this when you are arranging your loan.

E. ENGLISH IN ACTION

It's tax time, and Stella and Rubin decided to see an accountant about their taxes this year, rather than try to do them themselves. Listen in.

Mr. Genovese:	Let's see here, yes, here we are, Rubin and Stella, I have your taxes calculated for you.
Rubin:	Do we have to pay more money to the government?
Mr. Genovese:	Actually, you'll be getting a little money back.
Stella:	Oh! That's good news.
Mr. Genovese:	That's always good news.
Rubin:	How did we do that? I thought we would have to pay for sure. We had to pay in extra last year.
Mr. Genovese:	Well, for one thing, you bought a house.
Stella:	And that helped?
Mr. Genovese:	Absolutely. Let me show you. Your combined salary was about $75,000 last year, see?
Rubin:	But we made less money the year before, and we had to pay more taxes.
Mr. Genovese:	Yes, but last year you only took the standard deduction, which was about $10,000 for the two of you. And this year, we itemized your taxes. Look, your mortgage interest alone was about $16,000, and then add in about $2,500 in property taxes, plus there are several additional smaller deductions you can take, such as auto registration. See? Look here. Your itemized deductions added up to just about $30,000. That's $20,000 more than you were able to deduct last year.
Rubin:	But taxes go up every year, don't they?
Mr. Genovese:	Usually, but there are often new ways to save money on taxes, too, if you know where to look for them. For example, you have two children, and the deduction on having children goes up each year. When your kids start college, you'll be able to deduct some of their college expenses as well. You just have to pay attention to all the new tax laws. They change just about every year.
Stella:	Well, that helps keep you employed I guess.
Mr. Genovese:	Yes, it sure does. Most Americans get lost in the maze of tax law, but in my profession, we all have to keep up with it.
Rubin:	So how much did we save? Was it enough to pay your bill?
Stella:	Rubin!

F. PRACTICE

Fill in the blanks with one of the following words: *excise tax, deductions, in the black, in the red, W-4, filing, withholding, fiscal year, gross income, take-home pay*

1. Our company has been _____ for too long. We need to start bringing in more money.

2. We'll be _____ our income taxes as soon as we get our W-2s.

3. Did you know that we pay a(n) _____ on gasoline? The money is used to improve transportation.

4. Let's celebrate! The company's _____ for the first time since we opened!

5. When I started my first job, I asked my family to help me fill out my _____. I didn't understand a lot of the terms and questions that it asked.

6. Your _____ is about $65,000, but your taxable income with probably be much less than that.

7. The _____ for public education is from July 1st to June 30th the next year.

8. We need to see an accountant to help us find more _____, because we need to reduce our taxes.

9. After taxes, your _____ will be about $1,242 each pay period.

10. _____ taxes are taken out of your check based on how many dependents you have.

Choose the correct preposition for each of the following from the three choices given.

1. You can learn (with, about, through) your tax preparer what deductions you can take.

2. Together (from, for, with) my family, I want to thank you for all your help.

3. What can you tell me (about, for, besides) American tax laws?

4. (At, Besides, About) having income taxes and FICA taken out of our paychecks, we also have our insurance payments taken out.

5. I've finished all the work (except, in spite of, to) this project. I'll do it tomorrow.

6. If it weren't (by, through, for) taxes, we wouldn't have so many public parks.

7. Have you tried that new tax program (by, to, with) wedotaxes.com?

8. Many people are (for, against, without) any kind of new tax because they think their taxes will go up.

9. Have you received your refund (with, to, from) the IRS yet?

10. Americans pay far less in taxes compared (to, besides, by) taxes in many other countries.

G. TASK

Go to www.taxengine.com/information/gatherinfo.asp, or find another tax preparation checklist online, and see how organized you are for tax time. If you're not the kind of person who thinks about taxes except around April 14th, this is a great opportunity to get organized, and to make your life a whole lot easier next year!

H. REAL LIFE

Hey, you know, I have to tell you that doing taxes isn't ever easy, but it's possible to make them a whole lot easier. I know. I used to wait until the last minute to do my taxes. Instead of organizing my receipts, I used to throw everything in a shoebox. I always procrastinated because it was just too much work, and I hated doing it, and I never had any idea what the new tax laws were. So every year I'd wait until the last minute, go down to the post office, and pick up all of those horrible forms and booklets with indecipherable instructions and worksheets and tables. And I'd have to set aside a whole day just to figure out what I was doing! It was awful . . . But last year I decided that my New Year's resolution would be to get my taxes organized. So, now I have a file for all my receipts, bank statements, donations, and everything. And instead of frantically trying to do my taxes with those horrible paper forms on my own, or paying someone else to do them, I just do it online. It's so easy. The website walks you through the whole process, beginning to end, explains everything to you, automatically calculates everything, provides information on deductions so you can easily tell whether you qualify or not, and then, best of all, files everything for you electronically. And you're done! No forms, no photocopying, no hassle. If you want a printed record, it'll print everything out for you. And if you get a refund, you can have it automatically deposited in your bank account. I can't believe the way I used to do taxes . . . but no more!

I. RESOURCES

Internal Revenue Service (for up-to-date tax laws, information on filing taxes online, explanations of terms and tax process, refund status, change of address form, etc.):
www.irs.gov or call 1-800-829-1040 for any tax questions

Tax preparation programs and information on them:
www.turbotax.com
www.hrblock.com
www.rapidtax.com
www.taxengine.com

Additional tax help:
www.1040.com

Explanation of income tax process:
people.howstuffworks.com/income-tax.htm
taxes.yahoo.com/basics/filing/income.html

History and description of U.S. taxes:
www.treasury.gov/education/fact-sheets/taxes/economics.shtml

State-by-state taxes:
www.payroll-taxes.com/websites.html
www.taxadmin.org/fta/rate/tax_stru.html
www.taxsites.com/state.html

FICA:
www.ssa.gov/mystatement/fica.htm

ANSWER KEY
Practice 1: 1. in the red; 2. filing; 3. excise tax; 4. in the black; 5. W-4; 6. gross income; 7. fiscal year; 8. deductions; 9. take-home pay; 10. Withholding

Practice 2: 1. through; 2. with; 3. about; 4. Besides; 5. except; 6. for; 7. by; 8. against; 9. from; 10. to

CHAPTER 32

Government and Immigration:
U.S., State, and Local Government

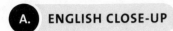
A. ENGLISH CLOSE-UP

Township of Alexandria
2007 OFFICIALS

Mayor, Robert H. Burgstrom

Council Member, Ralph J. Crum

Council Member, Fred Little

Council Member, John G. Shenk

Council Member, Ellen Murdock

Council Member, Jim Gilbert

Council Member, Leonard Oppenmeyer

Municipal Attorney, David Brown, Esq.

Borough Administrator, Annabelle Richards

Municipal Clerk, Rae Ann Gibbons

B. VOCABULARY ESSENTIALS

Administration—A group of individuals working together to administer or execute government, the executive branch of the U.S. government, or the period of time in office of any particular president. *Humankind began preparing to go to the moon during the Kennedy administration and landed on the moon during the Nixon administration.*

To amend (the U.S. Constitution)—To formally alter the Constitution. Amendments to the U.S. Constitution are the laws added to the Constitution. *In 1920, the Constitution of the United States was amended to give women the right to vote. This is the Nineteenth Amendment.*

Bicameral—Consisting of two chambers or two branches. *The United States Congress is bicameral, made up of the Senate and the House of Representatives.*

Bill—A bill is a proposed law before it becomes a law. *Congress spent considerable time on the bill, but the president chose to veto it.*

Checks and balances—The ability of each branch of the government to limit the power of the others. *The United States government has three branches, with a system of checks and balances to maintain equal power.*

Chief Justice—The primary or presiding judge of the Supreme Court. *Oliver Wendell Holmes, Jr., is one of the most famous Chief Justices of the Supreme Court.*

City charter (or town charter)—A document issued by a legislature to create a city or town. The charter defines the privileges and duties of that city or town. *The legislature granted Springfield their city charter on December 6, 1998.*

Coauthor, to coauthor—One of the authors of a bill. To be one of the authors of a bill. *Bella Abzug, a well-known representative from New York City, coauthored the Freedom of Information Act.*

Commander in Chief—The title for the president of the United States as leader of the U.S. military. *"Hail to the Chief" is a song that is played to introduce the Commander in Chief.*

Commonwealth—A government based on the common consent of the people. Four states in the U.S.—Massachusetts, Virginia, Kentucky, and Pennsylvania—have designated themselves commonwealths. *Puerto Rico, a self-governing territory of the United States, calls itself the Commonwealth of Puerto Rico.*

Congress—The legislative branch of the U.S. government that consists of the House of Representatives and the Senate. *Congress has two sessions for every term, and each term lasts for two years.*

Constituent—A person represented in a democracy, someone living in an area represented by an elected official. *Legislators must listen to their constituents or they could get voted out of office.*

Constitution—The governing set of principles of a nation, state, etc., usually recorded in a document. The U.S. Constitution is the highest law of the United States and was written and ratified in the late 1780s. *The first three words of the U.S. Constitution are "We the People."*

County—The largest level of local government in a state. A state is divided up into multiple counties. A county is called a borough in Alaska and a parish in Louisiana. *Many counties have the same name as the largest city within their borders.*

Executive branch—Branch of government that executes, or carries out, the laws of the land. The executive branch of the United States government consists of the president, vice president, and the president's cabinet and its departments, along with various other agencies and departments. *The job of the executive branch of the U.S. government is to enforce the laws that Congress enacts.*

Federal—National, concerning the United States government. *The executive branch of the federal government is headed by the president.*

Founding Fathers (of the United States)—Those who attended the First Constitutional Convention, where the Constitution was written. The term is sometimes also applied more generally to mean the group of people who helped to create the United States in its very early stages. *Thomas Jefferson and Benjamin Franklin are considered to be two of the Founding Fathers of the United States.*

To incorporate—To become united as one legal body. *Cities are incorporated by the state.*

Incumbent—An elected official running for reelection to the same office in an upcoming election. *It is very common for incumbents to win reelection.*

Judicial branch—Branch of government that interprets the law and administers justice. System of courts. *The judicial branch of the U.S. government includes the Supreme Court as well as the lower federal courts.*

Jurisdiction—Control or authority, the area of control or authority. *The Supreme Court has jurisdiction over the constitutionality of U.S. laws.*

Laws—Codes and regulations set down and enforced by the government. *There are federal laws governing everything from employment and voting to environmental protection.*

Legislative branch—Branch of government that makes the laws of the land. The United States legislative branch consists of Congress and its two chambers. *The Capitol building is the headquarters of the legislative branch of the United States.*

Lobby—A group of people representing a specific cause who try to influence members of Congress in their favor. *There are some lobbies that are very powerful and influential in Washington.*

Municipal—Of or relating to a local, self-governed area, such as a town or city. *Municipal services can include waste removal, public transportation, public housing, and public education.*

Unconstitutional—Outside the principles of the Constitution, not consistent with the Constitution. *It is unconstitutional to prohibit people from voting when they are legally registered to do so.*

Unincorporated area—An area that is not legally bound to any incorporated area or municipality. *The county provides services to the unincorporated areas.*

Veto, to veto—The power of U.S. president to refuse to sign into law the bills that Congress has enacted. To execute the power of veto on a bill. *If the president does not approve of a large part of a bill that Congress has presented, the president is likely to veto it and send it back to Congress.*

 ## C. GRAMMAR ESSENTIALS: THE SUBJUNCTIVE

The subjunctive is not a tense, but rather a mood, meaning that it is used not to convey a time of action, but rather a speaker's attitude toward the action. While the indicative mood expresses real actions, the subjunctive is used to express wishes, desires, rules, or contingencies. It is not very commonly used in English, and in fact many would say that the subjunctive will fall into disuse. But there are still many expressions and situations in which speakers use the subjunctive. Some common fixed expressions that use the subjunctive are: *God bless you, come what may, praise be to God, so be it, be that as it may,* and *heaven forbid.* The subjunctive looks like the present indicative, except that there is no *s* on the end of the verb in the third person singular (*he, she,* or *it*). Note that the subjunctive of the verb *to be* is *be.*

The subjunctive is typically used with *that* to express commands, suggestions, desires, or possibilities. The verbs with which the subjunctive is usually used are: *advise, ask, beg, decide, decree, demand, desire, dictate, insist, intend, move, order, petition, propose, recommend, request, require, resolve, suggest, urge,* and *vote.* Some examples include:
> *We recommend that you report concerns to the city council.*
> *Mrs. Zepeda insists that she learn her civic responsibilities.*
> *Sharon suggests that everyone visit Washington, D.C., someday.*

The adjectives *advisable, critical, desirable, essential, fitting, imperative, required, important, necessary,* and *vital* are used with *it* plus the subjunctive:
> *It is advisable that he contact the city attorney.*
> *It is desirable that we leave by 3:00 p.m. to avoid the traffic.*
> *It is important that she get this information from the building inspector.*
> *It is imperative that he make his voice heard.*
> *It is vital that he be on time.*

The following nouns can also be used with the subjunctive: *advice, condition, demand, directive, intention, order, proposal, recommendation, request, suggestion,* and *wish.* For example:
> *It is our recommendation that you use our website to find important city information.*
> *My advice is that he read the Declaration of Independence.*

Finally, note that the subjunctive is used in formal English following *if, although, whether,* and *lest:*

*If that be so, then the House must be called back into session.
Whether she be here or not, we have to begin.*

D. HOW-TO

The United States is a federal system, meaning that it is a union of states that recognize the power of a central government in certain spheres, but that maintain power and rights in other spheres. The federal government is the central power, seated of course in Washington, D.C., a district that is not part of any state. The Constitution of the United States is the supreme law of the land. Written by the Founding Fathers, it is a document that outlines the system of government found in the U.S. today. It is a government divided into three branches, the executive, the legislative, and the judicial. In order to keep any one branch or individual from gaining too much power in government, the U.S. Constitution contains a system of checks and balances, limiting power by granting each branch certain controls over the others.

The U.S. executive branch includes the president, vice president, the president's cabinet, and various department and agencies. The president of the United States is the head of the executive branch and the head of the country. He or she also serves as the Commander in Chief of the military and enacts the laws. The powers of the president include veto power, nomination of judges and occupants of certain other government positions, making of treaties, and granting of pardons. The president and the vice president are the only two officials that the entire population of the country votes for. They serve together for four years and may be elected to serve an additional four-year term, but no more. Both the president and vice president must be at least thirty-five years old, have lived in the U.S. for 14 years, and be natural born U.S. citizens.

The legislative branch of the U.S. government, Congress, is bicameral. It includes the Senate and House of Representatives. The House and Senate work together to make the laws of the land, which sometimes means making amendments to the Constitution. It is also their duty to ensure that the president acts within the bounds of the Constitution and hold him or her accountable if the Constitution is violated. Other powers of Congress are the ability to establish lower federal courts, to override a presidential veto, and to impeach the president. Two senators are elected from each state and are chosen for a term of six years. The number of representatives per state is based on the population of the state, about one representative per 650,000 people. Representatives' terms are for two years. Both senators and representatives may serve for longer periods, but at the end of each term they must face a new election. It is required that senatorial candidates be at least thirty years of age, U.S. citizens for at least nine years, and residents of the state they represent. Requirements to be a representative are similar, except candidates must be at least twenty-five years of age and have been a U.S. citizen for at least seven years.

The federal judicial branch is headed by the Supreme Court, but there are lower federal courts as well. The job of the judicial branch is to ensure that the Constitution is followed. This means guaranteeing the rights of the people of the United States against any unconstitutional acts, either by the president or by Congress. The power that the judiciary has over the other two branches is that it may declare any law or act unconstitutional. The Supreme Court also has the power to try federal cases and to interpret the laws of the nation. There are nine Supreme Court justices, including the Chief Justice, and they are all selected by the president of the United States and approved by Congress. They serve life terms or until they choose to retire. There are no legal requirements in order to be a Supreme Court justice, but there is the practical requirement that individuals selected have judicial experience.

Although the federal government holds jurisdiction over the states, the states are to a certain extent autonomous. Each state has its own constitution that gives authority to its own executive, legislative, and judicial branches. State governments in the U.S. all have governors as head of state, and lieutenant governors who serve as head of state in the absence of the governor. Each state has a house of representatives and a senate, and the state judicial branch is headed by the state supreme court. Qualifications for office in each state vary. As in the federal government, the legislative branch makes the laws, and the executive branch approves and then executes the laws. The judicial branch interprets the law. The governor and the members of the legislature are elected by the people of the state. Like the federal government, the state government collects taxes, but it also receives a share of federal funds. While states are under the jurisdiction of the federal government, each state makes its own laws as well. States concern themselves with driving laws, automobile safety, public health, insurance, education, the environment, state parks, and so on. Every state has a different set of laws and a different approach to state concerns. Attitudes and laws concerning such issues as environmental protection, gay rights, gambling, alcohol sales, and smoking vary greatly from state to state.

Local government varies from state to state, and even within states, so it is difficult to make generalizations. Most states are divided into counties (also known as boroughs in Alaska or parishes in Louisiana). Within the counties are municipalities that are towns, townships, or cities, or in some cases boroughs (not to be confused with the boroughs of Alaska) or villages. Each municipality and county has its own governmental body as well. Instead of a constitution, municipalities have charters. At the most local level, there's a mayor or city manager who is the executive head, the city council is the legislative body, and there is also a court system that is the judicial body. Municipal governments are responsible for police and fire protection, zoning within municipal limits, and other chiefly local concerns. At the county level there may be a county executive, a county board of legislators, and a district attorney. The county maintains local highways and is responsible for such issues as refuse collection and recycling in the areas that remain unincorporated. In addition, there may be local or regional districts that are designated for specific uses, such as fire protection, transit, sewer, and water services. Schools have their own special districts, as well, and may or may not necessarily fit into a specific municipal area. In short, the more local the government, the more varied its structure in order to deal with local conditions and population levels.

E. ENGLISH IN ACTION

Let's listen in on a citizenship class.

Mr. Egan: So, only Congress has the right to make laws . . . Yes, Adrian?
Adrian: I understand that Congress makes laws, but I was just wondering how something actually becomes a law.
Mr. Egan: Very good question. First of all, Congress is composed of . . .
Adrian: The House of Representatives and the Senate, right?
Mr. Egan: That's right. A bill must first originate in one of those two houses. Then it must pass by a majority before it can move on to the other house. Once both the Senate and the House of Representatives have passed it, it then goes to the president.
Adrian: Then the president signs it into law. Yeah, I get it.
Mr. Egan: Well, not always. If the president signs it, then yes, it becomes a law, but suppose the president doesn't like something about the bill.
Adrian: I guess he doesn't sign it.
Mr. Egan: That's right, he can veto it. That means he doesn't approve it. But if he vetoes the bill, he has to send it back to whichever house it originated in. If he doesn't send it immediately, within ten days of receiving it, not including Sunday of course, it becomes law, even though the president didn't sign it.
Adrian: Why would he do it that way?
Mr. Egan: Well, he might know that it'll pass anyway or he may not sign it just to register his disapproval of something within the law, but he thinks overall it's a good law. However, if he sends it back before the ten days are up, then both houses of Congress must approve it by a two-thirds majority. If they don't pass it by a two-thirds majority, it dies until they take it up again, or they may try to rewrite it so that the president will sign it, or they might wait until there's a new president who they believe will sign it.

Adrian: It must be difficult to get laws passed.

Mr. Egan: Yes, very often it is difficult. It really depends upon how much in agreement Congress is with the president on an issue. But a law is important, so it makes sense that the process of making laws should be careful.

F. PRACTICE

Fill in the blanks with the following words: *bill, checks and balances, constituent, administration, veto, incumbent, Founding Fathers, legislative branch, unconstitutional, municipal*

1. The U.S. Senate is part of the _____ of the U.S. government.
2. The Johnson _____ presented the idea of the Great Society.
3. The president has the right to _____ a law passed by Congress.
4. Yesterday, the Senate overwhelmingly passed a(n) _____.
5. As your _____, I'd like to request that you vote no on the upcoming bill.
6. One of the _____, Thomas Jefferson, wrote most of the Declaration of Independence.
7. You'll be tried in _____ court because your crime was committed within this county.
8. Taking away Americans' civil liberties is _____.
9. _____ presidents often win a second term.
10. That the judicial branch can declare an act by the president to be unconstitutional and that the president nominates Supreme Court Justices are examples of _____.

Rewrite each of the following indicative sentences using the subjunctive, as indicated.

1. You arrive at the appointment on time. (It's advisable that . . .)
2. He contacts his congressperson. (My advice is that . . .)
3. You are on time for your interview. (We insist that . . .)
4. You wait your turn. (Mr. Biggs insists . . .)
5. You are a permanent resident for five years before you can apply for citizenship. (It is required . . .)
6. The applicant has good moral character. (The government's condition is that . . .)
7. You remain in the U.S. territory for six months out of the year. (The government advises that . . .)

8. Each branch of government shares power equally. (It is the Constitution's intent that . . .)

9. A citizenship applicant is honest with the federal government. (It is essential that . . .)

10. We become citizens. (It is preferable that . . .)

 TASK

Go to the U.S. Office of Citizenship's website at www.uscis.gov/graphics/ citizenship/index.htm and download the "Civics Flash Cards." They will help you learn about U.S. history and government. Then answer the following questions. You can find the answers in the Answer Key of this lesson.

1. What is the Bill of Rights?

2. What are the names of the two senators from your state?

3. What do we call changes to the Constitution?

4. Who succeeds the president should he or she die in office?

H. REAL LIFE

Dear Sammy,

I have been a legal permanent resident of the United States for about four years and want to start preparing for my citizenship test on U.S. government and history. I don't think I can afford an expensive tutor or class or anything like that though. What should I do?

Please help!
Mila

Dear Mila,

Don't worry! There are many inexpensive or free resources available to help you study for the naturalization test that assesses your knowledge of U.S. government, citizens' rights, and history. First of all, the United States Office of Citizenship (you can visit them at www.uscis.gov/graphics/ citizenship/index.htm) provides many resources online for immigrants preparing for the civics test. These can include a practice naturalization test, civics flash cards and lessons, sample U.S. history and government questions, and more. The site also provides links to other websites that will help you locate English classes, if you need them (because you need to pass a test of your English too to become a citizen!). Furthermore, there are many free or very inexpensive citizenship classes, which teach U.S. government and history as well as teach you about the test itself, available through adult education/ESL programs at colleges and through community organizations and centers, religious institutions, some public school systems, and so on. Just do a basic search online or contact your local college, public school district, community center, or religious institution to see if they offer or know of any classes. You should also be able to find a wide variety of inexpensive citizenship test preparation guides in a bookstore or through an online bookseller. So as you can see, there are many resources available to you!

Good luck!
Sammy

I. RESOURCES

Contact Information:
The President of the United States
The White House, 1600 Pennsylvania Avenue NW, Washington, D.C. 20500
www.whitehouse.gov/contact or 1-202-456-1414

U.S. Senate www.senate.gov
United States Senate, Washington, D.C. 20510
Call the U.S. Capitol switchboard at (202) 224-3121

Contact information for individual senators can be found at
www.senate.gov/general/contact_information/senators_cfm.cfm

U.S. House of Representatives www.house.gov
United States Senate, Washington, D.C. 20515
Call the U.S. Capitol switchboard at (202) 224-3121

Contact information for individual representatives can be found at
clerk.house.gov/members/index.html

U.S. Supreme Court www.supremecourtus.gov
Supreme Court of the United States, Washington, D.C. 20543
(202) 479-3211

State and local governments:
www.loc.gov/rr/news/stategov/stategov.html (includes useful links to other online resources on state and local governments)
www.statelocalgov.net
www.govspot.com/state

U.S. Constitution:
www.usconstitution.net

ANSWER KEY
Practice 1: 1. legislative branch; 2. administration; 3. veto; 4. bill; 5. constituent; 6. Founding Fathers; 7. municipal; 8. unconstitutional; 9. Incumbent; 10. checks and balances

Practice 2: 1. It's advisable that you arrive at the appointment on time. 2. My advice is that he contact his congressperson. 3. We insist that you be on time for your interview. 4. Mr. Biggs insists that you wait your turn. 5. It is required that you be a permanent resident for five years before you can apply for citizenship. 6. The government's condition is that the applicant have good moral character. 7. The government advises that you remain in the U.S. territory for six months out of the year. 8. It is the Constitution's intent that each branch of government share power equally. 9. It is essential that a citizenship applicant be honest with the federal government. 10. It is preferable that we become citizens.

Task: 1. The first ten amendments to the Constitution. 2. Varies from state to state. 3. Amendments. 4. The vice president.

CHAPTER 33

Government and Immigration: Voting

A. ENGLISH CLOSE-UP

ELECTION DISTRICT (ED)	ASSEMBLY DISTRICT (AD)	SERIAL NUMBER
58	74	000520103

CONGRESSIONAL DISTRICT	STATE SENATORIAL DISTRICT	COUNCIL DISTRICT	CIVIL COURT DISTRICT
14	29	02	09

PARTY	DEMOCRAT		

John C. Bryans
782 Fourth Avenue
Apt. 803
New York, N.Y. 10003

B. VOCABULARY ESSENTIALS

527 organization—Named for an IRS tax code, an organization created to receive and disburse "soft money" in order to influence elections. *The contributions that 527 organizations raise are not taxed by the IRS.*

Absentee ballots—Ballots marked and mailed in prior to an election, used by registered voters who will not be in the jurisdiction on Election Day. *Because I'm going to be on a business trip on Election Day, I filled in an absentee ballot.*

Ballot—The list of candidates running for office, or the paper on which a voter notes his or her selection. *Once your ballot has been marked and turned in, you have voted.*

Blue state—A state with an overall political climate that favors the Democratic Party, generally (although not always) a state in the Northeast, Upper Midwest, or West Coast. *California and New York are blue states.*

Candidate—A person who is running for an elected position. *Everyone wants his or her candidate to win.*

Caucus—A meeting of members of a political party to nominate candidates or plan policy. *The House Democratic caucus will meet to decide how best to pass their version of the bill.*

Delegate—Someone selected to represent a block of voters. *State delegates for the Republican Party vote, mainly as a formality, for their preferred Republican candidate for president at the Republican national convention.*

Democrats—Members of the Democratic Party, one of the two major political parties in the U.S. To learn more about the Democratic Party, go to: www.democrats.org. *President Kennedy is one of the most well-known Democratic presidents from the 20th century.*

Electoral College—A group of electors, essentially voting representatives, chosen from each state to formally vote for the president and vice president of the United States, after the popular vote for the state is cast. Each state has a certain number of electoral votes, equal to the total number of seats it holds in Congress, and usually the candidate who wins the popular vote in a state wins that number of electoral votes. The candidates with the most electoral votes win the election. *Electors are pledged, but not always required, to vote for certain candidates for president and vice president. In 1976, an elector who was supposed to vote for Gerald Ford for president instead voted for Ronald Reagan.*

Enfranchised—Free, empowered, allowed to vote. *Women were enfranchised in 1920 when they were given the right to vote.*

Inauguration—The formal ceremony inducting an individual, such as the president, into office. *President Jimmy Carter began an inauguration tradition of walking from the Capitol to the White House.*

Midterm elections—Elections that do not coincide with the presidential election. *The state's governor was selected during the last midterm election.*

Mudslinging—The practice of presenting malicious information about or making personal attacks on an opposing candidate, an effort to win by casting the other candidate in a negative light, a "smear campaign." *Every year the candidates say there will be no mudslinging from their side, but they all do it anyway.*

Nomination—The official naming of a candidate. *The Republican candidate won the nomination in the primary among a group of candidates and will face his Democratic opponent in the general election in the fall.*

Political parties—Any one of several organizations representing a certain segment of the population in elections. *Democrats and Republicans are currently the two primary political parties in the U.S., although there are also other minor parties.*

Poll—A scientific sample of public opinion that gauges where most people stand on an issue or candidate. *The latest polls show that both presidential candidates are at about 48%.*

Polling station—Where voters go to cast their ballots during an election. *If you've moved recently, your polling station has changed. You need to reregister so you can vote.*

Popular vote—The method of selecting someone for a political office in which each voter casts one vote and the person with the majority of these votes wins. *Given the current system of selecting a president, it's possible for a candidate to lose the popular vote but still be elected by winning the electoral vote.*

Race—A competition for political office. *It can be confusing when there are many candidates running in the race for a particular office.*

Red state—A state with an overall political climate that favors the Republican Party, generally (although not always) a state in the South, Great Plains, and Intermountain West. *Texas and Kansas are red states.*

Republicans—Members of the Republican Party, one of the two major political parties in the U.S. To learn more about the Republican Party, go to: www.gop.com. *The Republican Party nominated Dwight Eisenhower for president in 1952.*

To run for office—To try to get elected to a political position. *It takes a strong stomach to run for office because anything you've ever done will become common knowledge, whether you want it to or not.*

Slate—The list of candidates selected by a political party. Often called a "ticket," which can also refer to political candidates running as a team and being voted for together rather than separately. One example of this is the presidential ticket—the candidates for president and vice president run together. *I'm calling to ask you to please vote for the slate of candidates selected by your party. Thank you.*

Soft money—Campaign contributions not regulated by federal election laws. *Senator Smith lost the election because of the soft money used to run ads against him.*

Straw poll—A vote that is not binding but is used only to gauge opinion. Also called a straw vote. *If they held a straw poll for president today, who do you think would be the victor?*

Suffrage—The right to vote. *The women's suffrage movement began to gain momentum in 1848.*

Swing state—A state that alternates between Democratic and Republican, where neither party tends to have a reliable majority. *Ohio and Florida have been considered important swing states.*

Two-party system—When two major political parties dominate the election process and win most of the elections. *The U.S. currently has a two-party system, so the president is always either a Democrat or a Republican.*

Voter registration—The process of signing forms and declaring one's address and political affiliation in order to vote. *If you see voter registration going on outside grocery stores, you'll know it's almost time for the next election.*

C. GRAMMAR ESSENTIALS: REAL CONDITIONALS

There are two types of conditionals: real conditionals, which express potential or possible results of an action, and unreal conditionals, which express purely hypothetical results of unreal actions. In this lesson we'll deal with real conditionals, and in the next lesson we'll tackle unreal conditionals. Conditionals have two clauses: the condition and the result. The condition is typically introduced by *if*, and the result by *then*, although *then* may not be expressed. In real conditionals, both the condition and the result clause are in the same tenses as they'd be in a regular, indicative sentence. The only difference is the presence of *if*, and the optional presence of *then*. However, keep in mind that the future tense is not used after *if*. Instead, it's replaced by the present:

Present	*If you vote, you participate in democracy.*
Past	*If he made it to the polling station on time, then he voted.*
Future	*If a candidate for president gets 270 electoral votes, he or she will win the presidency.*
Present Perfect	*If she has followed the election, she's heard about the polls.*
Present Progressive	*If they are contributing a lot of money to the party, then they must be strong supporters.*
Present Perfect Progressive	*If you have been following elections for so long, you know all about mudslinging.*

Note that the condition and result clauses are not always in the same tense; that depends on the logical relationship between cause and effect. Also note that you can reverse the order of clauses:

You participate in democracy if you vote.
Your vote is going to get counted if you send your absentee ballot in on time.

Should, when, and *whenever* can sometimes replace *if,* and *unless* can replace *if . . . not:*

> *Should you forget to send in your absentee ballot, your vote won't be counted.*
> *Your vote won't be counted unless you send in your absentee ballot.*
> *Whenever you vote, you are exercising democracy.*
> *When you take the time to study the candidates, you will make better decisions.*

D. HOW-TO

The United States Constitution does not outline a system for nominating candidates, and the process has gradually evolved into a two-party system. Although there are other political parties, the Republican Party and the Democratic Party have remained the dominant parties for more than a century. This two-party system has created its own system of checks and balances that does not allow any one party to remain in power for too long. Often within one administration, the White House is controlled by one party and Congress by another, which also allows for more checks and balances on power. Let's take a look at how parties come to power—in other words, how citizens vote in the U.S.

Before U.S. citizens can vote, they must be registered in the county of their residence. When Americans are at least eighteen years old, and they meet their state's requirements, they are eligible to register to vote. Registration can take place at the local registrar of voters office, state departments of motor vehicles, state offices providing public assistance, state offices providing state-funded programs for the disabled, armed forces recruitment offices, and in some states, in local libraries, post offices, and so on. Registration forms can also be downloaded online from the state registrar of voters and mailed in.

Elections in the United States are a two-step process. First, there is the primary election, and then later comes the general election. Beginning at the local level, a slate of candidates is chosen for each party through the primary election. These candidates belong to the same party; they vie with one another to be selected by the party as the candidate representing that party. The date of the primary election varies from state to state, but in most states, the voters choose their candidates from the ballot that represents only their political party. So, if you are registered as a Democrat, you have only a Democratic slate to choose from, and if you are Republican, you can only vote on the Republican slate of candidates. However, in some states, voters may vote in the primaries of parties that are not their own. After the primaries, each party holds a convention at which the one candidate chosen to represent the party is officially nominated to run against the member chosen from the other party. It is not until the general election that these candidates run against each other, and voters are offered the choice of not just the two major parties, but also all the other political parties on one ballot. Elections occur at fixed times. Every even-numbered year on the first Tuesday after the first Monday of November, the general election for all the representatives' seats and one-third of the senators' seats occurs. Every four years in November, the offices of president and vice president are up for reelection. Most governors are elected during the midterm election. Locally, there may be elections every year for such offices as mayor, council member, and school board member, as well as for propositions and bond measures.

On Election Day, most voters go to their designated polling station, which may be a school, a library, a fire station, or some other large public space. The poll workers (American citizens who are able to speak, read, and write English, are registered voters, and are not office holders at the time of the election nor have a relative running for office) check names off of one roster and addresses off another. Each voter is then given a ballot and the means to mark his or her choices. Then the voter steps into a private booth to vote. Once selections have been made, the paper ballot is slipped into a box or a voting machine records the vote. If the voting takes place on an electronic voting machine, the selection is made entirely on the machine. If American citizens do not reside in the United States, they can vote by absentee ballot. Absentee ballots can also be selected by voters who do reside in the U.S. but anticipate being unable to get to the polls on Election Day. Every election is held locally even if it is for a national office.

Of course, Election Day is the culmination of a long and arduous process of convincing voters whom to vote for. Prior to an election, candidates running for office travel around, give speeches, hold debates, seek endorsements from such organizations as newspapers or unions, run advertisements on television, on radio, and in print, all directed at urging voters to select them instead of their opponents. Unfortunately, there is often a good deal of mudslinging that occurs during races, especially tight ones. Political Action Committees, 527 Committees (also called "soft money" political action committees), and a whole host of other advocacy groups often enter the fray, endorsing one candidate or the other and stressing their particular agendas.

While candidates in local and state elections are always selected by popular vote, the presidential election (the president and vice president are voted for together, with presidential candidates choose their running mates, the vice presidential candidates) is determined instead by the Electoral College. In this system, which is outlined in the Constitution, each state has a certain number of electors, equal to its number of senators plus representatives in Congress. When voters vote for certain candidates in a presidential election, they are actually technically voting for electors who have pledged to vote for those candidates. For example, in general, if

Candidate A is running against Candidate B in State X, which has 10 electoral votes, each candidate has 10 electoral nominees that have pledged to vote for him or her. If Candidate A gets 49% of the popular vote in State X and Candidate B gets 51%, then all ten of Candidate B's electors go on to officially vote in the Electoral College for that candidate. In other words, the winner of the popular vote in a state usually gets all of that state's electoral votes (the exceptions are Maine and Nebraska). The candidate who gets the majority of the 358 total electoral votes wins the election. Occasionally, then, it is possible for a candidate to win the popular vote on a national level but to lose the electoral vote because of "election calculus." This same election calculus also often has candidates focusing on key battleground states, which are typically swing states with a great number of electoral votes. There is often some debate on whether to change to a direct popular vote for the highest office in the country. As a final note, it is important to keep in mind that each state can have a different electoral process, so you should visit your state's secretary of state's website to learn about the voting process where you live.

E. ENGLISH IN ACTION

Let's listen in on a citizenship class, where Mila asks about the Electoral College.

Mr. Stanley: Welcome to citizenship class, everyone. We recently had our national election, and I was wondering if anyone had any questions about the last election? Yes, you're Mila, right?

Mila: That's right, and I have a question about the election. I was confused by the difference between the popular vote and some kind of college. Why would a college choose the president?

Mr. Stanley: Very good question. I was hoping someone would ask about that. The Electoral College is not a college like a school, but rather a body of people who represent votes from their home states. You see, in the U.S., the people don't actually vote directly for the president. The president is chosen by the Electoral College, which reflects the vote of each state as a whole. The Electoral College was instituted by the Founding Fathers because it was thought to be a much fairer process than the popular vote, since it would give states with smaller populations more of an equal vote with states having a larger population, as well as avoid corruption, balance state and national concerns, and other issues. Each state is designated a number of electoral voters equal to its number of senators and representatives in Congress; however, no federal legislator can be an elector.

Mila: So how do the electors get to be electors?

Mr. Stanley: Another good question. It varies from state to state. But usually they are selected by party leaders because of their dedication to the party, or they campaign for the job and are then selected at their state's party convention. The Constitution doesn't give any qualifications for electors, only that they cannot be a representative or a senator, they cannot be a high-ranking U.S. official in position to profit in some way, nor can they be someone who has engaged in "insurrection or rebellion" against the United States.

Mila: But how do they decide who to choose?

Mr. Stanley: Once the general election has taken place and the voters have made their choices, in most states all the electoral votes go to the candidate that receives the most votes in the general election. This is called the "winner-takes-all" system. A few states use the "district system," where two electors go with the candidate that receives the most popular votes. The rest of the electors are divided between the candidates according to the popular vote in each congressional district.

Mila: So how many electoral votes does it take to win the presidency?

Mr. Stanley: If one candidate wins at least 270 votes, they win the election. That's over half of the 538 possible electoral votes.

Mila: It seems kind of complicated, but I think I understand.

Mr. Stanley: Yes, it can be very confusing. There are probably many American citizens who don't understand how it works. Now, we should probably move on to our next topic, bills and amendments . . .

F. PRACTICE

Fill in the blanks with the following words: *run for office, mudslinging, Electoral College, delegates, ballot, nomination, poll, candidates, voter registration, polling station*

1. There are 50 _____ from California and 32 from Texas who will help select the next union leader.

2. At the party national conventions, the Democratic and Republican _____ for president were made.

3. Hand your _____ to the poll worker after you have finished voting.

4. It seems like there's a new _____ taken every day during a presidential election.

5. Often, before elections, parties sponsor _____ drives to get new voters involved in the process.

6. There are often many _____ for a particular office who run in primaries, but only one gets chosen from each party's primary.

7. You'll be notified in the mail before the election about where your local _____ is.

8. Many voters lose interest or get frustrated when the candidates start _____.

9. A presidential candidate can't win without 270 votes from the _____.

10. You will need a lot of financial support if you want to _____.

Using the verbs in parentheses, finish the real conditional sentences. There may be more than one correct answer.

1. Jim _____ (get) to vote if he's eighteen or older.

2. If Maria becomes a citizen in time, she _____ (vote).

3. If someone _____ (want) to be mayor, she or he needs to win a majority of the popular vote.

4. If she _____ (win) the popular vote, that doesn't necessarily mean that she'll be elected president.

5. If he _____ (ask) for an absentee ballot before last week, then he got one.

6. Should you decide to run for office, you _____ (need) plenty of money.

7. You _____ (not know) the issues unless you follow the news.

8. You'll learn about voting when you _____ (take) your citizenship class.

9. A lot of candidates think they _____ (win) if they use mudslinging techniques.

10. When pollsters take a poll, they _____ (see) election trends.

G. TASK

Go to memory.loc.gov/learn/features/election/home.html, a government learning website on elections by the Library of Congress, click "elections," and using the information found there, answer the following questions. The answers are listed in the Answer Key of this lesson.

1. Who selects the president and vice president when there is a tie in the Electoral College?

2. What was the first year a presidential candidate tried to win a party's nomination through primary elections, and who was the candidate?

3. How does the Constitution suggest that candidates for president of the U.S. be nominated?

H. **REAL LIFE**

Ralph Ryland, a popular Constitution expert, talks about voting rights in his weekly syndicated radio show, *Democracy in America*:

When the framers of the Constitution first laid out the election process, their intention was that only property owners would be allowed to vote. That meant white males would be the only qualified voters, because women didn't own property, African-Americans were slaves, and Native Americans weren't considered citizens at that time. There were also many white men who did not own property and were therefore disenfranchised. By 1860, the previously disenfranchised white men had gained the right to vote. In 1870, after the Civil War, the Fifteenth Amendment was added to the Constitution, giving African-American men the right to vote. This amendment stated that the right to vote could not be denied on the basis of color, race, or previous enslavement. Some states resisted enforcing this amendment, and it was not until the Voting Rights Act of 1965, which allowed for more federal oversight of the voting process and outlawed certain practices that were prohibiting African-Americans from voting, that the amendment was almost fully put into effect. Women were left out of the voting process until 1920, when they were finally granted suffrage through the Nineteenth Amendment. Although the Fifteenth Amendment did in fact grant Native Americans the right to vote, they did not have full American citizenship rights until 1924. But because election rules were in the hands of the states, it was not really until 1948 that all Native Americans gained the right to vote. One more amendment, the Twenty-sixth Amendment, was added to the Constitution in 1971. This amendment gave eighteen-year-olds the right to vote, lowering the voting age from twenty-one.

I. **RESOURCES**

Democratic Party:
www.democrats.org

Republican Party:
www.gop.com

Background and information on elections and voting:
memory.loc.gov/learn/features/election/home.html
www.archives.gov/federal-register/electoral-college
www.fec.gov/index.shtml
www.infoplease.com/timelines/voting.html (voting rights history)

Information on current elections:

www.uselections.com

www.vote-smart.org/election_congress.php (Senate and House elections)

www.politics1.com

www.cnn.com/POLITICS

ANSWER KEY

Practice 1: 1. delegates; 2. nominations; 3. ballot; 4. poll; 5. voter registration; 6. candidates; 7. polling station; 8. mudslinging; 9. Electoral College; 10. run for office

Practice 2: 1. gets; 2. will vote; 3. wants; 4. wins; 5. asked; 6. will need; 7. won't/don't know; 8. take; 9. will win; 10. see

Task: 1. The president is selected by the House and the vice president by the Senate. 2. 1912, Theodore Roosevelt. 3. The Constitution gives no guidelines.

CHAPTER 34

Government and Immigration: Court System

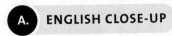

A. **ENGLISH CLOSE-UP**

NOTICE FOR TRIAL JURY SERVICE

By order of the court, you are summoned by the Superior Court of the state of _____ in the county of _____ for service as a trial juror.

FAILURE TO APPEAR WITHOUT EXCUSE OR POSTPONEMENT IS PUNISHABLE BY CONTEMPT AND/OR FINE PURSUANT TO THE CODE OF CIVIL PROCEDURE, SECTON 201

Reporting Date: **August 10, 2007**   **Court Location**

Reporting Time: **7:45 a.m.**   **Hall of Justice**

B. **VOCABULARY ESSENTIALS**

Alibi—A defense given by the accused to prove that he or she did not commit the crime, usually by saying that he or she was somewhere else at the time. *Mr. Naylor's alibi is that he was at the stadium watching the baseball game at the time the crime was committed, and his friends will vouch for him.*

To appeal—To take a case to a higher court in order to challenge a ruling of the lower court and ask the higher court to review or reverse the judgment of the lower court. *After a great deal of deliberation, the judge granted the defendant an appeal.*

Bail—Money paid to permit a defendant (a suspect, someone believed to have committed a crime) to remain out of jail before a trial, a type of security to ensure that the defendant will return to court for the trial. The amount of the bail is set by a judge. If the defendant is "released on his or her own recognizance," then no bail is required for that person to go free before returning for the trial. *Once the defendant is acquitted, he or she can usually get his or her bail returned.*

Civil court—A court having jurisdiction over civil matters or the private rights of individuals, which are usually claims related to such matters as personal injury, divorce, adoptions, guardianship, landlord/tenant issues, and so on. Small claims cases, where the claim usually has to be worth less than a certain amount (such as $5,000) and/or conform to other conditions, are tried in civil court. *When Raymond couldn't get his security deposit back from his landlord, he sued his landlord in the small-claims court of civil court.*

Criminal court—A court that tries criminal cases, or cases involving crimes. Crimes are acts in violation of the law, such as theft, sexual assault, treason, tax evasion, and murder, and are punished. Crimes are usually categorized according to how serious they are, from misdemeanor (such as disorderly conduct or the theft of something low in value) to felony (such as arson or murder). *If you use someone else's personal information, such as his or her Social Security number or financial information, you could be tried in criminal court on felony charges.*

Defendant—The person who has a legal action filed against him or her. *The defendant chose not to take the witness stand for fear he might incriminate himself.*

Defense attorney—A lawyer that represents the defendant. *The defense attorney closed the case with an emotional appeal for the defendant.*

To deliberate—To consider carefully, to consult. *The jury deliberated for several hours before concluding that the defendant was guilty.*

Deterrent—A means of discouraging someone from criminal behavior, such as the fear of being punished. *People in favor of the death penalty often say that it is a deterrent against murder.*

To dismiss—To remove a case or appeal from consideration in court, without allowing for a complete trial. *A judge can dismiss a case if there isn't enough evidence against a defendant, if the plaintiff has failed to appear, or for other reasons.*

District attorney (DA)—The primary prosecuting attorney for criminal cases in a district, representing the government. *The district attorney proceeded with her case against the former mayor in spite of pleas from other city officials not to.*

Felony—A serious crime, such as murder, kidnapping, or burglary. *When someone is found guilty of a felony, it usually involves a jail sentence.*

Hung jury—A jury that is unable to reach a verdict. *If there is a hung jury, the judge will declare a mistrial, or a void trial without a verdict, and the case can be retried under certain conditions.*

Judge—An official of the government who has the authority to decide and preside over legal cases. *Mike was very nervous when he appeared before the judge in traffic court.*

Judgment—The court's formal ruling or decision. A judgment can sometimes refer to a judge's decision, as opposed to a jury's decision, which is a verdict. *The judge signed the final judgment awarding the plaintiff $1,000,000.*

Jury—A group of people who have been selected and have sworn to listen to a case and deliver a verdict based on the facts presented to them. A *grand jury* does not deliver a verdict but instead decides whether or not there is enough evidence against someone to proceed to trial. A member of a jury is called a *juror. Mary was surprised when she was selected to serve on a jury after appearing for jury duty.*

Litigation—A legal proceeding, a lawsuit, an action in a court. *Defending yourself against litigation can be very expensive.*

Misdemeanor—A less serious crime, such as a traffic violation or disorderly conduct. *If you are found guilty of a misdemeanor, the penalty is often a fine and community service.*

To object—To contest an argument or a procedure in a trial. *"I object!" boomed Jim Jerrod's lawyer from across the courtroom. She didn't like the direction the testimony was heading.*

Parole—When a convicted criminal is allowed to leave prison before his or her sentence is over under certain conditions. *Hello Ms. Steele, I'm Ralph Ramos, your husband's parole officer. I'm just calling to check up on him and to make sure he's adjusting to life outside of prison.*

Plaintiff—The party in a court case who brings an action against someone. *The plaintiff claimed that the defendant had wrecked his car.*

To plead/take the Fifth—To exercise the right against self-incrimination granted under the Fifth Amendment of the Constitution. In other words, if you say that you plead the Fifth, you refuse to say something because you believe it could incriminate you. Can also be used informally to mean that you don't want to answer a question. *The defendant pleaded the Fifth and refused to testify.*

Probation—A type of sentence allowing someone convicted of a crime to remain free, but usually under supervision, after a conviction or a guilty plea, instead of being imprisoned (or sometimes in addition to jail time). While on probation, the individual has to abide by certain conditions. *Instead of jail time, she was sentenced to six months probation.*

To prosecute—To make formal charges against someone and present a case against that person. *The district attorney vowed to prosecute the case against Larson even though the majority of the public sided with the defendant.*

Prosecuting attorney (prosecutor)—A lawyer who prosecutes cases as a representative of the government. *Many prosecutors' offices have victim* assistance programs that will guide victims of crimes through the legal process, help them with recovery, and provide other aid.

Public defender—An attorney employed by the government to represent defendants who cannot afford to pay for an attorney. *The public defender was young and idealistic, but he lacked enough experience to win his first case.*

Restitution—Compensation made for loss, damage, or injury. *For restitution to occur, you are hereby ordered to pay the plaintiff $3,000.*

Sentence—The judgment of a court that states the punishment to be given to a convicted offender, such as jail time or hours of community service. *The defendant's sentence was three years probation and 200 hours of community service.*

To sequester—To set apart, to seclude. *In high-profile cases where the case is in the news every day, the jurors must be sequestered for the duration of the trial.*

Settlement—A possible result of a lawsuit, where both parties come to an agreement before a final court judgment is reached. Often refers to an amount of money received as part of the agreement. *Instead of going to trial, the company reached a settlement with the employee who had filed the lawsuit.*

Subpoena—A written order to appear in court to give testimony. *Once the witness got a subpoena, he was offered protection by the authorities.*

To sue, a suit—To start legal proceedings against someone else. A suit, or lawsuit, is a case brought before a court of law with a defendant and a plaintiff who is seeking some form of remedy for alleged wrongs done by the defendant. *Bill sued his neighbor in small claims court for cutting down trees that were entirely on his property.*

Summons—A notice to appear in court. *Marilyn just received her summons to appear in traffic court.*

To try—To put someone on trial. *Charles Manson was tried and convicted for the Tate-LaBianca murders.*

Verdict—A jury's formal decision in a trial, such as a decision as to whether a defendant is guilty or not guilty. *"Do you have a verdict?" the judge asked the jury.*

Voir dire—The questioning of jurors under oath to determine competence and suitability for a jury. *Nita must have passed inspection during her voir dire because she was selected as a juror.*

C. GRAMMAR ESSENTIALS: UNREAL CONDITIONALS

The unreal conditional describes actions that are unreal, hypothetical, or contrary to fact. Different verb forms are used in the *if* condition clause and the *then* result clause. The *if* clause is similar to reported speech, in that the verb tense "shifts back." For the future in the *if* clause, the construction *were to* + verb is used: *if I were to be, if they were to go, if we were to see,* and so on. A *would* conditional is used in the result clause, either present/future (*would* + bare verb) or past (*would have* + past participle):

Present	*If you received a subpoena, you would go to court.*
Past	*If you had received a subpoena last week, you would have gone to court.*
Future	*If you were to receive a subpoena tomorrow, you would go to court.*
Present Perfect	*If you had ever received a subpoena, you would already have gone to court.*

Note that in conversational English, many speakers do not use *were to* + verb to express future *if* condition clauses. Instead, they may use the simple past, or even *was to* + verb (for *I, he, she,* and *it;* other forms take *were*):
> *If Jenny took you to court tomorrow, you'd lose.*
> *If Jenny was to take you to court tomorrow, you'd lose.*

The past unreal conditional is often used to scold, or teach lessons, or even to make excuses:
> *If you had prepared for court, you could have won your case!*
> *If he had dressed better, the judge would have respected him more.*
> *If I hadn't had jury duty today, I would have been home on time.*

Finally, don't forget that you can reverse the order of clauses, just as in the real conditional:
> *I would have been home on time if I hadn't had jury duty.*

D. HOW-TO

Now let's lay out some major points about the legal system in the U.S. and go through what you should expect if you're ever involved in a civil or criminal case. Let's start with the two major types of cases handled by state courts, civil and criminal. Criminal cases are those in which the law has been broken, so they involve things like larceny, assault, racketeering, or murder. Criminal cases may involve felonies, which are serious or egregious crimes, or misdemeanors, which are lesser offenses. Even though these crimes may be committed against an individual, they are viewed as crimes against the government (state or federal), making the government the plaintiff. The attorney representing the government in criminal cases is the prosecutor, and the person charged with a crime is the defendant. Civil cases, on the other hand, involve disputes between at least two individuals rather than between the government and an individual. The party bringing the charge is called the plaintiff; the person being charged is the defendant. Civil cases can involve contract law, pertaining to oral or written agreements that have not been met, or tort law, which concerns either intentional or negligent harm caused by one individual to another. Whereas in criminal trials a defendant might be found guilty and sentenced to jail time as well as fined, in a civil case a defendant might be found liable, meaning legally responsible to pay some amount. In civil cases, defendants who are found liable cannot be incarcerated as part of their punishment.

Criminal and civil cases also differ in the burden placed on the prosecutor or plaintiff to show the guilt or liability of the defendant, who is always considered innocent until proven guilty. In a criminal case, the prosecutor must prove that the defendant is guilty beyond a reasonable doubt. While this does not mean guilty beyond the shadow of a doubt, there is a very high burden of proof to be met by the prosecutor, and jurors must be persuaded by the evidence laid before them that a defendant is guilty. At the end of a criminal trial, they must usually reach that decision unanimously. Not all criminal cases have juries, however, and cases are sometimes decided solely by a judge (a bench trial); the same is true for civil cases. There is also a great deal of trial law that protects the rights of the accused, and rules of evidence often err on the side of caution in favor of the defendant. The defense attorney in a criminal trial tries to show that there is reason to doubt the prosecutor's case. In a civil case, the burden is lower than in criminal cases, the phrase most often used to describe it being "a preponderance of the evidence." Basically, that means that a judge or jury must be persuaded that it's more likely that the facts support the plaintiff's case than the defendant's defense in order for the defendant to be found liable.

Court cases vary greatly from one another, but the general flow of events is as follows: The trial begins with opening statements, which allow each side to present their version of the issues and a description of the evidence to be presented. Opening statements are made first by the prosecuting attorney then by the defendant's attorney. Then witnesses are called, again first by the prosecuting attorney and then by the defendant's attorney. Each attorney has the opportunity to cross-examine (question) the other's witnesses. Additional evidence may be presented by either attorney. Finally, the attorneys issue their closing statements, which do not present evidence but summarize events from their viewpoint. From time to time throughout the trial, the judge may issue instructions to the jury, if there is one, but once the attorneys have gone over all of the evidence and given their closing statements, the judge gives instructions to the jury on how to consider the evidence presented during the trial. Then comes jury deliberation. Once the jury has made their determination in the case, they return to the courtroom to announce their verdict. If it is a civil case, a final judgment is entered, determining, for example, how much a defendant has to pay. If it is a criminal case and the defendant is found guilty, sentencing occurs at a later date. During the sentencing phase, the two attorneys give their arguments for and against the severity of the sentence to be imposed. In serious crimes, the jury may decide on a sentence, and then the judge weighs the jury's recommendation and sentences the defendant. Once a defendant is sentenced, he or she must serve that sentence. The sentence could be a fine, but it is often imprisonment. However, both criminal and civil cases are often appealed, which means that the verdict is challenged in a higher court. The losing party in a case is often the party to appeal, hoping to reverse or otherwise change the decision of the lower court by proving that errors occurred in the lower court's trial. In a criminal case, an appellate court (any court that hears appeals from a lower court) can, for example, reduce a sentence or overturn a conviction, while in a civil case, an appellate court could choose, for instance, to reduce monetary damages. The U.S. Supreme Court is the highest court appeals can go to.

The three ways you're most likely to have contact with the court system are as a juror, as a plaintiff, or as a defendant. Let's start with the role of jurors. Every citizen eighteen years of age or older who meets certain conditions will be called for jury duty at some point. The list of people called for jury duty is pulled from lists of registered voters and driver's licenses. You'll be summoned for jury duty by receiving notification in the mail, which will tell you when to report to court and where to go. Jury service is a responsibility of U.S. citizenship, and you must attend at the appointed time unless you opt to reschedule or postpone for legitimate reasons. You can visit your state or county website for more information. If you do attend, instructions are usually very clear. First, you'll go to a room where you'll wait to be called as a potential juror for one case or another. You may spend a lot of time there just waiting, so make sure you bring a book or something to occupy your time! You may then be called for a process known as voir dire. During voir dire, as a prospective juror you'll be questioned by both the prosecutor and the defense attorneys to determine your suitability as a juror for the particular case at hand. You may be asked if you know someone who is in jail or who has been accused of the particular crime for which the defendant is on trial, if you've ever participated in a similar trial, if you have any previous knowledge of or prejudice toward the defendant or the defendant's company, and so on. Basically, both the prosecution and the defense teams want to know that you'll be fair and impartial, and that you'll follow the law when it comes time to make a decision about guilt or innocence. If you are found to be a suitable juror, you'll be notified that you are now on a case, and you'll be told where and when to go for the actual trial.

During the trial, jurors must follow certain rules. They must dress appropriately, be on time, and not talk about the case until the judge instructs them to. Jurors are not allowed to eat during the trial. Breaks will be given throughout the proceedings that allow jurors to eat or drink something. In many cases, jurors are given paid time off to serve on a jury (and most companies have jury duty policies because employees need to take time off from work for it; check with your human resources department for more information on your company's policy). They are also paid a small amount while the trial is going on. The judge oversees the trial, instructing the jurors to consider or to disregard evidence presented to them. For the duration of the trial, jurors must not discuss the case with anyone, not even other jurors, until deliberation takes place. At this point, depending on district policy, either the jurors or the judge selects a foreperson to preside over the deliberation. The jurors then deliberate until they come to a verdict. In high-profile cases, the jurors will usually be sequestered. In a criminal case, the verdict must be unanimous in order to either convict or acquit the defendant. When the jury has reached a verdict, court is called back into session and their verdict is delivered by the foreperson. The jurors may or may not be asked individually whether they agree with the verdict. After the verdict is read, the judge thanks the jurors and discharges them.

There may come a time when you feel that you have a civil case against some person or organization. This usually means that efforts to resolve the issue out of court have failed. In this case, the first thing is to find a lawyer to represent you, the plaintiff. Then a complaint stating your version of events must be filed with the proper court, and a summons is issued notifying the defendant that a lawsuit has been filed against him or her. Once this action has been taken, settlement may occur—many civil cases do not ever go to court. Your lawyer will prepare for the trial by getting the facts of the case as you see them. She or he will then gather evidence and determine the order of witnesses. Your counsel will likely organize your case around a central theme. The court may order the plaintiff and defendant to take their case to a mediator. Civil cases never end in incarceration; in general, if the defendant's conduct is found to be caused by malicious intent, gross negligence, or willful disregard for the plaintiff's rights, he or she usually reimburses the plaintiff for losses caused by that conduct. Of course, the defendant could always appeal this decision.

You may also find yourself in the unfortunate position of being a defendant in either a civil or a criminal case. In a civil case you are likely to be notified by a summons. Should you receive a summons, be sure to appear in court. Failure to appear can result in a default judgment against you. As the defendant, you should also select an attorney to represent you. Your attorney will then prepare the case in a similar manner to the plaintiff's attorney. In a civil trial you may choose to file a counterclaim against the plaintiff. If so, allow your lawyer to advise you on this. Once the case goes to trial it is important to present yourself well in court. A neat, clean, businesslike appearance will work in your favor. If you lose a criminal case you may be fined, given a jail sentence, put on probation, and/or sentenced to do a certain number of hours of community service. Sentencing in a civil case does not result in jail time. However, you may have to pay damages to the plaintiff. As a criminal defendant, you are entitled to a speedy trial, a trial by a jury of your peers, and a court-appointed attorney should you not have the funds to pay for a criminal defense attorney yourself. In a criminal case, it is the government arguing the case against you, the defendant, and a district attorney represents the state or county. Prior to trial and jury selection, the defendant meets with the judge either in public or private session to state his or her guilt or innocence. If the accused pleads guilty, that person admits guilt; he or she will not have a trial and will not be able to appeal. A person who pleads guilty is then sentenced but allowed to speak on his or her behalf. If the accused pleads not guilty, then a court date is set. Due to the Fifth Amendment, a defendant cannot be forced to take the stand against him- or herself; a witness may also be allowed to exercise this right. The burden of proof is on the prosecuting attorney, and the case must be proved beyond a reasonable doubt. If the trial appears to be going in the favor of the prosecution, the defense attorney may suggest a plea bargain, which means the defendant will plead guilty in exchange for a lesser sentence. If the defendant is found guilty, a sentencing date will be set. If the defendant is found not guilty, he or she is released. A mistrial can be declared if the jury cannot reach a unanimous verdict or if prejudicial misconduct or a procedural error has occurred. A jury that fails to reach a unanimous verdict is considered a hung jury, and the defendant is released. The case is usually retried.

E. ENGLISH IN ACTION

Raul, a new American citizen, is talking to his friend Melissa, because he has just gotten his first summons for jury duty.

Raul: Melissa, I just got a summons for jury duty. I'm a little bit nervous about it.

Melissa: Yeah, they do make it kind of scary when you open that envelope and it says SUMMONS!, failure to appear, and all that stuff.

Raul: Well, that's scary, too, but I'm talking about not knowing exactly what to do and what to expect. You know . . .

Melissa: Well, there are a few things you need to be aware of, like you shouldn't wear shorts and flip-flops or anything like that, and then you may have to go through that voir dire or whatever it's called.

Raul: Yeah, voir dire, where both the prosecuting and defense attorney question you to see if you'd make a good juror. I learned about that in my citizenship class. I learned about the whole process, but that's not the same as actually doing it. Have you ever been called to jury duty?

Melissa: Of course. Anybody who registers to vote or has a driver's license is going to get called sometime. Usually they tell you to call the Thursday before the Monday you're supposed to appear or the night before, or something like that. When you call in, though, they may tell you that you don't have to show up on that day or that you should call back the next day.

Raul: Well, that's not what my summons says. It just says to report that Monday morning at 7:45.

Melissa: Okay, well, take a good book or your laptop or something. You may just sit there all day. It can be really boring unless you like to people-watch.

Raul: Don't I have to go back the next day?

Melissa: Usually if you don't get selected they send you home and you don't hear from them again for another year or so. It just kind of depends whether your group number gets called up or not.

Raul: I'm a part of a group?

Melissa: That's just how they organize it, I guess. But if you get called, you'll all be called together. It really all depends upon how much action there is in court that week.

Raul: So did you ever sit on a jury?

Melissa: Yeah, once. It was pretty interesting. Everything's so formal. You all stand up when the judge comes in and you have to wait until he or she is seated before you can sit down. Everyone has to be quiet. You can take notes, but you can't ask any questions.

Raul: But how did you decide, I mean, you know? Did you find the guy guilty?

Melissa: Actually, we did. But we all went into this room and discussed it. Everyone got to say what they thought. The guy who was the foreman was pretty evenhanded, I thought. He made sure we didn't just decide he was guilty so we could go home. We really took it seriously and discussed things, voted, deliberated, and then came to a decision together as a group.

Raul: Wow! This is starting to sound exciting. I kind of hope I get a trial.

Melissa: Yeah? I think you'd enjoy it, actually. A lot of people complain about jury duty, and I used to be the same way. But after sitting on my first case, I realized, this really is a civic duty, and if, God forbid, I'm ever the one accused of a crime, I really want to know that the people on my jury are taking their responsibility to me seriously!

F. PRACTICE

Fill in the blanks with the following words: *appeal, defendant, deterrent, sentence, litigation, plaintiff, probation, to sue, restitution, summons*

1. Will the _____ please rise and hear the charges brought against him?
2. Knowing that you'll pay a huge fine for littering may work as a(n) _____.
3. Once her client was convicted, the defense attorney pushed for a light _____. She argued that community service and probation were more appropriate than jail time, considering the crime.
4. Even though we lost this case, I think we can win it on _____.
5. This case has been in _____ for such a long time, I'm ready to give up!
6. Because it's a misdemeanor, you'll probably get a short jail sentence with _____.
7. It looks like the _____ is willing to deal if you agree to pay for her car repair.
8. Once you receive a(n) _____, you are obligated to go to court.
9. The company decided _____ its rival, claiming that the other company had violated its patent on the product.
10. It looks like you're going to lose your house in order to pay _____ to the plaintiff.

Fill in the blanks with the correct form of the verb.

1. If you _____ (be) to go to court, you would have to dress more formally than usual.
2. If that other witness had been called, we _____ (win) the case.
3. If you had arrived at court on time, you _____ (get) in.
4. If the accused _____ (be) actually guilty, she wouldn't have such a good alibi.
5. I wouldn't go into the courtroom if I _____ (not have) a pass.
6. The jury _____ (accept) your alibi if they thought it had merit.
7. If you had driven more carefully, we never _____ (have) this whole problem!
8. If you were to try take a gun into the justice building, you _____ (be) arrested on the spot.
9. If anybody _____ (deserve) a good lawyer, it would be Michael.
10. If Michael _____ (stay) at home that night, he wouldn't be on trial right now.

G. TASK

Did you know you can watch a trial? Contact your local superior court to check the schedule. To find your local court, go to www.govspot.com/judicial, enter your state, and then click on superior court under judicial. Each state has a different website setup, so navigate the site until you find a list of courts. Then click on the one you want. See if you can then answer the following questions. If you can't go to court to find out the answers, you can probably answer them after doing some research on the internet, in books, or by watching the news or court cases on TV. The answers are listed in the Answer Key of this lesson.

1. What do the people do when the judge walks in?
2. Observe how a lawyer questions a witness or suspect. What does the other lawyer say when he or she doesn't like the way a question is asked?
3. What is proper courtroom behavior?
4. What does the bailiff do?

H. REAL LIFE

John Rankin is a high school civics teacher. Today he's giving this class an overview of the court system in the United States:

We're going to be spending the next several weeks on the court system in the U.S. The federal court system is fairly straightforward. Think of the federal court system as a pyramid. On the bottom is the U.S. district court system. There are 650 judges and about 95 courts throughout the country and the U.S. territories. These courts have original jurisdiction over federal cases. On the next tier is the U.S. Circuit Court of Appeals. This system has 167 judges and 13 courts. They mostly look for error in the lower courts. At the top of our pyramid is the U.S. Supreme Court. This court has nine judges, or justices, one of them being the chief justice. They hear about 100 cases a year, usually involving questions of constitutional law.

Then we have the state court system. This system is a lot more difficult to navigate, especially since the names of these courts are not the same in every state. Every city has state trial courts, sometimes called inferior courts. There are 13,000 of these courts in the U.S., and they see only minor cases that involve a judge but not a jury. Above that, we have the state trial court or superior court. There are 3,000 of these courts in the U.S. They hold felony trials where the defendant has a right to a trial by jury. Next, we have the state intermediate appellate courts, of which there are 39. Obviously, not all states have one. They hear appeals from state courts, usually with a panel of three judges. Finally, we have the state superior courts. There's one in each of the 50 states. Each court has between five and nine judges. They hear appeals from the state court. Their cases usually end in the state supreme courts, but occasionally they do go to the federal Supreme Court.

 RESOURCES

The U.S. court system:
www.uscourts.gov

Explanation of court system:
usinfo.state.gov/products/pubs/legalotln
usinfo.state.gov/usa/infousa/politics/judbranc.htm
www.uscourts.gov/understando2

Listing of websites of U.S. courts and websites with information on the court system:
www.govspot.com/judicial

Criminal vs. civil information:
www.usdoj.gov/crt/crim/faq.htm

ANSWER KEY
Practice 1: 1. defendant; 2. deterrent; 3. sentence; 4. appeal; 5. litigation; 6. probation; 7. plaintiff; 8. summons; 9. to sue; 10. restitution

Practice 2: 1. were; 2. would have won; 3. would have gotten; 4. were; 5. didn't have; 6. would accept; 7. would have had; 8. would be; 9. deserved; 10. had stayed

Task: 1. Everyone stands up. 2. I object!/Objection! 3. Everyone must be quiet. Only sit when the judge sits. Stand when the judge stands. Be respectful to the judge, attorneys, bailiff, other courtroom employees, and witnesses. 4. He or she helps the judge in a variety of ways and makes sure that order is kept in the court.

CHAPTER 35

Government and Immigration: Services and Immigration

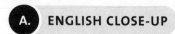

A. ENGLISH CLOSE-UP

APPLICATION FOR FOOD STAMPS

Information for non-citizens
Eligible family members can get food stamps even if other family members are not eligible because of immigration status.

Using food stamp benefits will not affect your immigration status, nor will it affect the immigration status of your family.

---

1. Applicant's name:

_____ SSN_____
(Last)   (First)   (MI) (Maiden)

Resident Address:
(The place where you actually live.)

_____
(Number and Street or RFD)   (City)   (State)   (Zip Code)

Address where your mail goes: *(If different from your resident address.)*

_____
(P.O. Box, Street Address, or RFD)   (City)   (State)   (Zip Code)

B. VOCABULARY ESSENTIALS

Alien—A person who is not a citizen or national of a country, a foreigner. A resident alien, or an alien living in the U.S., has a different tax status from a non-resident alien. *The IRS considers you a resident alien if you have a green card or if you pass the substantial presence test, which means you have been physically present in the country for 31 days during the current year and 183 days over the past three years, which includes the current year.*

Allegiance—Loyalty. The Pledge of Allegiance is an oath of loyalty to the U.S. that is often spoken at public events and in schools. It is said facing the U.S. flag with your right hand over your heart. *The Pledge of Allegiance is: "I pledge allegiance to the flag of the United States of America and to the republic for which it stands, one nation under God, indivisible, with liberty and justice for all."*

Attachment to the Constitution—Applicants to naturalization must declare their "attachment to the Constitution" under oath, which means they understand and are willing to support and defend the Constitution. *When you take the Oath of Allegiance, you will be declaring your attachment to the Constitution.*

CCR&R agencies—Child Care Resource and Referral agencies are centers that refer parents to a qualified child-care provider and provide parents with other child-care aid and information. CCR&Rs also provide support and training for child-care providers. NACCRRA is the National Association of Child Care Resource & Referral Agencies and is the non-profit network of over 850 CCR&R centers throughout the country. *By going to NACCRRA's website at www.naccrra.org, you can find the location of your local CCR&R center.*

Continuous residency—An eligibility requirement for naturalization meaning that you must have lived in the U.S. as a permanent resident for a certain period of time, usually five years. *If you are married to a U.S. citizen, you must be in continuous residence as a permanent resident for three years.*

Fingerprints, to get fingerprinted—Impressions made by the lines on the fingers, or the inked prints of such, used as a means of identification. *Some immigration applications, often including naturalization applications, may require the applicants' fingerprints. Usually, you pay a fee and then the USCIS fingerprints you at a designated location.*

Food stamps—A government USDA-issued EBT (electronic benefits transfer) card that allows low-income qualified applicants to purchase food for their families. *You can't buy cigarettes with your food stamp card; it's only for legitimate food purchases.*

"Good moral character"—An eligibility requirement for naturalization. This includes honesty and not having committed certain crimes. *Whatever you do, don't ever lie to the USCIS agent, because this will suggest that you do not have good moral character.*

Green card (permanent resident card)—An (originally green) alien registration card that shows permanent residency status. *Trent has been in the U.S. on a work visa for two years, but he hopes to get his green card.*

Immigrant—Someone migrating to another country, often in order to live there permanently. The USCIS usually equates a legal immigrant with a permanent resident. *There are many steps you must go through to become a legal immigrant to the U.S.*

Naturalization—The process of becoming a citizen in a country not of one's birth. *July 4th is a popular day for naturalization ceremonies.*

Naturalized citizen—A person who becomes a citizen of a country that is not the one he or she was born in. *A naturalized citizen has all the legal rights of a* *natural born citizen, except he or she may not become president or vice president of the United States.*

Oath of Allegiance—The last step in the citizenship process, where you swear allegiance to the U.S. during a ceremony. People with certain disabilities may not have to recite the oath. *Once you have officially taken the Oath of Allegiance at the naturalization ceremony, you are a U.S. citizen and you will receive your Certificate of Naturalization.*

Permanent residency—Immigration status that is the first step to American citizenship, being a foreigner who is legally allowed to work and reside permanently in the U.S., having a green card. *If someone of foreign birth marries an American, it's fairly easy to get permanent residency status.*

Port of entry—An area where people from other countries enter a country under governmental supervision, such as an airport. *In the past, Ellis Island was the port of entry for almost all immigrants to the U.S.*

Record—An official listing of illegal activities held by the police authorities. *If you have an aggravated felony on your record, such as murder or trafficking in drugs, you can never be granted citizenship to the United States.*

SBA—Small Business Association. A government organization dedicated to helping small businesses get started and also to providing disaster assistance to those people who are trying to rebuild homes and businesses after a disaster. *If you need help with a small business loan, check with the SBA.*

Selective service—A government program to call people to serve in the military in times of need, also known as the draft. *Every American male, including some non-citizens, must register with selective service once he turns 18 and/or is between the ages of 18 and 25.*

Substance abuse—Dependence on an addictive substance, such as alcohol or a narcotic drug. *There are plenty of substance abuse programs sponsored by the state or federal government.*

USCIS—United States Citizenship and Immigration Services. The agency that handles immigration and naturalization, formerly the INS. *Contact the USCIS if you are interested in becoming a U.S. citizen.*

 C. **GRAMMAR ESSENTIALS: PHRASAL AND PREPOSITIONAL VERBS**

There are many verbs in English that consist of a main verb along with one or more "particles," or other words, typically prepositions or adverbs. Examples are: *to go with, to look up, to get by, to eat up, to do over, to get along with, to put up with,* and so on. These verbs are often challenging for students of

English for a few reasons. First of all, their meanings aren't always obviously related to the sum of the parts, and many are in fact rather idiomatic. For example, the meaning of *to put up with* has little to do with the meanings of *put* or *up*. There are also some slight pronunciation differences in stress in spoken English—for example, "he's LOOKing for his friends" compared to "things are looking UP these days." And finally, there are important structural differences with regard to word order of objects in relation to the particle. For example, both "he looked up the word in the dictionary" and "he looked the word up in the dictionary" are correct, but only "he looked up the stairs to see if anyone was coming down" is correct.

All of these differences can be understood more easily if we divide these verbs into two different categories, prepositional verbs and phrasal verbs. Let's start with prepositional verbs. Prepositional verbs are combinations of verbs and prepositions, and the meanings of these combinations are often (but not always) clearly related to the sum of the two parts. The prepositions always have an object:

> I'm <u>looking for</u> my keys.
> They <u>walked across</u> the office.

The object, whether it's a noun or a pronoun, always comes right after the preposition, and nothing can come between the two. But you can add an adverb between the verb and the preposition:

> I look carefully for them every day. (Not: I look for carefully them . . .)
> They walked slowly across the office. (Not: They walked across slowly the office.)

In speech, there is an intonation stress on the verb, not on the preposition:

> We need to LOOK for a new babysitter.
> Don't WALK across the street outside of the crosswalk.

Some examples (and meanings) of common prepositional verbs are: *to look for* (to search for), *to run into* (to meet by accident), *to get through* (to finish, to endure), *to count on* (to rely or depend on), *to deal with* (to handle, as in a problem), *to get over* (to recover from), *to end up* (to end in a particular state), *to get on* (to board, as in a train or plane), *to get off* (to exit a large vehicle), *to get into* (to enter a car, or to become involved in a situation), *to fall for* (to begin to love someone), *to look after* (to watch, to take care of).

Phrasal verbs are combinations of verbs and adverbs, and the meanings of these combinations are often not obviously related to the individual parts. Phrasal verbs can be intransitive, meaning that they don't take objects, or transitive, meaning that they do:

> The government helps many poor families <u>get by</u>.
> Don't worry; something is bound to <u>turn up</u>.

Could you <u>turn down your music</u>?
I need to <u>look up a word</u> in the dictionary.

With transitive phrasal verbs, if the direct object is a noun, there are two possible word orders: verb + particle + object, or verb + object + particle:

He looked up the word in the dictionary.	*He looked the word up in the dictionary.*
The editor looked over the manuscript.	*The editor looked the manuscript over.*
I can't figure out the answers.	*I can't figure the answers out.*
We called up our friend.	*We called our friend up.*

But if the object is a pronoun, there is only one possible one word order: verb + pronoun + particle:

He looked it up in the dictionary. (Not: *He looked up it in the dictionary.*)
The editor looked it over.
I can't figure them out.
We called her up.

With phrasal verbs, the stress is normally either evenly divided between verb and particle, or just on the particle, but not just on the verb.

The editor looked the manuscript OVER.
We CALLED UP our friend.

Unlike with prepositional verbs, it's not possible to separate a phrasal verb from its particle with an adverb:

He looked up the word quickly. (Not: *He looked quickly up the word.*)
They easily figured out the answer. (Not: *They figured easily out the answer.*)

Some common examples of transitive phrasal verbs are: *to figure out* (to understand), *to look up* (to find, as in a meaning), *to make up* (to invent), *to turn in* (to hand over, to submit), *to try on* (to wear clothes to see if they fit), *to put on* (to begin to wear an article of clothing), *to take off* (to remove an article of clothing), *to call off* (to cancel), *to close down* (to close an establishment), *to set up* (to arrange, to organize), *to drop off* (to leave in a place), *to pick up* (to meet and collect by car, to gather), *to fill in/out* (to write a form), *to give up* (to stop, to surrender), *to let down* (to fail to fulfill expectations), *to rule out* (to eliminate as a possibility), *to turn down* (to reject), *to throw out/away* (to put into the garbage), *to stand up* (to fail to appear for an appointment), *to kick out* (to force to leave), *to bring up* (to raise, as in children, or to introduce, as in a topic), *to put off* (to leave for later).

Some examples of common intransitive phrasal verbs are: *to break down* (to stop working), *to break up* (to cease being romantic), *to catch on* (to gain popularity), *to check in* (to register, as in a hotel or a flight), *to check out* (to leave a hotel), *to clear up* (to become clear), *to come back* (to return), *to fall through* (to not work as expected), *to get up* (to rise from bed, a couch, or a chair), *to get back* (to return), *to go back* (to return), *to give up* (to admit defeat), *to grow up* (to become an adult), *to look out* (to be wary of danger), *to show up* (to appear), *to show off* (to boast), *to stand up* (to move from sitting to standing), *to take over* (to assume control), *to take off* (to depart, as in a plane), *to wake up* (to stop sleeping).

Finally, there are a number of three-part verbs that are actually combinations of phrasal verbs along with prepositions, such as *to get along with*. These verbs follow the rules of prepositional verbs when it comes to taking objects—they do take objects, and these objects always follow the preposition:

> *He doesn't get along with his brother.*
> *We checked up on the baby five minutes ago.*

Since the first part of these combinations is actually a phrasal verb, you cannot separate the verb from the first particle by an adverb. But you can sometimes put an adverb between the second and third particles:

> *He doesn't get along well with his brother.* (Not: *He doesn't get well along with his brother.*)
> *We checked up a few minutes ago on the baby.* (Not: *We checked a few minutes ago up on the baby.*)

Some examples of three-part verbs are: *to get along with* (to enjoy a good relationship with), *to check up on* (to periodically examine for well-being or progress), *to break up with* (to end a romantic relationship with), *to walk out on* (to desert, such as family or a romantic partner), *to look forward to* (to await with anticipation), *to catch up with* (to chat with a friend to find out about his or her life), *to catch up on* (to spend a lot of time doing something in order to make up for missed opportunities), *to come down with* (to catch an illness), *to look up to* (to respect), *to look down on* (to regard with contempt), *to put up with* (to tolerate), *to get through to* (to reach, as on a telephone).

D. HOW-TO

Now let's talk about programs that the government or organizations make available to families. First we'll cover child-care services; then we'll talk about food stamps, family counseling, healthcare and insurance, and Americans with disabilities. We will then cover immigration issues.

CHILD CARE

Every state in the U.S. has a child-care licensing program, which means the state regulates those who help care for and supervise young children so that licensed child-care providers meet certain standards of care. To get information about licensed child care in your state, you can visit your local CCR&R. CCR&Rs are centers throughout the country that provide child-care information and support to parents, employers, and the community, as well as help child-care providers. To find your local CCR&R, you can go to www.childcareaware.org, a site available through NACCRRA, and enter your zip code under "To find your local CCR&R."

The federal and state governments also facilitate free preschool and prenatal programs for low-income children and families. Head Start, Early Head Start, and Even Start are some of these programs. Head Start helps prepare children for kindergarten and includes immunizations, physical and dental exams, and information and resources for treatment when needed. Early Head Start helps promote prenatal care, which is medical care, information, and advice, as well as other services needed by a mother-to-be. Early Head Start is also involved in care for infants and toddlers. Even Start helps with family literacy and education by engaging parents in their children's education, providing adult literacy and education as well as parenting classes, and other intensive early childhood education services for low-income families. These are just a few of the early childhood programs available to low-income families. For more information, go to www.whitehouse.gov/infocus/earlychildhood/sect3.html or the websites of the Department of Health and Human Services (Administration for Children and Families) and the Department of Education.

COUNSELING

Low-cost government-sponsored family counseling is also available. To find out more information about family counseling with issues concerning the welfare of children, such as child abuse, child behavioral problems, and unplanned pregnancies, you can check www.childwelfare.gov and look up their service array, or ask your family physician for a referral. Apart from family counseling, other counseling programs that are available include mental health care, adolescent/youth counseling specific to their needs (such as depression and behavioral problems), and substance abuse and alcoholism programs. There are also counseling services for job assistance and for housing. And if you wish to start a small business, the SBA even provides counseling to help you get started. For more information on that, go to www.sba.gov.

FOOD STAMPS

Originally issued as coupons or stamps for food, the food stamp program no longer issues "stamps" and now uses a card like an ATM debit card. It is available to certain low-income U.S. citizens and permanent residents. Legal immigrants who have lived in the U.S. for at least five years, who are receiving disability-related assistance, or who are children may be eligible for food stamps if the qualifying income is low enough. There are also a few other categories of legal immigrants who may qualify. For more information on immigrant qualifications and other food stamp questions, check out the USDA's food stamp site at www.fns.usda.gov/fsp. You can also call 1-800-221-5689 to check your eligibility and for more information. If you think you qualify for food stamps, it is a relatively simple procedure to enroll. You can get an application either from the local food stamp office, call the office and ask them to mail the form to you, or (if possible) download an application from your state's website. You can find your local food stamp office by calling the 800 number above or by looking the office up in your phone book under "Social/Human Services." Fill out the application and turn it in to the food stamp office, and then make an appointment for an interview. They will tell you what legal documents you will need to bring to your interview. If you have trouble filling out the application, the food stamp workers will help you. Additionally, if you find that you are not approved and you believe you should be, you can ask for a "fair hearing," which is a free meeting between you, the food stamp worker, and a representative from the state. If are approved for food stamps, it's important to keep in mind that you can only purchase food for you and your family with food stamps. Cigarettes, alcohol, paper goods, pet foods, etc., do not qualify to be purchased with food stamps.

HEALTHCARE OPTIONS

Whether your child is insured or not, he or she can get free or very low-cost immunizations (certain immunizations are required for children entering school from kindergarten through college, as discussed in Chapters 14 and 17). Just contact www.cdc.gov/nip, which is the Centers for Disease Control and Prevention's National Immunization Program, for information on where to get these immunizations and to find other information about vaccinations. You can also call the CDC Information Center at 1-800-232-4636. For women who are pregnant, each state offers free or reduced-cost prenatal care. To find the prenatal program in your state, call 1-800-311-2229. You can find additional information about pregnancy and other women's health issues at the women's health website www.womenshealth.gov/tools. The girls' health website girlshealth.gov offers guidance for girls on health, diet, fitness, relationships, etc. These are both U.S. government–sponsored websites. Also, the USDA provides health and nutrition information for all Americans, as well as food programs in addition to the food stamp program, through its Food and Nutrition Service at www.fns.usda.gov.

DISABILITIES

The U.S. has a lot of special accommodations for the disabled, such as special handicapped parking, seating, ramps in place of stairs, entrances, etc. There are also such services as education, employment, housing, transportation, health, financial benefits, technology, and community life accessible to the handicapped so that they can enjoy the full life that all Americans are entitled to. These services are made available due to the Americans with Disabilities Act, signed into law in July of 1990, which essentially prohibits discrimination due to disability and gives civil rights to those with disabilities. Under the ADA, anyone with a physical or mental impairment that is severe enough to have a lasting and adverse effect on one's ability to carry out normal, everyday activities is usually considered disabled. This act is divided into five titles: education, public services, public accommodations, telecommunications, and miscellaneous, which primarily includes the right of the disabled and those helping the disabled not to be coerced or threatened in any way. For more information, you can visit the Americans with Disabilities Act website at www.usdoj.gov/crt/ada. To check your local disability services, go to your community's website and look under services. Your state's website will also list disability services available.

INSURANCE

If you cannot afford health insurance, there may be a few options available to you. Medicare offers a program called Medicaid that you may qualify for. Medicaid is health insurance provided through the government for those who cannot afford to pay some or all of their medical bills. The program sends payments to health-care providers to help pay for your bills. You can check your eligibility and find out more information by going to www.cms.hhs.gov/medicaid/whoiseligible.asp. Even though Medicaid is a federally funded program, it is facilitated by each state. If your family does not qualify for Medicaid, you cannot afford private insurance, and you have a child under 18, you may be able to get low-cost health, dental, and vision-care insurance through your state of residence for your child. But your family must meet income requirements, and your child must usually be a citizen, a non-U.S. citizen national, or an eligible qualified immigrant. He or she will be covered for one year; renewal will be annual with an eligibility process repeated each year. For more information, check www.insurekidsnow.gov or call 1-877-543-7669.

IMMIGRATION AND NATURALIZATION

If you want to become a citizen of the United States, you must first get permanent resident status. The first step in becoming a permanent resident is to receive approval for an immigrant petition from the USCIS filed through a sponsor. An employer or family member is usually the sponsor that files this petition for the applicant. For eligibility information for both the immigrant and the sponsor, as well as information on other methods of applying for permanent resident status (for example, as a refugee or investor, or through the lottery described below), visit the USCIS website. Once the immigrant petition has been approved, the applicant—whether residing in or outside of the U.S.—must wait for a visa number to become available. Those who are immediate relatives of U.S. citizens will usually receive a visa number relatively quickly. But because U.S. law limits the number of immigrant visa numbers available each year, others may not get one for a while, and depending upon various factors like what country they are from, it could be several years before they get one. Applicants in the U.S. may apply to adjust their status to permanent residency once an immigrant visa number is available to them. Those living outside the U.S. will be given a local U.S. consulate address to go to for completing the application process. Those who have special circumstances for wanting to immigrate and/or become permanent legal residents may want to hire an attorney sometime during or at the start of the immigration process. Getting legal advice and/or hiring an attorney might be advisable for many applicants. To see if you need a lawyer, you can check with your local legal aid center for advice. Whatever you do, be aware that there are people out there who claim they can help you get a green card if you pay them something. You might want to be suspicious of the following: anyone claiming they have a special relationship with immigration officers, promising you a green card even though you were previously rejected, and/or suggesting a meeting with you in a public place rather than meeting with you in an office. If someone tells you he or she is a lawyer, ask for proof. Lawyers don't make promises, and no one can promise they'll get you a green card.

For citizens of countries having low rates of immigration to the U.S., there is a lottery they can enter. Every year, the State Department's National Visa Center has a lottery that grants 50,000 winners (selected at random from a computer-generated program) the opportunity to apply for an immigrant visa. There is an educational requirement of having a high school diploma or its equivalent, or a job-training requirement of having two years' work experience in a job requiring at least two years of training and/or experience in order to do it. The lottery is free to enter, and a lawyer is not needed to enter. Just follow the government guidelines available at travel.state.gov (under their "Visas" section) to apply through the U.S. State Department. For more information on the lottery, you can check the following website: www.ftc.gov/bcp/conline/pubs/alerts/lottery.htm.

Once approved for permanent residency and you have your green card, there are several qualifications that you usually have to pass through to apply for citizenship (certain people do not have to follow these rules; check with USCIS for more information):

- Age—You must be at least eighteen years old.
- Continuous residence—Most applicants must reside in the U.S. for five years before applying for citizenship and be physically present for at least 30 months of those five years. Usually, if you leave the country for one year or more, you must start your five years over. In order to return at all as a permanent resident if you leave the country for over a year, you'll need to get a reentry permit before you leave. You may also have problems if you were gone for over six months at a time.
- You must have lived within a specific state or district for at least three months before starting the application process.
- Good moral character—To become a citizen you must have good moral character according to the laws of the Constitution. This means not having a criminal record involving certain types of crimes, such as being convicted of gambling, prostitution, the smuggling of illegal aliens, or for being a habitual

drunkard. You will be barred from naturalization (cannot become a citizen) if you are convicted of an aggravated felony. It is very important that applicants not lie to the U.S. government at any point during your citizenship application. If you are granted citizenship but are later found to have lied during your interview, your citizenship may be revoked.

- English and civics—You must have a fundamental grasp of reading, writing, and speaking English, as well as a basic knowledge of American civics—essentially, history, government, and citizens' rights and responsibilities. Some people do not need to fulfill the English and civics requirement (see pages 26–27 of the immigration handbook at www.uscis.gov/graphics/services/natz/English.pdf.) You must usually still be able to take the oath of citizenship, though.

- Oath of Allegiance—Be prepared to declare your attachment to the United States Constitution when you take your Oath of Allegiance during your naturalization ceremony. You must also be willing to renounce any foreign allegiances.

Once you are ready to apply for citizenship, you must first fill out the N-400 form (there is a fee to file this form) and send it to your local USCIS office along with two photographs and the necessary documents. Once you have received your appointment for an interview, you'll need to get fingerprinted. They may ask for some additional forms; if there are any additional forms, you need be sure to mail them in as soon as possible. You will receive an interview appointment that you cannot miss unless you write a letter asking for an appointment change. You should go to your interview on time with identification and any additional requested documents. You will answer some questions about your background and your application. Then, as discussed in Chapter 32, you will take the English and civics naturalization tests (either orally or written). You may receive a decision at your interview, or it may come later. You may be administered your Oath that same day or be given an appointment for the administering of your Oath. You will turn in your permanent residency card when you take your Oath and get your Certificate of Naturalization in its place. For additional information, see the USCIS website at www.uscis.gov or call 1-800-375-5283.

E. ENGLISH IN ACTION

Rubin Ayala wants to be an American citizen. Let's listen in as he interviews with the USCIS agent, Mr. Pearson.

Mr. Pearson: Okay, Mr. Ayala, let's get started on the testing portion of the interview.

Rubin: Okay.

Mr. Pearson: We're going to be testing your English skills and civics knowledge. For English, we'll be testing your reading, writing, and speaking, okay?

Rubin: Of course, I'm ready.

Mr. Pearson: All right, take a look at your application and read these few lines to me, okay?

Rubin: Okay. Umm, it says, *Provide the following information about all of your sons and daughters ... If you need more space, use a separate sheet or sheets of paper ... How many sons and daughters have you had? For more information on which sons and daughters you should include and how to complete this section, see the Instructions.*

Mr. Pearson: Okay, that's enough. Now, here's a piece of paper. I'd like you to write these few sentences. I'll dictate and you write.

Rubin: Okay. I'm ready.

Mr. Pearson: Here goes. "Martha Washington was the first First Lady."

Rubin: Okay.

Mr. Pearson: Next, "The children bought a newspaper."

Rubin: Okay.

Mr. Pearson: "The Constitution is the supreme law of the land."

Rubin: Okay.

Mr. Pearson: Okay. Now we'll do the oral interview. Your civics knowledge, as well as your speaking ability, will be tested here.

Rubin: Okay.

Mr. Pearson: How many changes or amendments to the Constitution are there?

Rubin: Um, 27.

Mr. Pearson: Okay, who was Martin Luther King, Jr.?

Rubin: A civil rights leader.

Mr. Pearson: What is a head executive of a state government called?

Rubin: Governor.

Mr. Pearson: Who was president during the civil war?

Rubin: Abraham Lincoln.

Mr. Pearson: What are the first ten amendments to the ...

F. PRACTICE

Fill in the blanks with the following words: *allegiance, continuous residence, fingerprinted, food stamps, green card, naturalization, oath, port of entry, record, selective service*

1. All prospective government employees must have a background check and get _____ before they can go to work.

2. An international airport is a(n) _____, and many immigrants arrive in the U.S. this way.

3. If you are applying for citizenship and you left the country for over a year recently, you will most likely have to begin your _____ requirement over again.

4. If you are not born an American citizen, you can become a citizen through _____.

5. If you have a(n) _____ or a work visa, you can legally work in the U.S.

6. If you are a male and want to become a citizen, you will have to also register for _____.

7. To become a citizen, you must renounce your _____ to all other governments.

8. You can't buy cigarettes or alcohol with _____.

9. Once your application for naturalization has been approved, you must attend a naturalization ceremony and take a(n) _____ of allegiance to the U.S.

10. As long as your _____ is clean, you should be able to pass the good moral character test for becoming a U.S. citizen.

For each of the following sentences, determine whether or not you can rewrite it with a different order of the main verb and its particle(s). If so, rewrite the sentence.

1. We pick out a good child-care provider.
2. They turned around the chair so it faced the wall.
3. Make sure you look down the street before you pull out.
4. I still haven't gotten over my jet lag.
5. Who let out the dog?
6. Look out the window.
7. I want to try on that pair of pants.
8. If we go up the hill we can get a better view of the sunset.
9. Many people count on food stamps.
10. The agent looked over my application.

G. TASK

One of the things an applicant for citizenship must do is pass a citizenship test. Do you know the answers to these questions? (The answers to these questions are listed in the Answer Key of this lesson.)

1. Who are your state senators?
2. What country did the U.S. gain independence from?
3. Can you name some countries the U.S. fought during World War II?
4. Why did the pilgrims come to the U.S.?

You can find the answers to these questions, as well as a comprehensive guide to naturalization, at www.uscis.gov/graphics/services/natz/English.pdf.

H. REAL LIFE

Good morning. We're Simon and Lubov Chikonov, and we wanted to share with you our experience immigrating to the United States. When we were in Russia, we wanted to immigrate to the U.S. so much, but many people also wanted to immigrate. We didn't have any sponsors or any job promises in the United States, so we knew it would take a very long time for us to get permission. And, well, look at us—we are old; we don't have so many years left. We found out from some American friends that there's a lottery for permanent resident visas. When we found out, we looked at each other and said, "Why not try?" We found out that there are countries that cannot join this lottery, but fortunately for us, Russia was on the list of countries where people could apply. But, you know, you have to be really careful because there are so many rules. For example, you can only apply once during each registration period, and if you apply twice, both applications are eliminated immediately. But other family members can apply also. For example, we both applied separately to increase our chances. You also have to include a photograph of every single immediate family member, but it can't be a family photo. You have to have one recent photo for each person and child under twenty-one, unless the child is a citizen or legal permanent resident. You must submit a photo even if the person or child isn't living with you anymore. If your children are over twenty-one, they can't apply with you. They have to apply for themselves. We had to prove that we had at least a high school education, too. Oh, and the photographs have to be very special. They have to be a certain size. They must be pictures of your face only, with no hats. So much work! There are only three months out of the year— October to December, I think—when you can apply. If you want to apply, you have to follow the instructions precisely. You don't really need a lawyer. You just have to do everything exactly the way they tell you. So maybe if you aren't sure, you can hire a lawyer to help. You don't have to pay a fee to apply, but you will have to pay any U.S. immigration fees if you're selected. Anyway, we waited and waited until, maybe six or seven months later, we got our letter saying we had won! And now, here we are in the U.S., preparing for our citizenship test!

I. RESOURCES

USCIS:
www.uscis.gov or 1-800-375-5283

Other immigrant information:
travel.state.gov or 1-202-663-1225 (for visa information)
www.ftc.gov/bcp/conline/pubs/alerts/lottery.htm

Child care and family counseling information:
nccic.org or 1-800-616-2242
www.naccrra.org
www.childwelfare.gov

Immunization information:
www.cdc.gov/nip or 1-800-232-4636 (government's national immunization program)
cispimmunize.org

U.S. Small Business Administration www.sba.gov or 1-800-827-5722

Early childhood education programs:
www.whitehouse.gov/infocus/earlychildhood/sect3.html
www.ed.gov/programs/landing.jhtml (Department of Education)
www.acf.hhs.gov (Department of Health and Human Services)
Food stamps:
www.fns.usda.gov/fsp or 1-800-221-5689

Americans with Disabilities Act:
ADA Services Phone Line at 1-800-514-0301 (voice); www.ada.gov

Health insurance:
www.cms.hhs.gov/medicaid/whoiseligible.asp (Medicaid)
www.insurekidsnow.gov or 1-877-543-7669

Health care and nutrition information:
www.womenshealth.gov/tools
girlshealth.gov
www.fns.usda.gov

ANSWER KEY
Practice 1: 1. fingerprinted; 2. port of entry; 3. continuous residence; 4. naturalization; 5. green card; 6. selective service; 7. allegiance; 8. food stamps; 9. oath; 10. record

Practice 2: 1. We picked a good child-care provider out. 2. They turned the chair around so it faced the wall. 3. No. 4. No. 5. Who let the dog out? 6. No. 7. I want to try that pair of pants on. 8. No. 9. No. 10. The agent looked my application over.

Task: 1. Answers will vary by state. 2. England. 3. Germany, Italy, Japan. 4. For religious freedom.